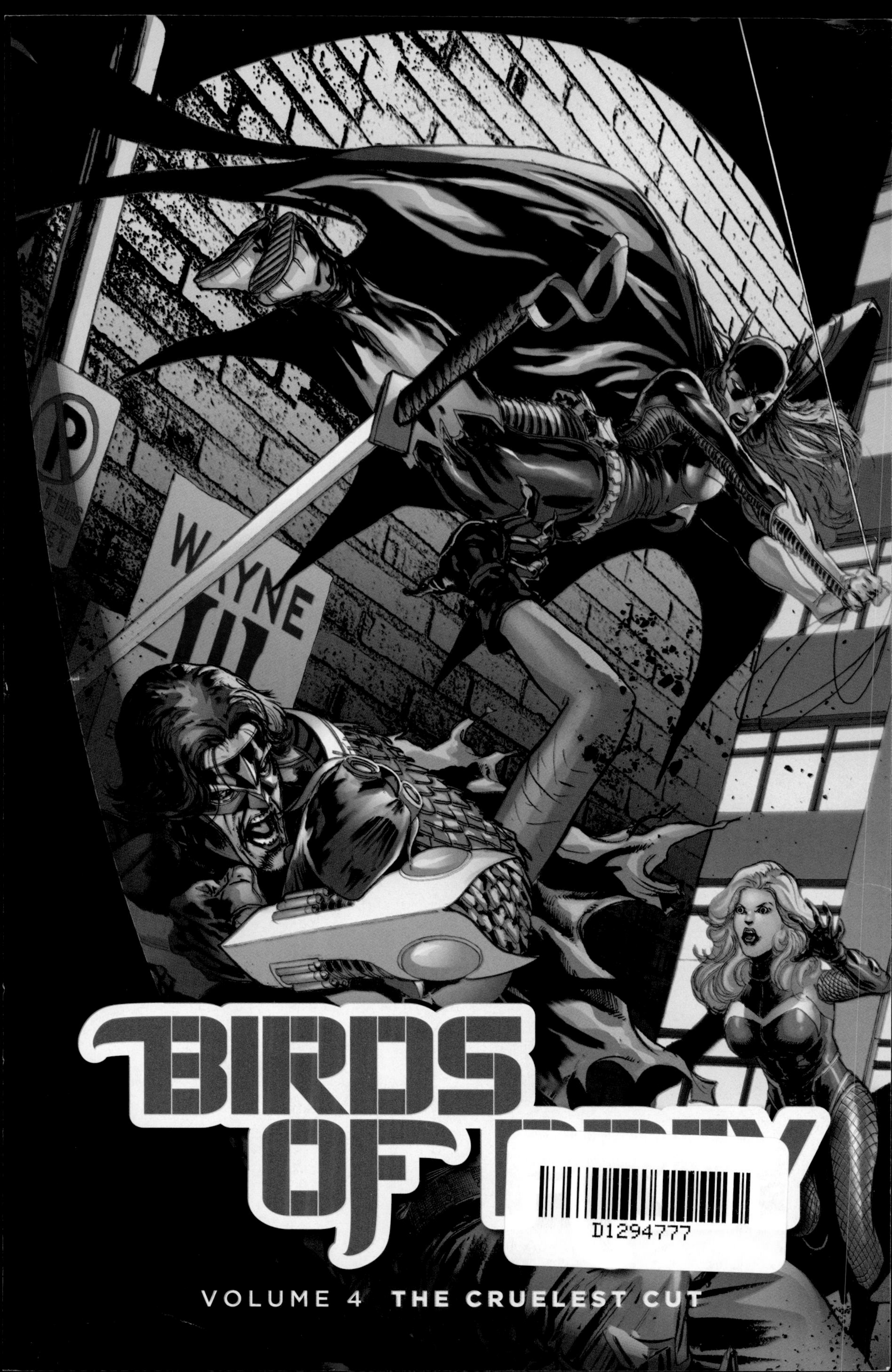

BIRDS
OF
VOLUME 4 THE CRUELEST CUT

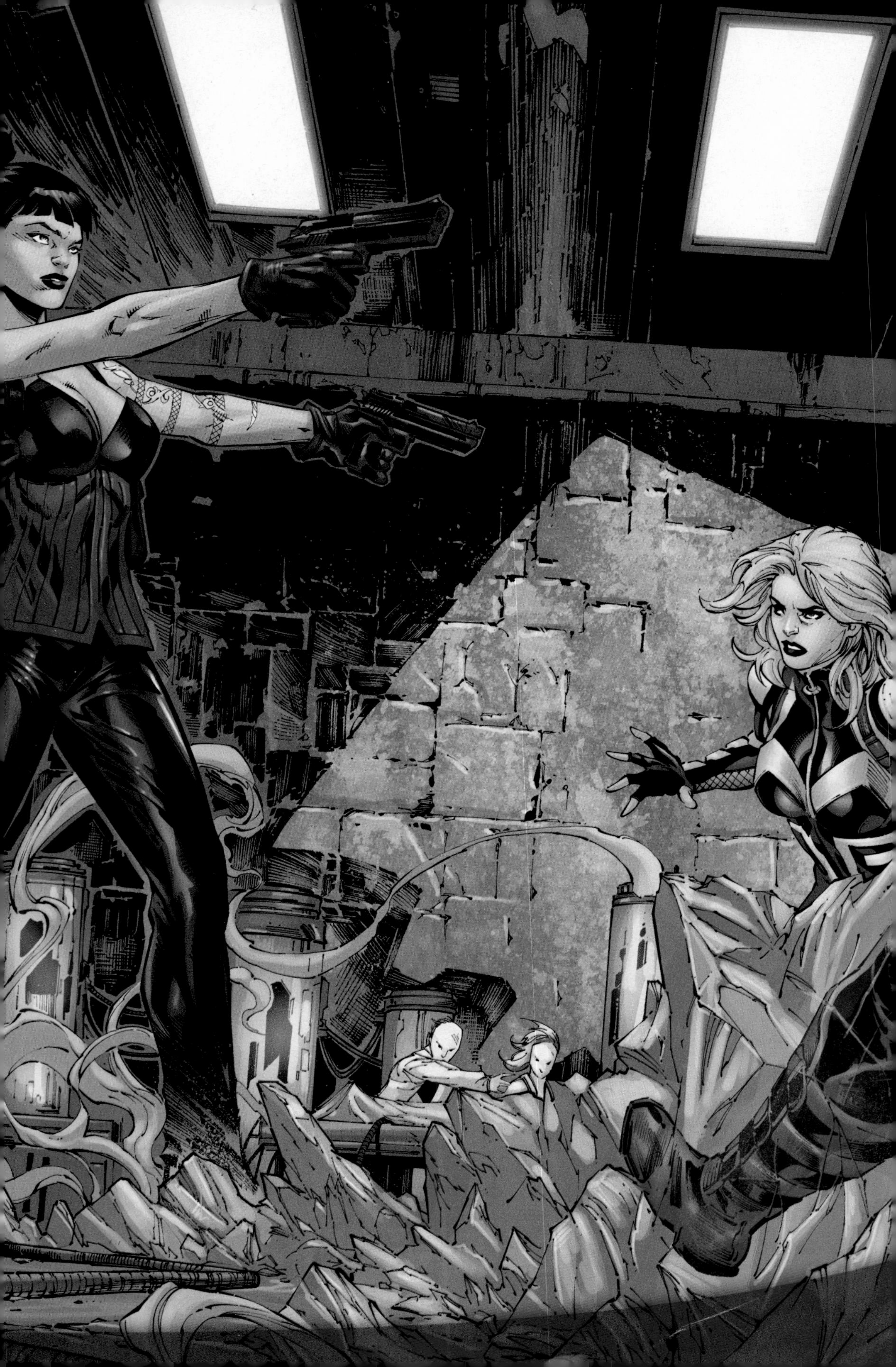

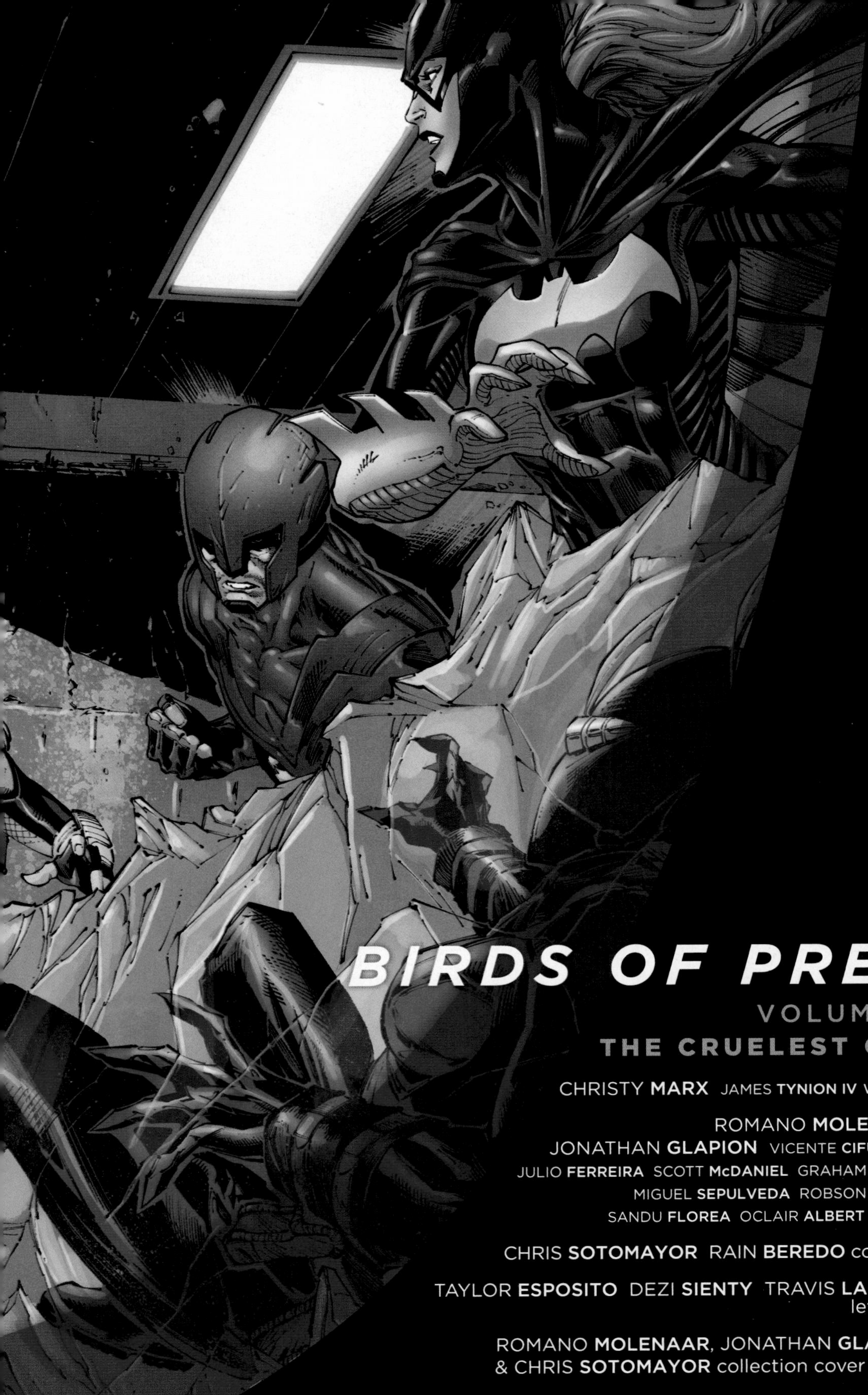

BIRDS OF PREY

VOLUME

THE CRUELEST CU

CHRISTY **MARX** JAMES **TYNION IV** write

ROMANO **MOLENAA**
JONATHAN **GLAPION** VICENTE **CIFUENT**
JULIO **FERREIRA** SCOTT **McDANIEL** GRAHAM **NOLA**
MIGUEL **SEPULVEDA** ROBSON **ROCH**
SANDU **FLOREA** OCLAIR **ALBERT** artis

CHRIS **SOTOMAYOR** RAIN **BEREDO** coloris

TAYLOR **ESPOSITO** DEZI **SIENTY** TRAVIS **LANHA**
lettere

ROMANO **MOLENAAR**, JONATHAN **GLAPIO**
& CHRIS **SOTOMAYOR** collection cover artis

TALON created by SCOTT **SNYDER** & GREG **CAPULL**

RACHEL GLUCKSTERN KATIE KUBERT Editors – Original Series
RICKEY PURDIN DARREN SHAN Assistant Editors – Original Series ROWENA YOW Editor
ROBBIN BROSTERMAN Design Director – Books ROBBIE BIEDERMAN Publication Design

BOB HARRAS Senior VP – Editor-in-Chief, DC Comics

DIANE NELSON President DAN DIDIO and JIM LEE Co-Publishers
GEOFF JOHNS Chief Creative Officer
JOHN ROOD Executive VP – Sales, Marketing and Business Development
AMY GENKINS Senior VP – Business and Legal Affairs NAIRI GARDINER Senior VP – Finance
JEFF BOISON VP – Publishing Planning MARK CHIARELLO VP – Art Direction and Design
JOHN CUNNINGHAM VP – Marketing TERRI CUNNINGHAM VP – Editorial Administration
ALISON GILL Senior VP – Manufacturing and Operations HANK KANALZ Senior VP Vertigo and Integrated Publishing
JAY KOGAN VP – Business and Legal Affairs, Publishing JACK MAHAN VP – Business Affairs, Talent
NICK NAPOLITANO VP – Manufacturing Administration SUE POHJA VP – Book Sales
COURTNEY SIMMONS Senior VP – Publicity BOB WAYNE Senior VP – Sales

BIRDS OF PREY VOLUME 4: THE CRUELEST CUT

DC Comics, 1700 Broadway, New York, NY 10019
A Warner Bros. Entertainment Company.
Printed by RR Donnelley, Owensville, MO, USA. 6/18/14. First Printing.

ISBN: 978-1-4012-4635-8

SUSTAINABLE
FORESTRY
INITIATIVE

Certified Chain of Custody
20% Certified Forest Content,
80% Certified Sourcing
www.sfiprogram.org
SFI-01042
APPLIES TO TEXT STOCK ONLY

Library of Congress Cataloging-in-Publication Data

Marx, Christy.
Birds of Prey. Volume 4, The Cruelest Cut / Christy Marx ; [illustrated by] Romano Molenaar, Vicente Cifuentes.
pages cm
ISBN 978-1-4012-4635-8 (paperback)
1. Graphic novels. I. Molenaar, Romano, 1971- illustrator. II. Cifuentes, Vicente, illustrator. III. Title. IV. Title: Cruelest Cut.
PN6728.B497M34 2014
741.5'973—dc23
                    2014010797

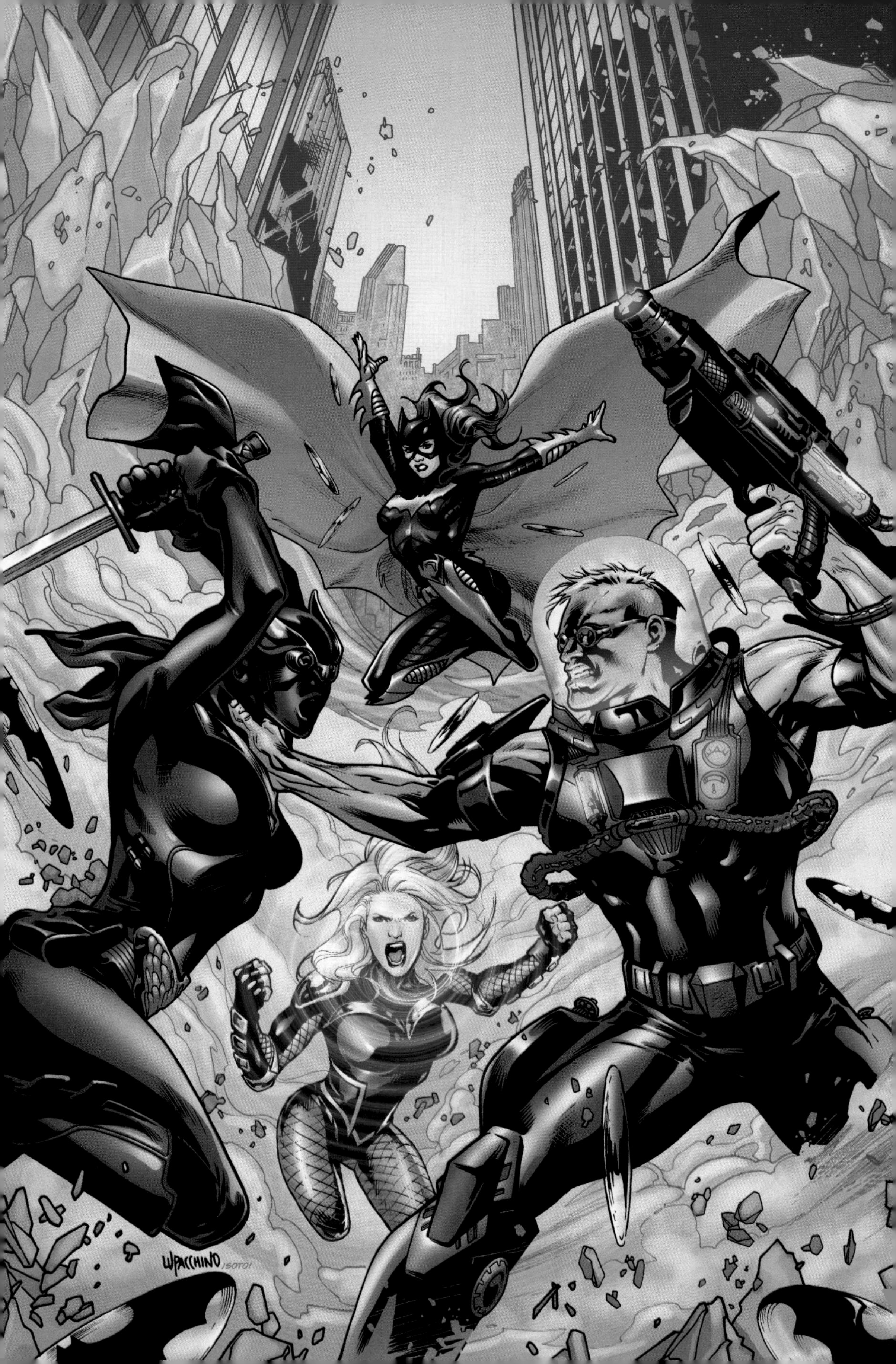
WPACCHINO
¡SOTO!

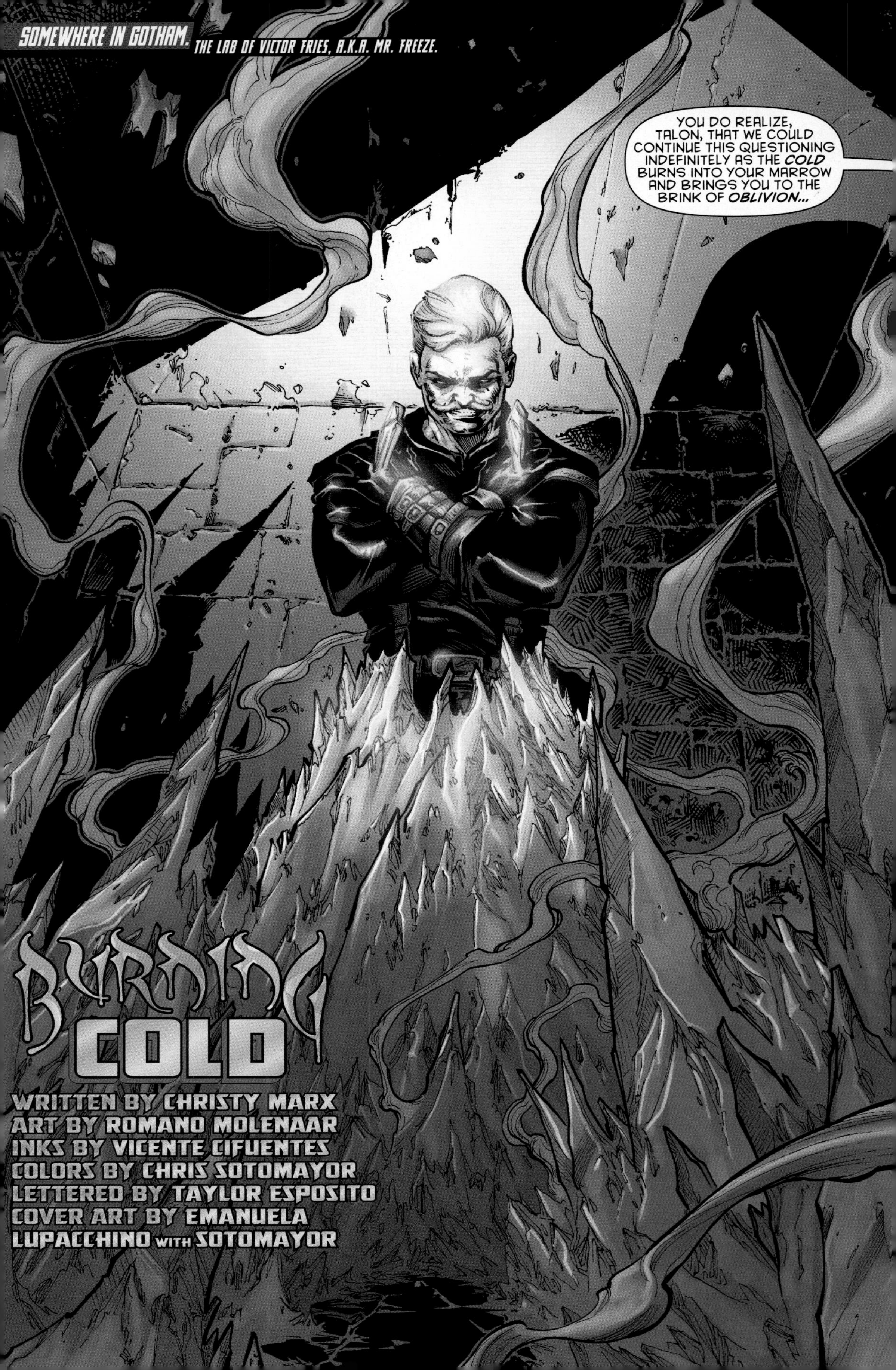
SOMEWHERE IN GOTHAM.
THE LAB OF VICTOR FRIES, A.K.A. MR. FREEZE.
YOU DO REALIZE, TALON, THAT WE COULD CONTINUE THIS QUESTIONING INDEFINITELY AS THE COLD BURNS INTO YOUR MARROW AND BRINGS YOU TO THE BRINK OF OBLIVION...
BURNING COLD
WRITTEN BY CHRISTY MARX
ART BY ROMANO MOLENAAR
INKS BY VICENTE CIFUENTES
COLORS BY CHRIS SOTOMAYOR
LETTERED BY TAYLOR ESPOSITO
COVER ART BY EMANUELA LUPACCHINO WITH SOTOMAYOR

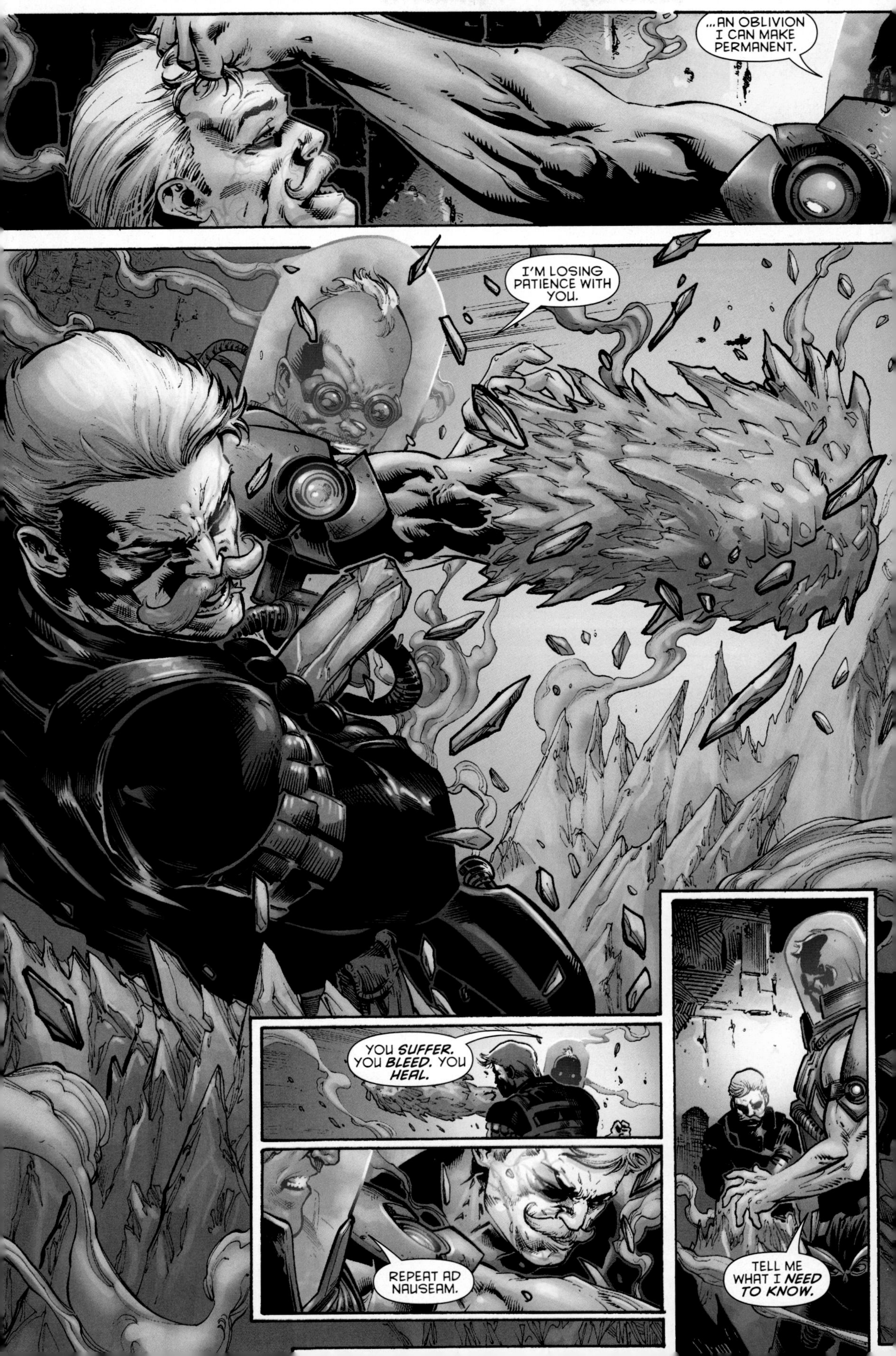
...AN OBLIVION I CAN MAKE PERMANENT.
I'M LOSING PATIENCE WITH YOU.
YOU SUFFER. YOU BLEED. YOU HEAL.
REPEAT AD NAUSEAM.
TELL ME WHAT I NEED TO KNOW.

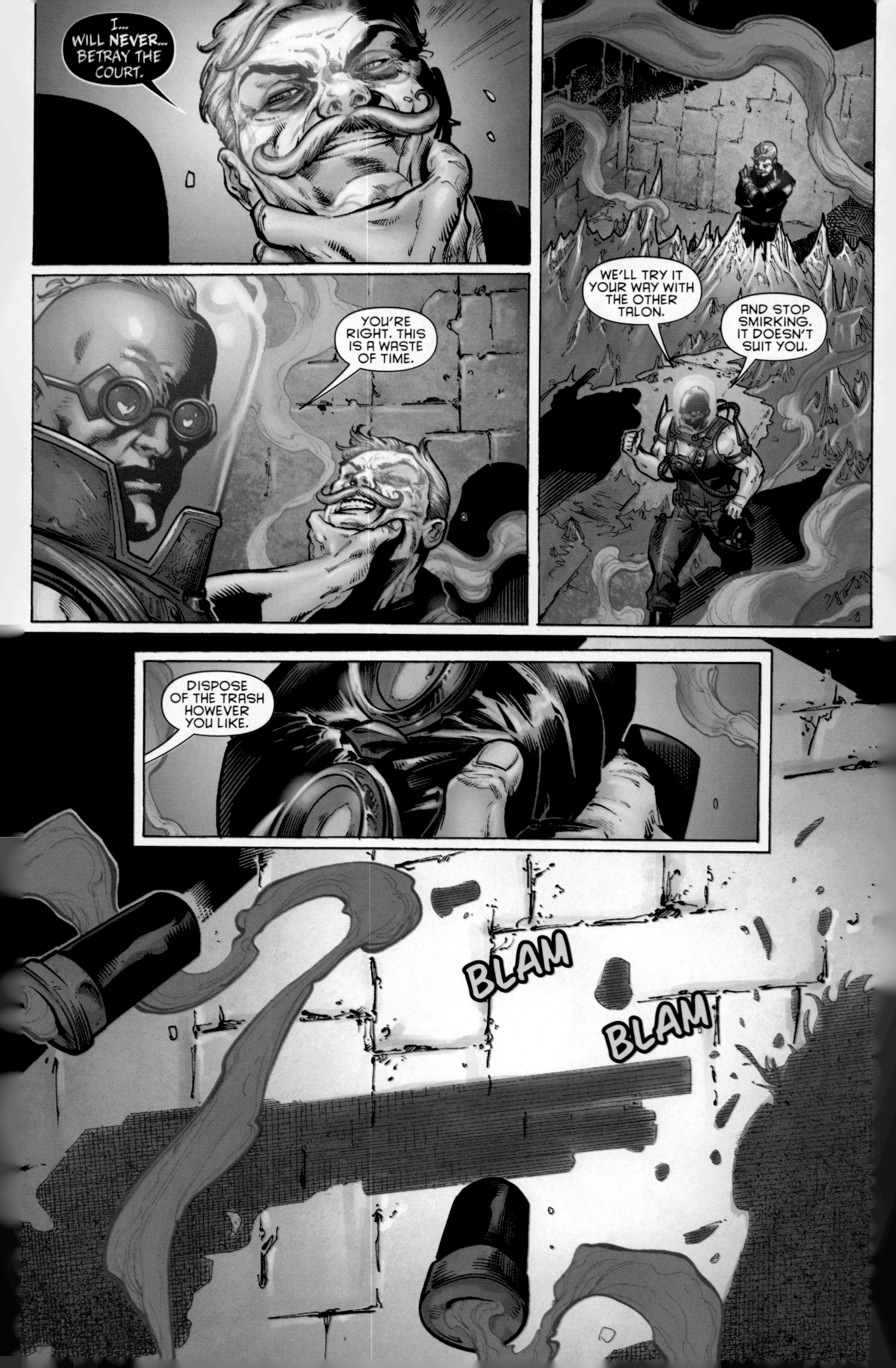
I... WILL NEVER... BETRAY THE COURT.
YOU'RE RIGHT. THIS IS A WASTE OF TIME.
WE'LL TRY IT YOUR WAY WITH THE OTHER TALON.
AND STOP SMIRKING. IT DOESN'T SUIT YOU.
DISPOSE OF THE TRASH HOWEVER YOU LIKE.
BLAM
BLAM

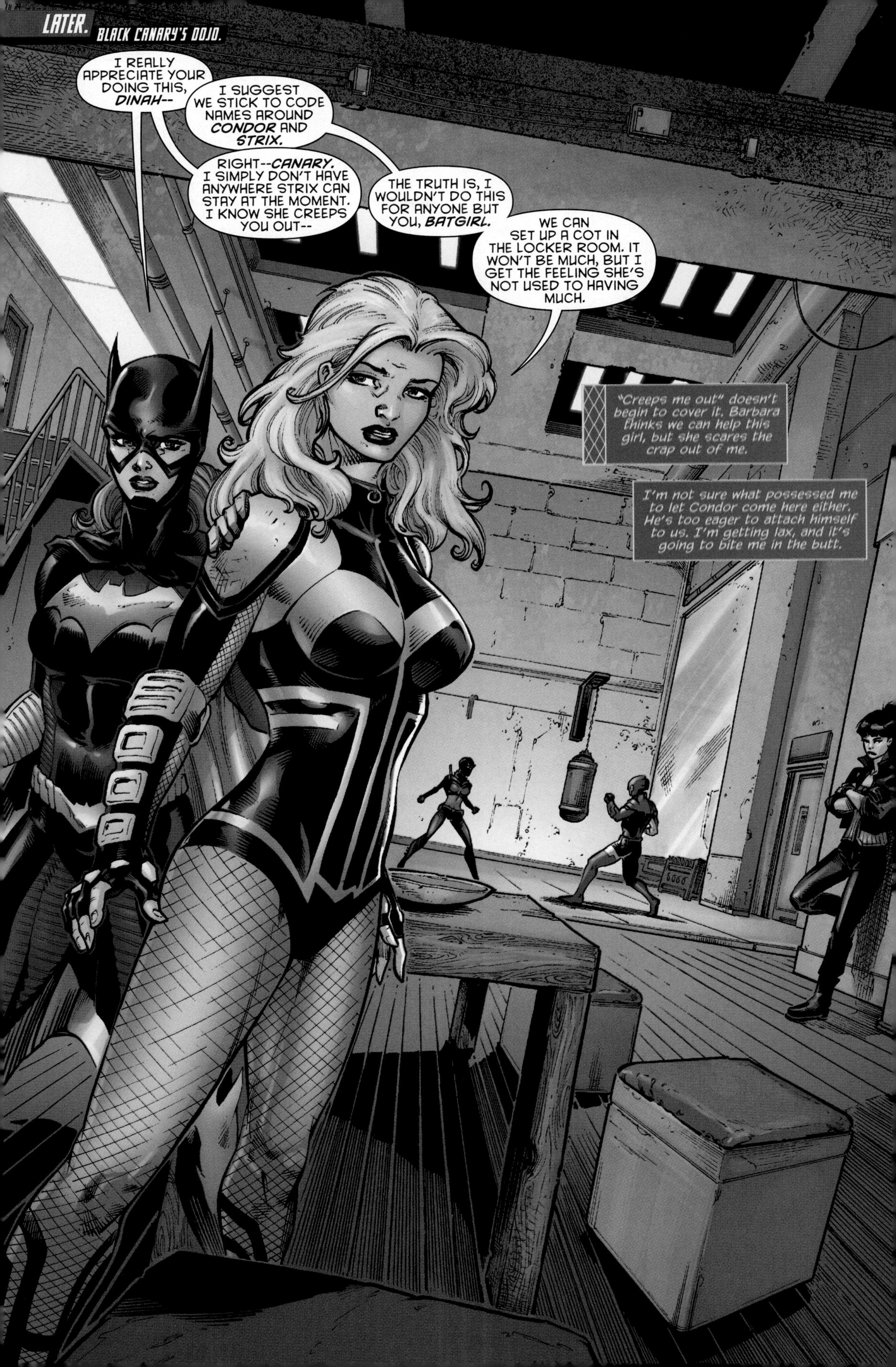
LATER.
BLACK CANARY'S DOJO.
I REALLY APPRECIATE YOUR DOING THIS, DINAH--
I SUGGEST WE STICK TO CODE NAMES AROUND CONDOR AND STRIX.
RIGHT--CANARY. I SIMPLY DON'T HAVE ANYWHERE STRIX CAN STAY AT THE MOMENT. I KNOW SHE CREEPS YOU OUT--
THE TRUTH IS, I WOULDN'T DO THIS FOR ANYONE BUT YOU, BATGIRL.
WE CAN SET UP A COT IN THE LOCKER ROOM. IT WON'T BE MUCH, BUT I GET THE FEELING SHE'S NOT USED TO HAVING MUCH.
"Creeps me out" doesn't begin to cover it. Barbara thinks we can help this girl, but she scares the crap out of me.
I'm not sure what possessed me to let Condor come here either. He's too eager to attach himself to us. I'm getting lax, and it's going to bite me in the butt.

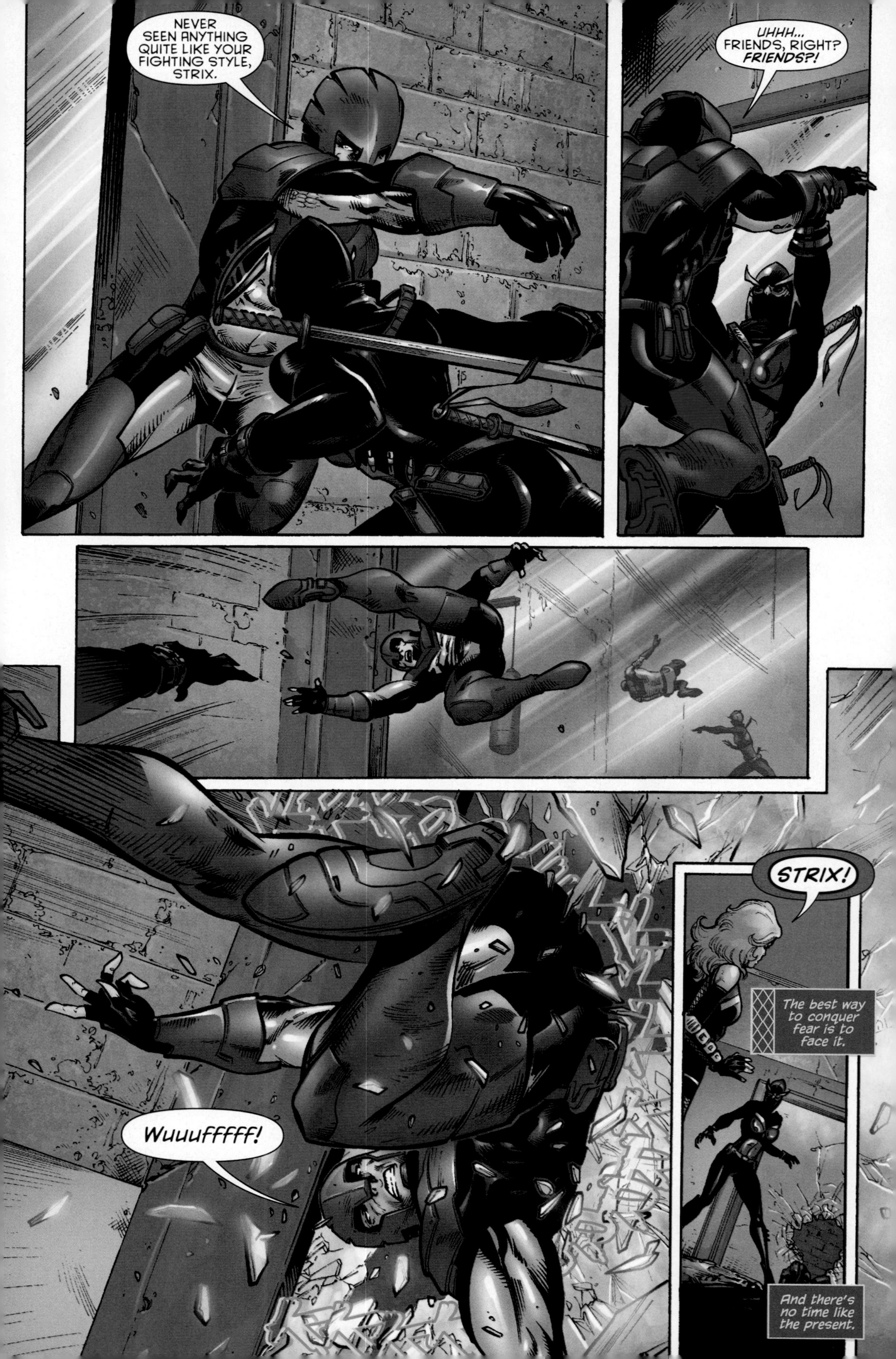

NEVER SEEN ANYTHING QUITE LIKE YOUR FIGHTING STYLE, STRIX.
UHHH... FRIENDS, RIGHT? FRIENDS?!
Wuuufffff!
STRIX!
The best way to conquer fear is to face it.
And there's no time like the present.

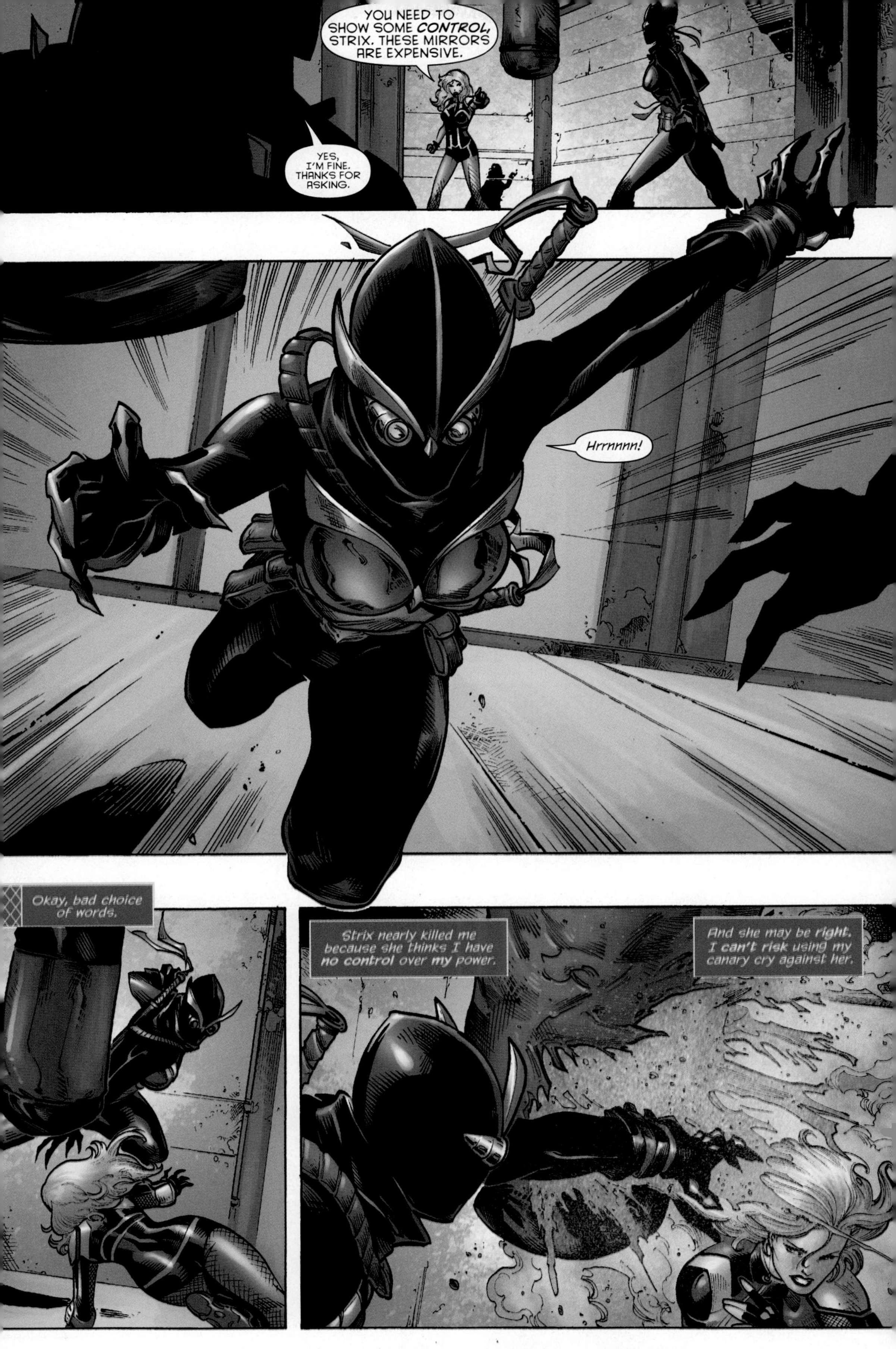
YOU NEED TO SHOW SOME CONTROL, STRIX. THESE MIRRORS ARE EXPENSIVE.
YES, I'M FINE. THANKS FOR ASKING.
Hrrnnnn!
Okay, bad choice of words.
Strix nearly killed me because she thinks I have no control over my power.
And she may be right. I can't risk using my canary cry against her.

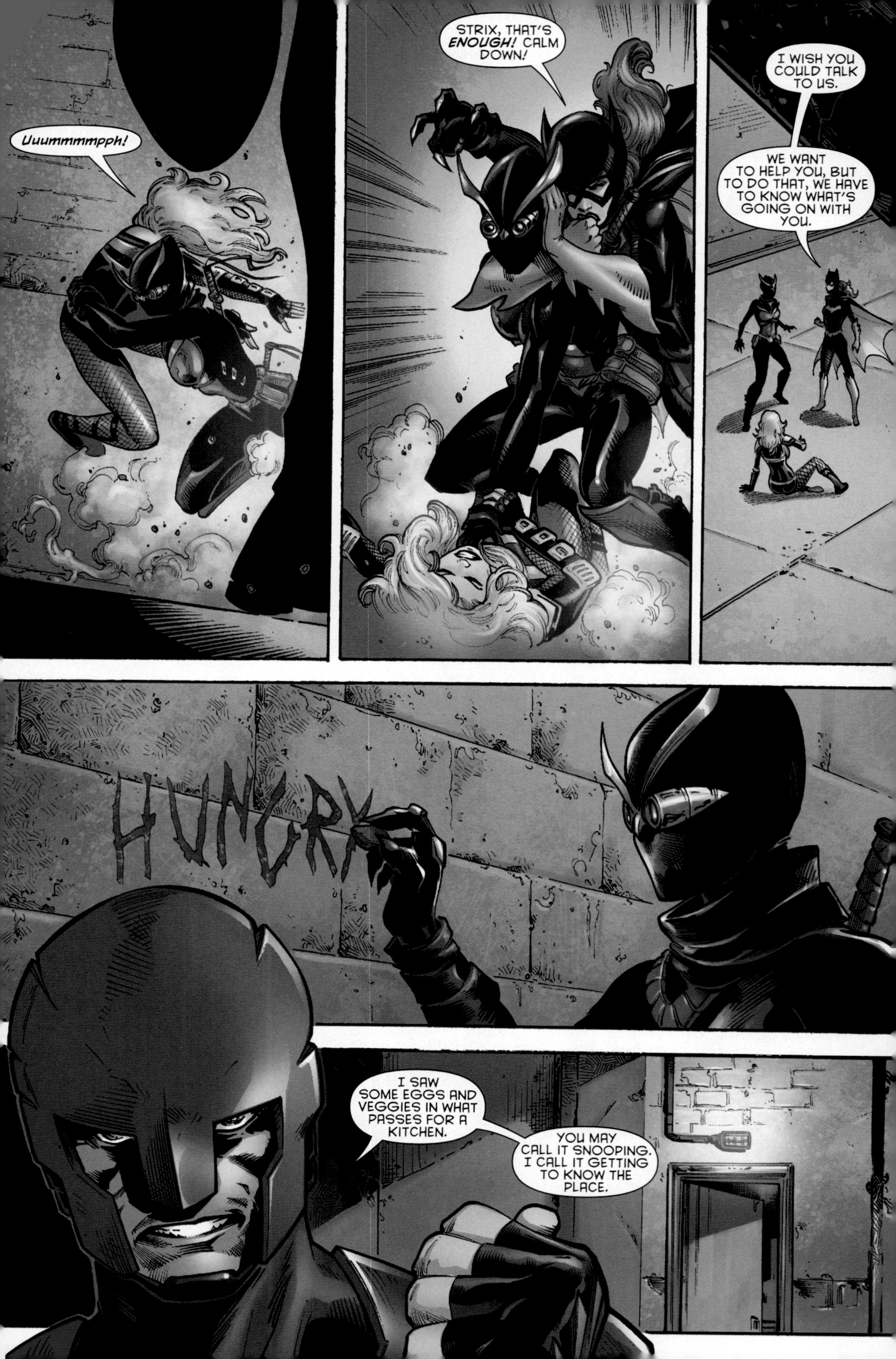
Uuummmmpph!
STRIX, THAT'S *ENOUGH!* CALM DOWN!
I WISH YOU COULD TALK TO US.
WE WANT TO HELP YOU, BUT TO DO THAT, WE HAVE TO KNOW WHAT'S GOING ON WITH YOU.
HUNGRY
I SAW SOME EGGS AND VEGGIES IN WHAT PASSES FOR A KITCHEN.
YOU MAY CALL IT SNOOPING. I CALL IT GETTING TO KNOW THE PLACE.

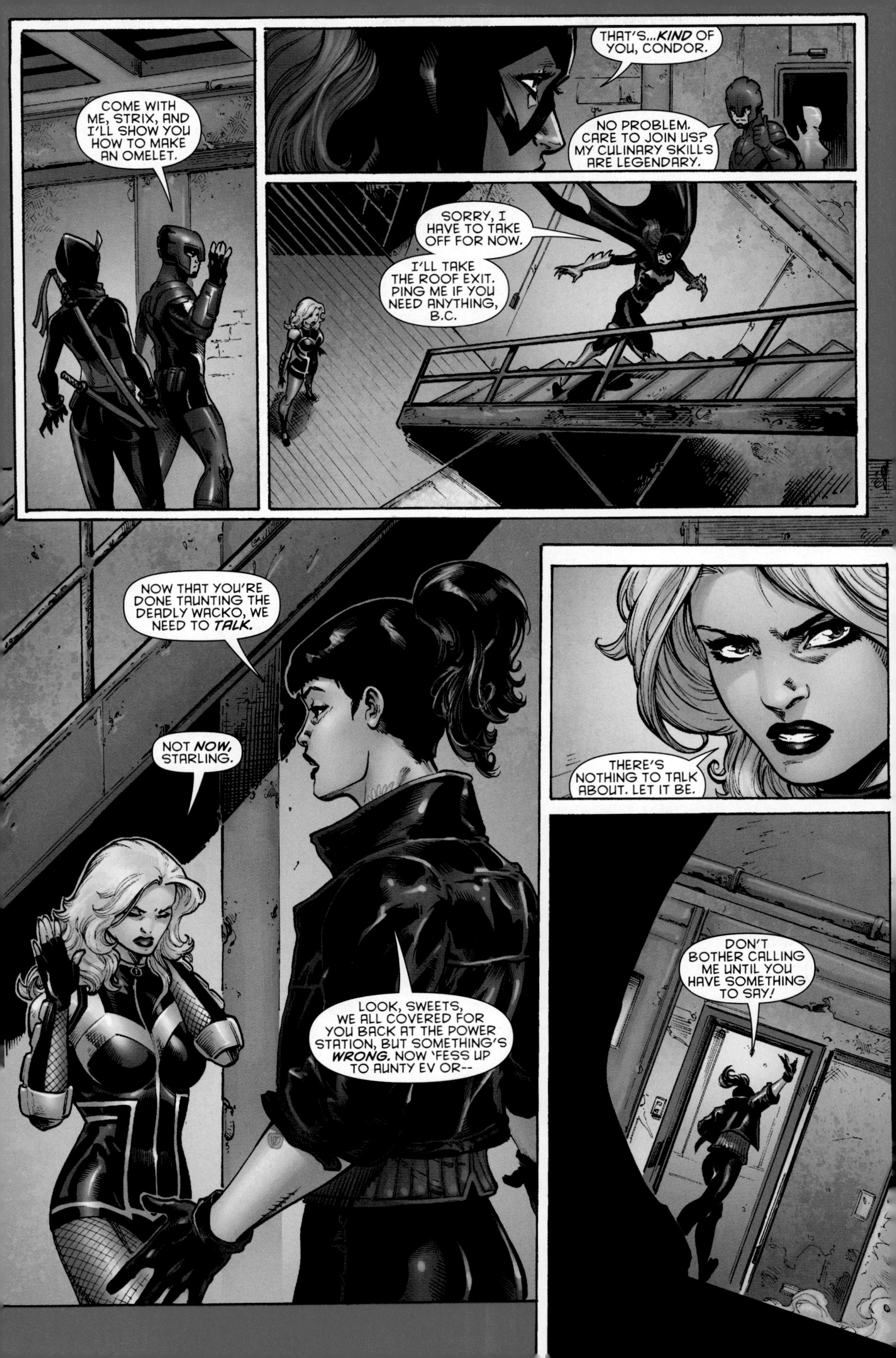
COME WITH ME, STRIX, AND I'LL SHOW YOU HOW TO MAKE AN OMELET.
THAT'S...KIND OF YOU, CONDOR.
NO PROBLEM. CARE TO JOIN US? MY CULINARY SKILLS ARE LEGENDARY.
SORRY, I HAVE TO TAKE OFF FOR NOW.
I'LL TAKE THE ROOF EXIT. PING ME IF YOU NEED ANYTHING, B.C.
NOW THAT YOU'RE DONE TAUNTING THE DEADLY WACKO, WE NEED TO TALK.
NOT NOW, STARLING.
LOOK, SWEETS, WE ALL COVERED FOR YOU BACK AT THE POWER STATION, BUT SOMETHING'S WRONG. NOW 'FESS UP TO AUNTY EV OR--
THERE'S NOTHING TO TALK ABOUT. LET IT BE.
DON'T BOTHER CALLING ME UNTIL YOU HAVE SOMETHING TO SAY!

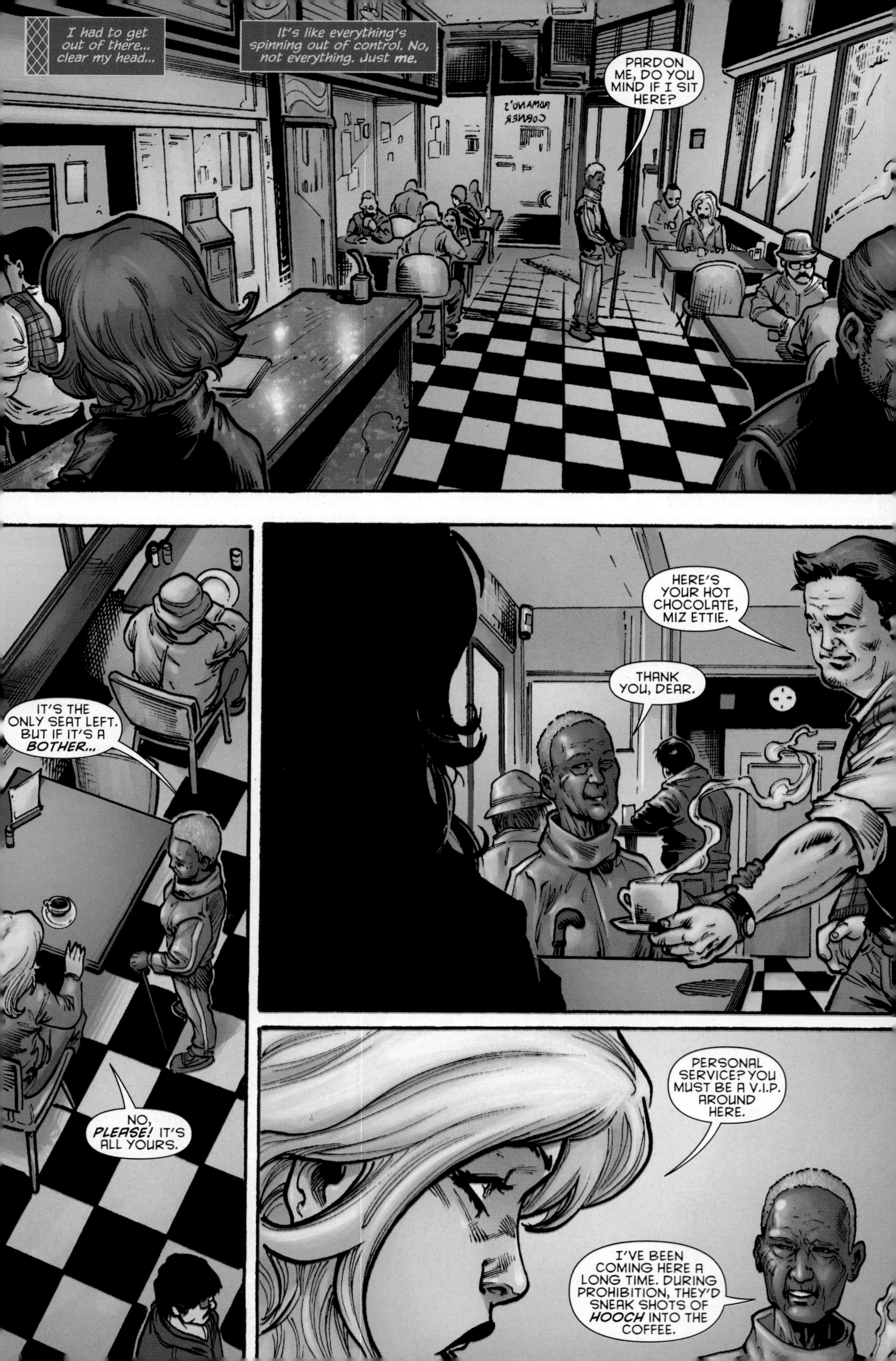
I had to get out of there... clear my head...
It's like everything's spinning out of control. No, not everything. Just *me.*
PARDON ME, DO YOU MIND IF I SIT HERE?
ROMANO'S CORNER
IT'S THE ONLY SEAT LEFT. BUT IF IT'S A *BOTHER*...
NO, *PLEASE!* IT'S ALL YOURS.
HERE'S YOUR HOT CHOCOLATE, MIZ ETTIE.
THANK YOU, DEAR.
PERSONAL SERVICE? YOU MUST BE A V.I.P. AROUND HERE.
I'VE BEEN COMING HERE A LONG TIME. DURING PROHIBITION, THEY'D SNEAK SHOTS OF *HOOCH* INTO THE COFFEE.

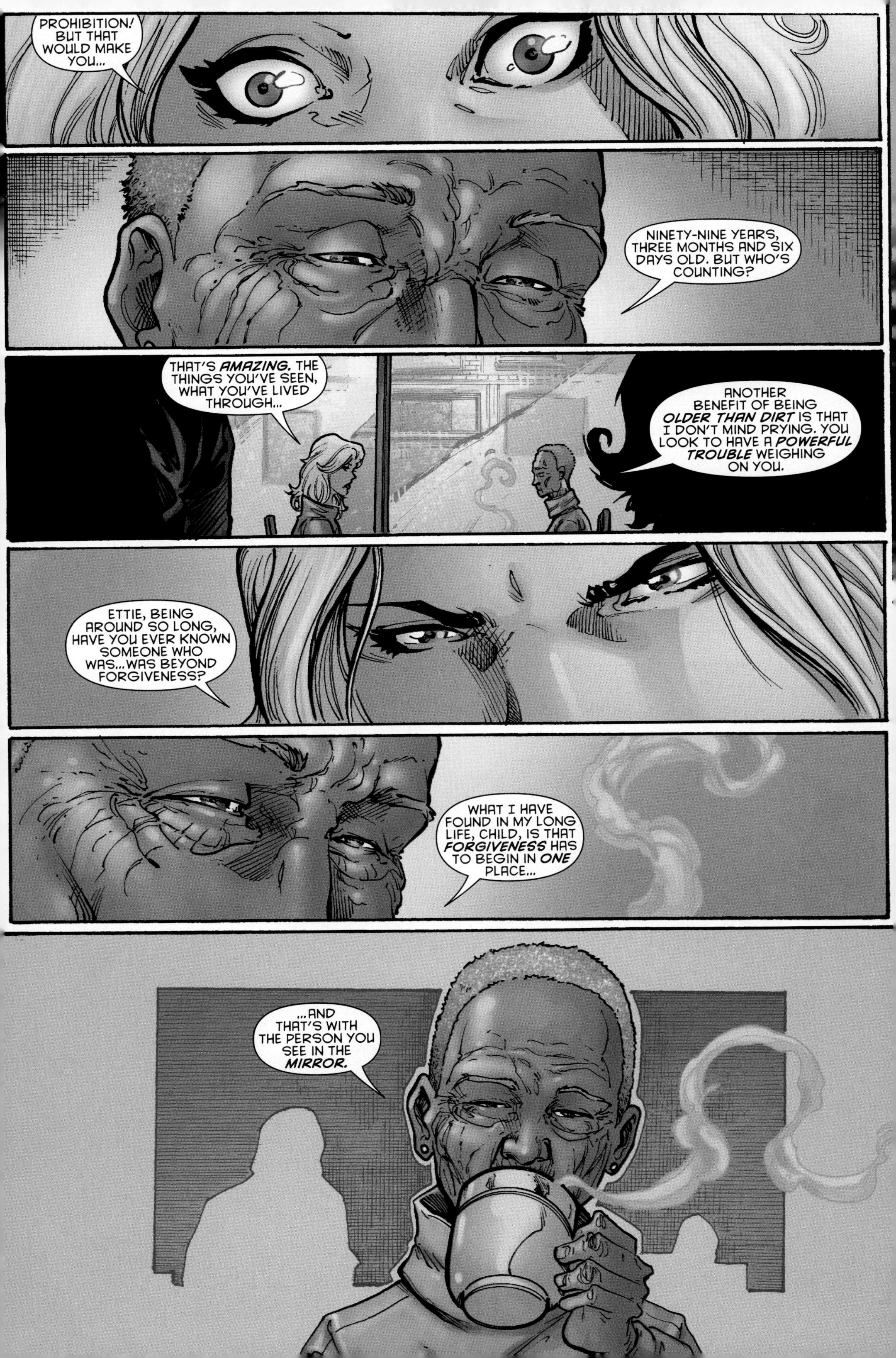
PROHIBITION! BUT THAT WOULD MAKE YOU...
NINETY-NINE YEARS, THREE MONTHS AND SIX DAYS OLD. BUT WHO'S COUNTING?
THAT'S AMAZING. THE THINGS YOU'VE SEEN, WHAT YOU'VE LIVED THROUGH...
ANOTHER BENEFIT OF BEING OLDER THAN DIRT IS THAT I DON'T MIND PRYING. YOU LOOK TO HAVE A POWERFUL TROUBLE WEIGHING ON YOU.
ETTIE, BEING AROUND SO LONG, HAVE YOU EVER KNOWN SOMEONE WHO WAS...WAS BEYOND FORGIVENESS?
WHAT I HAVE FOUND IN MY LONG LIFE, CHILD, IS THAT FORGIVENESS HAS TO BEGIN IN ONE PLACE...
...AND THAT'S WITH THE PERSON YOU SEE IN THE MIRROR.

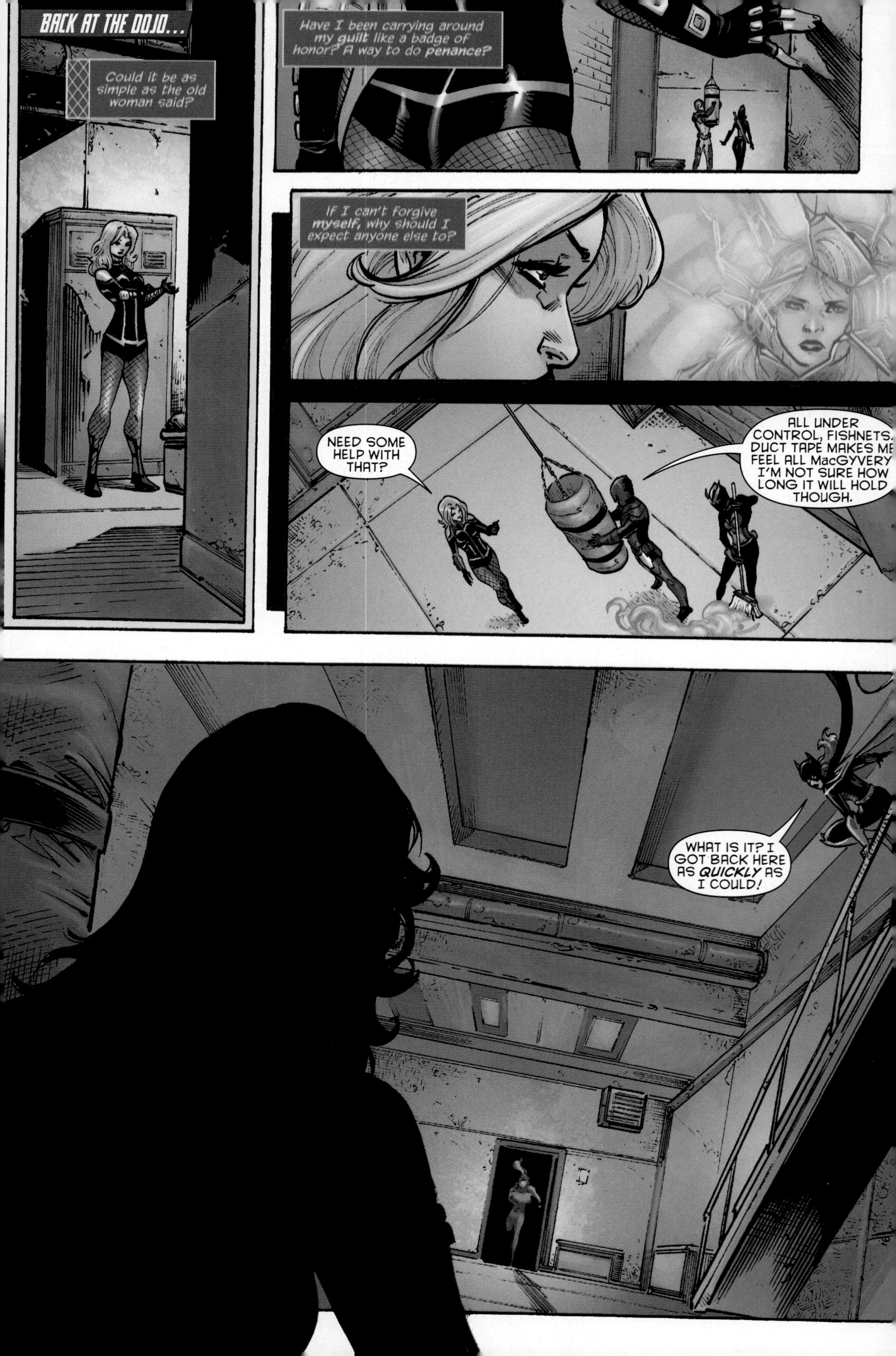
BACK AT THE DOJO...
Could it be as simple as the old woman said?
Have I been carrying around my guilt like a badge of honor? A way to do penance?
If I can't forgive myself, why should I expect anyone else to?
NEED SOME HELP WITH THAT?
ALL UNDER CONTROL, FISHNETS. DUCT TAPE MAKES ME FEEL ALL MacGYVERY. I'M NOT SURE HOW LONG IT WILL HOLD THOUGH.
WHAT IS IT? I GOT BACK HERE AS QUICKLY AS I COULD!

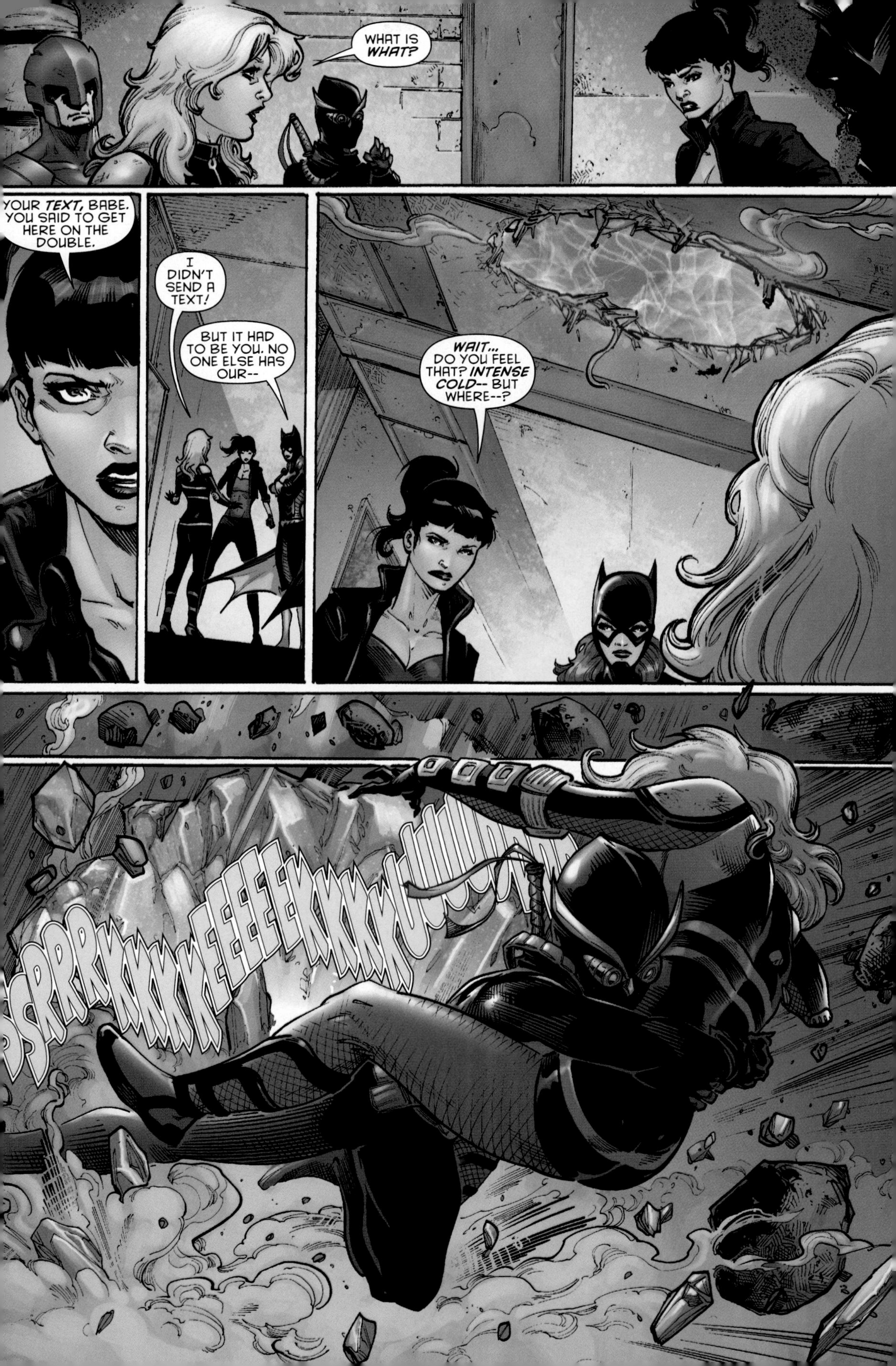

WHAT IS *WHAT?*
YOUR *TEXT,* BABE. YOU SAID TO GET HERE ON THE DOUBLE.
I DIDN'T SEND A TEXT!
BUT IT HAD TO BE YOU. NO ONE ELSE HAS OUR--
WAIT... DO YOU FEEL THAT? *INTENSE COLD--* BUT WHERE--?
SRRRKKKKKEEEEEKKKKKOOOOO

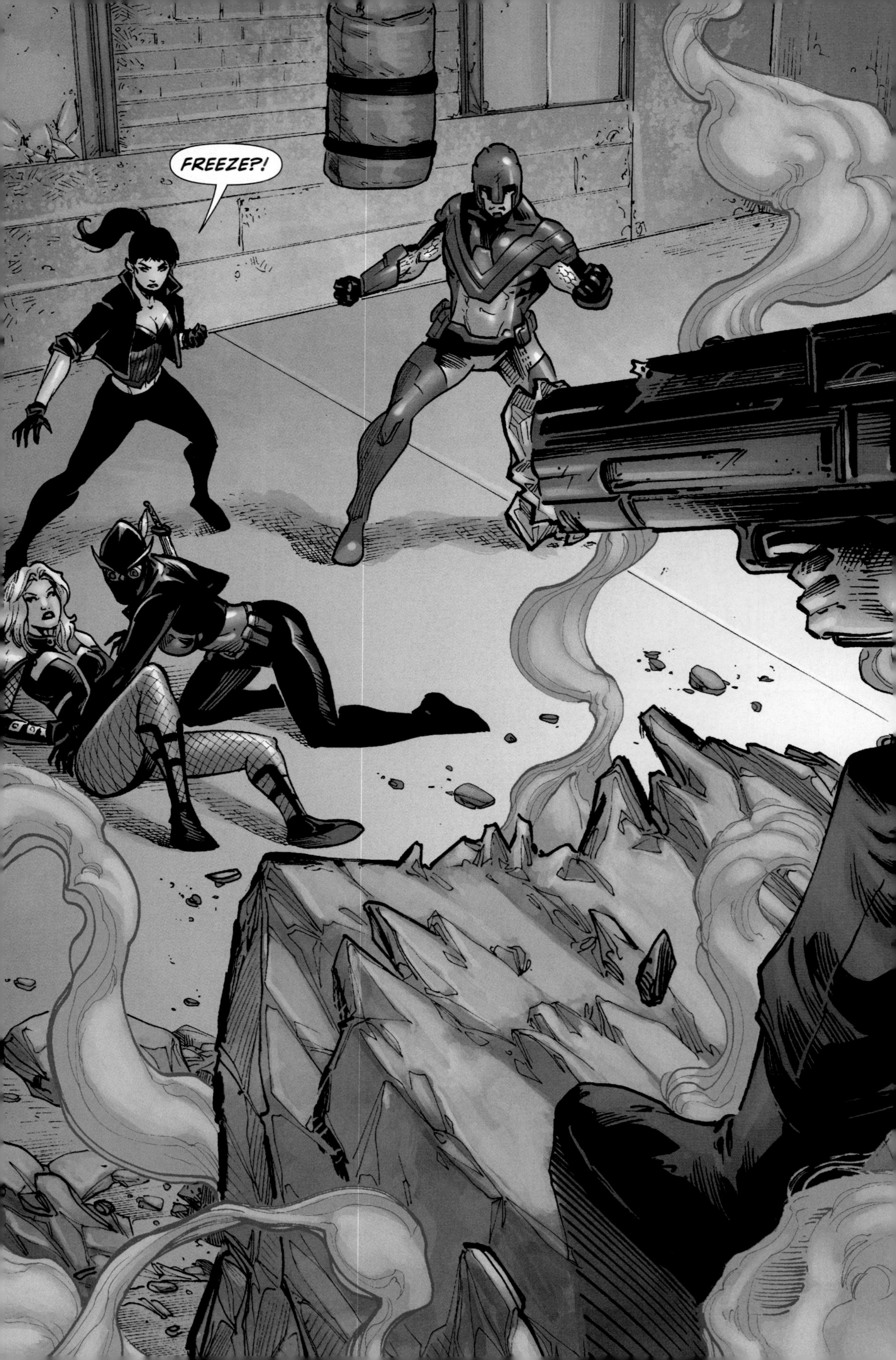
FREEZE?!

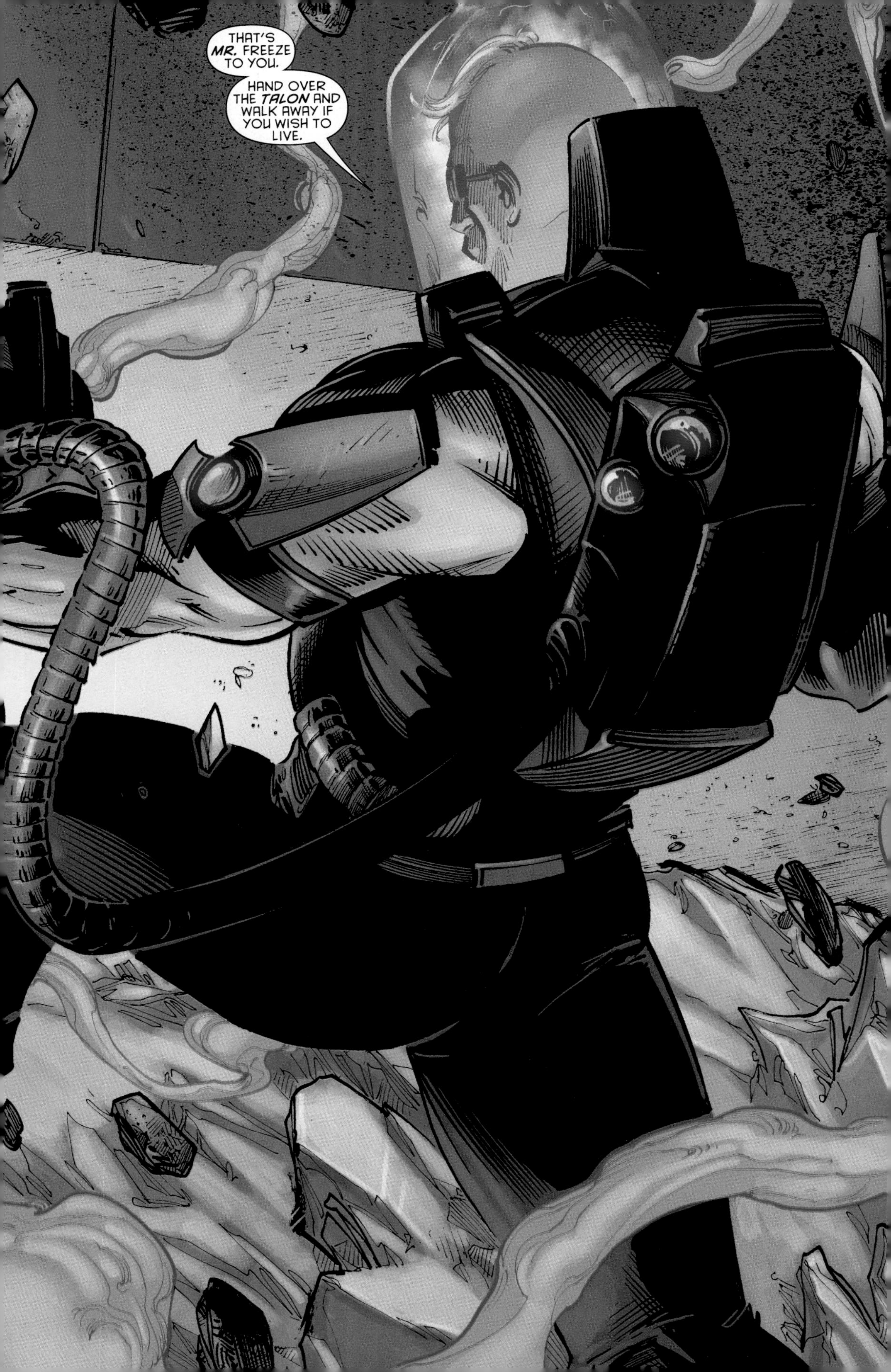
THAT'S MR. FREEZE TO YOU.
HAND OVER THE TALON AND WALK AWAY IF YOU WISH TO LIVE.

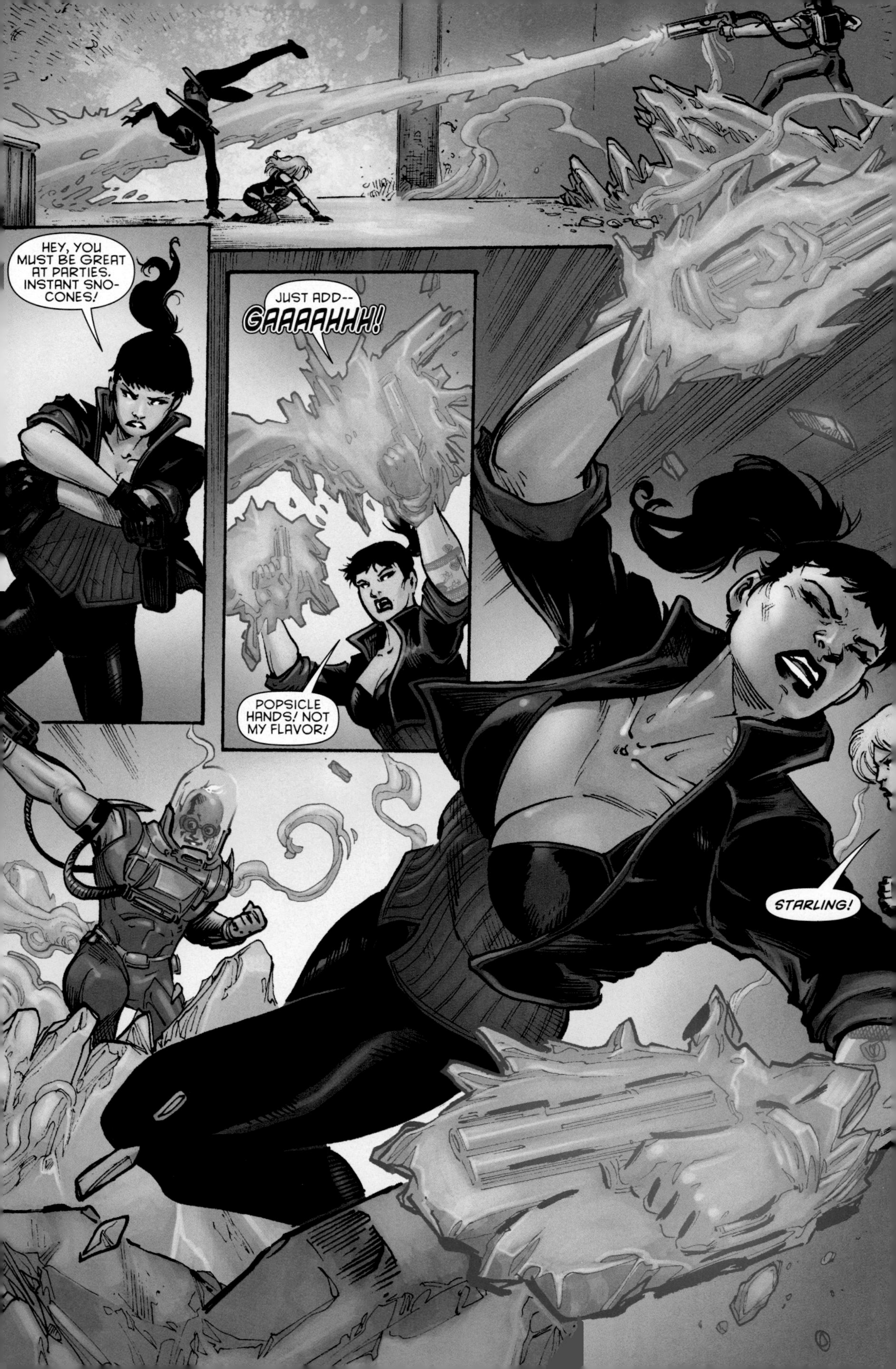
HEY, YOU MUST BE GREAT AT PARTIES. INSTANT SNO-CONES!
JUST ADD--
GAAAAHHH!
POPSICLE HANDS! NOT MY FLAVOR!
STARLING!

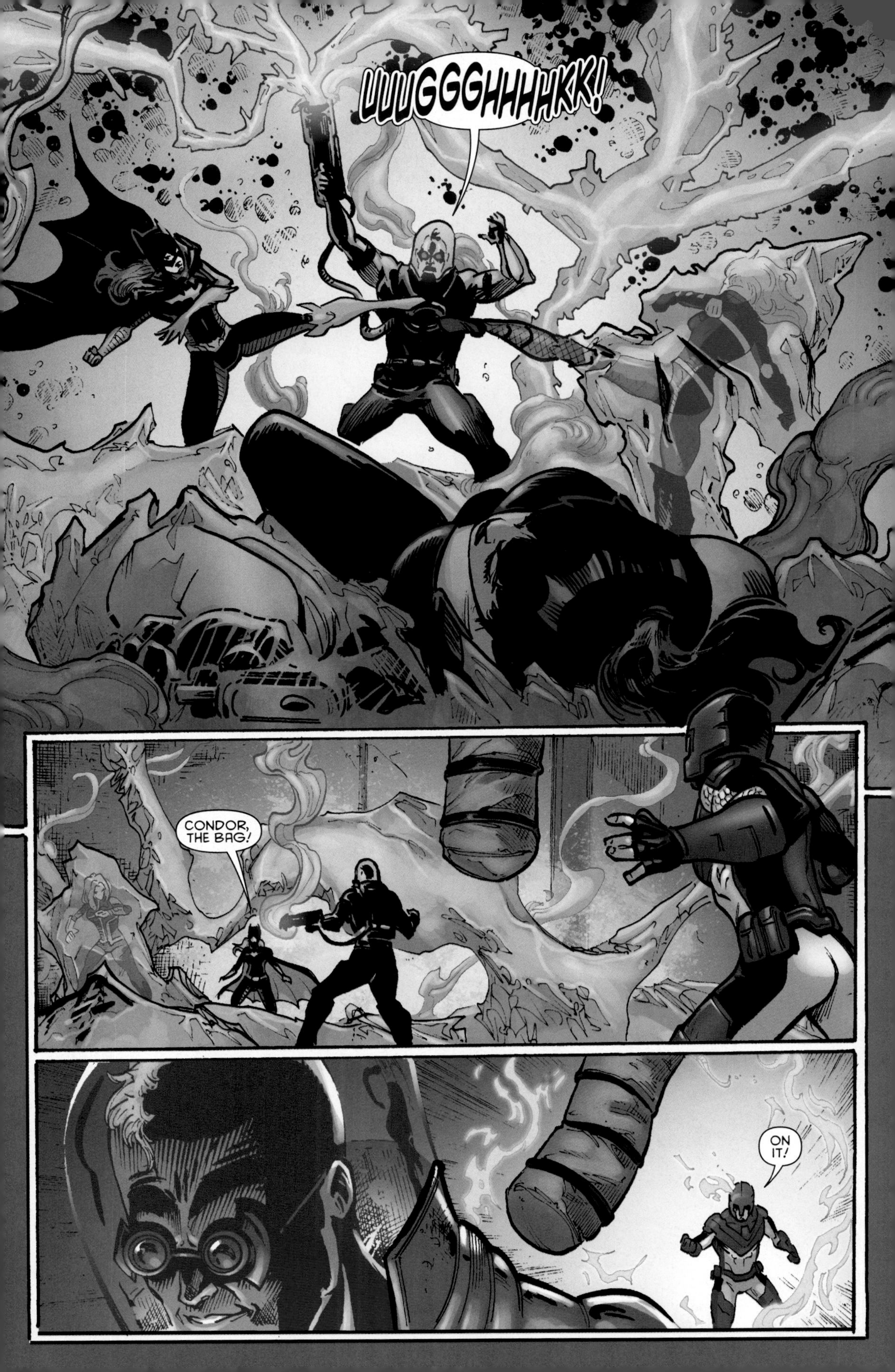
UUUGGGHHHHKK!
CONDOR, THE BAG!
ON IT!

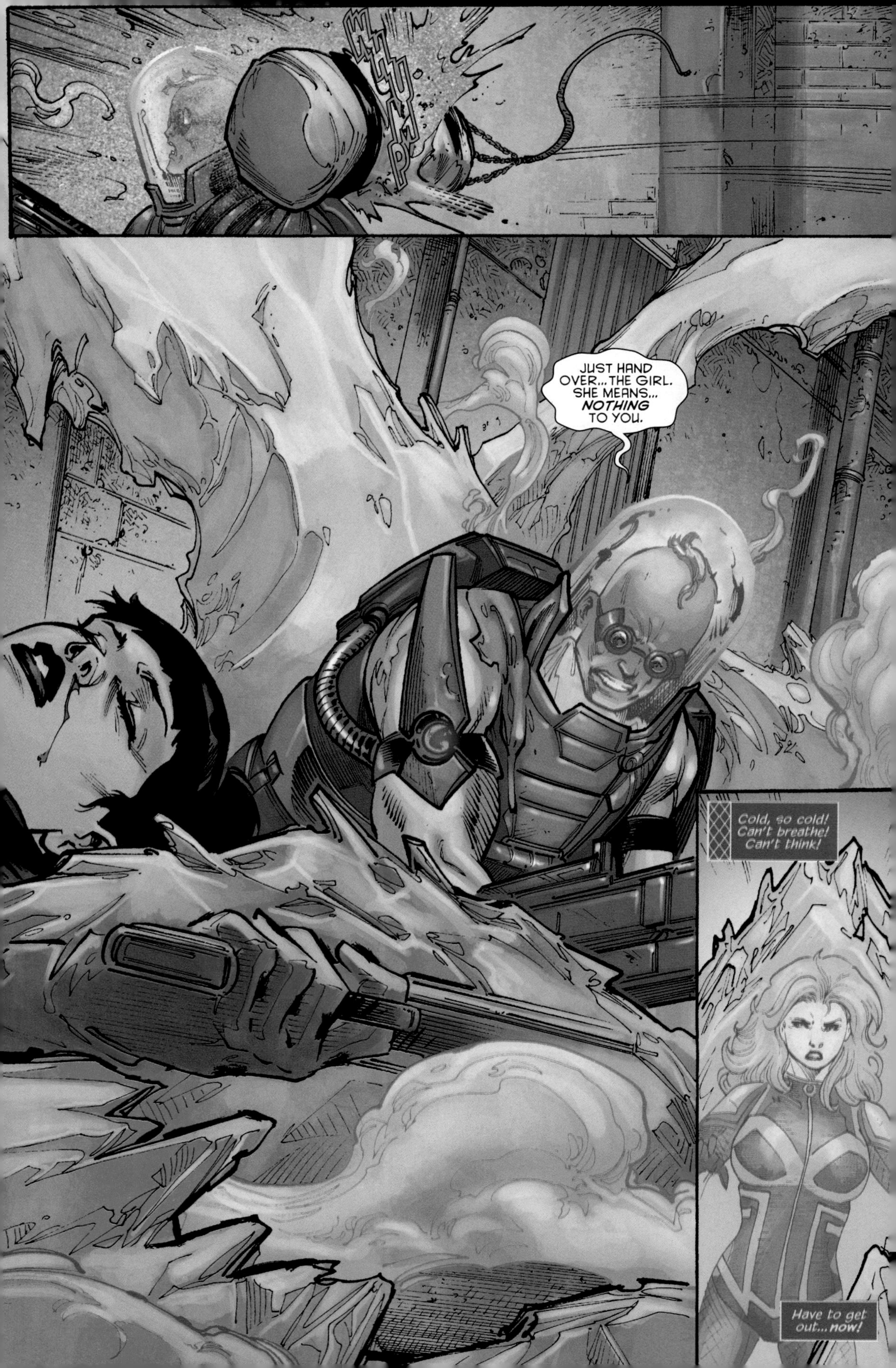
JUST HAND OVER... THE GIRL. SHE MEANS... *NOTHING* TO YOU.
Cold, so cold! Can't breathe! Can't think!
Have to get out... now!

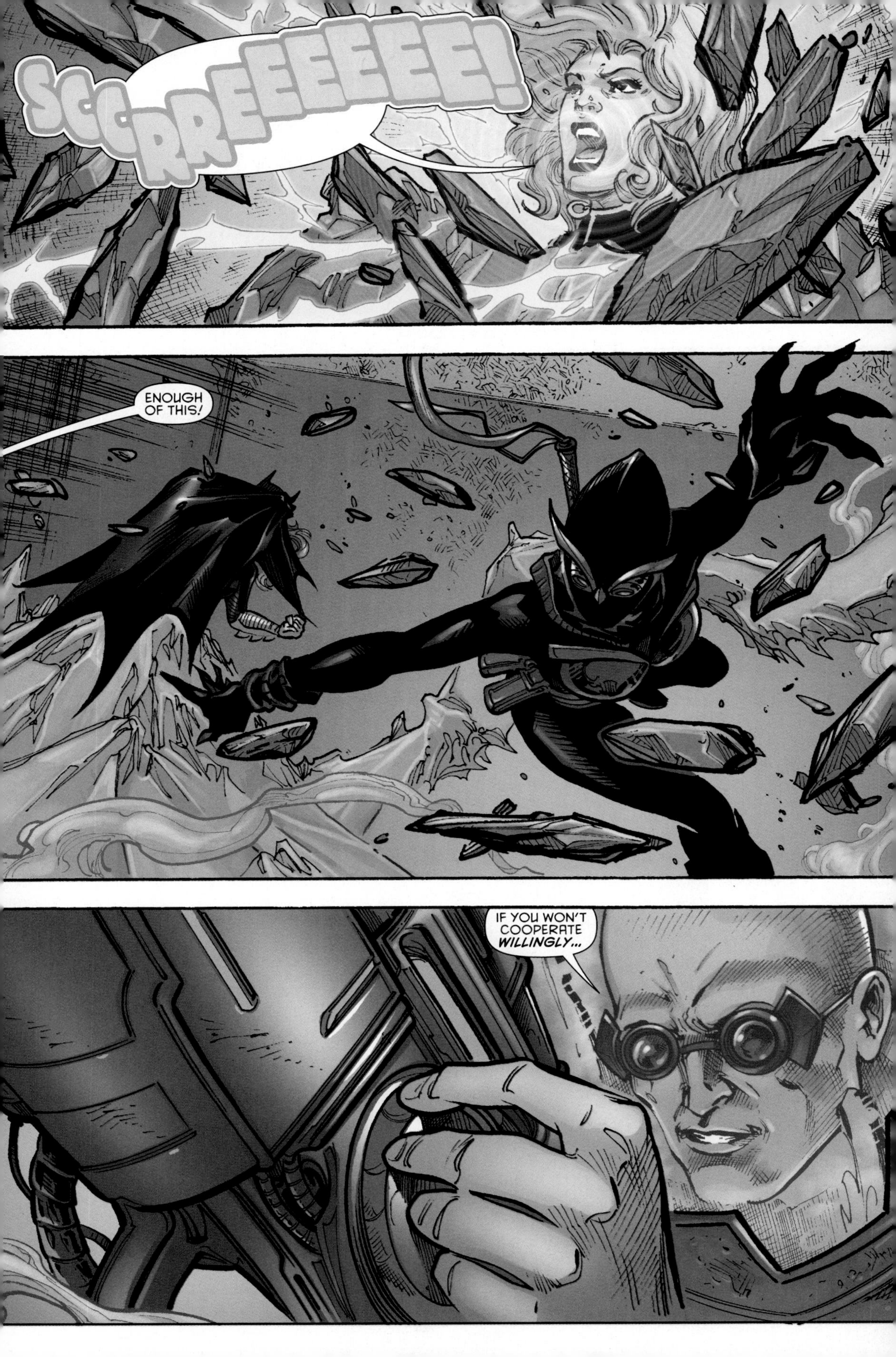
SCCRREEEEEEE!
ENOUGH OF THIS!
IF YOU WON'T COOPERATE *WILLINGLY*...

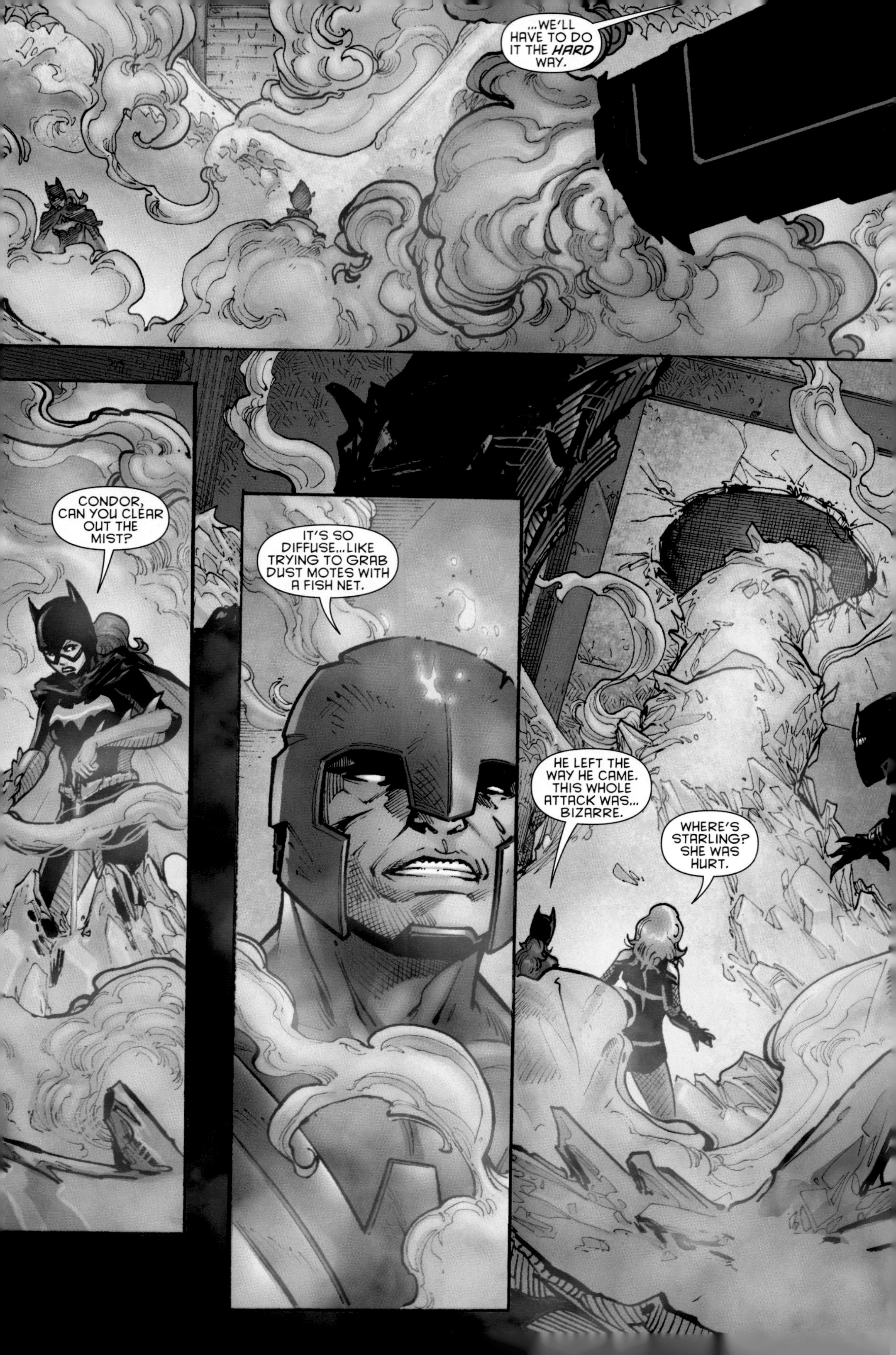
...WE'LL HAVE TO DO IT THE HARD WAY.
CONDOR, CAN YOU CLEAR OUT THE MIST?
IT'S SO DIFFUSE...LIKE TRYING TO GRAB DUST MOTES WITH A FISH NET.
HE LEFT THE WAY HE CAME. THIS WHOLE ATTACK WAS... BIZARRE.
WHERE'S STARLING? SHE WAS HURT.

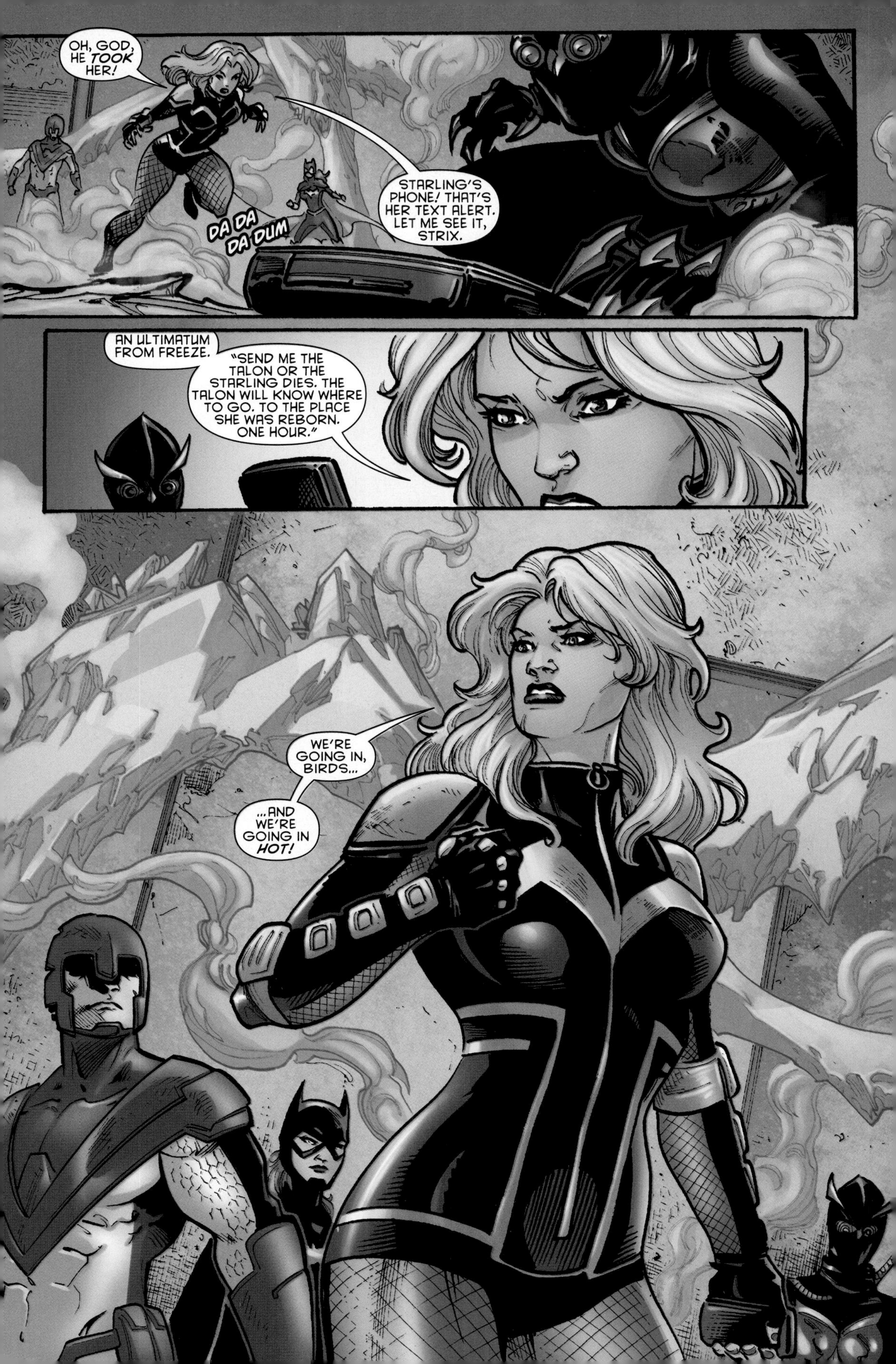
OH, GOD, HE *TOOK* HER!
STARLING'S PHONE! THAT'S HER TEXT ALERT. LET ME SEE IT, STRIX.
DA DA DA DUM
AN ULTIMATUM FROM FREEZE.
"SEND ME THE TALON OR THE STARLING DIES. THE TALON WILL KNOW WHERE TO GO. TO THE PLACE SHE WAS REBORN. ONE HOUR."
WE'RE GOING IN, BIRDS...
...AND WE'RE GOING IN *HOT!*

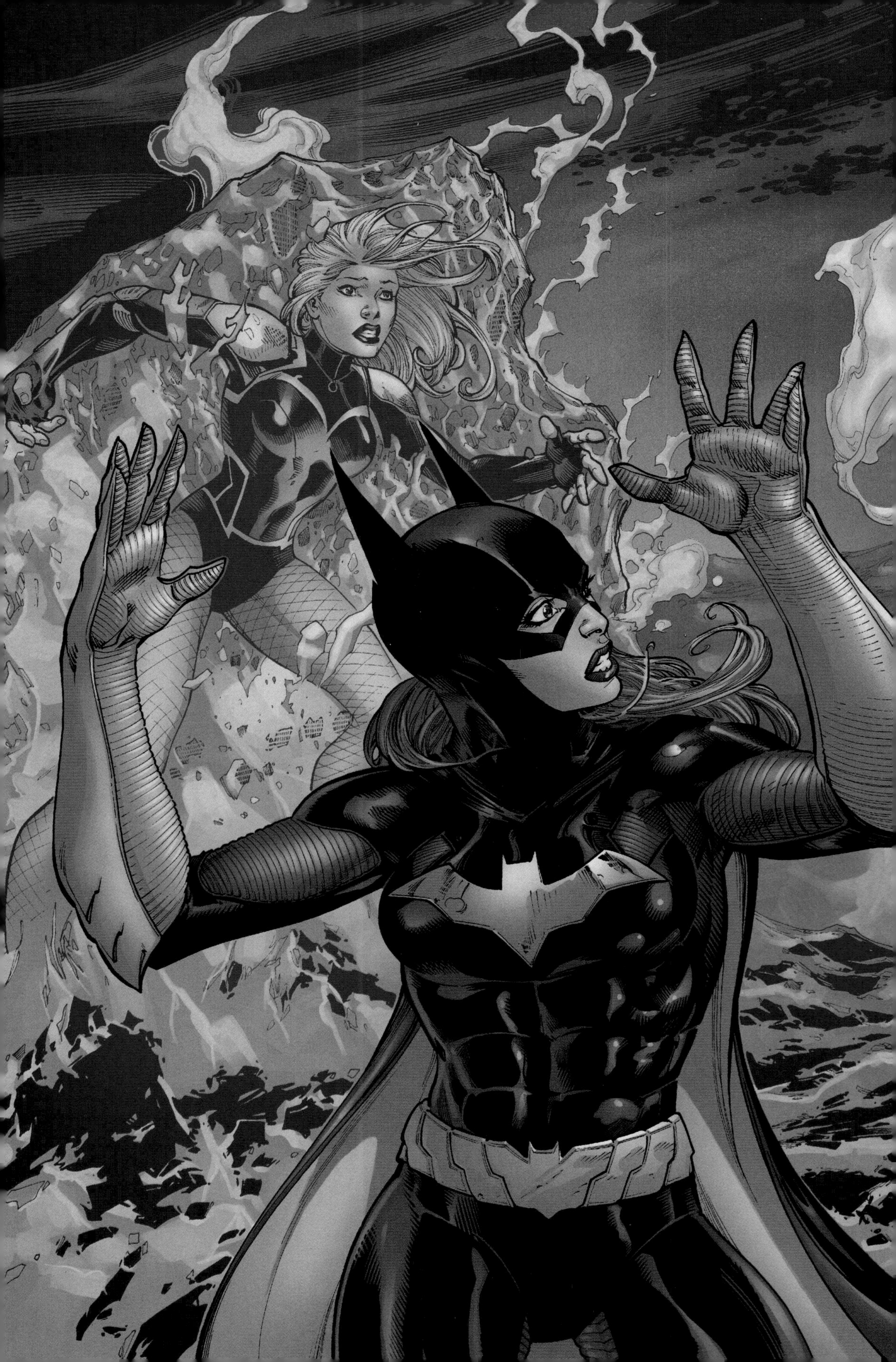

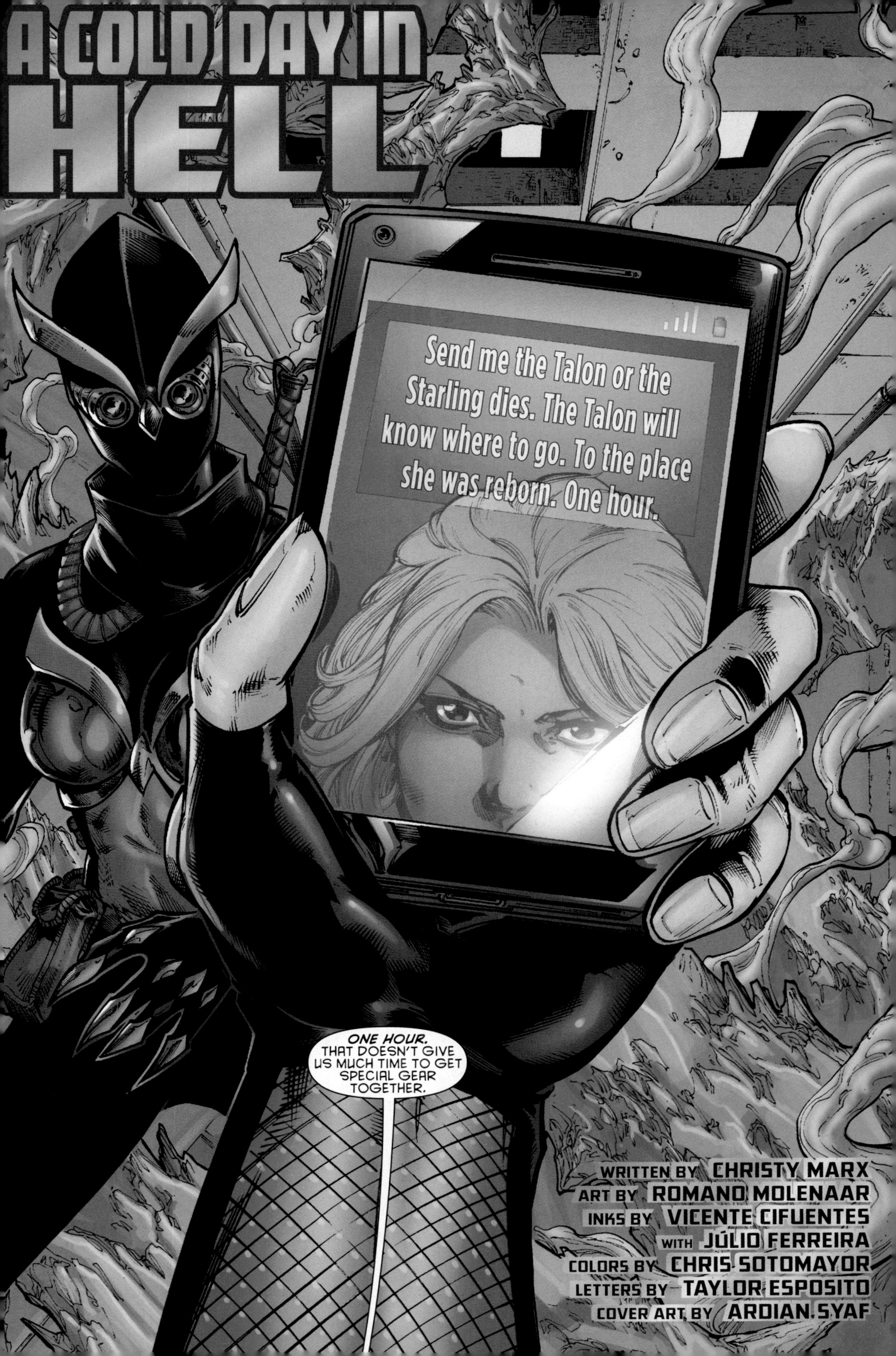
A COLD DAY IN HELL
Send me the Talon or the Starling dies. The Talon will know where to go. To the place she was reborn. One hour.
ONE HOUR. THAT DOESN'T GIVE US MUCH TIME TO GET SPECIAL GEAR TOGETHER.
WRITTEN BY CHRISTY MARX
ART BY ROMANO MOLENAAR
INKS BY VICENTE CIFUENTES
WITH JÚLIO FERREIRA
COLORS BY CHRIS SOTOMAYOR
LETTERS BY TAYLOR ESPOSITO
COVER ART BY ARDIAN SYAF

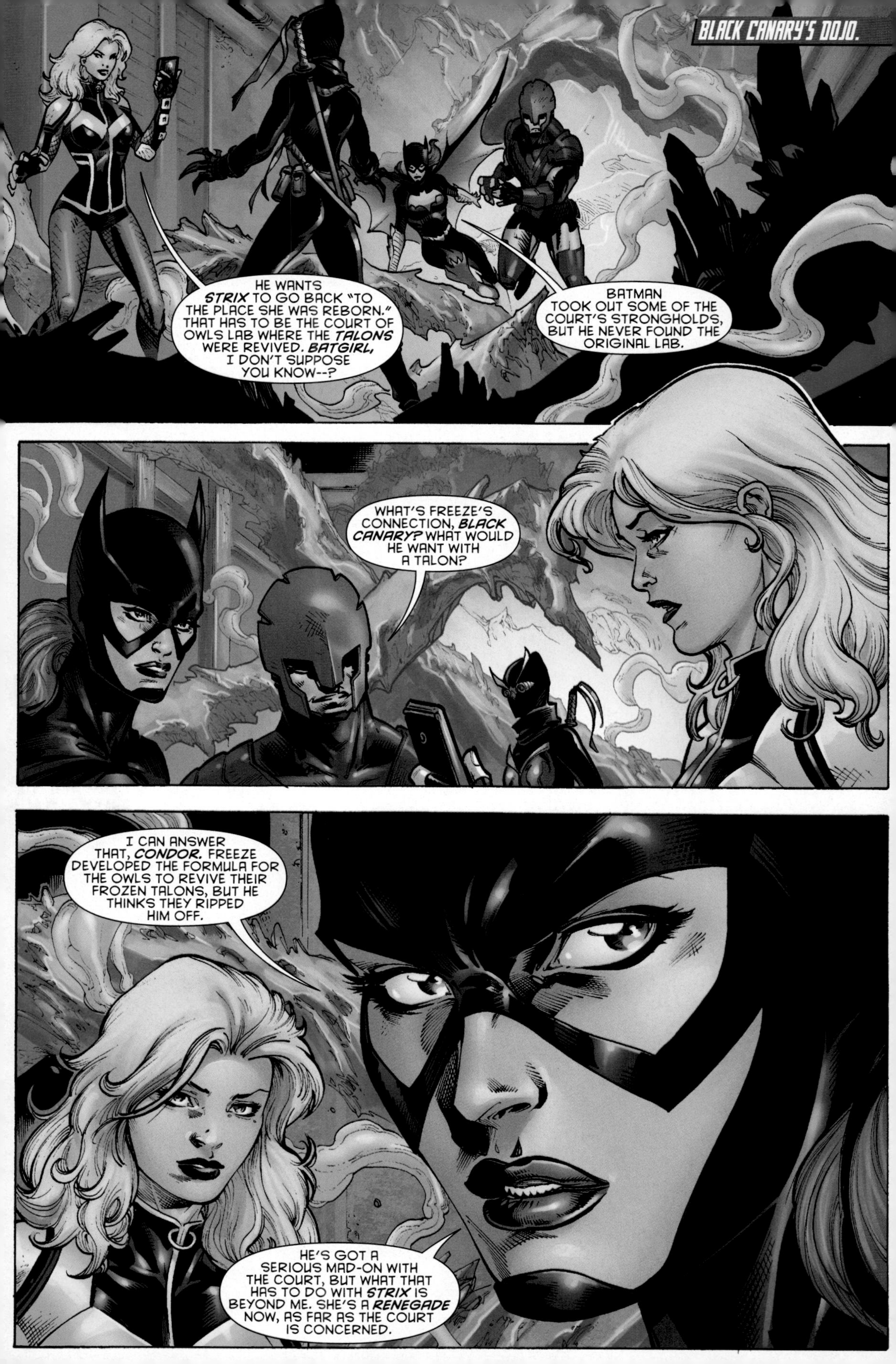
BLACK CANARY'S DOJO.
HE WANTS STRIX TO GO BACK "TO THE PLACE SHE WAS REBORN." THAT HAS TO BE THE COURT OF OWLS LAB WHERE THE TALONS WERE REVIVED. BATGIRL, I DON'T SUPPOSE YOU KNOW--?
BATMAN TOOK OUT SOME OF THE COURT'S STRONGHOLDS, BUT HE NEVER FOUND THE ORIGINAL LAB.
WHAT'S FREEZE'S CONNECTION, BLACK CANARY? WHAT WOULD HE WANT WITH A TALON?
I CAN ANSWER THAT, CONDOR. FREEZE DEVELOPED THE FORMULA FOR THE OWLS TO REVIVE THEIR FROZEN TALONS, BUT HE THINKS THEY RIPPED HIM OFF.
HE'S GOT A SERIOUS MAD-ON WITH THE COURT, BUT WHAT THAT HAS TO DO WITH STRIX IS BEYOND ME. SHE'S A RENEGADE NOW, AS FAR AS THE COURT IS CONCERNED.

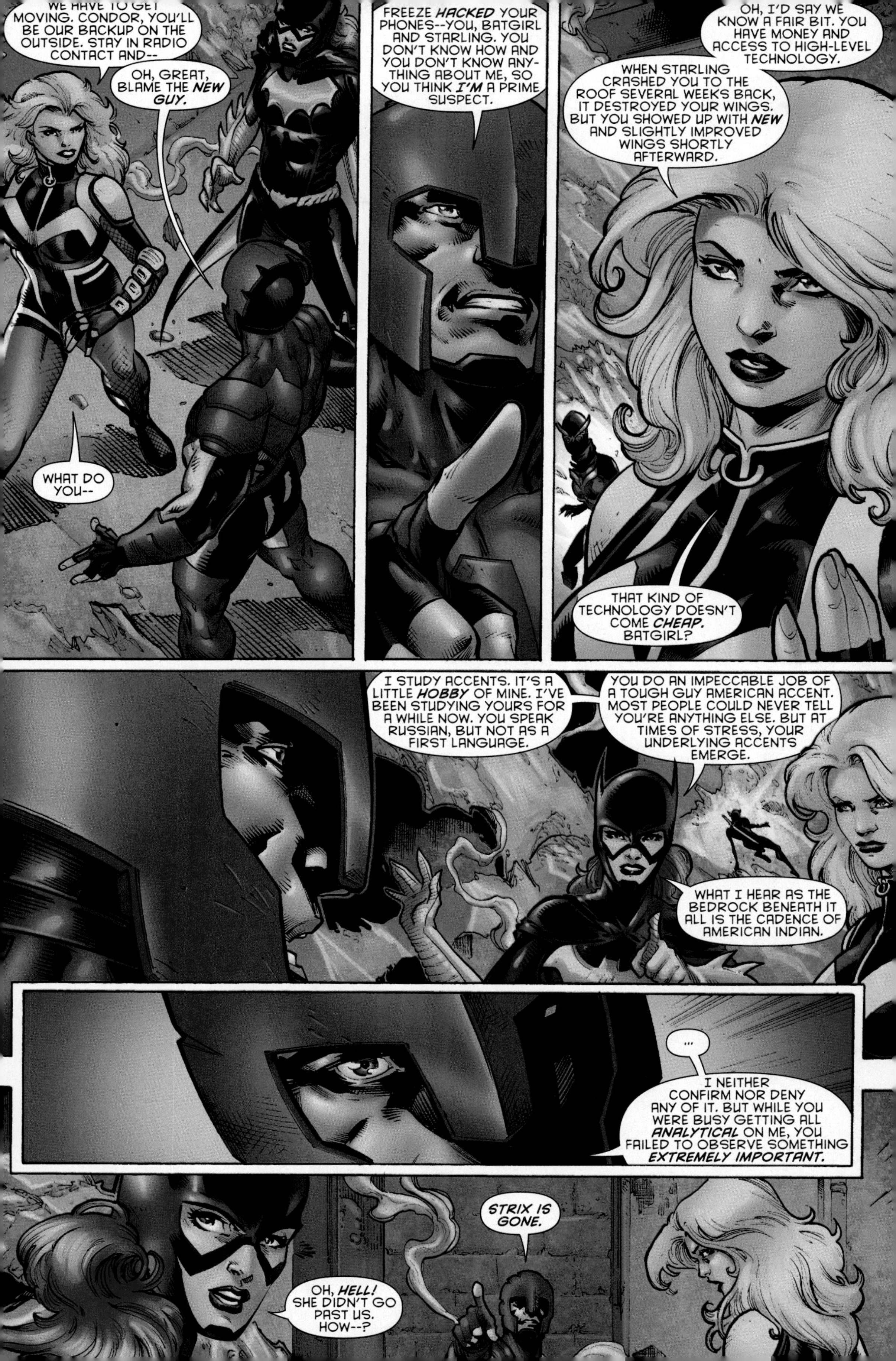
WE HAVE TO GET MOVING. CONDOR, YOU'LL BE OUR BACKUP ON THE OUTSIDE. STAY IN RADIO CONTACT AND--
OH, GREAT, BLAME THE NEW GUY.
WHAT DO YOU--
FREEZE HACKED YOUR PHONES--YOU, BATGIRL AND STARLING. YOU DON'T KNOW HOW AND YOU DON'T KNOW ANYTHING ABOUT ME, SO YOU THINK I'M A PRIME SUSPECT.
OH, I'D SAY WE KNOW A FAIR BIT. YOU HAVE MONEY AND ACCESS TO HIGH-LEVEL TECHNOLOGY.
WHEN STARLING CRASHED YOU TO THE ROOF SEVERAL WEEKS BACK, IT DESTROYED YOUR WINGS. BUT YOU SHOWED UP WITH NEW AND SLIGHTLY IMPROVED WINGS SHORTLY AFTERWARD.
THAT KIND OF TECHNOLOGY DOESN'T COME CHEAP. BATGIRL?
I STUDY ACCENTS. IT'S A LITTLE HOBBY OF MINE. I'VE BEEN STUDYING YOURS FOR A WHILE NOW. YOU SPEAK RUSSIAN, BUT NOT AS A FIRST LANGUAGE.
YOU DO AN IMPECCABLE JOB OF A TOUGH GUY AMERICAN ACCENT. MOST PEOPLE COULD NEVER TELL YOU'RE ANYTHING ELSE. BUT AT TIMES OF STRESS, YOUR UNDERLYING ACCENTS EMERGE.
WHAT I HEAR AS THE BEDROCK BENEATH IT ALL IS THE CADENCE OF AMERICAN INDIAN.
...
I NEITHER CONFIRM NOR DENY ANY OF IT. BUT WHILE YOU WERE BUSY GETTING ALL ANALYTICAL ON ME, YOU FAILED TO OBSERVE SOMETHING EXTREMELY IMPORTANT.
STRIX IS GONE.
OH, HELL! SHE DIDN'T GO PAST US. HOW--?

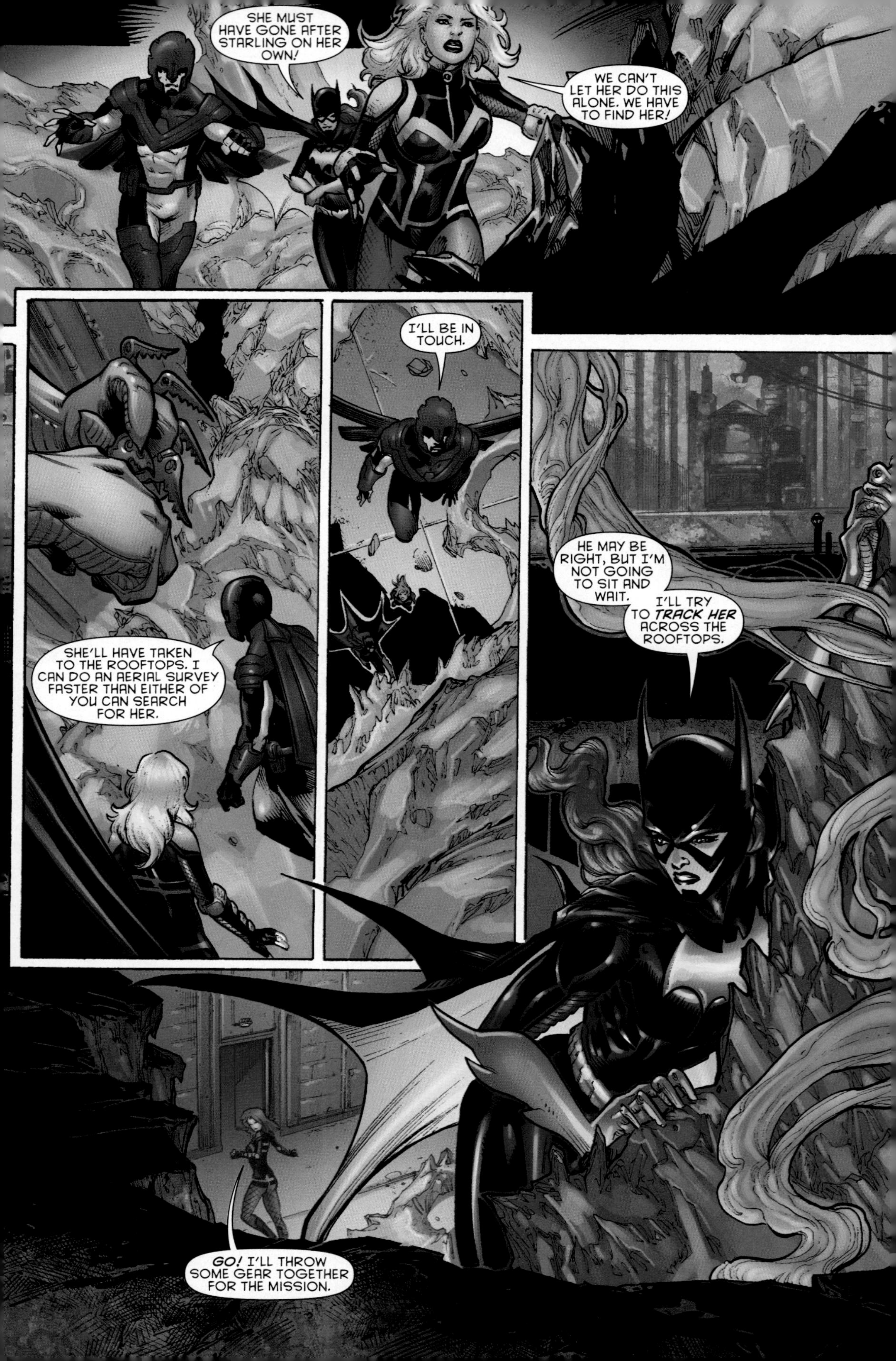
SHE MUST HAVE GONE AFTER STARLING ON HER OWN!
WE CAN'T LET HER DO THIS ALONE. WE HAVE TO FIND HER!
SHE'LL HAVE TAKEN TO THE ROOFTOPS. I CAN DO AN AERIAL SURVEY FASTER THAN EITHER OF YOU CAN SEARCH FOR HER.
I'LL BE IN TOUCH.
HE MAY BE RIGHT, BUT I'M NOT GOING TO SIT AND WAIT.
I'LL TRY TO TRACK HER ACROSS THE ROOFTOPS.
GO! I'LL THROW SOME GEAR TOGETHER FOR THE MISSION.

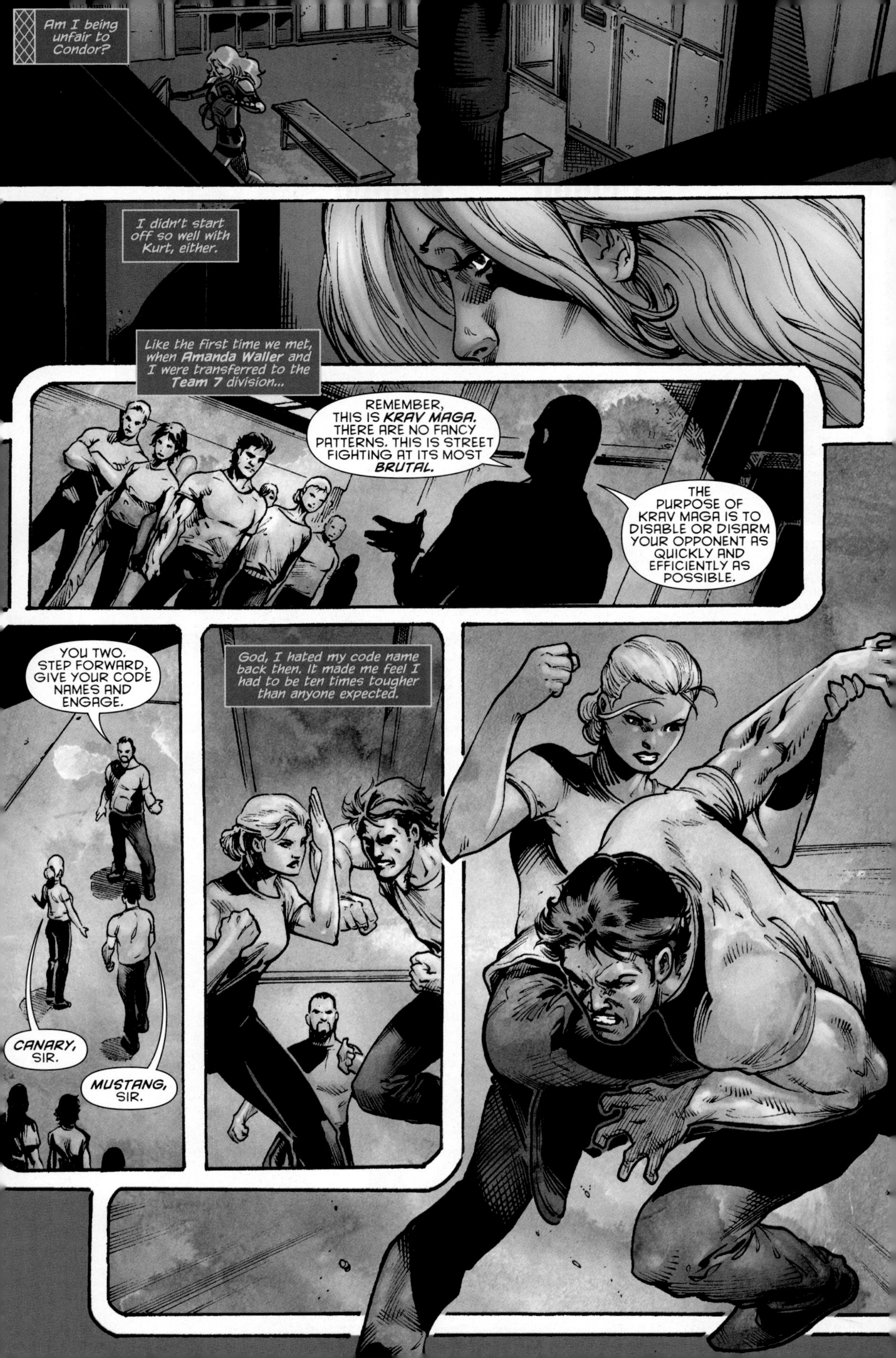
Am I being unfair to Condor?
I didn't start off so well with Kurt, either.
Like the first time we met, when Amanda Waller and I were transferred to the Team 7 division...
REMEMBER, THIS IS KRAV MAGA. THERE ARE NO FANCY PATTERNS. THIS IS STREET FIGHTING AT ITS MOST BRUTAL.
THE PURPOSE OF KRAV MAGA IS TO DISABLE OR DISARM YOUR OPPONENT AS QUICKLY AND EFFICIENTLY AS POSSIBLE.
YOU TWO. STEP FORWARD, GIVE YOUR CODE NAMES AND ENGAGE.
CANARY, SIR.
MUSTANG, SIR.
God, I hated my code name back then. It made me feel I had to be ten times tougher than anyone expected.

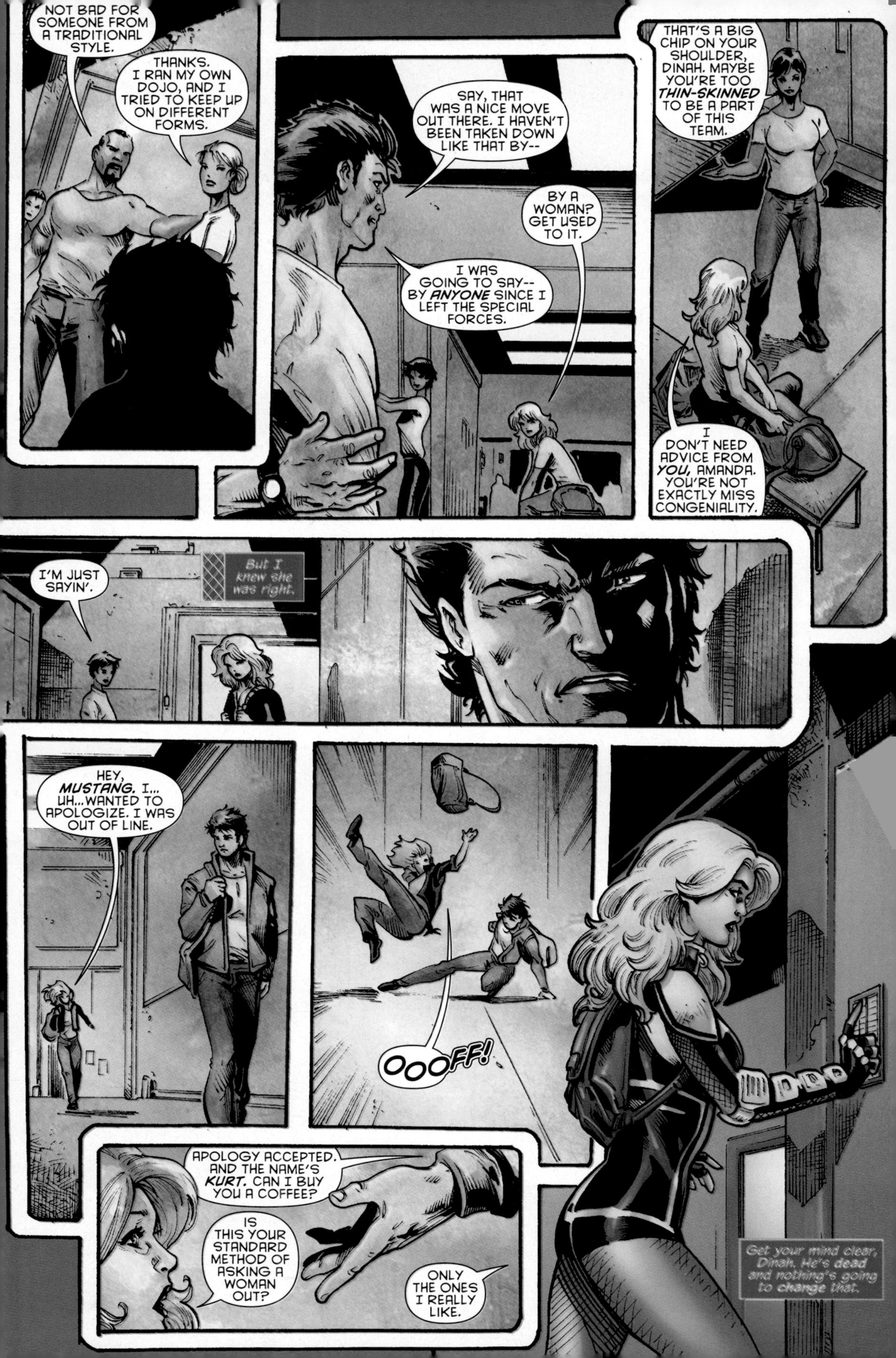
NOT BAD FOR SOMEONE FROM A TRADITIONAL STYLE.
THANKS. I RAN MY OWN DOJO, AND I TRIED TO KEEP UP ON DIFFERENT FORMS.
SAY, THAT WAS A NICE MOVE OUT THERE. I HAVEN'T BEEN TAKEN DOWN LIKE THAT BY--
BY A WOMAN? GET USED TO IT.
I WAS GOING TO SAY-- BY ANYONE SINCE I LEFT THE SPECIAL FORCES.
THAT'S A BIG CHIP ON YOUR SHOULDER, DINAH. MAYBE YOU'RE TOO THIN-SKINNED TO BE A PART OF THIS TEAM.
I DON'T NEED ADVICE FROM YOU, AMANDA. YOU'RE NOT EXACTLY MISS CONGENIALITY.
I'M JUST SAYIN'.
But I knew she was right.
HEY, MUSTANG. I... UH...WANTED TO APOLOGIZE. I WAS OUT OF LINE.
OOOFF!
APOLOGY ACCEPTED. AND THE NAME'S KURT. CAN I BUY YOU A COFFEE?
IS THIS YOUR STANDARD METHOD OF ASKING A WOMAN OUT?
ONLY THE ONES I REALLY LIKE.
Get your mind clear, Dinah. He's dead and nothing's going to change that.

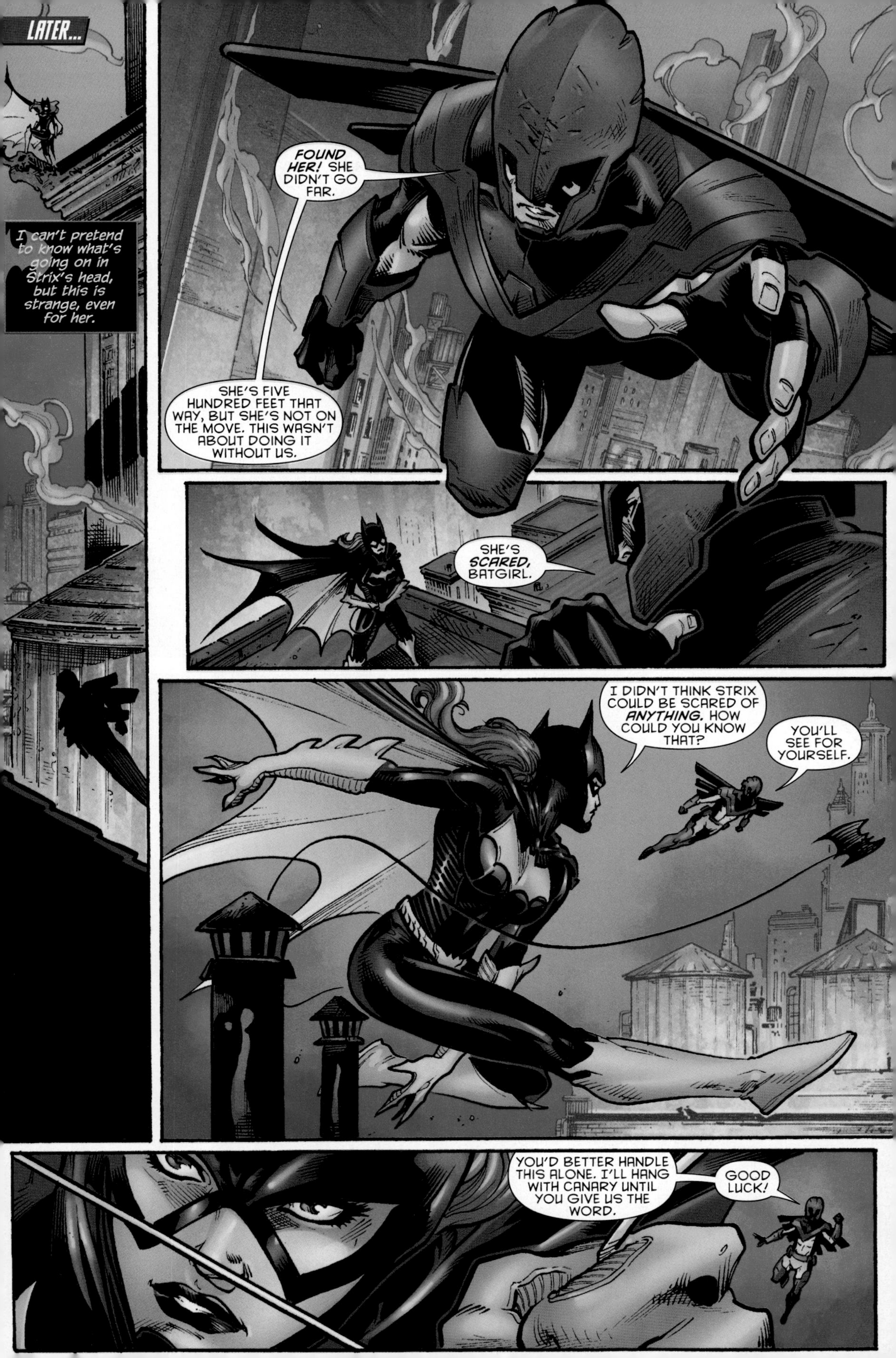
LATER...
I can't pretend to know what's going on in Strix's head, but this is strange, even for her.
FOUND HER! SHE DIDN'T GO FAR.
SHE'S FIVE HUNDRED FEET THAT WAY, BUT SHE'S NOT ON THE MOVE. THIS WASN'T ABOUT DOING IT WITHOUT US.
SHE'S SCARED, BATGIRL.
I DIDN'T THINK STRIX COULD BE SCARED OF ANYTHING. HOW COULD YOU KNOW THAT?
YOU'LL SEE FOR YOURSELF.
YOU'D BETTER HANDLE THIS ALONE. I'LL HANG WITH CANARY UNTIL YOU GIVE US THE WORD.
GOOD LUCK!

STRIX?

PLEASE, WE'RE RUNNING OUT OF TIME. CAN YOU SHOW US THE WAY?

BAD PLACE NOT. GO BACK

MARY... I'LL NEVER ASK YOU TO DO SOMETHING YOU CAN'T DO, BUT FREEZE WILL KILL STARLING IF WE DON'T GET THERE IN TIME.

WE CAN'T ABANDON ONE OF OUR OWN. GIVE ME AN ADDRESS OR DRAW ME A MAP. YOU DON'T HAVE TO COME WITH US.

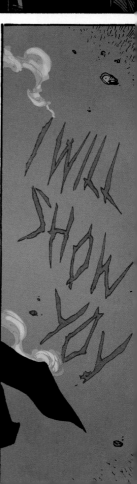

I WILL SHOW YOU

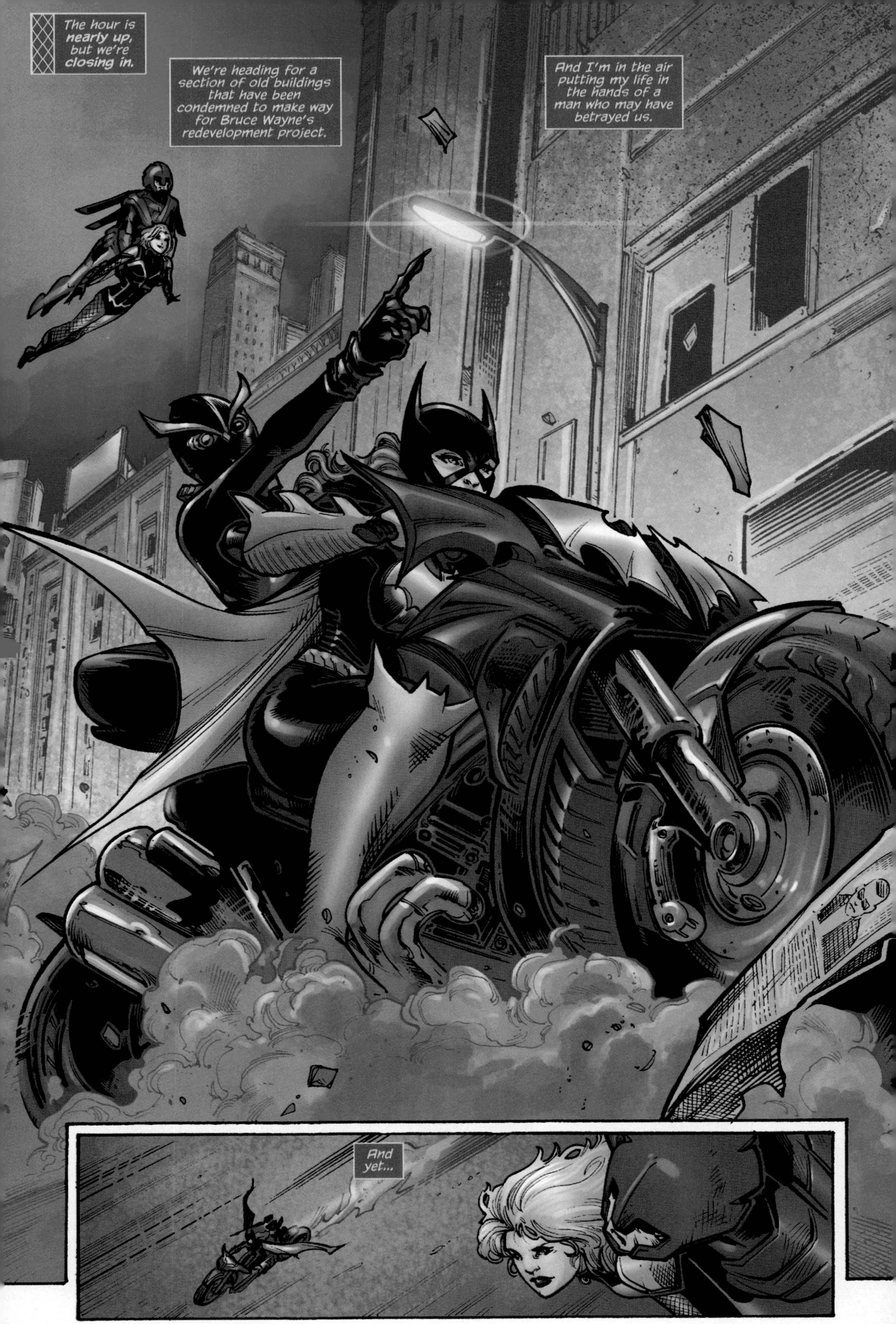
The hour is nearly up, but we're closing in.
We're heading for a section of old buildings that have been condemned to make way for Bruce Wayne's redevelopment project.
And I'm in the air putting my life in the hands of a man who may have betrayed us.
And yet...

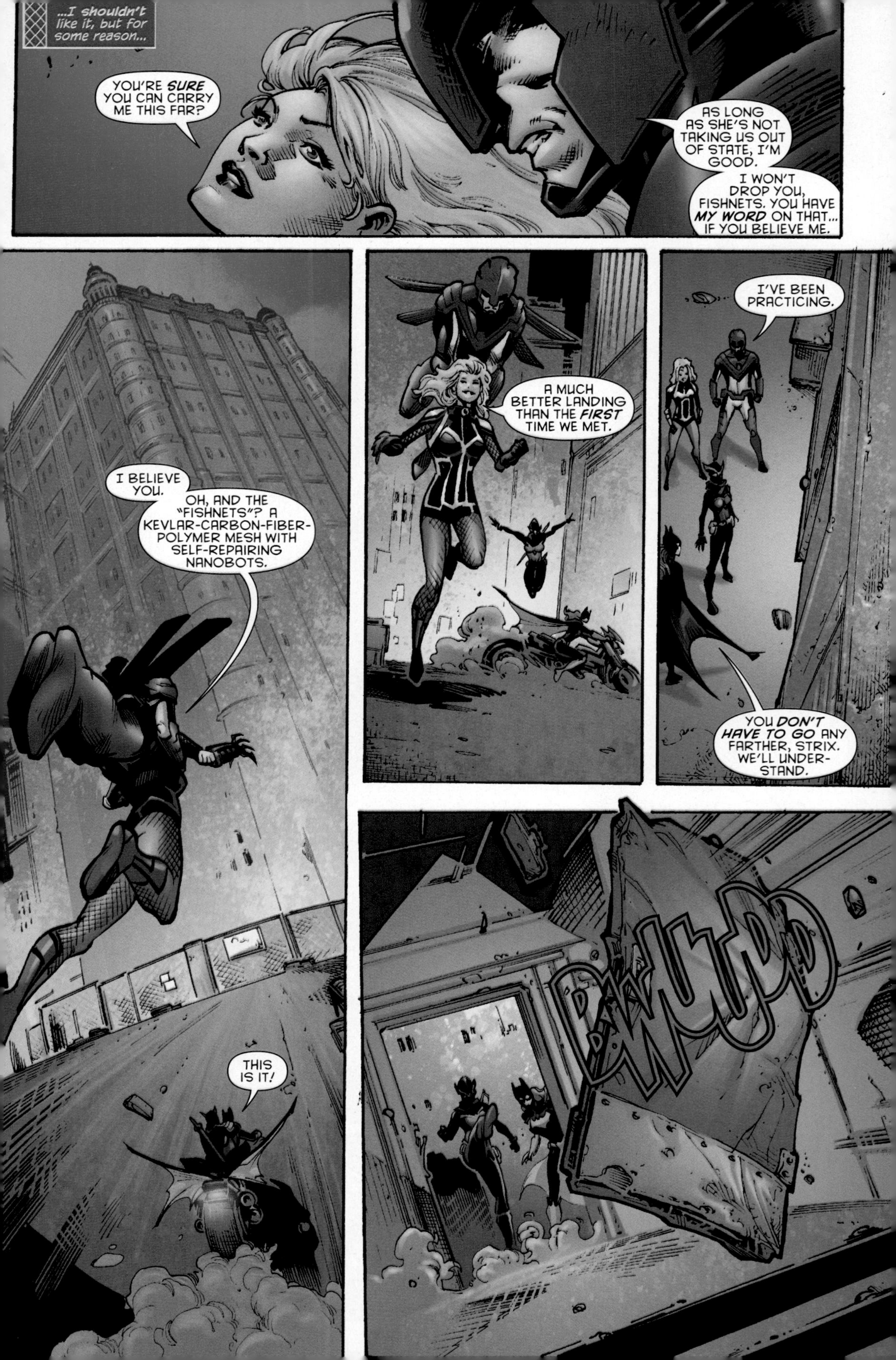
...I shouldn't like it, but for some reason...
YOU'RE SURE YOU CAN CARRY ME THIS FAR?
AS LONG AS SHE'S NOT TAKING US OUT OF STATE, I'M GOOD.
I WON'T DROP YOU, FISHNETS. YOU HAVE MY WORD ON THAT... IF YOU BELIEVE ME.
I BELIEVE YOU.
OH, AND THE "FISHNETS"? A KEVLAR-CARBON-FIBER-POLYMER MESH WITH SELF-REPAIRING NANOBOTS.
THIS IS IT!
A MUCH BETTER LANDING THAN THE FIRST TIME WE MET.
I'VE BEEN PRACTICING.
YOU DON'T HAVE TO GO ANY FARTHER, STRIX. WE'LL UNDER-STAND.
DWUDD

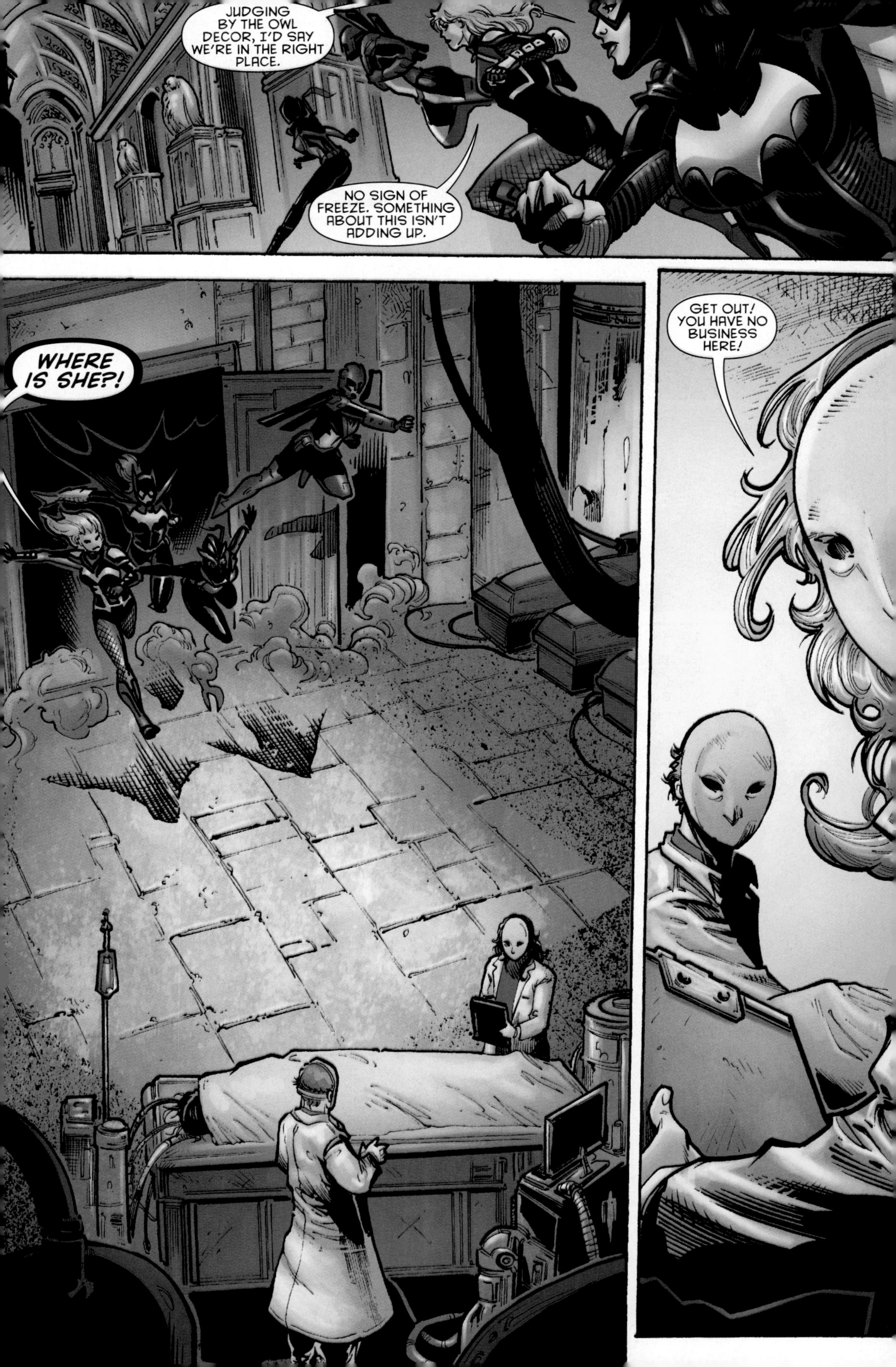
JUDGING BY THE OWL DECOR, I'D SAY WE'RE IN THE RIGHT PLACE.
NO SIGN OF FREEZE. SOMETHING ABOUT THIS ISN'T ADDING UP.
WHERE IS SHE?!
GET OUT! YOU HAVE NO BUSINESS HERE!

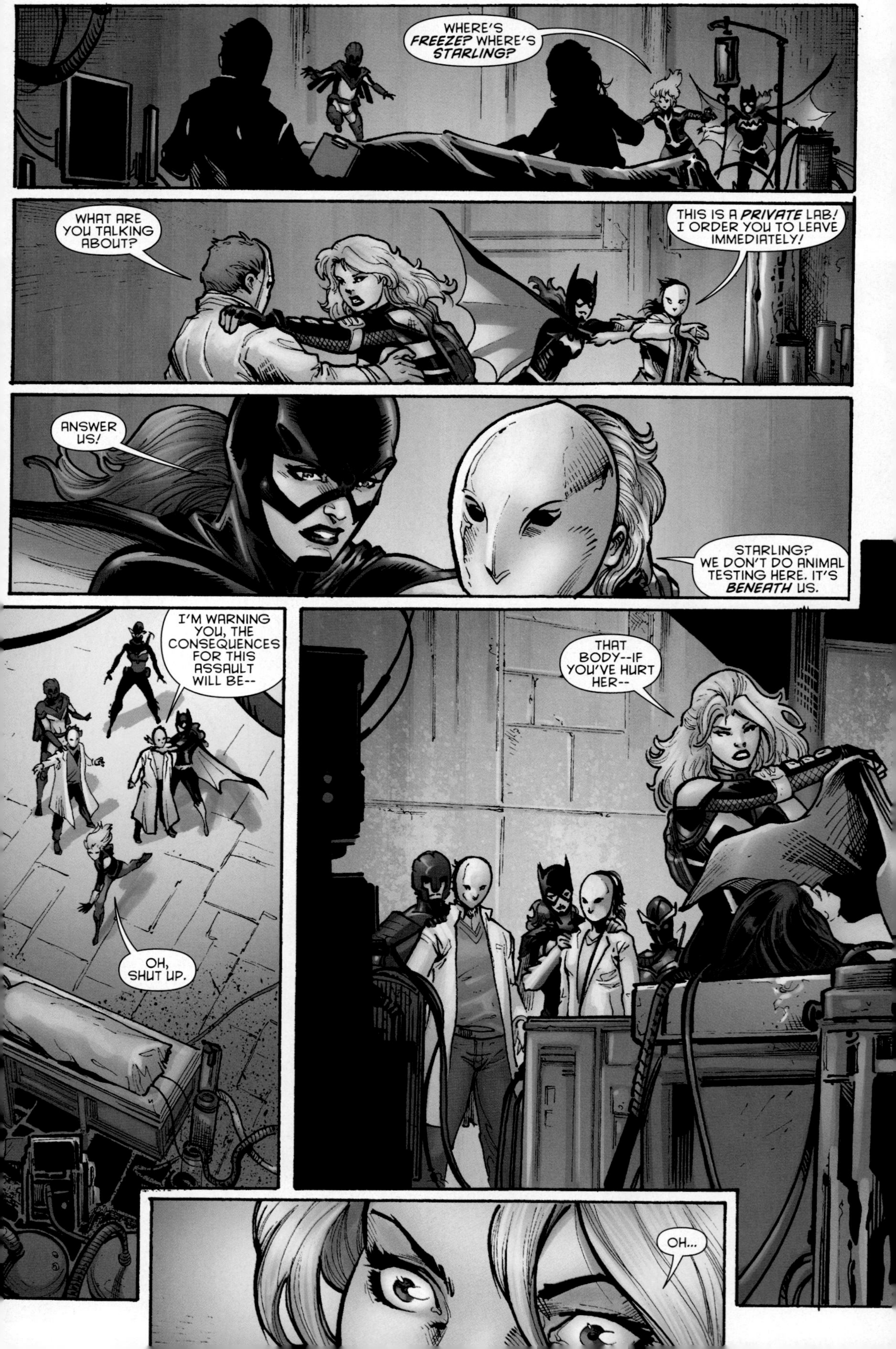

WHERE'S FREEZE? WHERE'S STARLING?
WHAT ARE YOU TALKING ABOUT?
THIS IS A PRIVATE LAB! I ORDER YOU TO LEAVE IMMEDIATELY!
ANSWER US!
STARLING? WE DON'T DO ANIMAL TESTING HERE. IT'S BENEATH US.
I'M WARNING YOU, THE CONSEQUENCES FOR THIS ASSAULT WILL BE--
OH, SHUT UP.
THAT BODY--IF YOU'VE HURT HER--
OH...

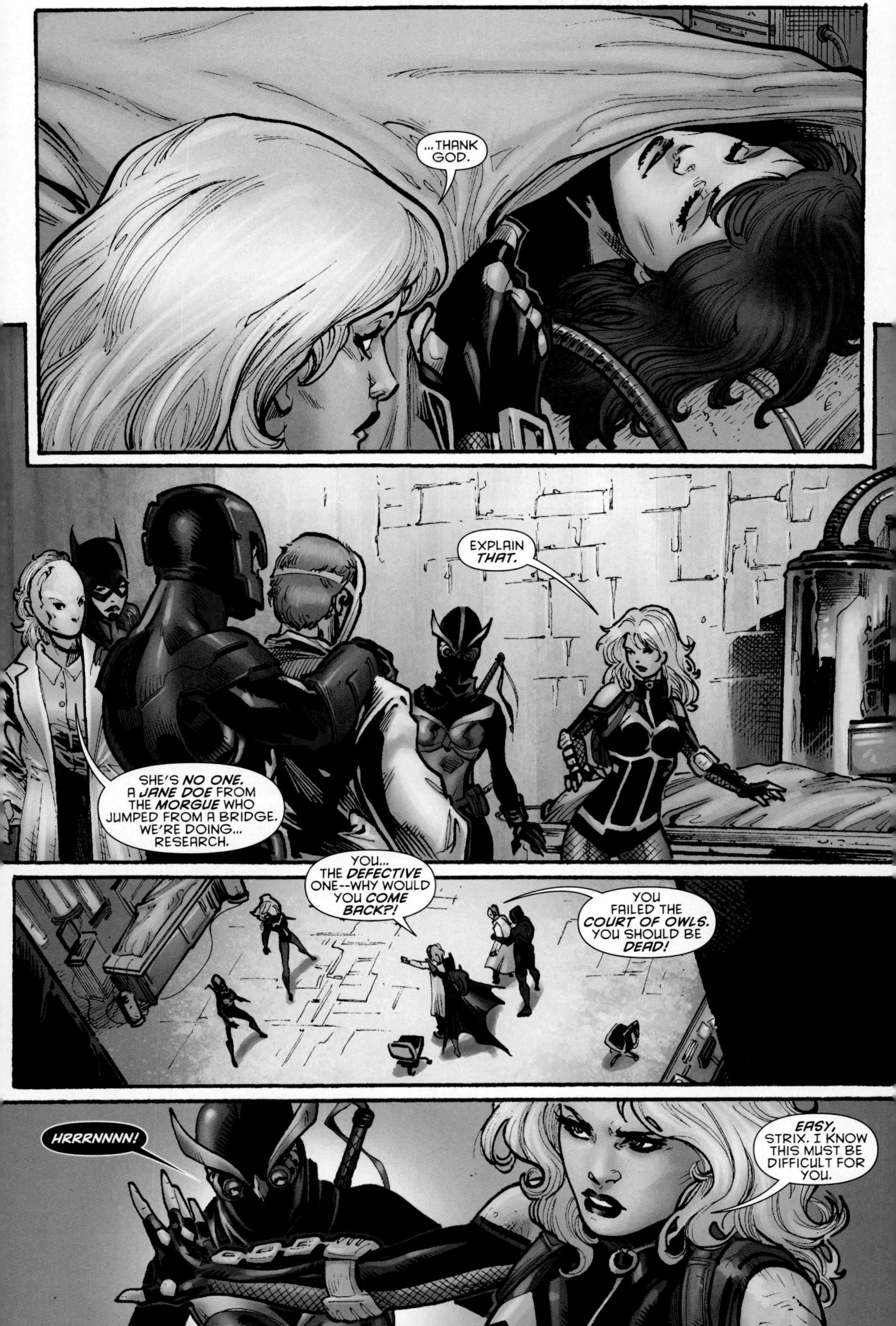

...THANK GOD.
EXPLAIN THAT.
SHE'S NO ONE. A JANE DOE FROM THE MORGUE WHO JUMPED FROM A BRIDGE. WE'RE DOING... RESEARCH.
YOU... THE DEFECTIVE ONE--WHY WOULD YOU COME BACK?!
YOU FAILED THE COURT OF OWLS. YOU SHOULD BE DEAD!
HRRRNNNN!
EASY, STRIX. I KNOW THIS MUST BE DIFFICULT FOR YOU.

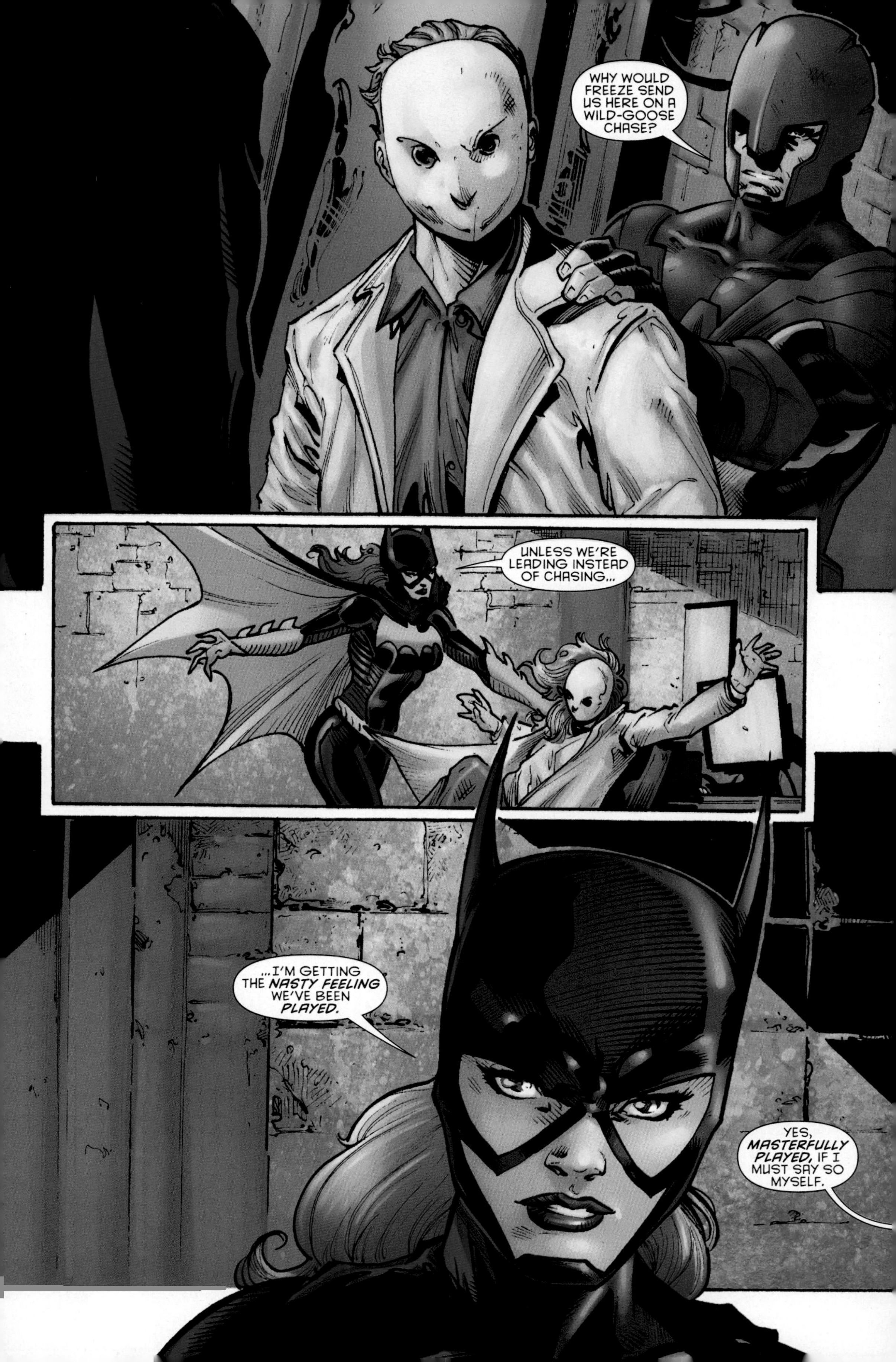
WHY WOULD FREEZE SEND US HERE ON A WILD-GOOSE CHASE?
UNLESS WE'RE LEADING INSTEAD OF CHASING...
...I'M GETTING THE NASTY FEELING WE'VE BEEN PLAYED.
YES, MASTERFULLY PLAYED, IF I MUST SAY SO MYSELF.

I'VE BEEN SEARCHING FOR THIS LAB FOR MONTHS, BUT THE TALONS HAVE BEEN...UNHELPFUL IN GIVING ME THE LOCATION.
IT WAS FAR EASIER TO GET YOUR TALON TO LEAD YOU TO IT, THEREBY LEADING ME TO IT AS WELL.

SCREW YOU AND YOUR PERSONAL VENDETTA, MR. FREEZE. WHERE'S STARLING?
ALIVE AND WELL, I ASSURE YOU. AND SHE'LL REMAIN THAT WAY AS LONG AS WE KEEP OUR HEADS AND BEHAVE RATIONALLY.

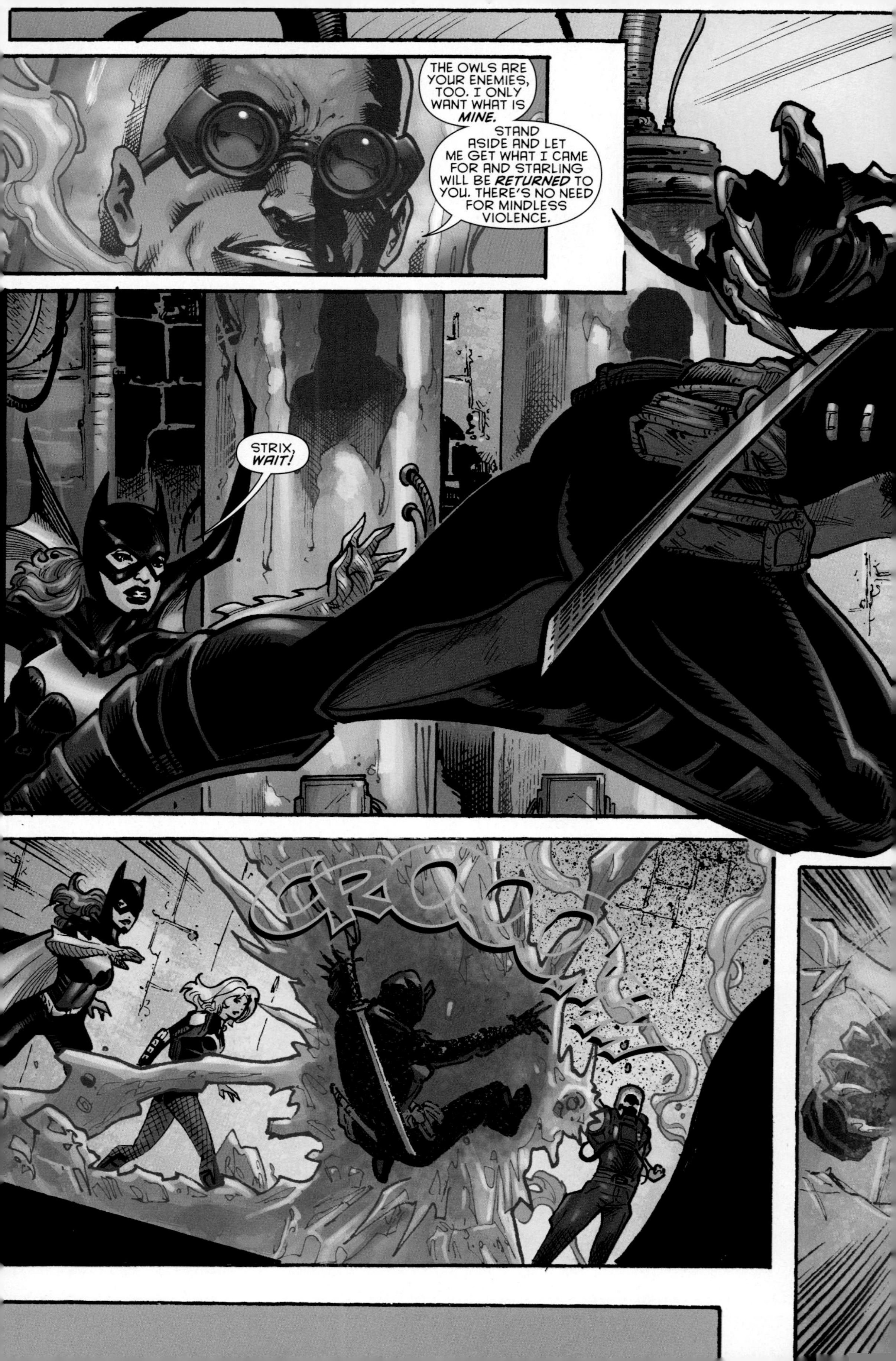
THE OWLS ARE YOUR ENEMIES, TOO. I ONLY WANT WHAT IS *MINE.*
STAND ASIDE AND LET ME GET WHAT I CAME FOR AND STARLING WILL BE *RETURNED* TO YOU. THERE'S NO NEED FOR MINDLESS VIOLENCE.
STRIX, *WAIT!*
CRO

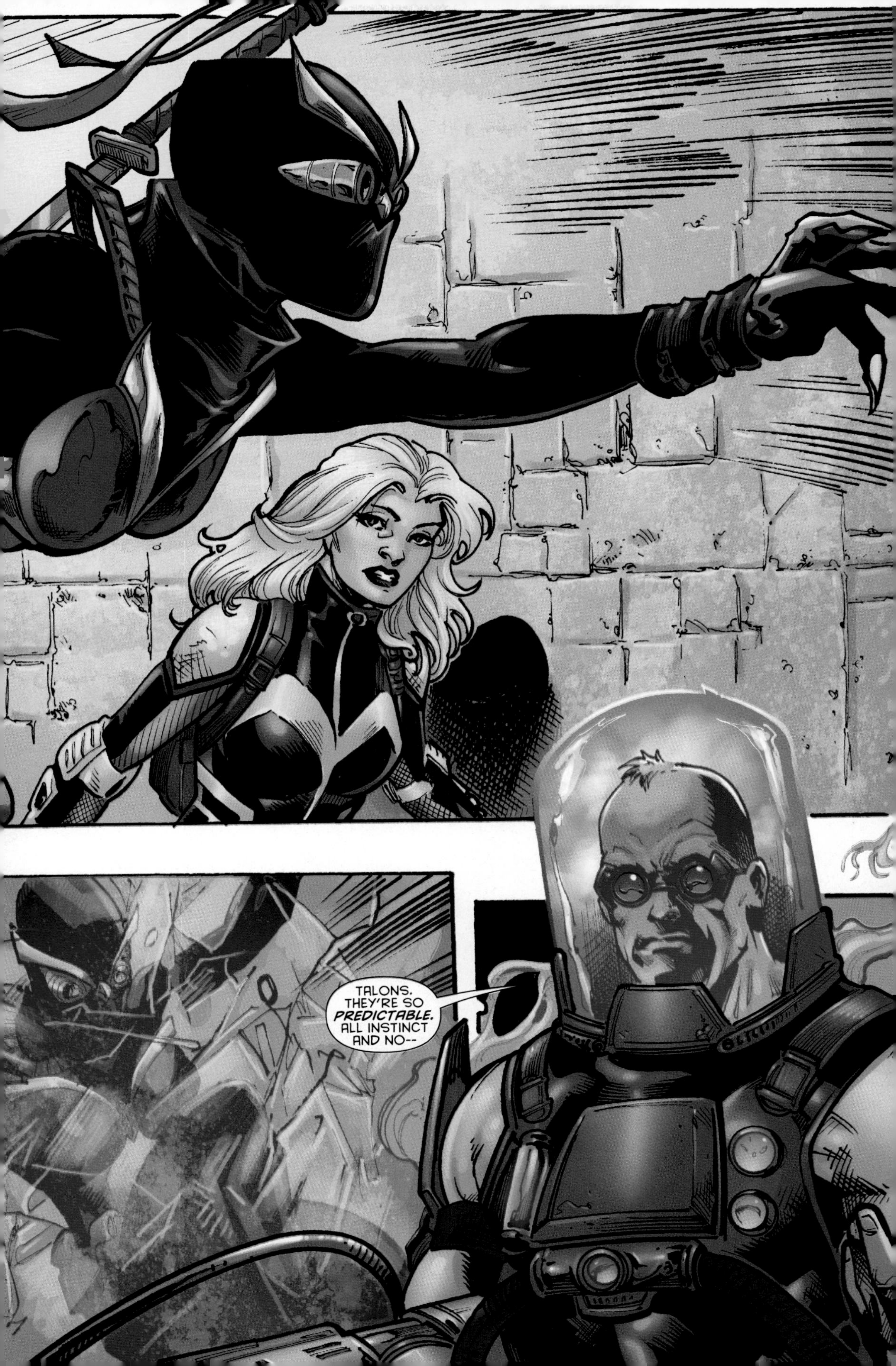
TALONS. THEY'RE SO PREDICTABLE. ALL INSTINCT AND NO--

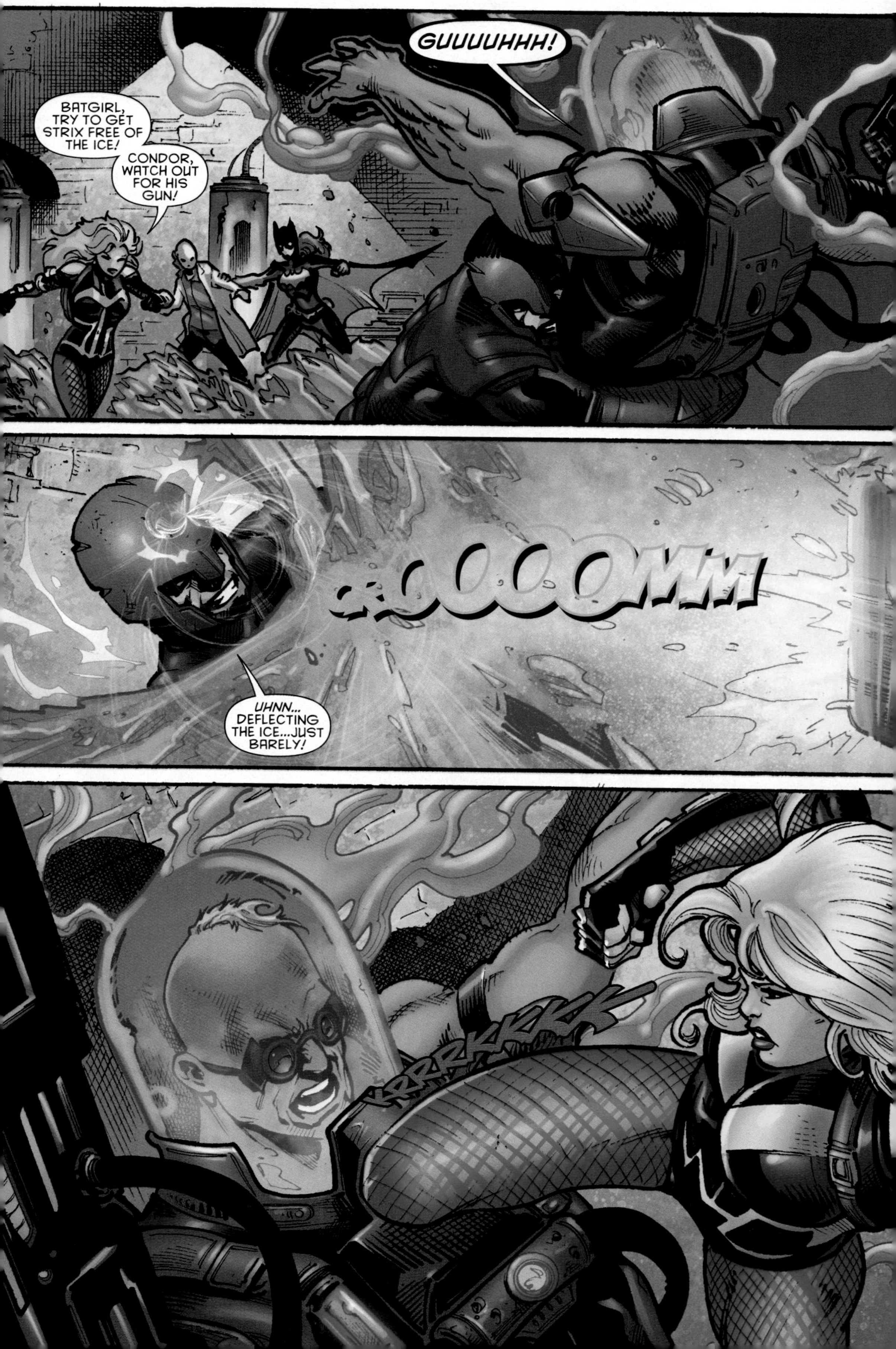
GUUUUHHH!
BATGIRL, TRY TO GET STRIX FREE OF THE ICE!
CONDOR, WATCH OUT FOR HIS GUN!
UHNN... DEFLECTING THE ICE...JUST BARELY!
KRRRKKKKK

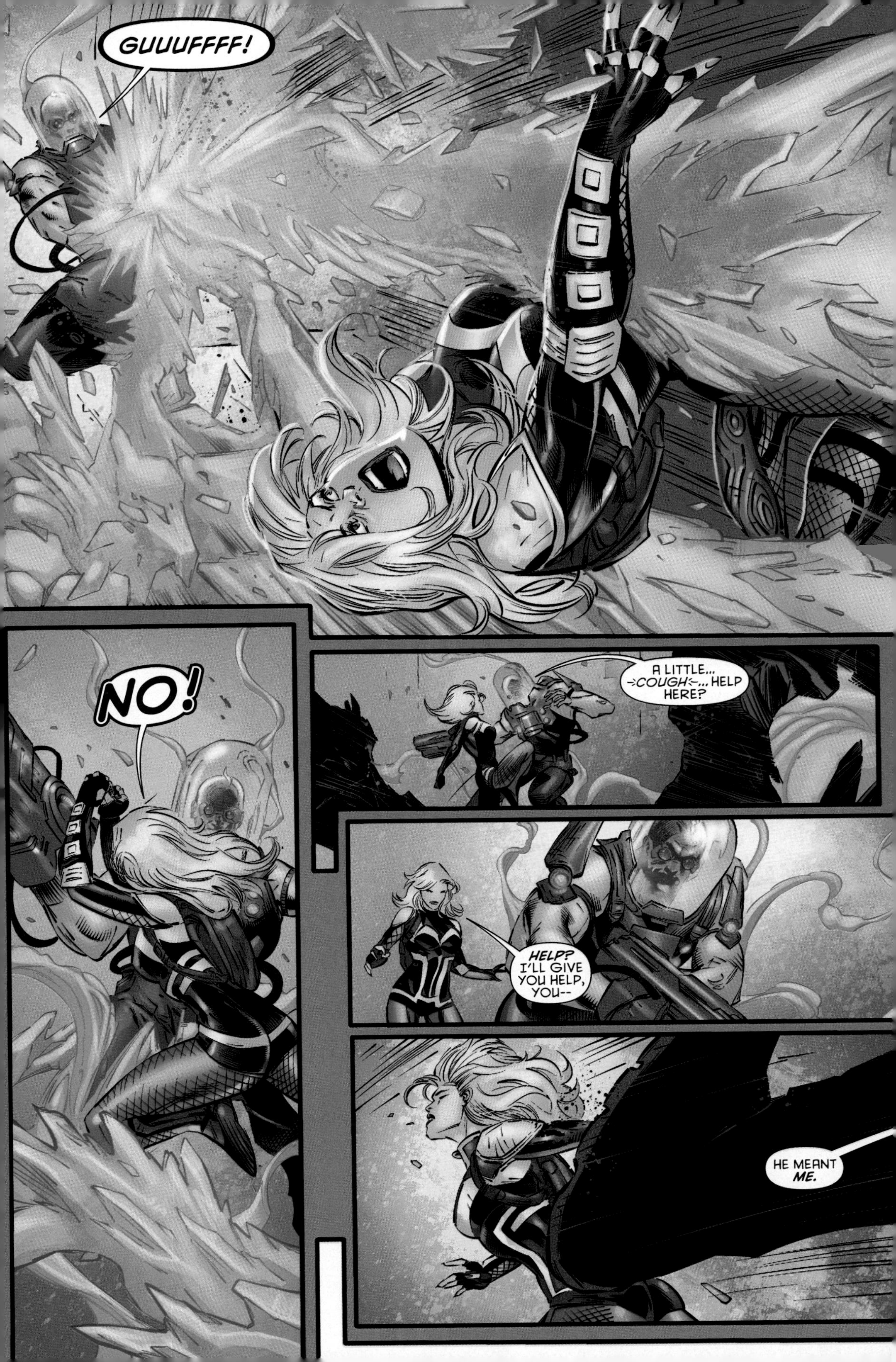
GUUUFFFF!
NO!
A LITTLE... -COUGH-... HELP HERE?
HELP? I'LL GIVE YOU HELP, YOU--
HE MEANT ME.

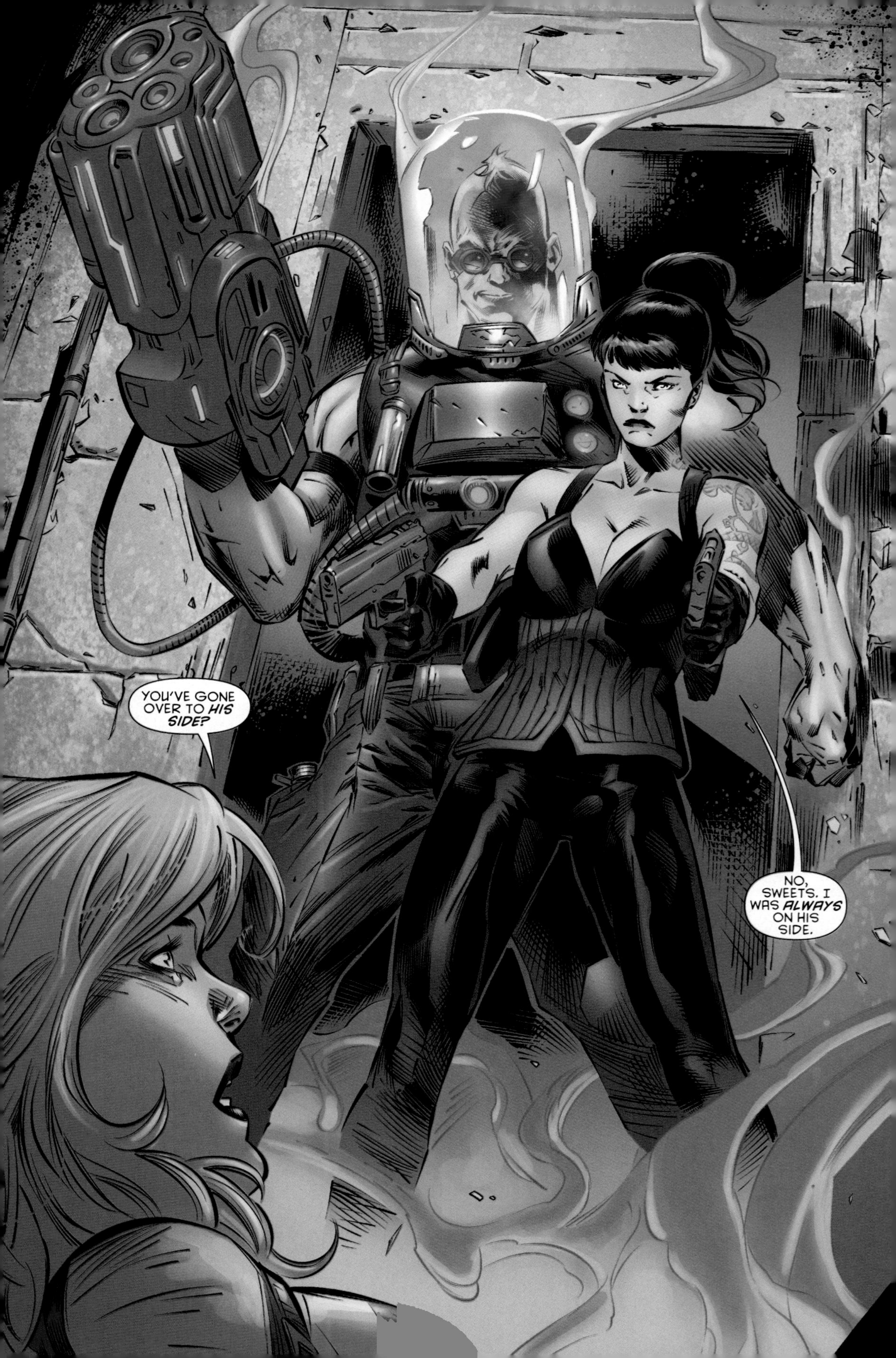
YOU'VE GONE OVER TO *HIS SIDE?*
NO, SWEETS. I WAS *ALWAYS* ON HIS SIDE.

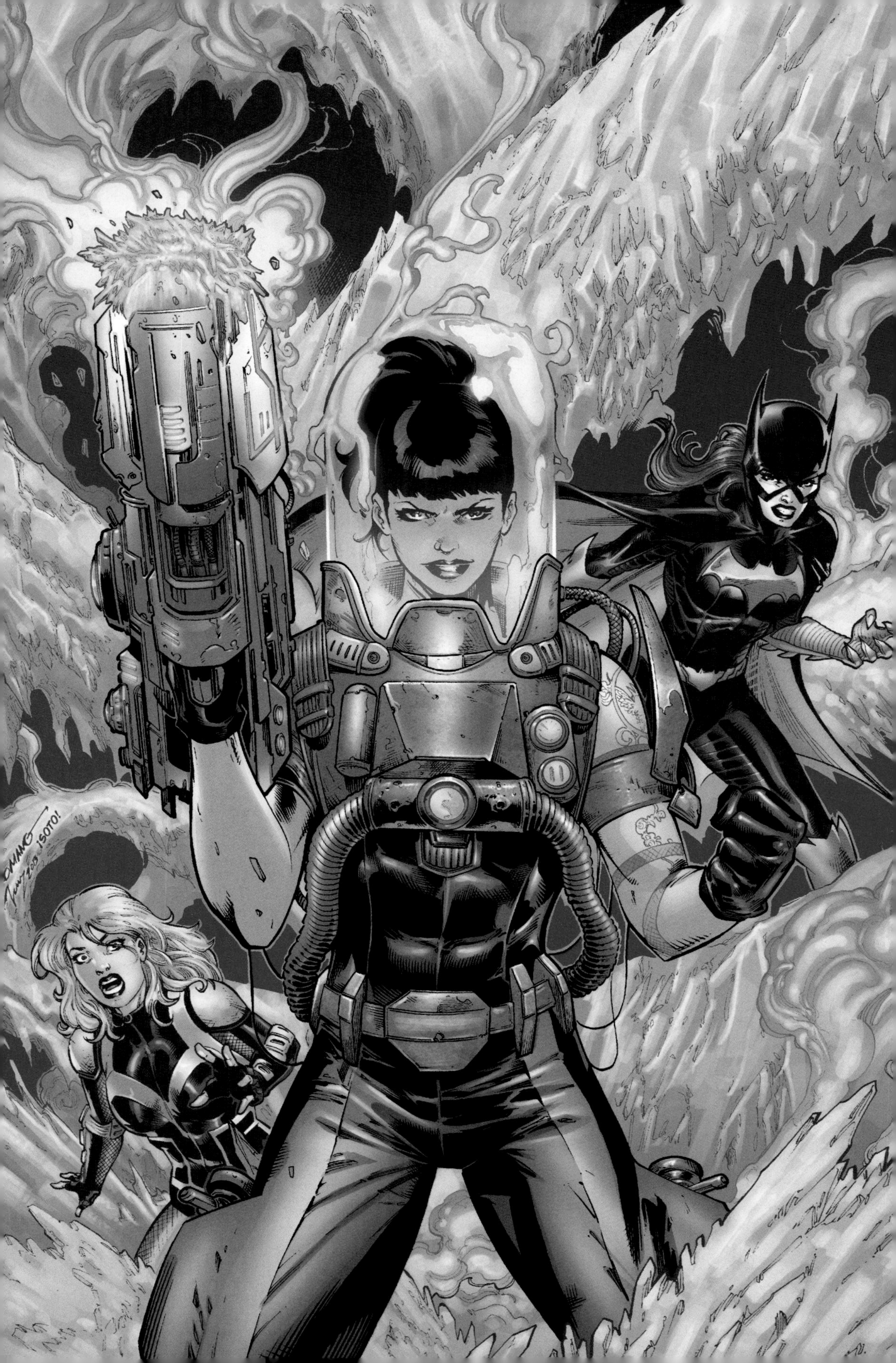

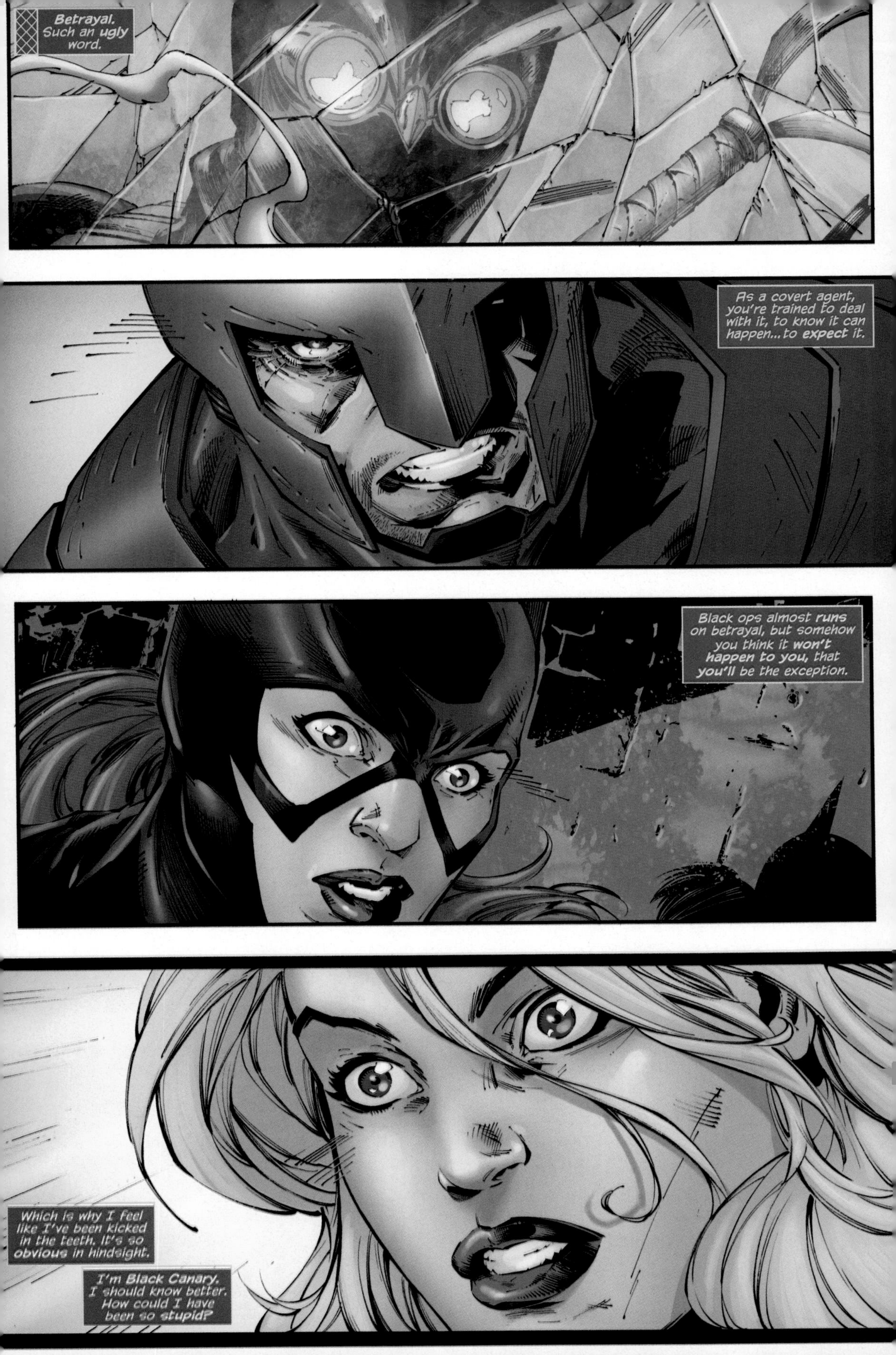

Betrayal. Such an ugly word.
As a covert agent, you're trained to deal with it, to know it can happen...to expect it.
Black ops almost runs on betrayal, but somehow you think it won't happen to you, that you'll be the exception.
Which is why I feel like I've been kicked in the teeth. It's so obvious in hindsight.
I'm Black Canary. I should know better. How could I have been so stupid?

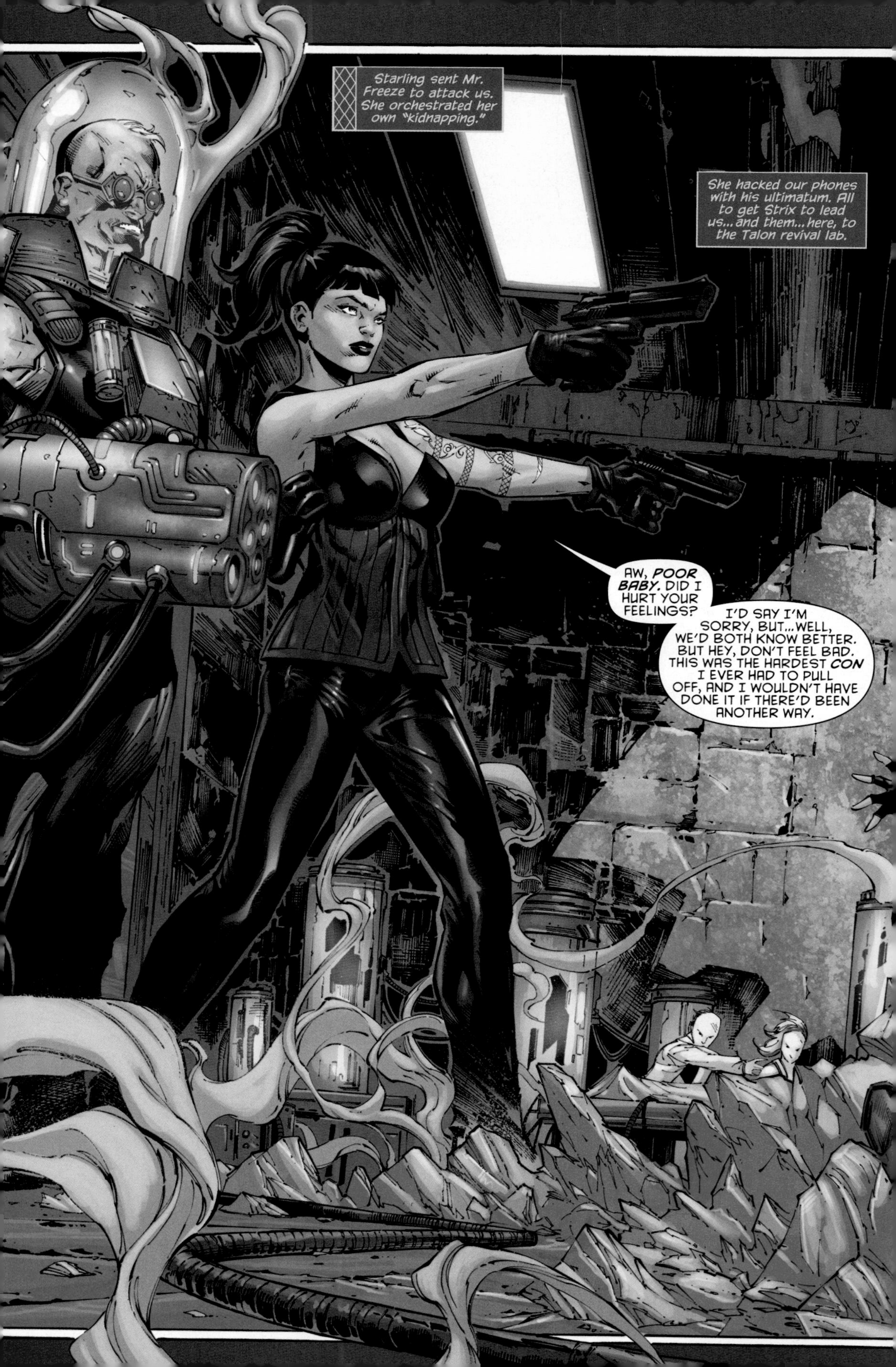
Starling sent Mr. Freeze to attack us. She orchestrated her own "kidnapping."
She hacked our phones with his ultimatum. All to get Strix to lead us... and them... here, to the Talon revival lab.
AW, POOR BABY. DID I HURT YOUR FEELINGS?
I'D SAY I'M SORRY, BUT... WELL, WE'D BOTH KNOW BETTER. BUT HEY, DON'T FEEL BAD. THIS WAS THE HARDEST CON I EVER HAD TO PULL OFF, AND I WOULDN'T HAVE DONE IT IF THERE'D BEEN ANOTHER WAY.

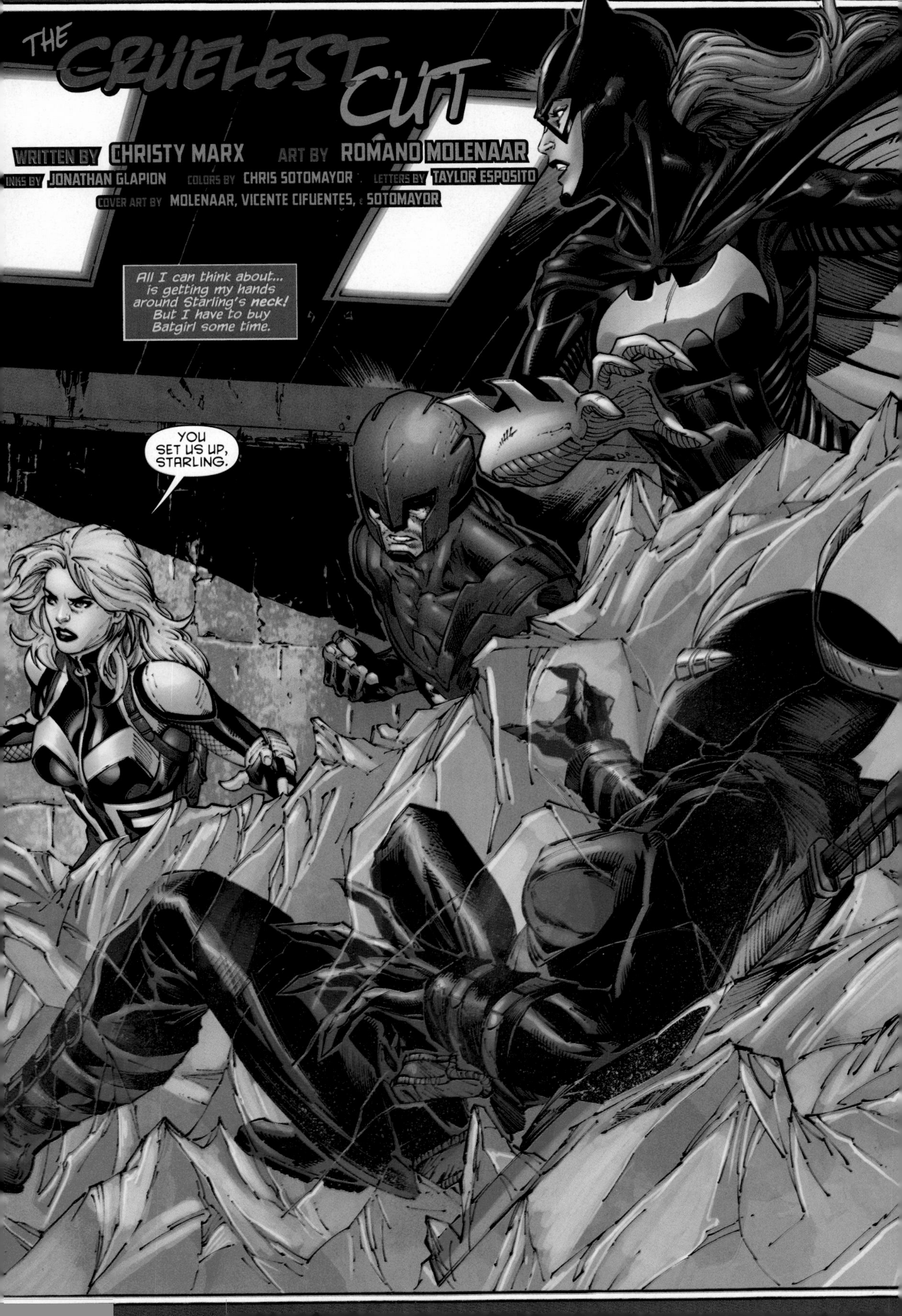
THE CRUELEST CUT
WRITTEN BY CHRISTY MARX ART BY ROMANO MOLENAAR
INKS BY JONATHAN GLAPION COLORS BY CHRIS SOTOMAYOR LETTERS BY TAYLOR ESPOSITO
COVER ART BY MOLENAAR, VICENTE CIFUENTES, & SOTOMAYOR
All I can think about... is getting my hands around Starling's neck! But I have to buy Batgirl some time.
YOU SET US UP, STARLING.

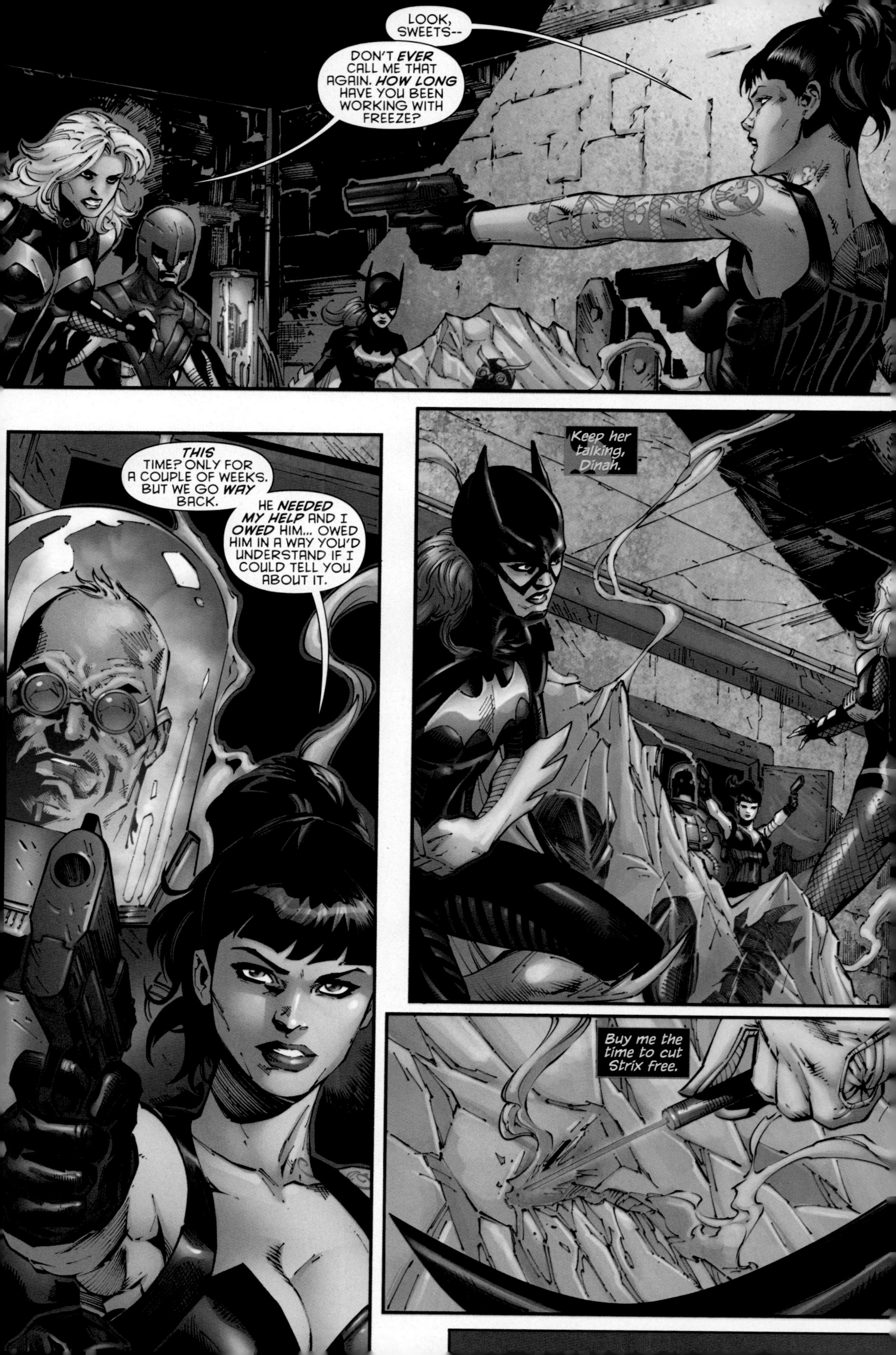
LOOK, SWEETS--
DON'T EVER CALL ME THAT AGAIN. HOW LONG HAVE YOU BEEN WORKING WITH FREEZE?
THIS TIME? ONLY FOR A COUPLE OF WEEKS. BUT WE GO WAY BACK.
HE NEEDED MY HELP AND I OWED HIM... OWED HIM IN A WAY YOU'D UNDERSTAND IF I COULD TELL YOU ABOUT IT.
Keep her talking, Dinah.
Buy me the time to cut Strix free.

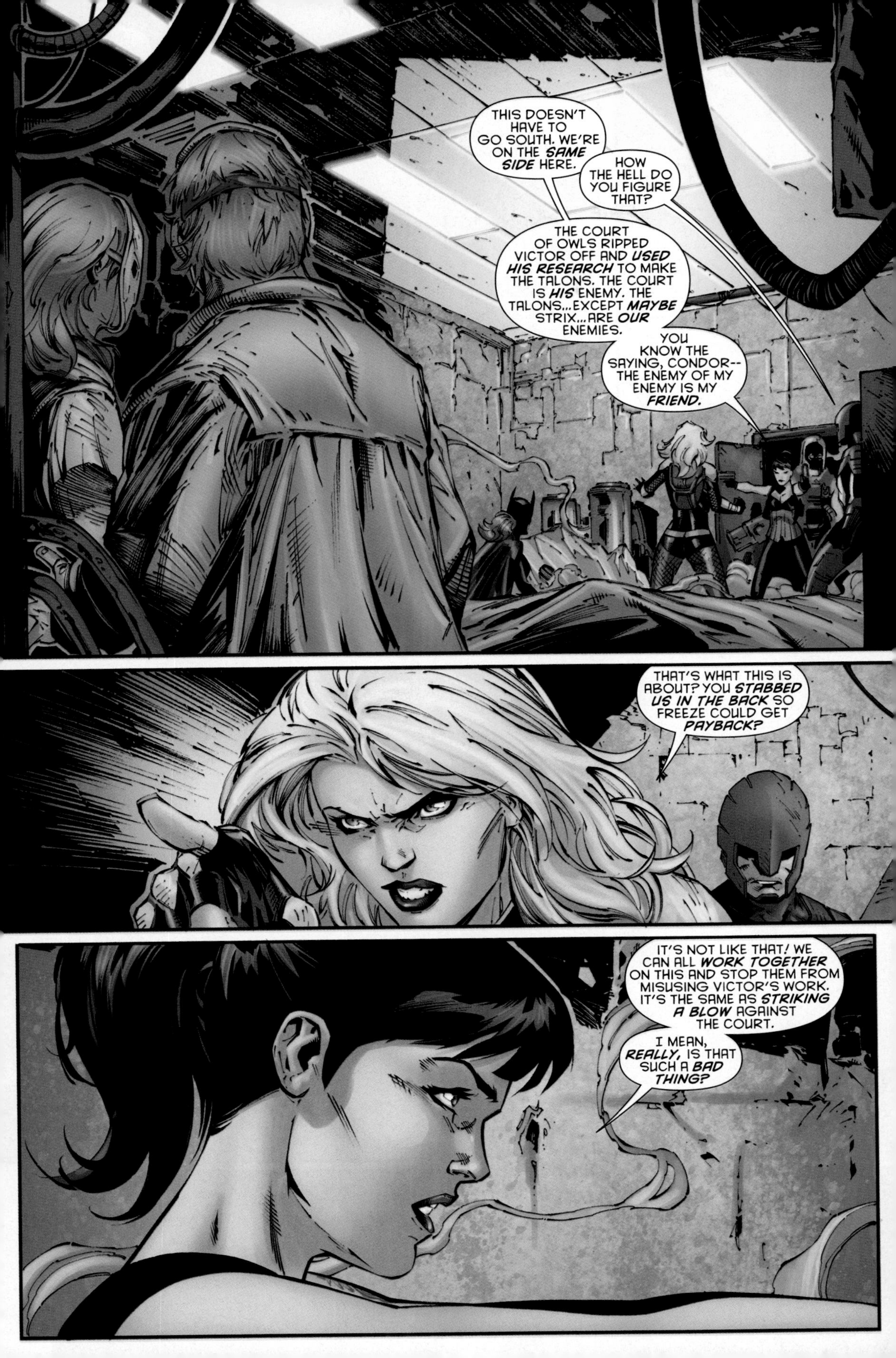
THIS DOESN'T HAVE TO GO SOUTH. WE'RE ON THE SAME SIDE HERE.
HOW THE HELL DO YOU FIGURE THAT?
THE COURT OF OWLS RIPPED VICTOR OFF AND USED HIS RESEARCH TO MAKE THE TALONS. THE COURT IS HIS ENEMY. THE TALONS...EXCEPT MAYBE STRIX...ARE OUR ENEMIES.
YOU KNOW THE SAYING, CONDOR-- THE ENEMY OF MY ENEMY IS MY FRIEND.
THAT'S WHAT THIS IS ABOUT? YOU STABBED US IN THE BACK SO FREEZE COULD GET PAYBACK?
IT'S NOT LIKE THAT! WE CAN ALL WORK TOGETHER ON THIS AND STOP THEM FROM MISUSING VICTOR'S WORK. IT'S THE SAME AS STRIKING A BLOW AGAINST THE COURT.
I MEAN, REALLY, IS THAT SUCH A BAD THING?

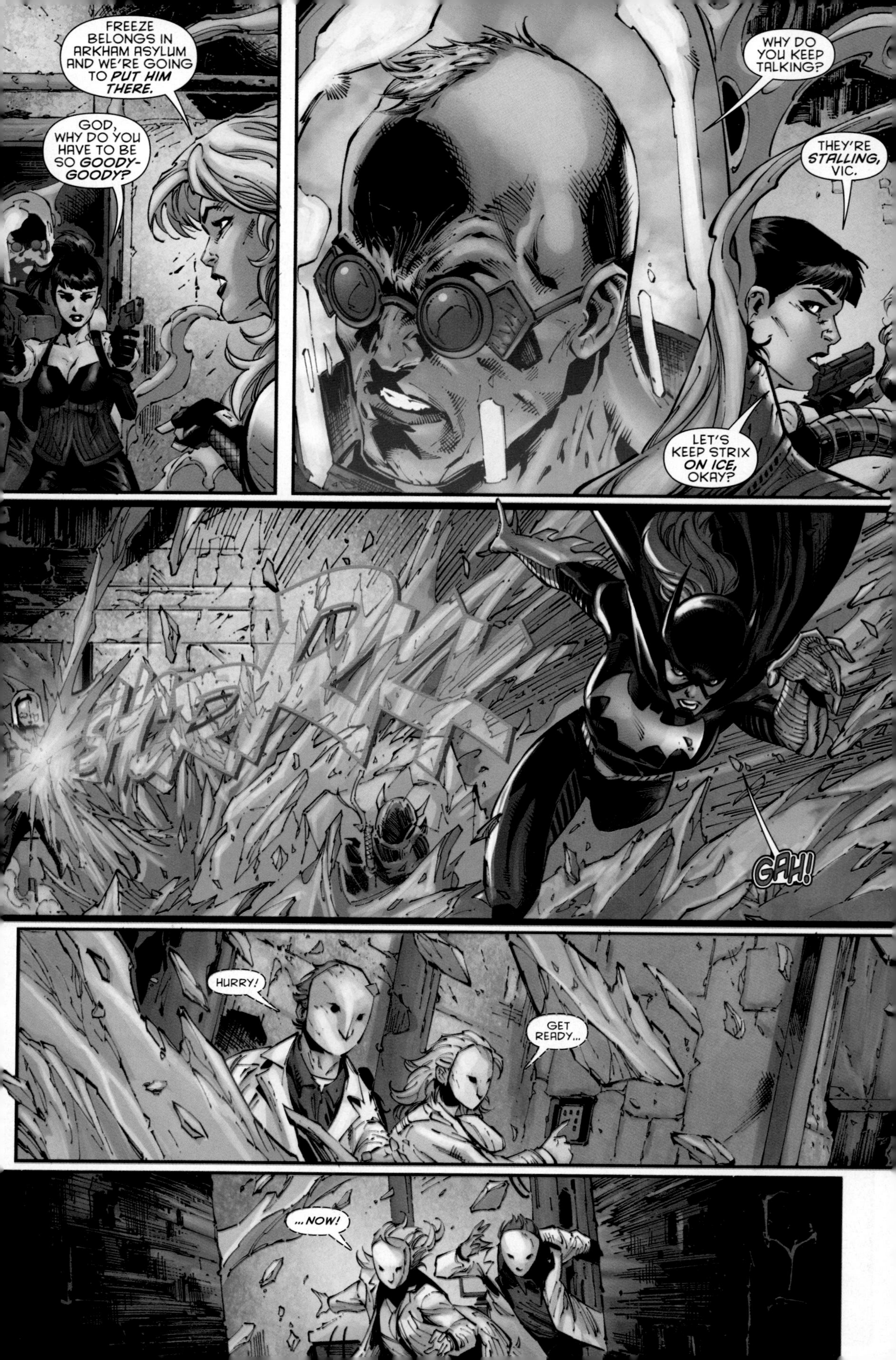
FREEZE BELONGS IN ARKHAM ASYLUM AND WE'RE GOING TO PUT HIM THERE.
GOD, WHY DO YOU HAVE TO BE SO GOODY-GOODY?
WHY DO YOU KEEP TALKING?
THEY'RE STALLING, VIC.
LET'S KEEP STRIX ON ICE, OKAY?
GAH!
HURRY!
GET READY...
...NOW!

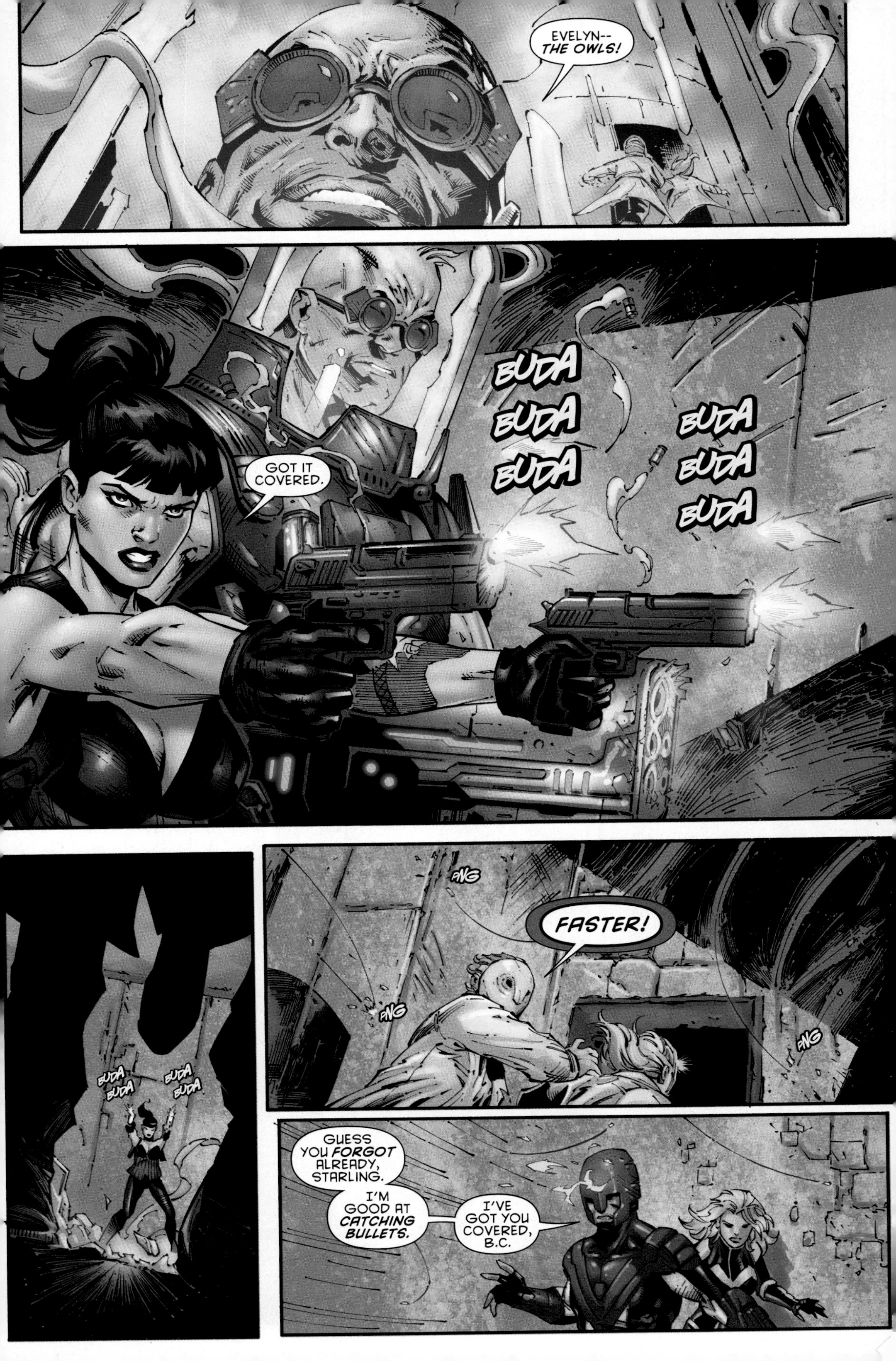
EVELYN-- THE OWLS!
GOT IT COVERED.
BUDA BUDA BUDA
BUDA BUDA BUDA
BUDA BUDA
BUDA BUDA
PNG
FASTER!
PNG
PNG
GUESS YOU FORGOT ALREADY, STARLING.
I'M GOOD AT CATCHING BULLETS.
I'VE GOT YOU COVERED, B.C.

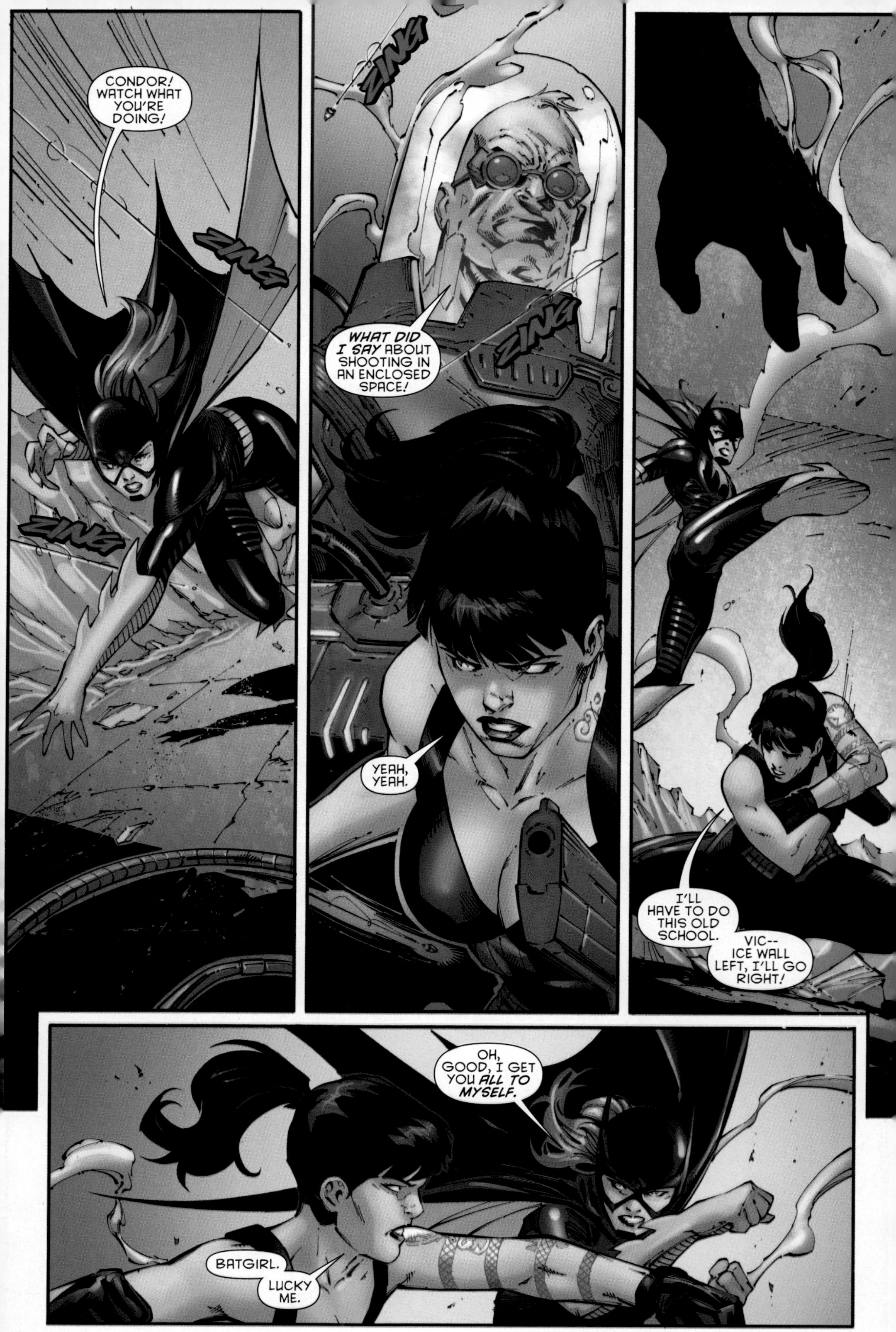

CONDOR! WATCH WHAT YOU'RE DOING!
ZING
ZING
ZING
WHAT DID I SAY ABOUT SHOOTING IN AN ENCLOSED SPACE!
ZING
YEAH, YEAH.
I'LL HAVE TO DO THIS OLD SCHOOL.
VIC-- ICE WALL LEFT, I'LL GO RIGHT!
OH, GOOD, I GET YOU ALL TO MYSELF.
BATGIRL.
LUCKY ME.

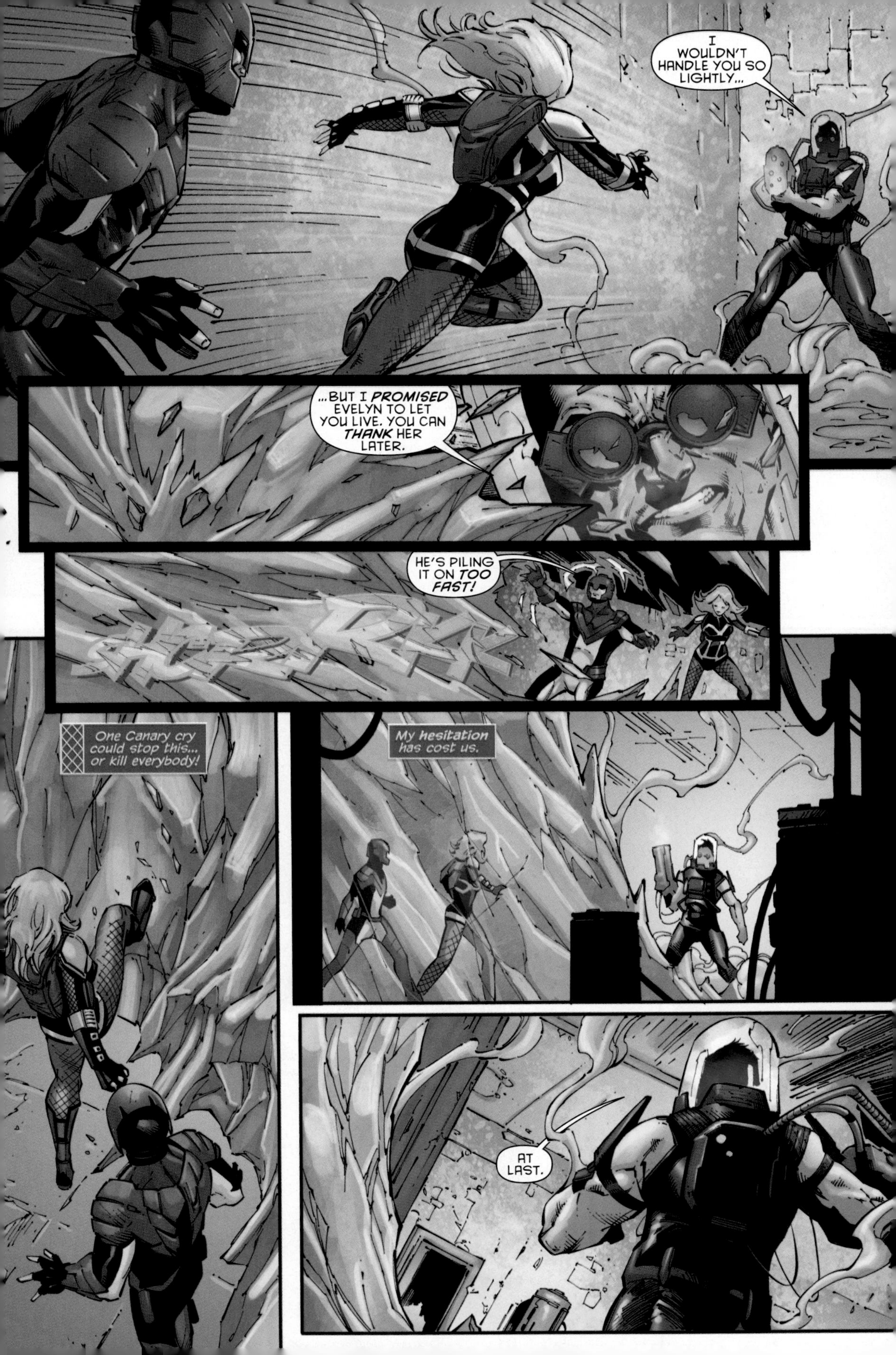
I WOULDN'T HANDLE YOU SO LIGHTLY...
...BUT I PROMISED EVELYN TO LET YOU LIVE. YOU CAN THANK HER LATER.
HE'S PILING IT ON TOO FAST!
One Canary cry could stop this... or kill everybody!
My hesitation has cost us.
AT LAST.

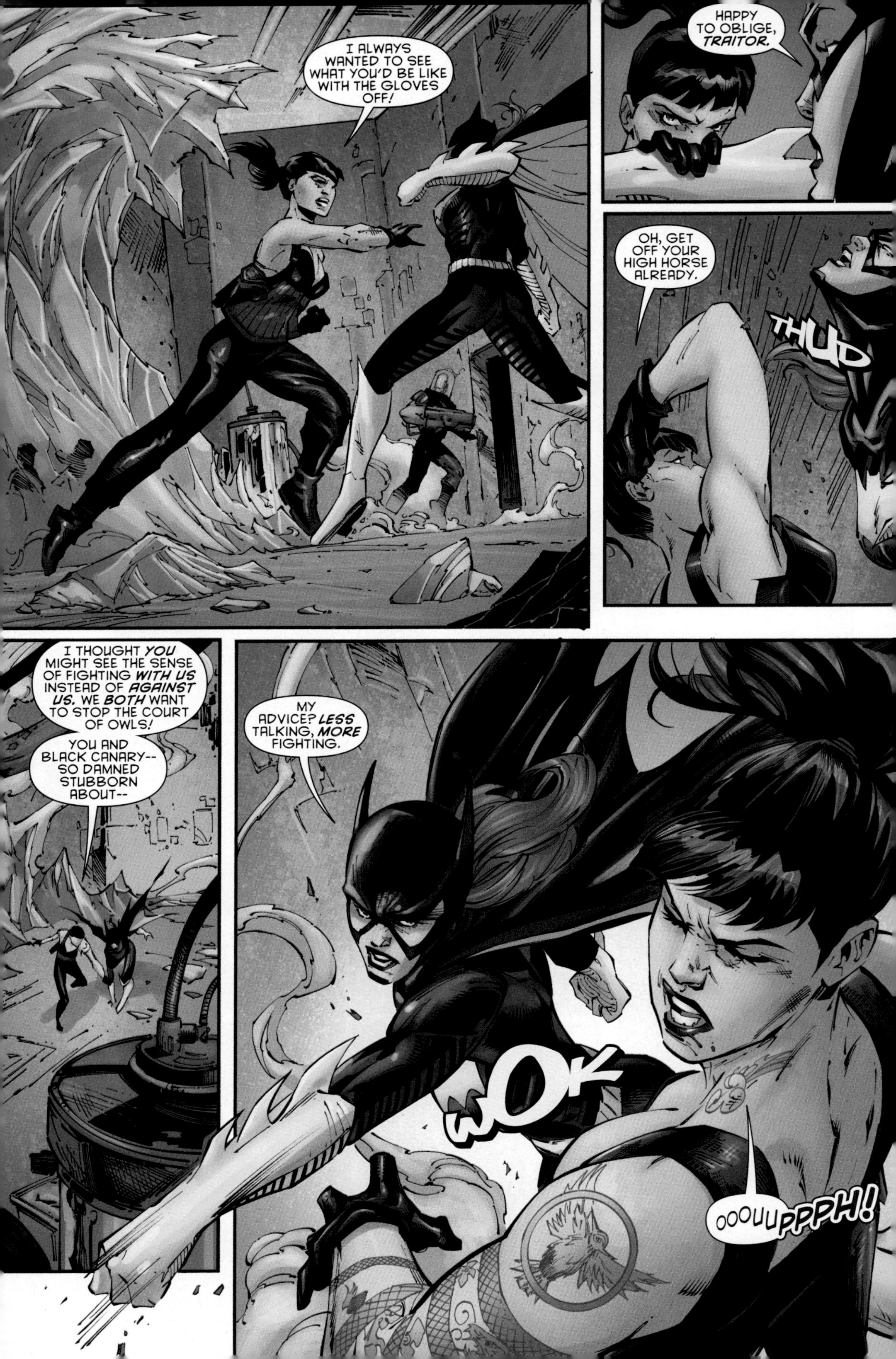

I ALWAYS WANTED TO SEE WHAT YOU'D BE LIKE WITH THE GLOVES OFF!
HAPPY TO OBLIGE, *TRAITOR.*
OH, GET OFF YOUR HIGH HORSE ALREADY.
THUD
I THOUGHT *YOU* MIGHT SEE THE SENSE OF FIGHTING *WITH US* INSTEAD OF *AGAINST US.* WE *BOTH* WANT TO STOP THE COURT OF OWLS!
YOU AND BLACK CANARY-- SO DAMNED STUBBORN ABOUT--
MY ADVICE? *LESS* TALKING, *MORE* FIGHTING.
WOK
OOOUUPPPH!

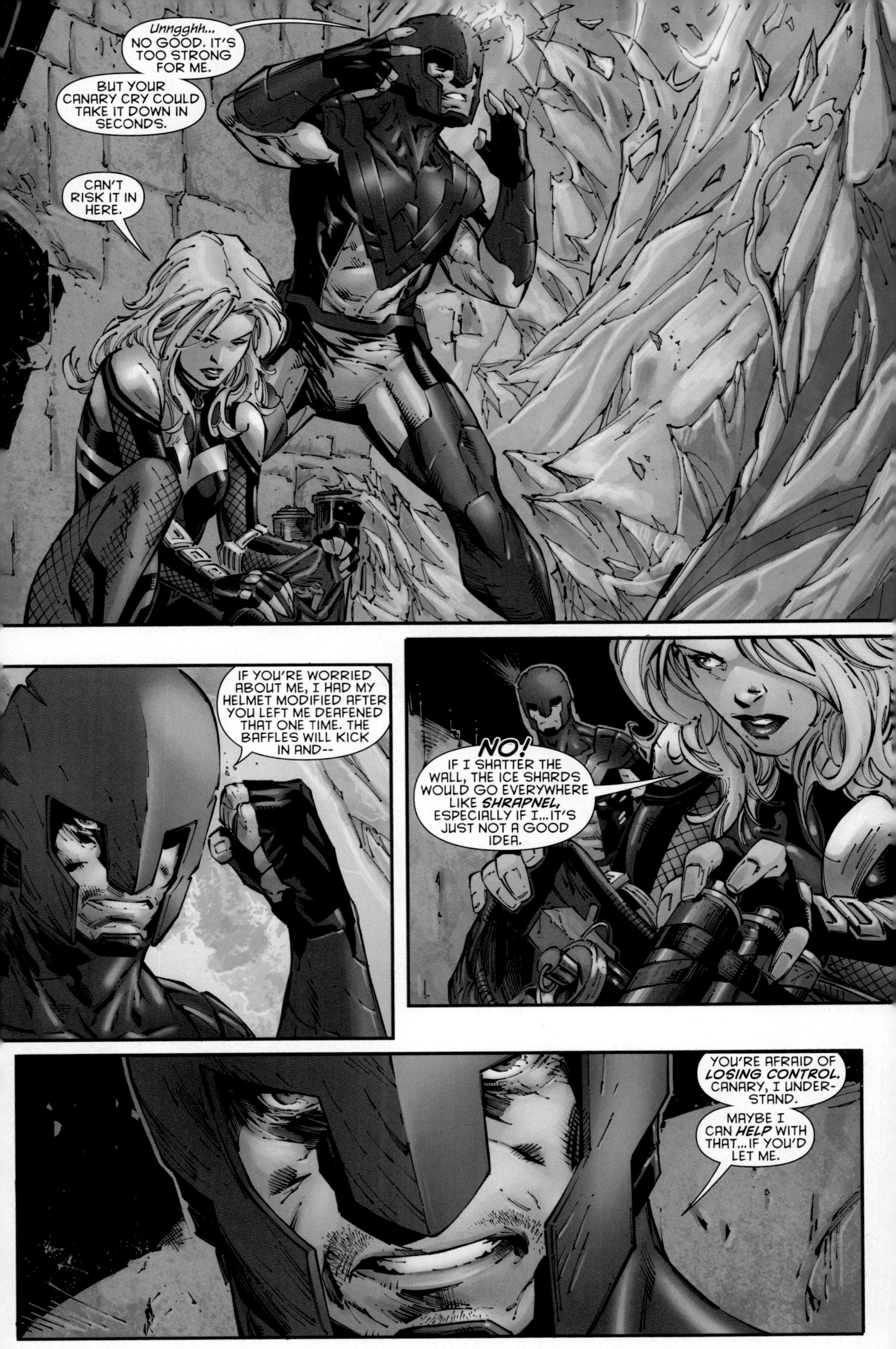

Unngghh... NO GOOD. IT'S TOO STRONG FOR ME.
BUT YOUR CANARY CRY COULD TAKE IT DOWN IN SECONDS.
CAN'T RISK IT IN HERE.
IF YOU'RE WORRIED ABOUT ME, I HAD MY HELMET MODIFIED AFTER YOU LEFT ME DEAFENED THAT ONE TIME. THE BAFFLES WILL KICK IN AND--
NO! IF I SHATTER THE WALL, THE ICE SHARDS WOULD GO EVERYWHERE LIKE SHRAPNEL, ESPECIALLY IF I...IT'S JUST NOT A GOOD IDEA.
YOU'RE AFRAID OF LOSING CONTROL. CANARY, I UNDERSTAND.
MAYBE I CAN HELP WITH THAT...IF YOU'D LET ME.

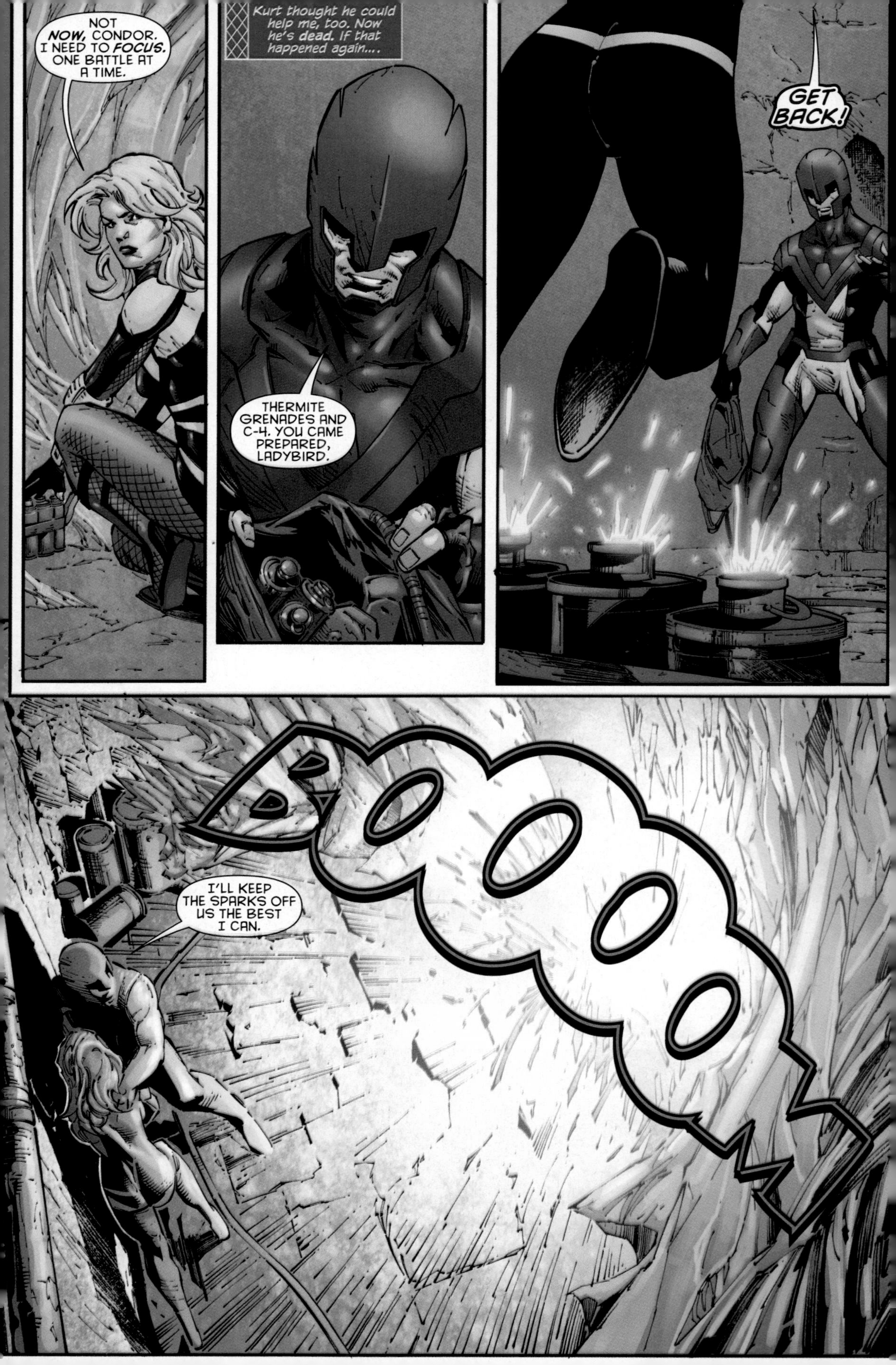
NOT *NOW,* CONDOR. I NEED TO *FOCUS.* ONE BATTLE AT A TIME.
Kurt thought he could help me, too. Now he's ***dead.*** *If that happened again....*
THERMITE GRENADES AND C-4. YOU CAME PREPARED, LADYBIRD.
GET BACK!
BOOOOOM
I'LL KEEP THE SPARKS OFF US THE BEST I CAN.

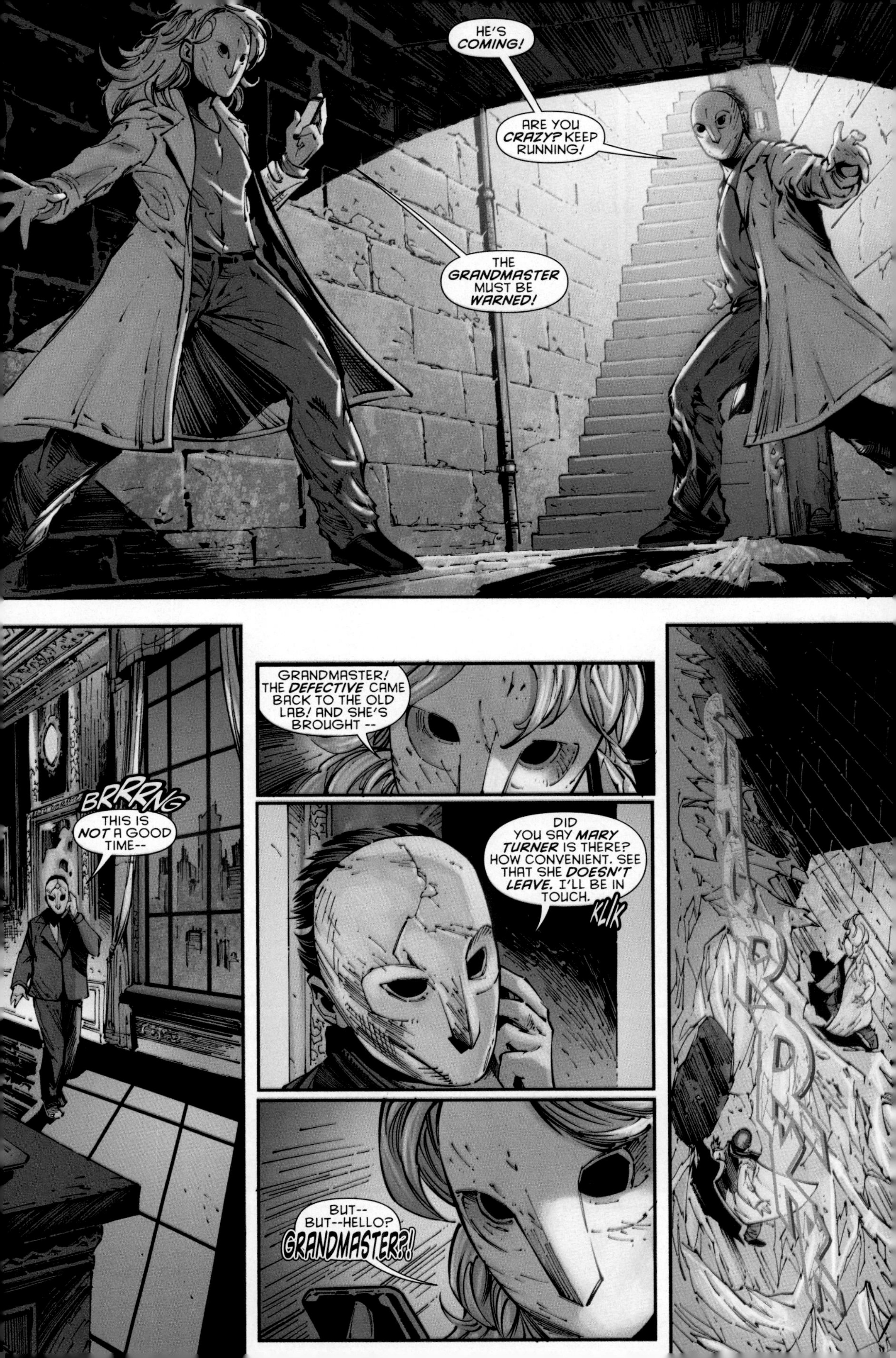
HE'S COMING!
ARE YOU CRAZY? KEEP RUNNING!
THE GRANDMASTER MUST BE WARNED!
BRRRNG
THIS IS NOT A GOOD TIME--
GRANDMASTER! THE DEFECTIVE CAME BACK TO THE OLD LAB! AND SHE'S BROUGHT --
DID YOU SAY MARY TURNER IS THERE? HOW CONVENIENT. SEE THAT SHE DOESN'T LEAVE. I'LL BE IN TOUCH.
KLIK
BUT-- BUT--HELLO? GRANDMASTER?!

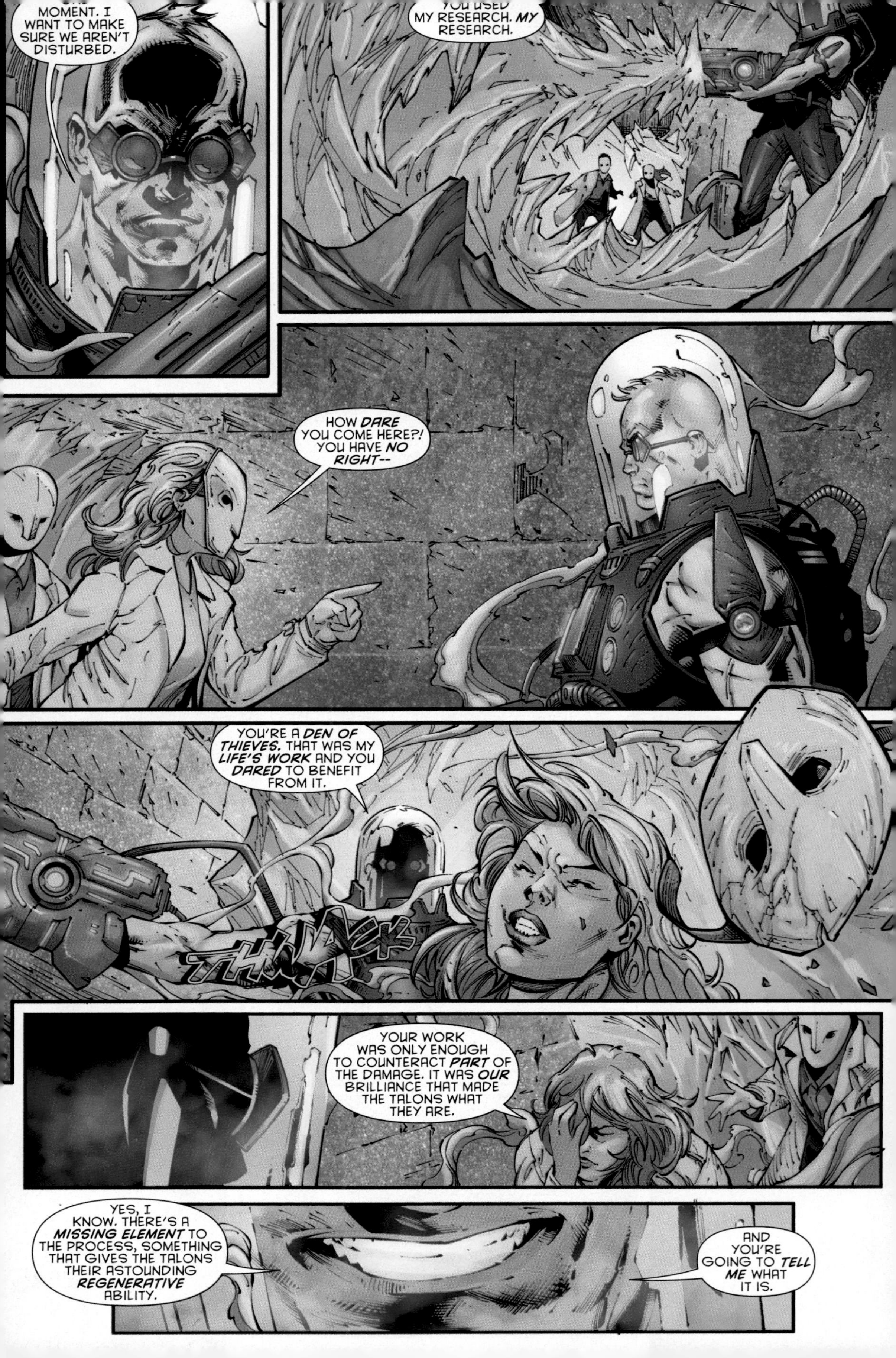
MOMENT. I WANT TO MAKE SURE WE AREN'T DISTURBED.
YOU USED MY RESEARCH. MY RESEARCH.
HOW DARE YOU COME HERE?! YOU HAVE NO RIGHT--
YOU'RE A DEN OF THIEVES. THAT WAS MY LIFE'S WORK AND YOU DARED TO BENEFIT FROM IT.
THWACK
YOUR WORK WAS ONLY ENOUGH TO COUNTERACT PART OF THE DAMAGE. IT WAS OUR BRILLIANCE THAT MADE THE TALONS WHAT THEY ARE.
YES, I KNOW. THERE'S A MISSING ELEMENT TO THE PROCESS, SOMETHING THAT GIVES THE TALONS THEIR ASTOUNDING REGENERATIVE ABILITY.
AND YOU'RE GOING TO TELL ME WHAT IT IS.

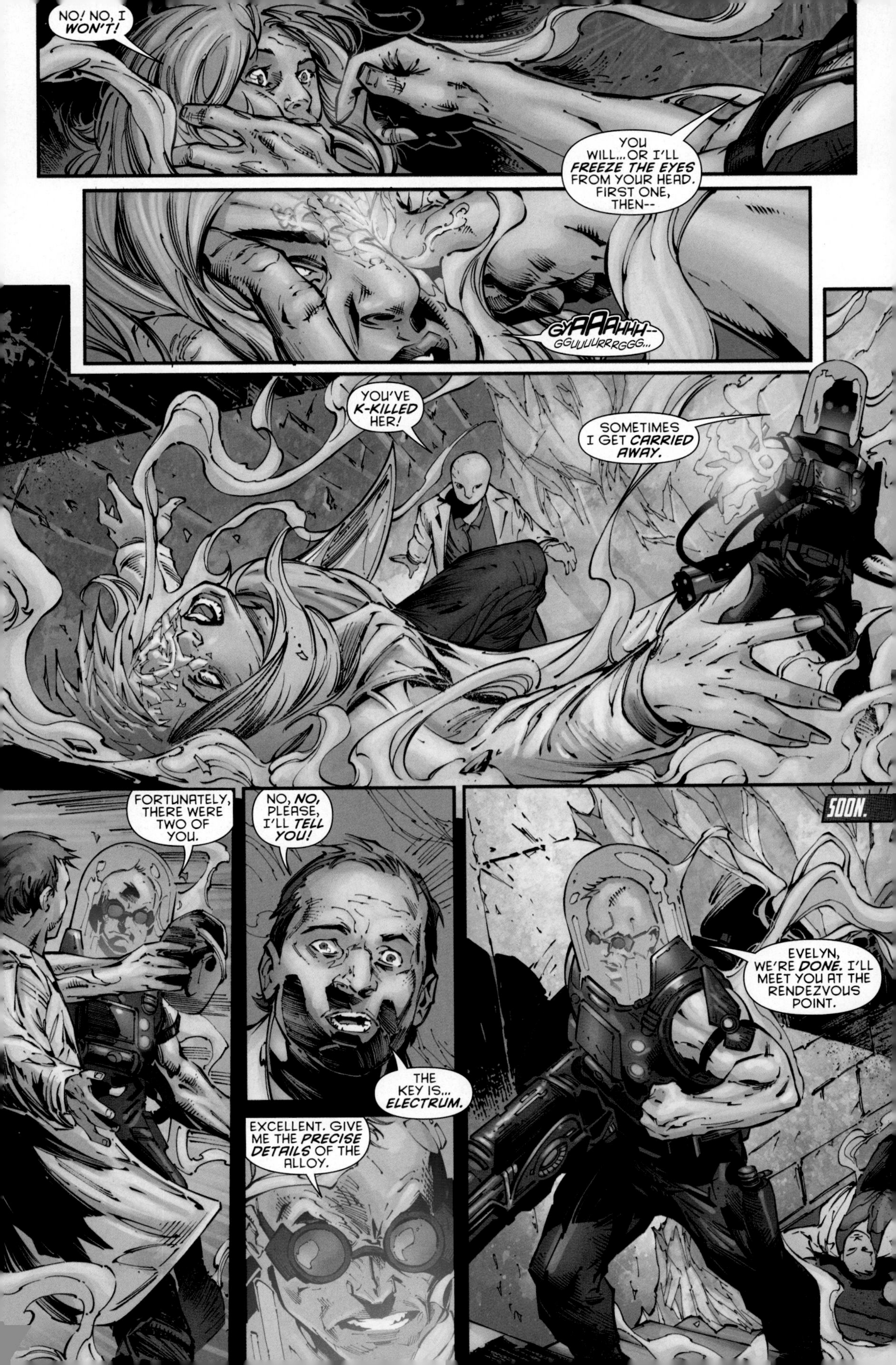
NO! NO, I WON'T!
YOU WILL...OR I'LL FREEZE THE EYES FROM YOUR HEAD. FIRST ONE, THEN--
GYAAAHHH-- GGUUUURRRGGG...
YOU'VE K-KILLED HER!
SOMETIMES I GET CARRIED AWAY.
FORTUNATELY, THERE WERE TWO OF YOU.
NO, NO, PLEASE, I'LL TELL YOU!
THE KEY IS... ELECTRUM.
EXCELLENT. GIVE ME THE PRECISE DETAILS OF THE ALLOY.
SOON.
EVELYN, WE'RE DONE. I'LL MEET YOU AT THE RENDEZVOUS POINT.

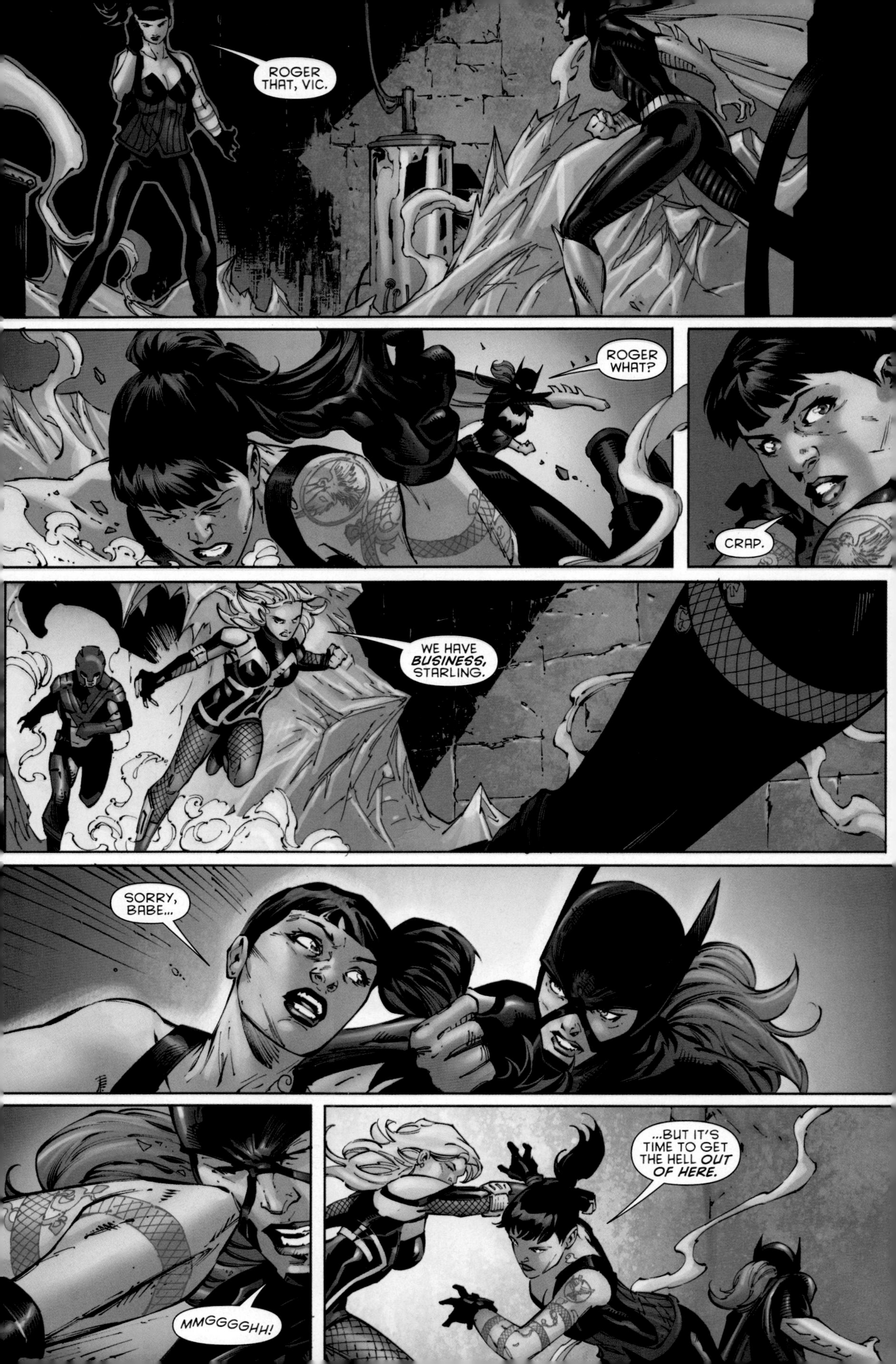
ROGER THAT, VIC.
ROGER WHAT?
CRAP.
WE HAVE *BUSINESS,* STARLING.
SORRY, BABE...
MMGGGGHH!
...BUT IT'S TIME TO GET THE HELL *OUT OF HERE.*

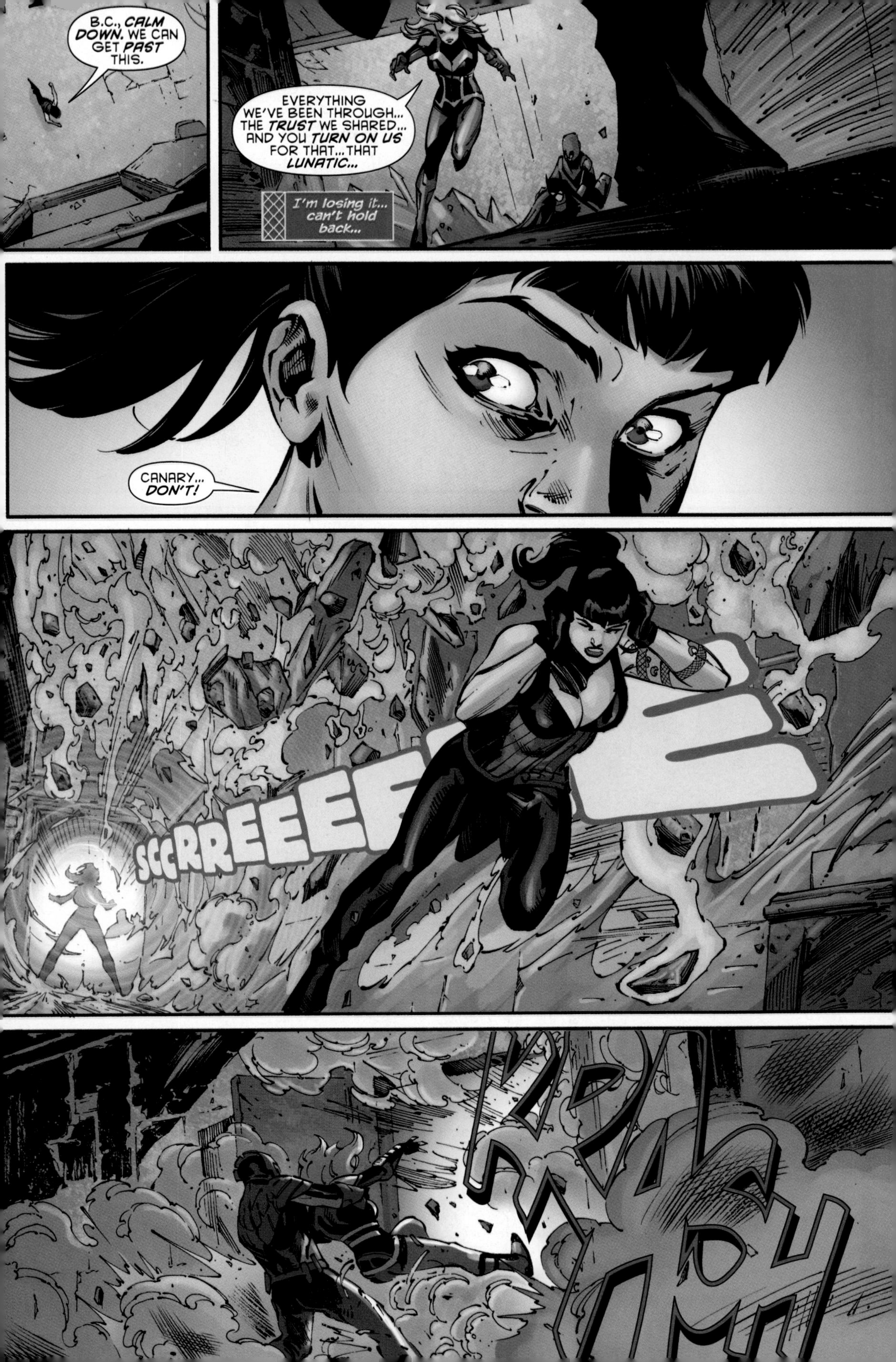
B.C., CALM DOWN. WE CAN GET PAST THIS.
EVERYTHING WE'VE BEEN THROUGH... THE TRUST WE SHARED... AND YOU TURN ON US FOR THAT...THAT LUNATIC...
I'm losing it... can't hold back...
CANARY... DON'T!
SCCRREEEE

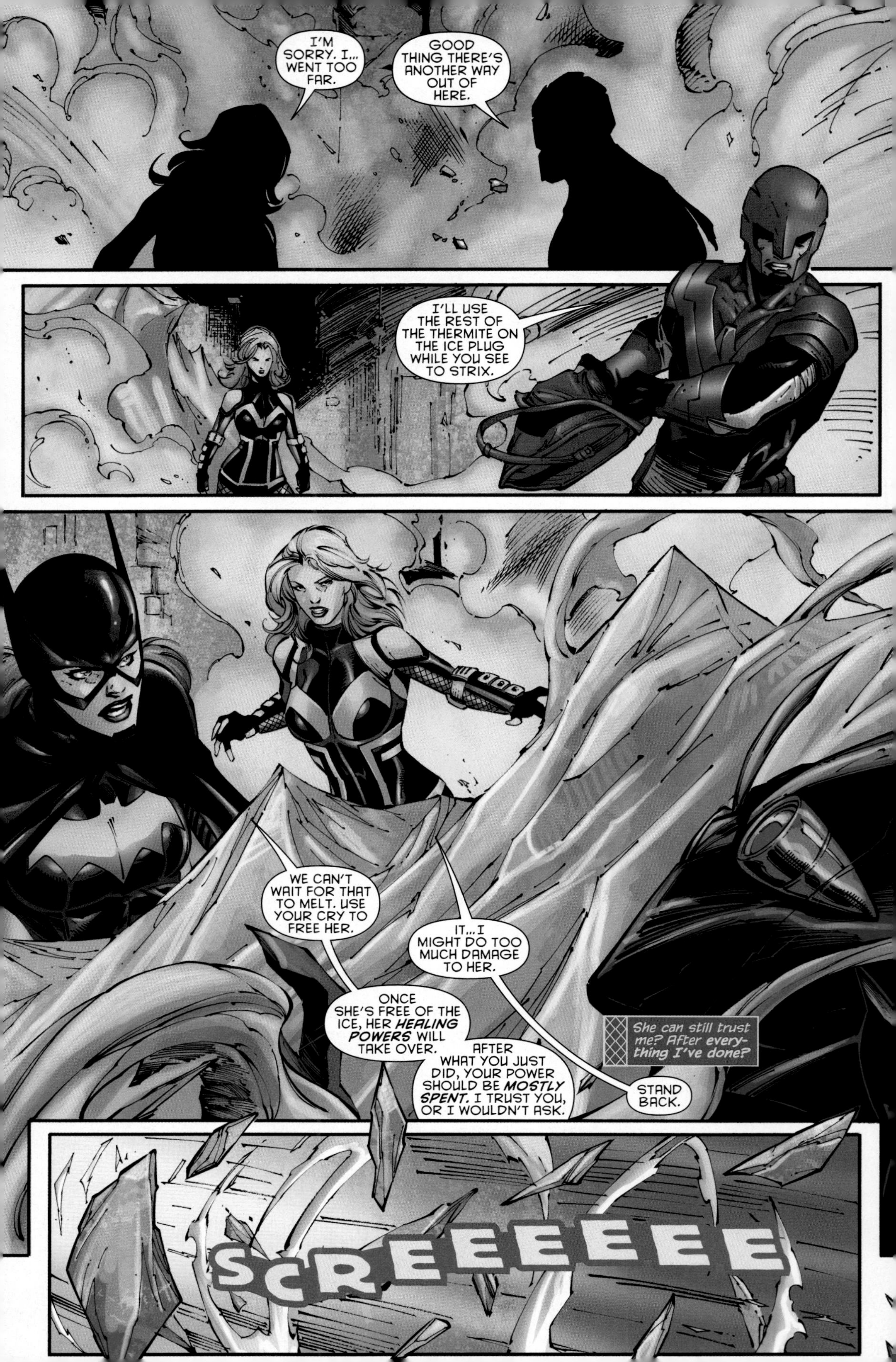

I'M SORRY. I... WENT TOO FAR.
GOOD THING THERE'S ANOTHER WAY OUT OF HERE.
I'LL USE THE REST OF THE THERMITE ON THE ICE PLUG WHILE YOU SEE TO STRIX.
WE CAN'T WAIT FOR THAT TO MELT. USE YOUR CRY TO FREE HER.
IT...I MIGHT DO TOO MUCH DAMAGE TO HER.
ONCE SHE'S FREE OF THE ICE, HER *HEALING POWERS* WILL TAKE OVER.
AFTER WHAT YOU JUST DID, YOUR POWER SHOULD BE *MOSTLY SPENT.* I TRUST YOU, OR I WOULDN'T ASK.
She can still trust me? After everything I've done?
STAND BACK.
SCREEEEEE

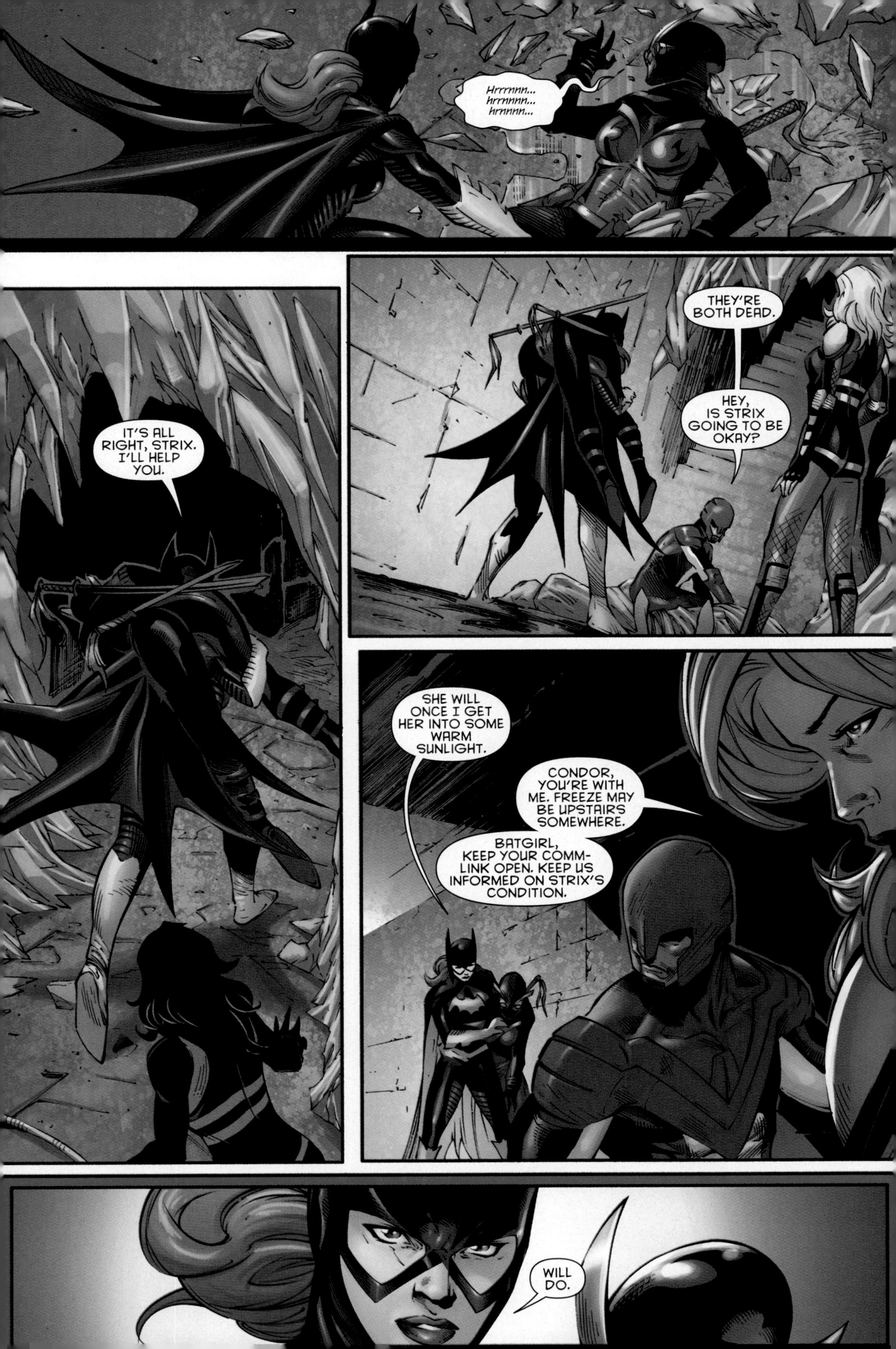
Hrrrnnn... hrrnnnn... hrnnnn...
IT'S ALL RIGHT, STRIX. I'LL HELP YOU.
THEY'RE BOTH DEAD.
HEY, IS STRIX GOING TO BE OKAY?
SHE WILL ONCE I GET HER INTO SOME WARM SUNLIGHT.
CONDOR, YOU'RE WITH ME. FREEZE MAY BE UPSTAIRS SOMEWHERE.
BATGIRL, KEEP YOUR COMM-LINK OPEN. KEEP US INFORMED ON STRIX'S CONDITION.
WILL DO.

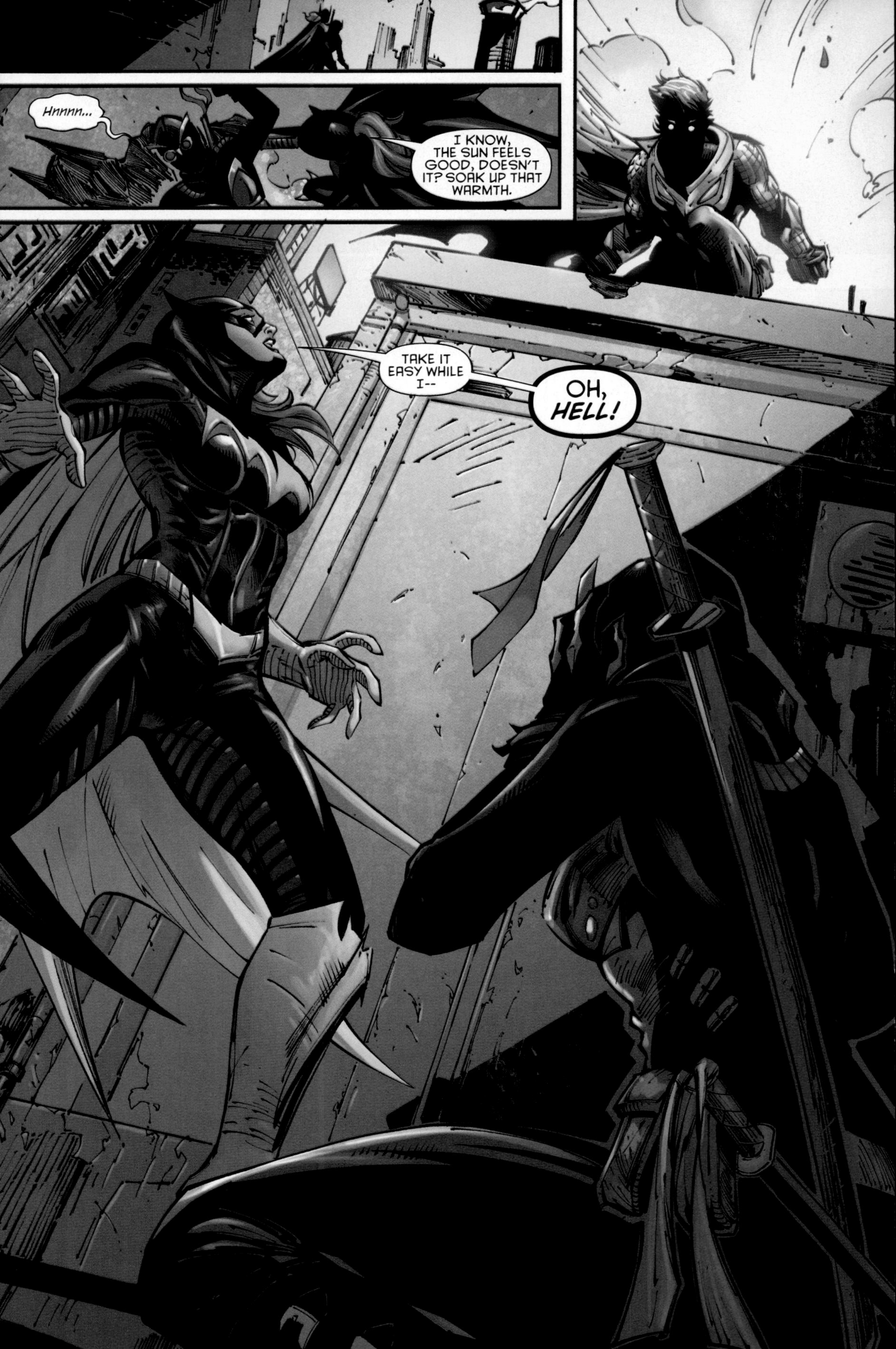
Hnnnn...
I KNOW, THE SUN FEELS GOOD, DOESN'T IT? SOAK UP THAT WARMTH.
TAKE IT EASY WHILE I--
OH, HELL!

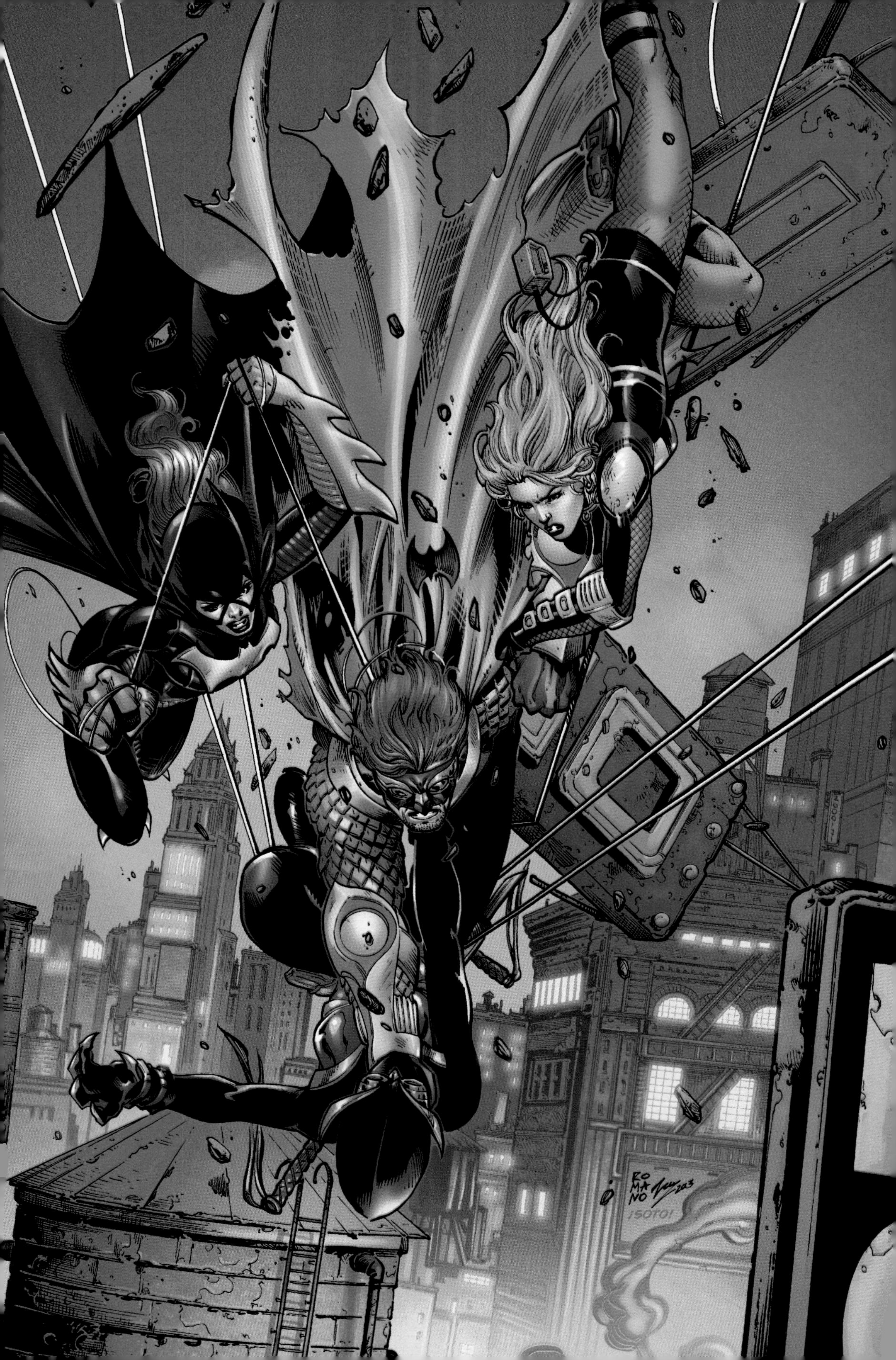
ROMANO
2013
¡SOTO!

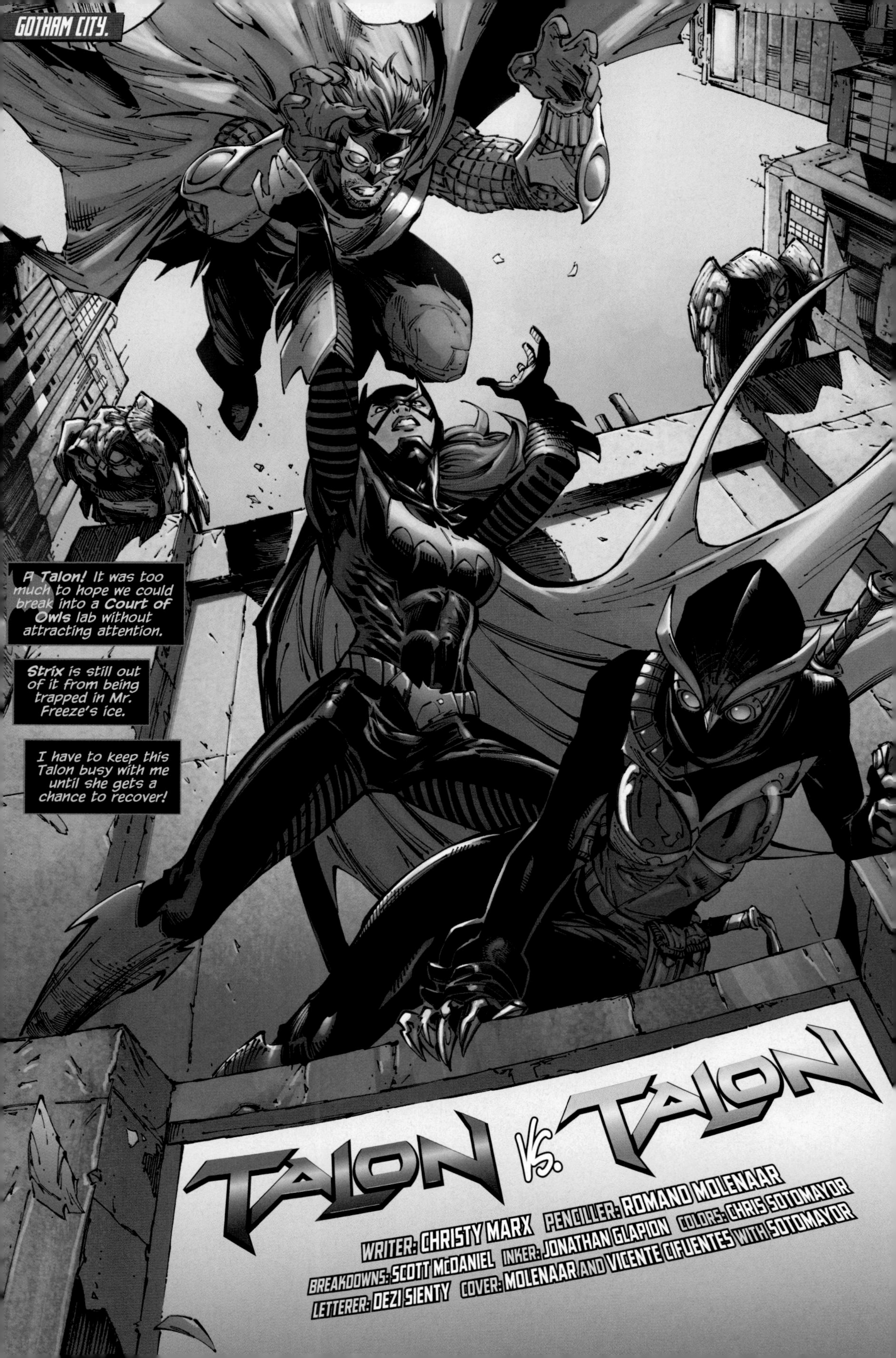
GOTHAM CITY.
A Talon! It was too much to hope we could break into a Court of Owls lab without attracting attention.
Strix is still out of it from being trapped in Mr. Freeze's ice.
I have to keep this Talon busy with me until she gets a chance to recover!
TALON VS. TALON
WRITER: CHRISTY MARX PENCILLER: ROMANO MOLENAAR
BREAKDOWNS: SCOTT McDANIEL INKER: JONATHAN GLAPION COLORS: CHRIS SOTOMAYOR
LETTERER: DEZI SIENTY COVER: MOLENAAR AND VICENTE CIFUENTES WITH SOTOMAYOR

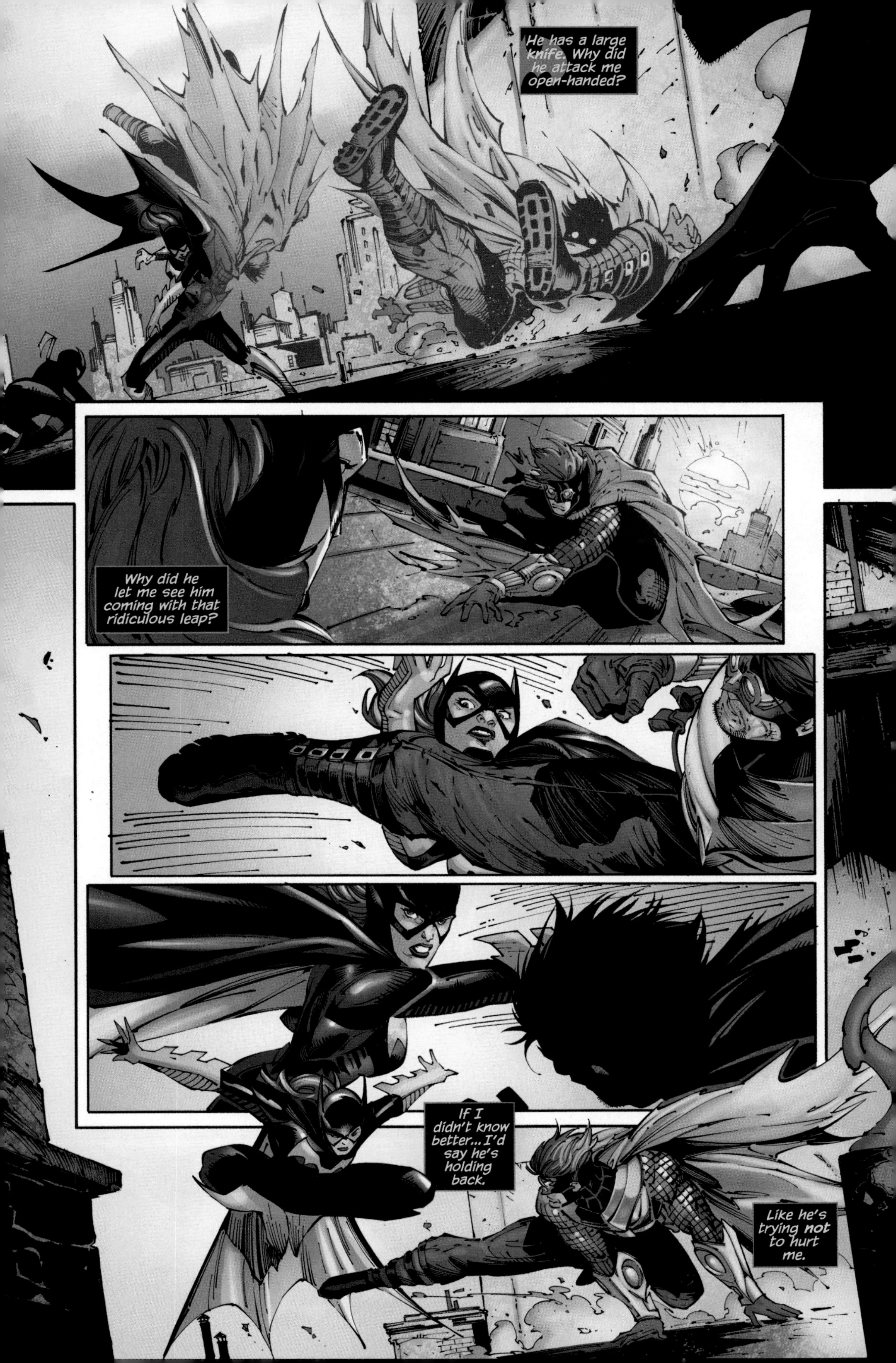
He has a large knife. Why did he attack me open-handed?
Why did he let me see him coming with that ridiculous leap?
If I didn't know better...I'd say he's holding back.
Like he's trying **not** to hurt me.

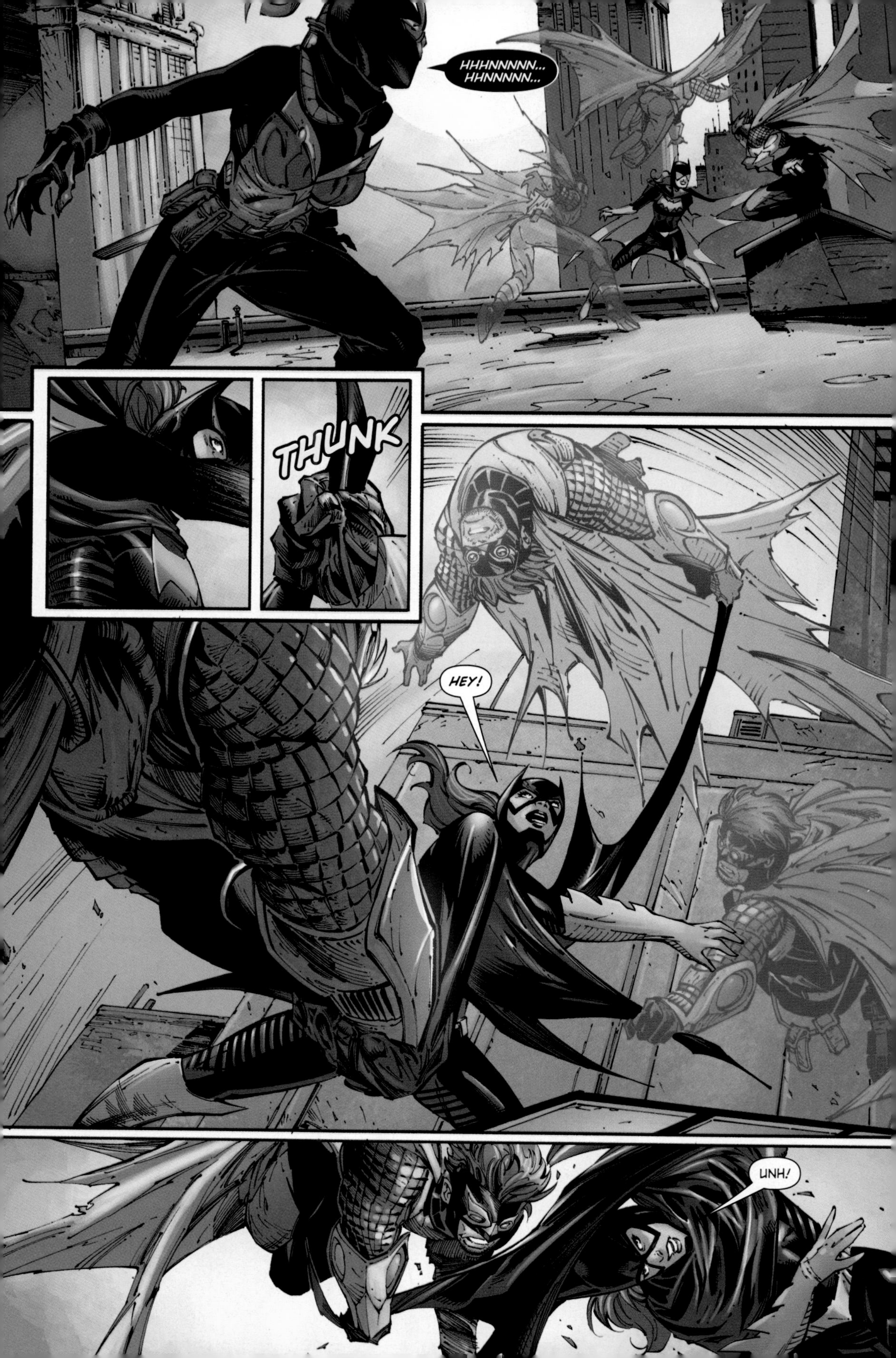
HHHNNNNN...
HHNNNNN...
THUNK
HEY!
UNH!

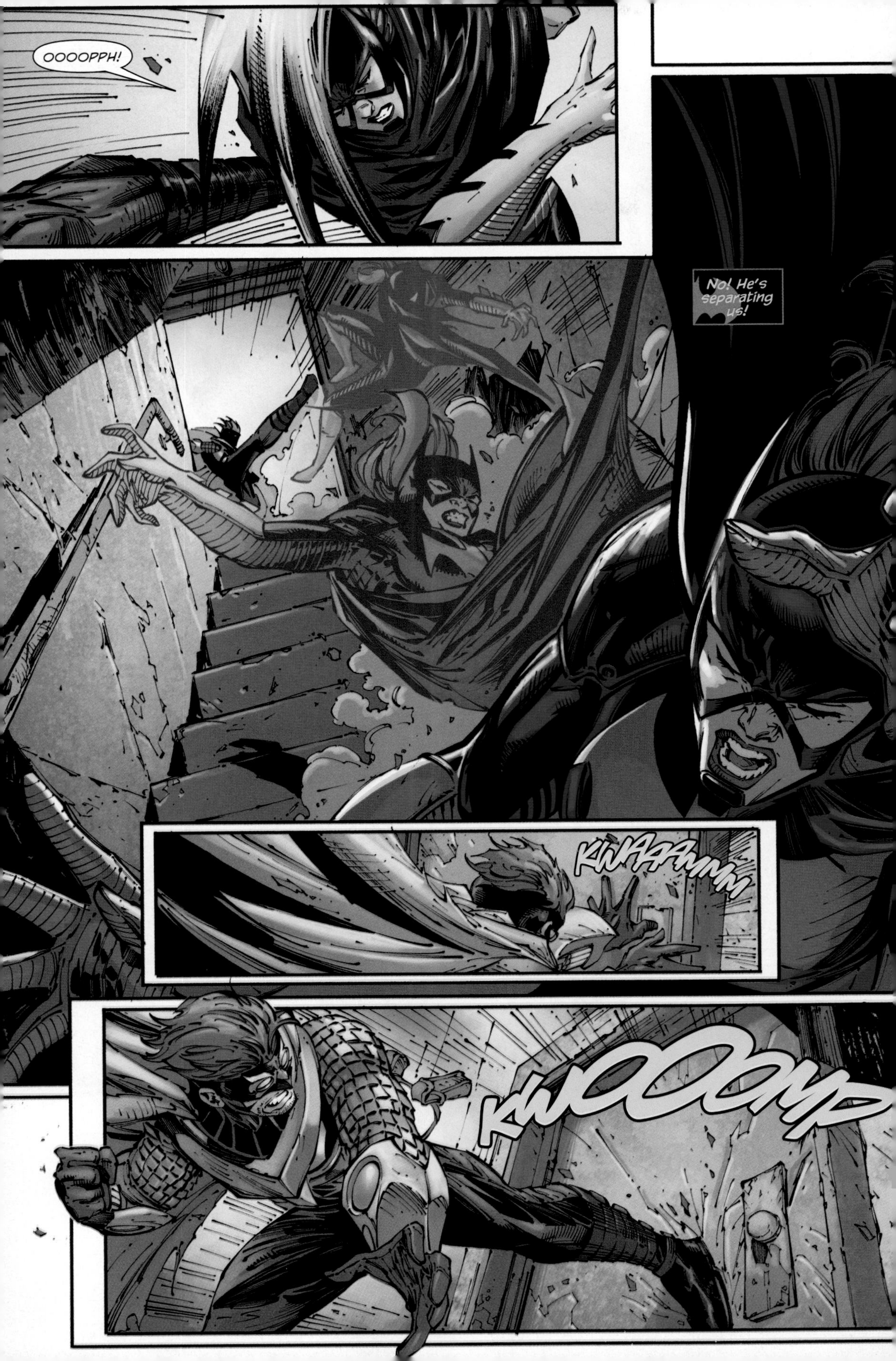
OOOOPPH!
No! He's separating us!
KWAAAMMM
KWOOOMP

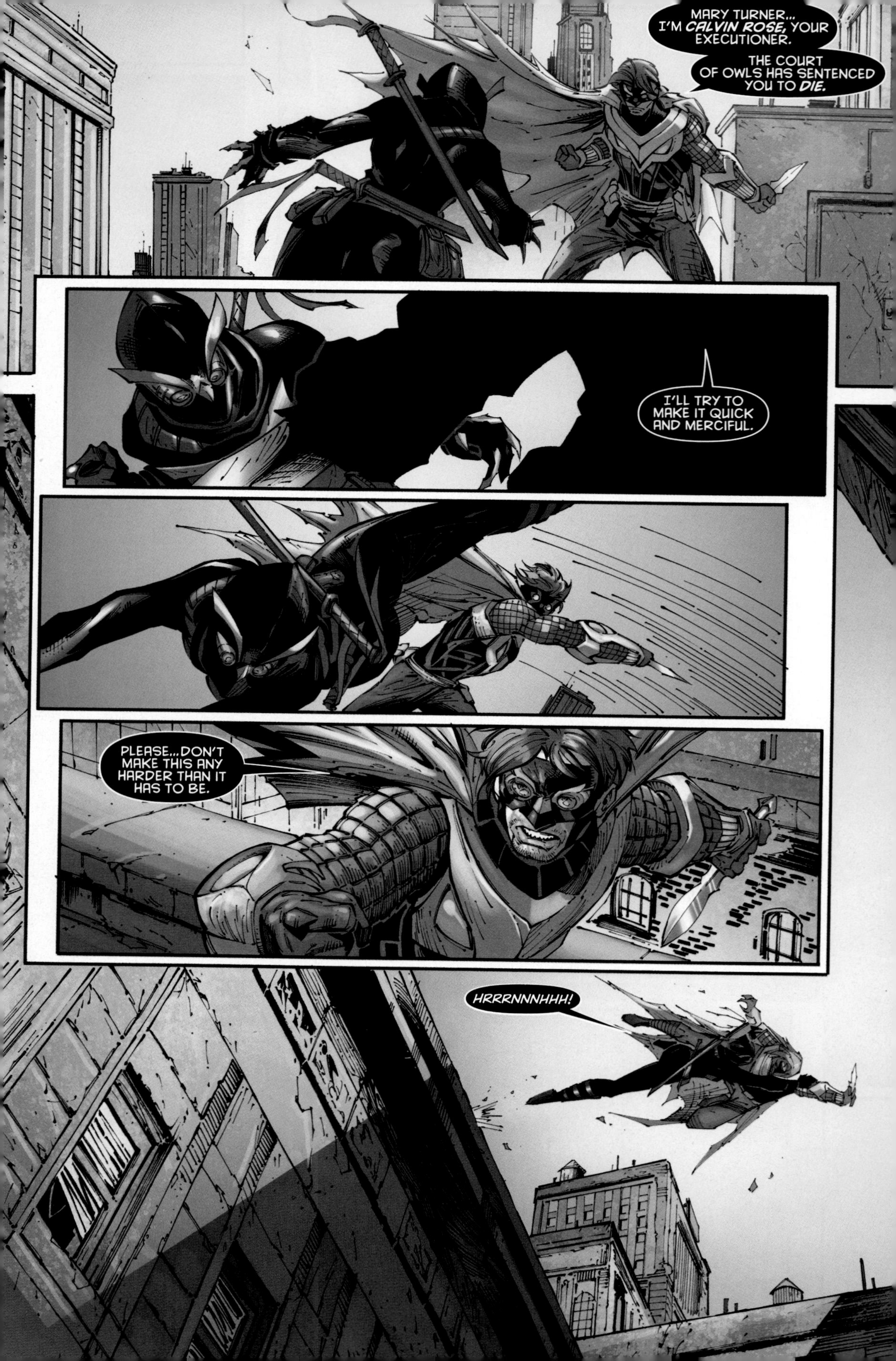
MARY TURNER... I'M CALVIN ROSE, YOUR EXECUTIONER.
THE COURT OF OWLS HAS SENTENCED YOU TO DIE.
I'LL TRY TO MAKE IT QUICK AND MERCIFUL.
PLEASE...DON'T MAKE THIS ANY HARDER THAN IT HAS TO BE.
HRRRNNNHHH!

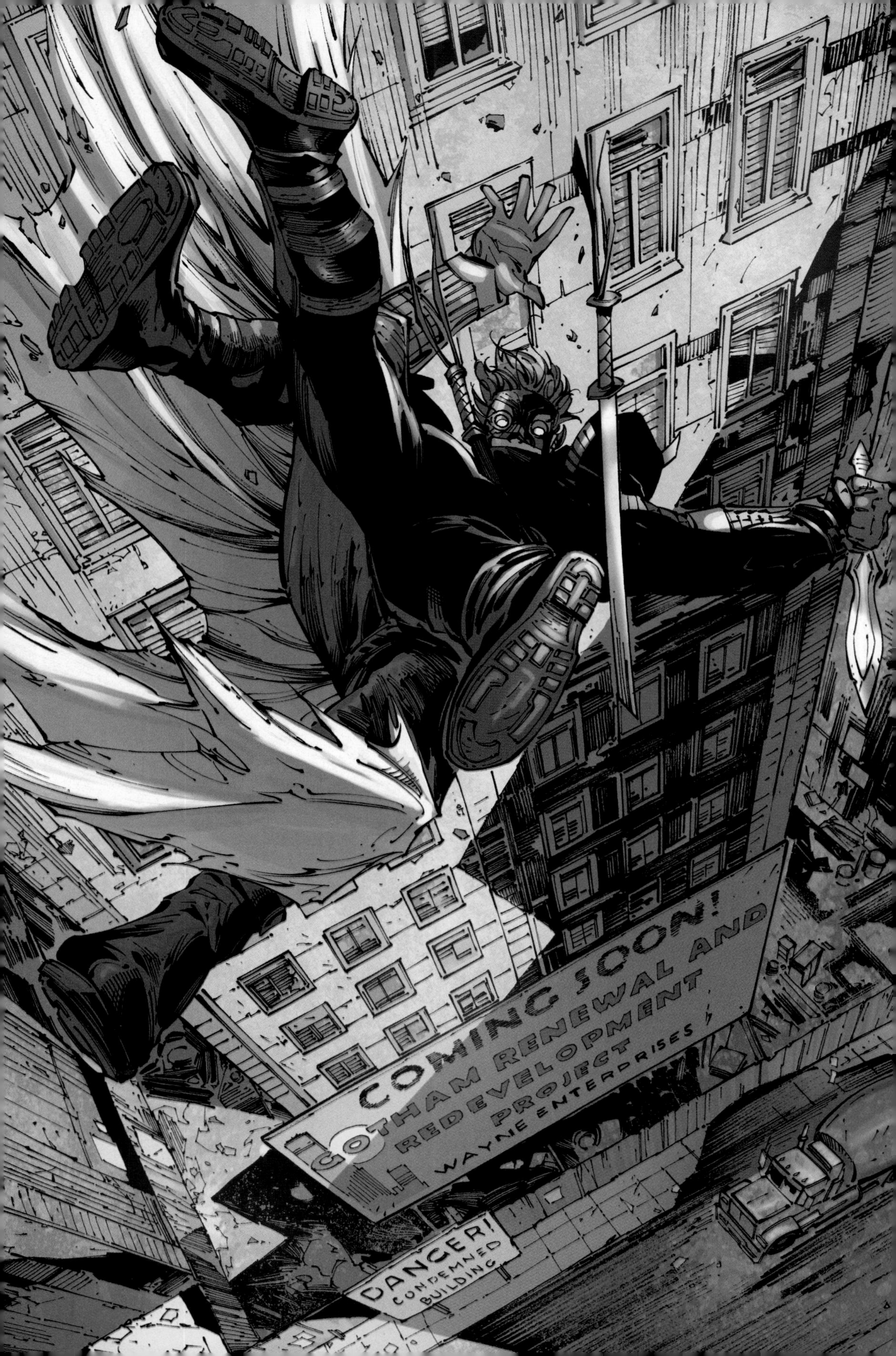
COMING SOON!
GOTHAM RENEWAL AND REDEVELOPMENT PROJECT
WAYNE ENTERPRISES
DANGER! CONDEMNED BUILDING

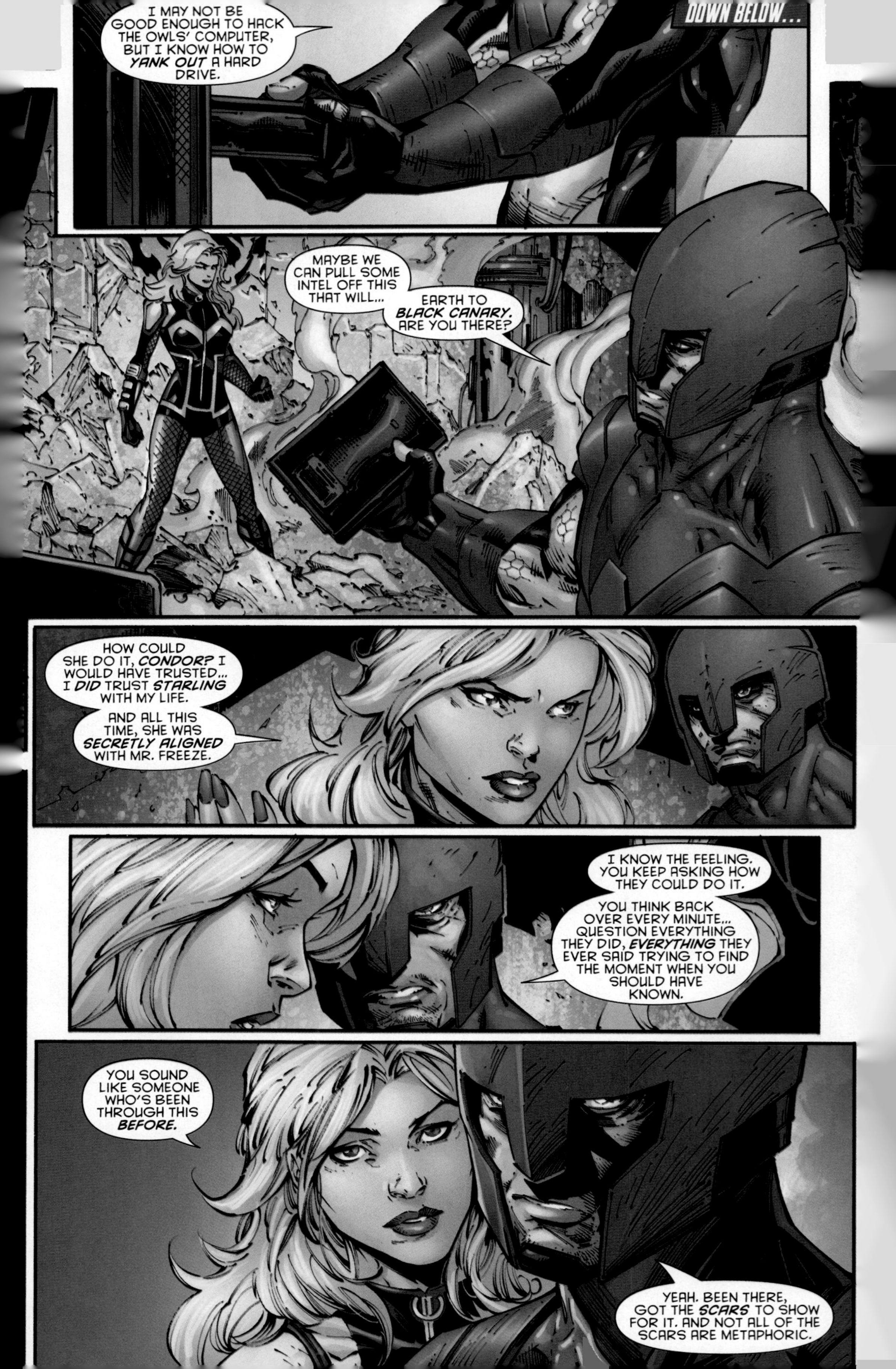

DOWN BELOW...
I MAY NOT BE GOOD ENOUGH TO HACK THE OWLS' COMPUTER, BUT I KNOW HOW TO YANK OUT A HARD DRIVE.
MAYBE WE CAN PULL SOME INTEL OFF THIS THAT WILL...
EARTH TO BLACK CANARY. ARE YOU THERE?
HOW COULD SHE DO IT, CONDOR? I WOULD HAVE TRUSTED... I DID TRUST STARLING WITH MY LIFE.
AND ALL THIS TIME, SHE WAS SECRETLY ALIGNED WITH MR. FREEZE.
I KNOW THE FEELING. YOU KEEP ASKING HOW THEY COULD DO IT.
YOU THINK BACK OVER EVERY MINUTE... QUESTION EVERYTHING THEY DID, EVERYTHING THEY EVER SAID TRYING TO FIND THE MOMENT WHEN YOU SHOULD HAVE KNOWN.
YOU SOUND LIKE SOMEONE WHO'S BEEN THROUGH THIS BEFORE.
YEAH. BEEN THERE, GOT THE SCARS TO SHOW FOR IT. AND NOT ALL OF THE SCARS ARE METAPHORIC.

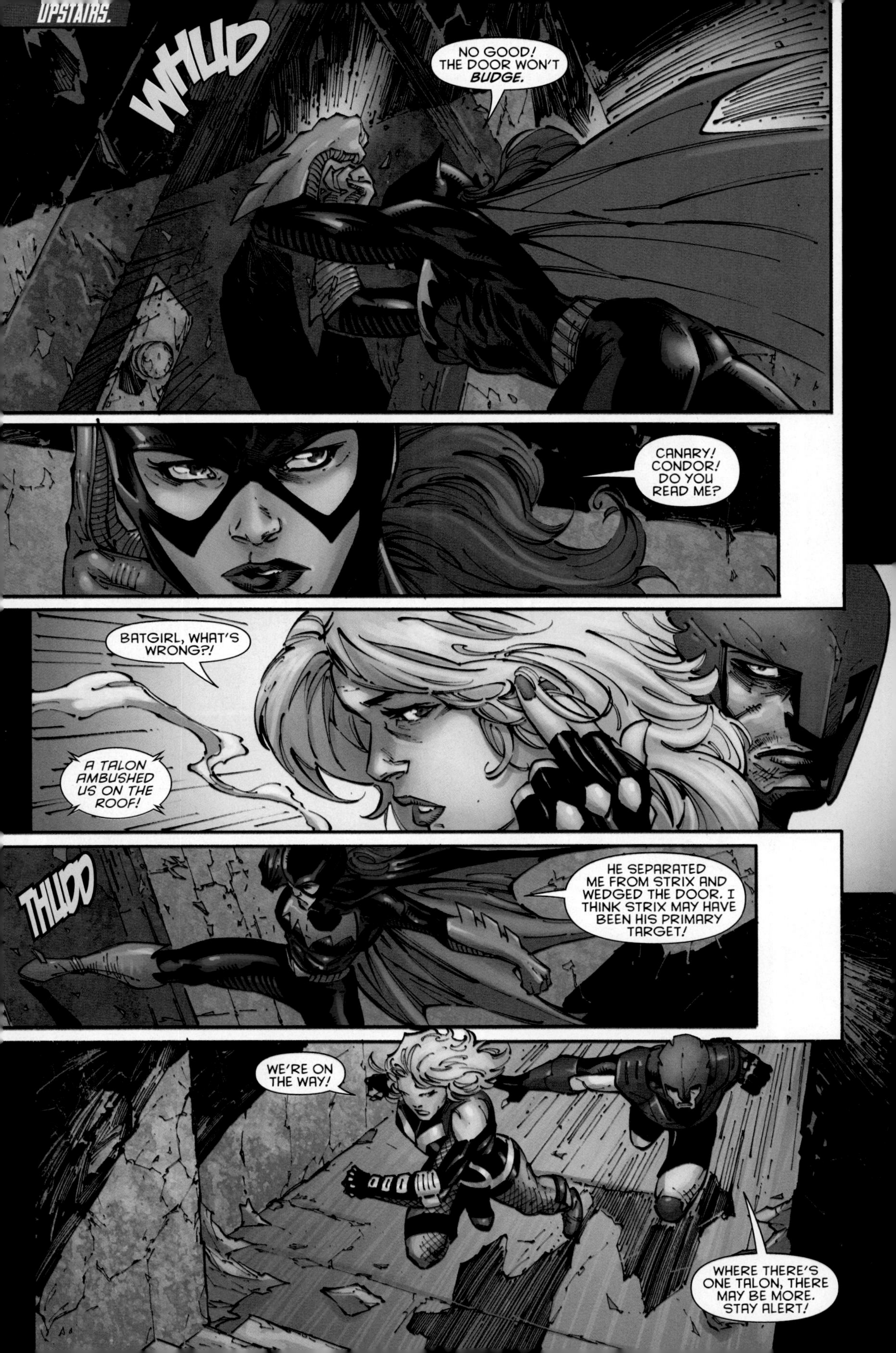
UPSTAIRS.
WHUD
NO GOOD! THE DOOR WON'T BUDGE.
CANARY! CONDOR! DO YOU READ ME?
BATGIRL, WHAT'S WRONG?!
A TALON AMBUSHED US ON THE ROOF!
THUDD
HE SEPARATED ME FROM STRIX AND WEDGED THE DOOR. I THINK STRIX MAY HAVE BEEN HIS PRIMARY TARGET!
WE'RE ON THE WAY!
WHERE THERE'S ONE TALON, THERE MAY BE MORE. STAY ALERT!

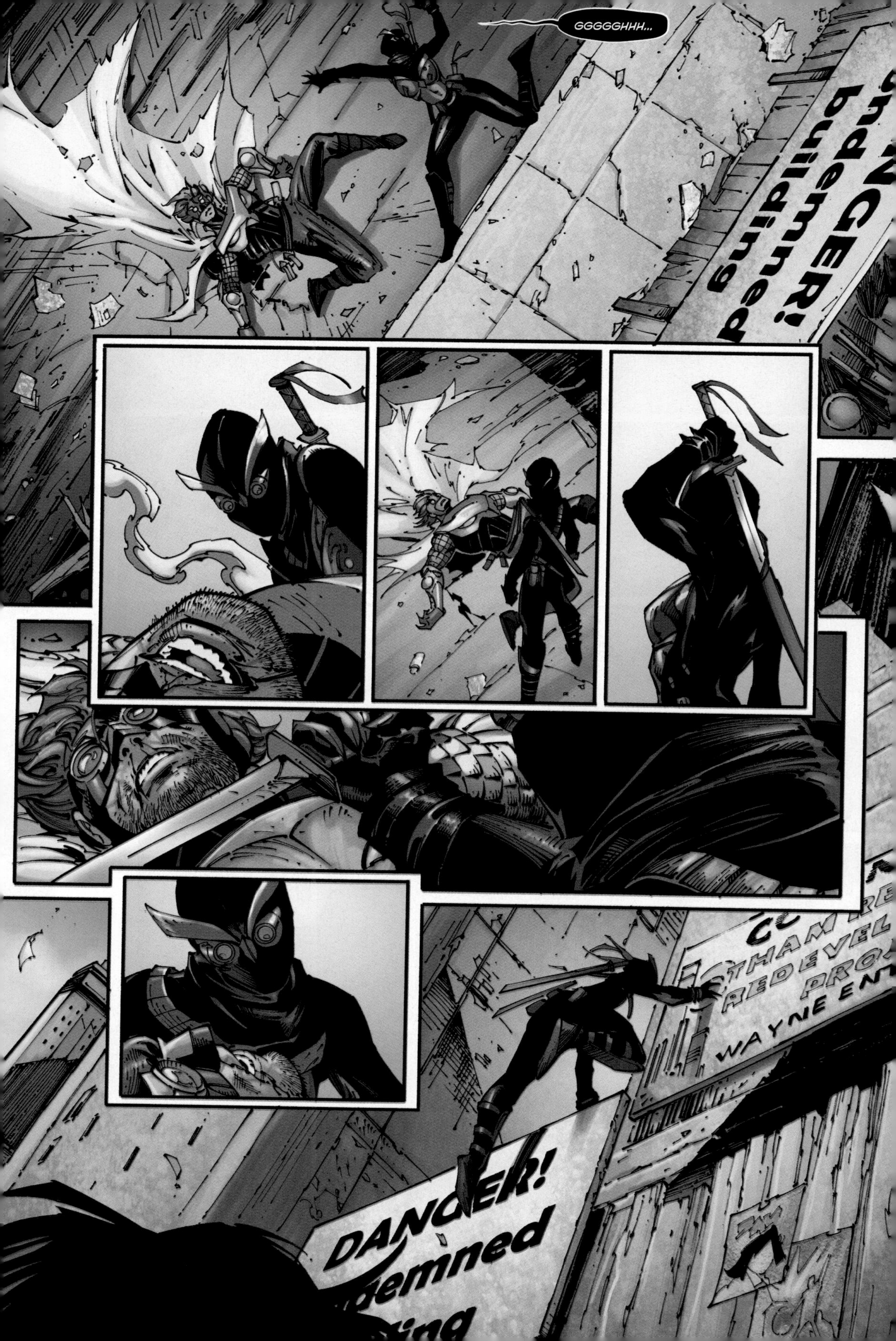
GGGGGHHH...
DANGER!

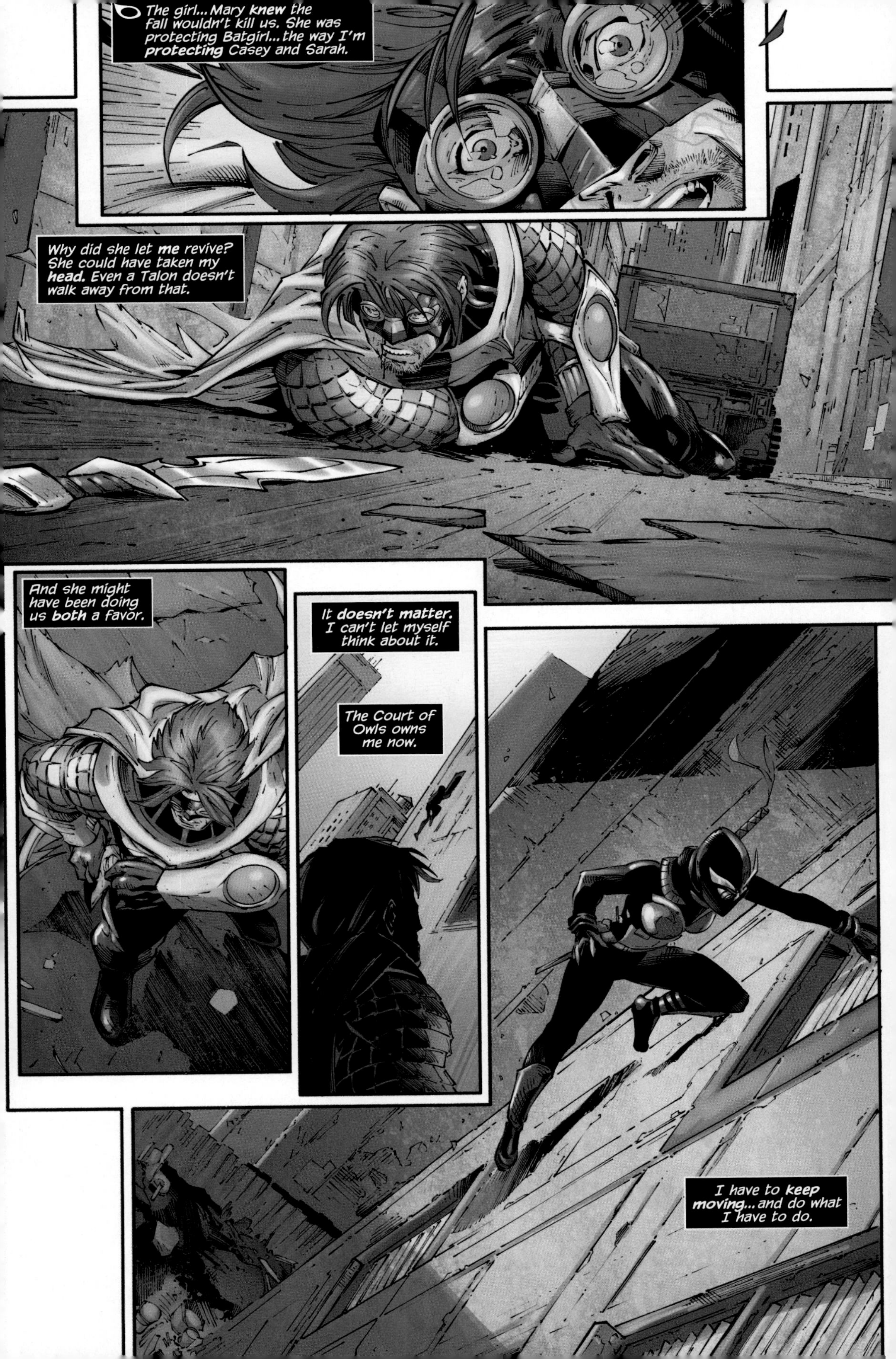
The girl... Mary knew the fall wouldn't kill us. She was protecting Batgirl... the way I'm protecting Casey and Sarah.
Why did she let me revive? She could have taken my head. Even a Talon doesn't walk away from that.
And she might have been doing us both a favor.
It doesn't matter. I can't let myself think about it.
The Court of Owls owns me now.
I have to keep moving... and do what I have to do.

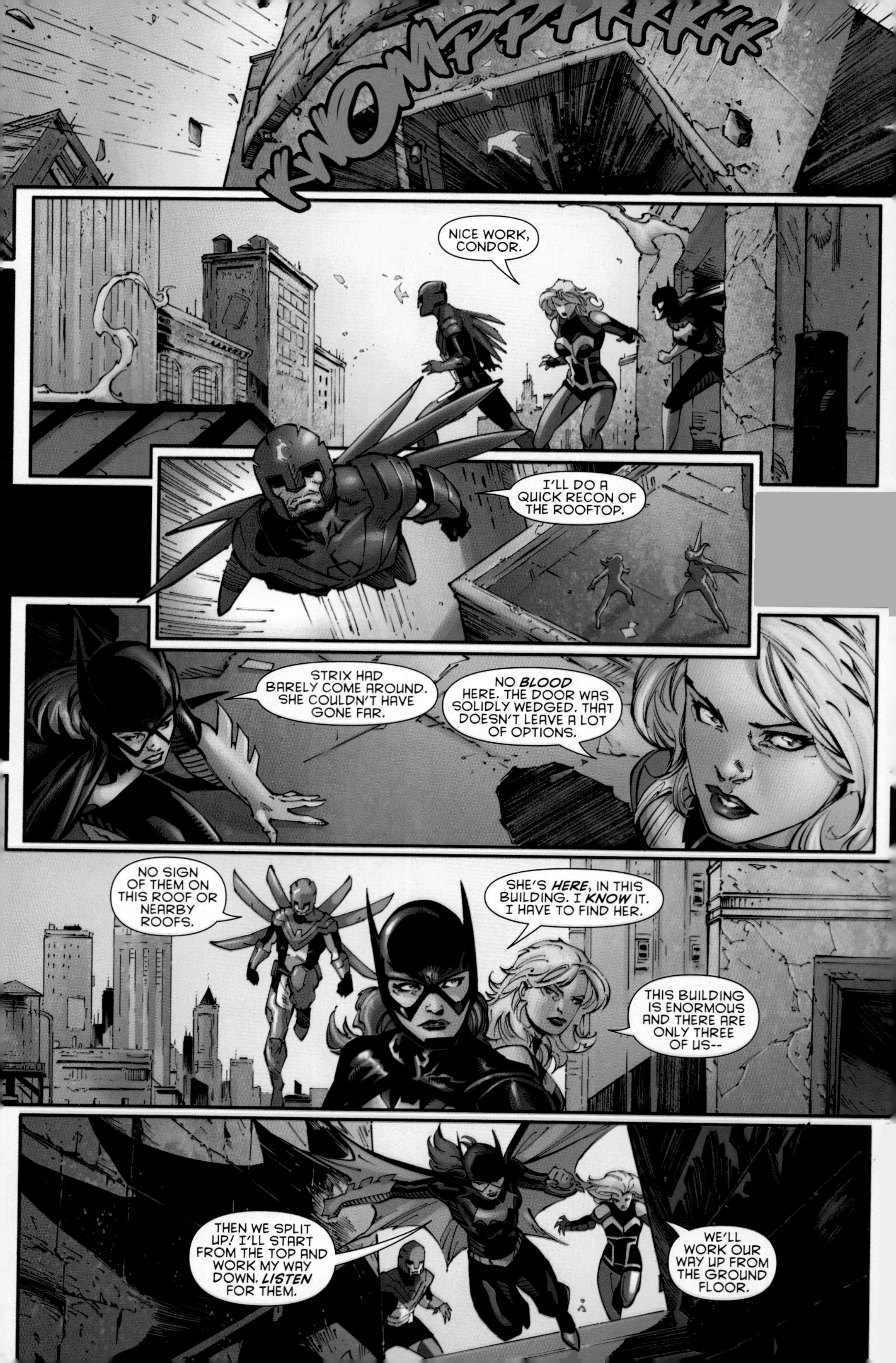
KWOMPKKKKKK
NICE WORK, CONDOR.
I'LL DO A QUICK RECON OF THE ROOFTOP.
STRIX HAD BARELY COME AROUND. SHE COULDN'T HAVE GONE FAR.
NO *BLOOD* HERE. THE DOOR WAS SOLIDLY WEDGED. THAT DOESN'T LEAVE A LOT OF OPTIONS.
NO SIGN OF THEM ON THIS ROOF OR NEARBY ROOFS.
SHE'S *HERE*, IN THIS BUILDING. I *KNOW* IT. I HAVE TO FIND HER.
THIS BUILDING IS ENORMOUS AND THERE ARE ONLY THREE OF US--
THEN WE SPLIT UP! I'LL START FROM THE TOP AND WORK MY WAY DOWN. *LISTEN* FOR THEM.
WE'LL WORK OUR WAY UP FROM THE GROUND FLOOR.

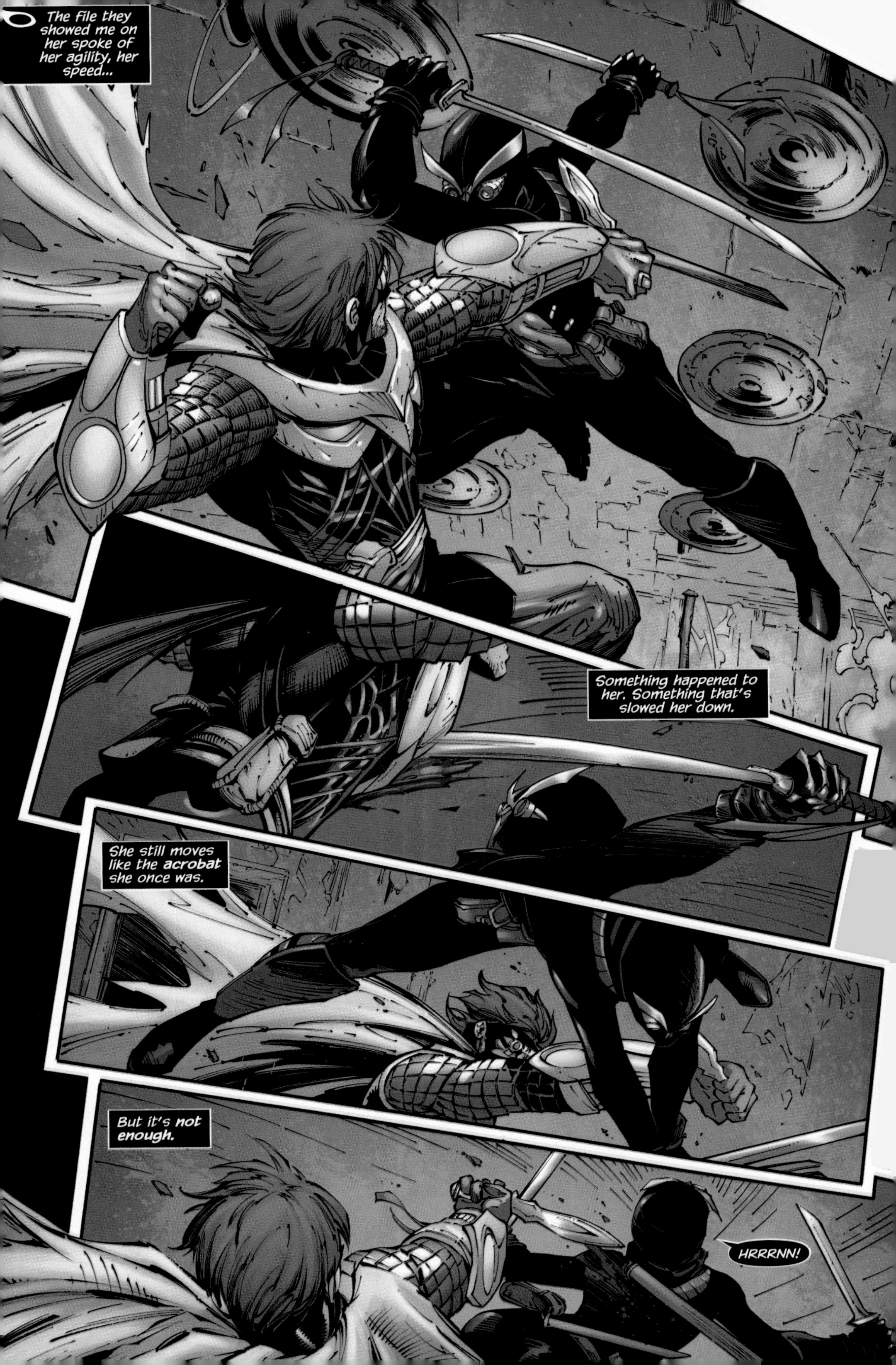

The file they showed me on her spoke of her agility, her speed...
Something happened to her. Something that's slowed her down.
She still moves like the **acrobat** she once was.
But it's **not enough.**
HRRRNN!

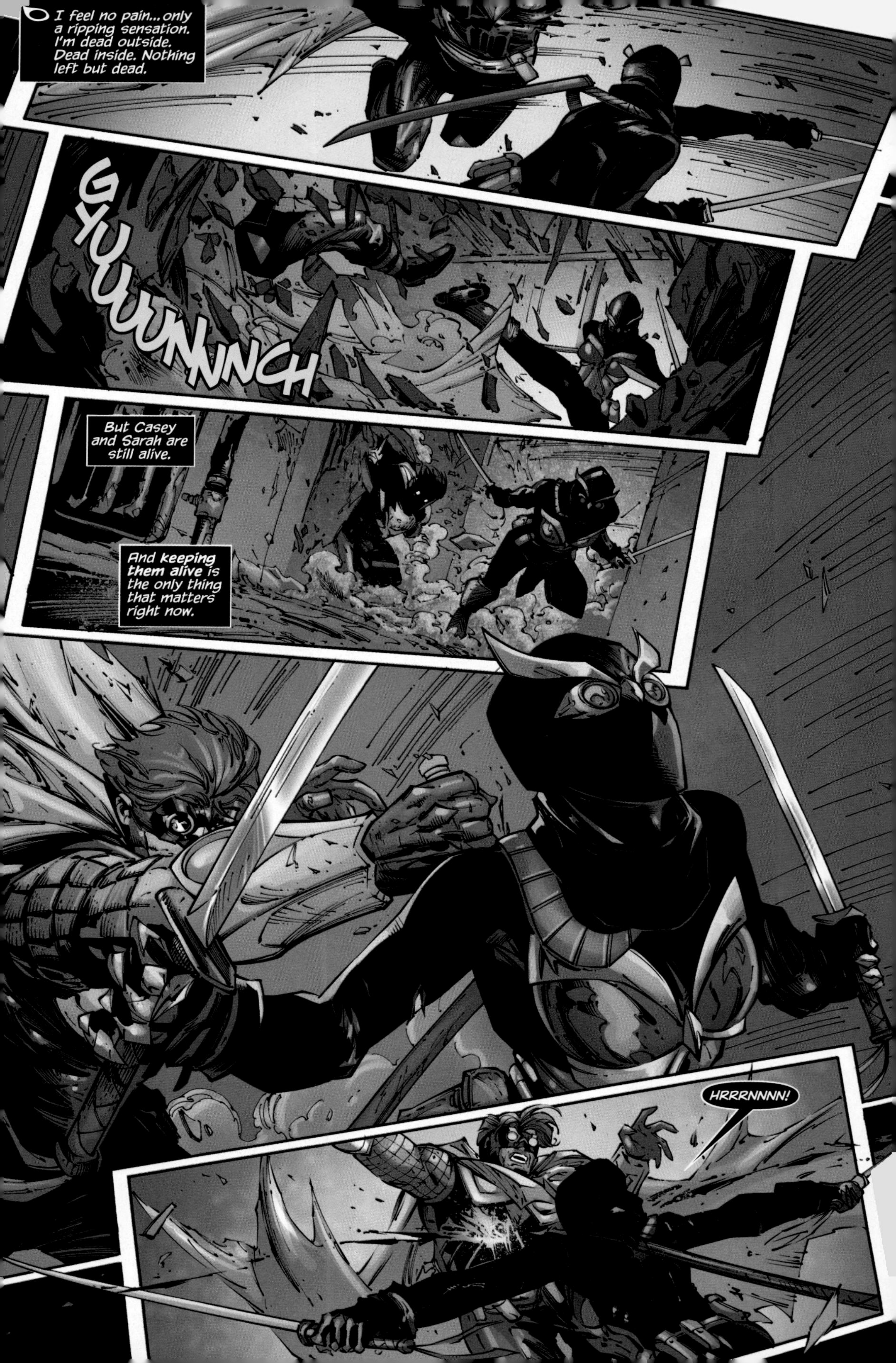
I feel no pain...only a ripping sensation. I'm dead outside. Dead inside. Nothing left but dead.
GYUUUNNNCH
But Casey and Sarah are still alive.
And keeping them alive is the only thing that matters right now.
HRRRNNNN!

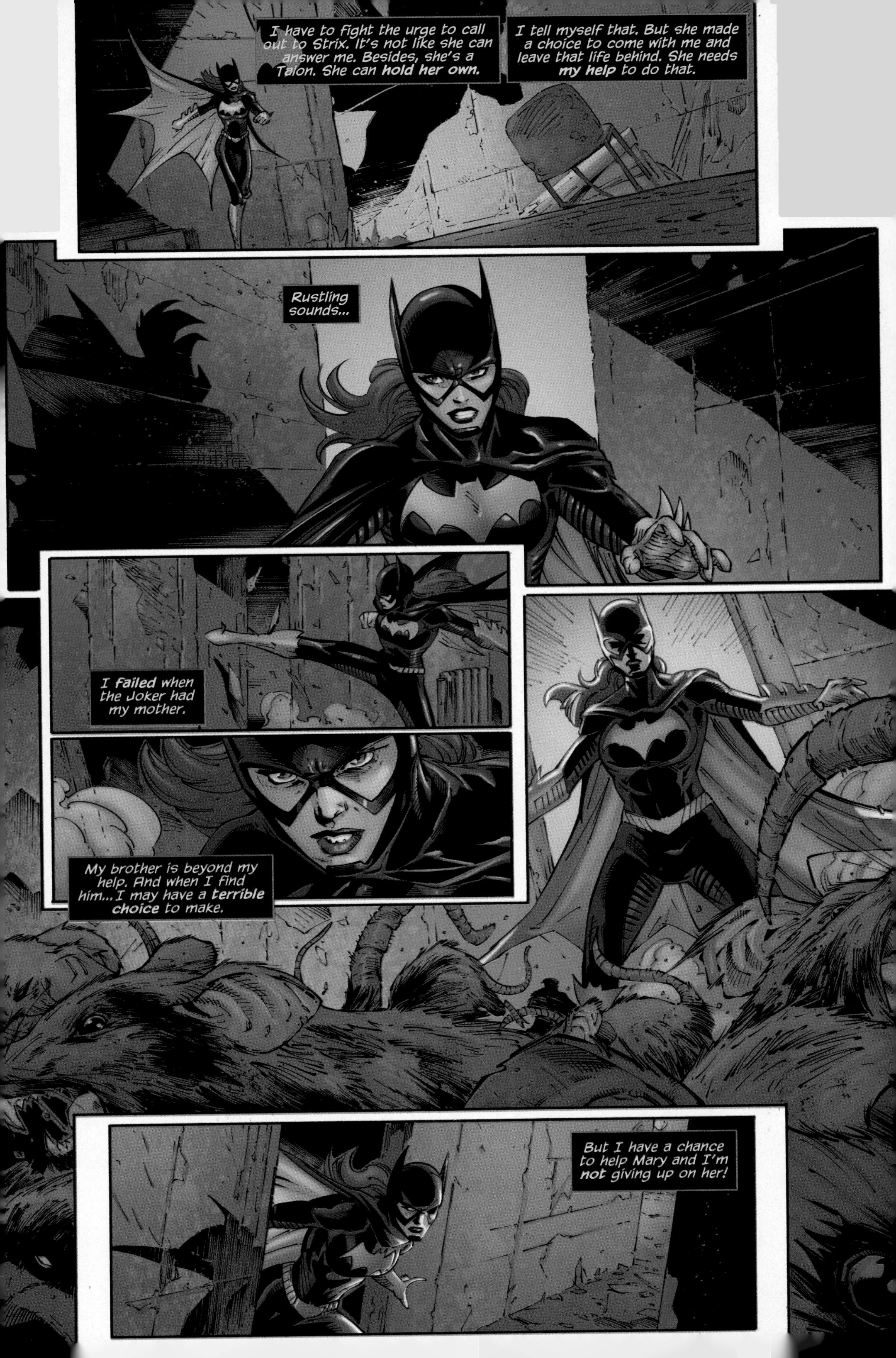
I have to fight the urge to call out to Strix. It's not like she can answer me. Besides, she's a Talon. She can **hold her own.**
I tell myself that. But she made a choice to come with me and leave that life behind. She needs **my help** to do that.
Rustling sounds...
I **failed** when the Joker had my mother.
My brother is beyond my help. And when I find him... I may have a **terrible choice** to make.
But I have a chance to help Mary and I'm **not** giving up on her!

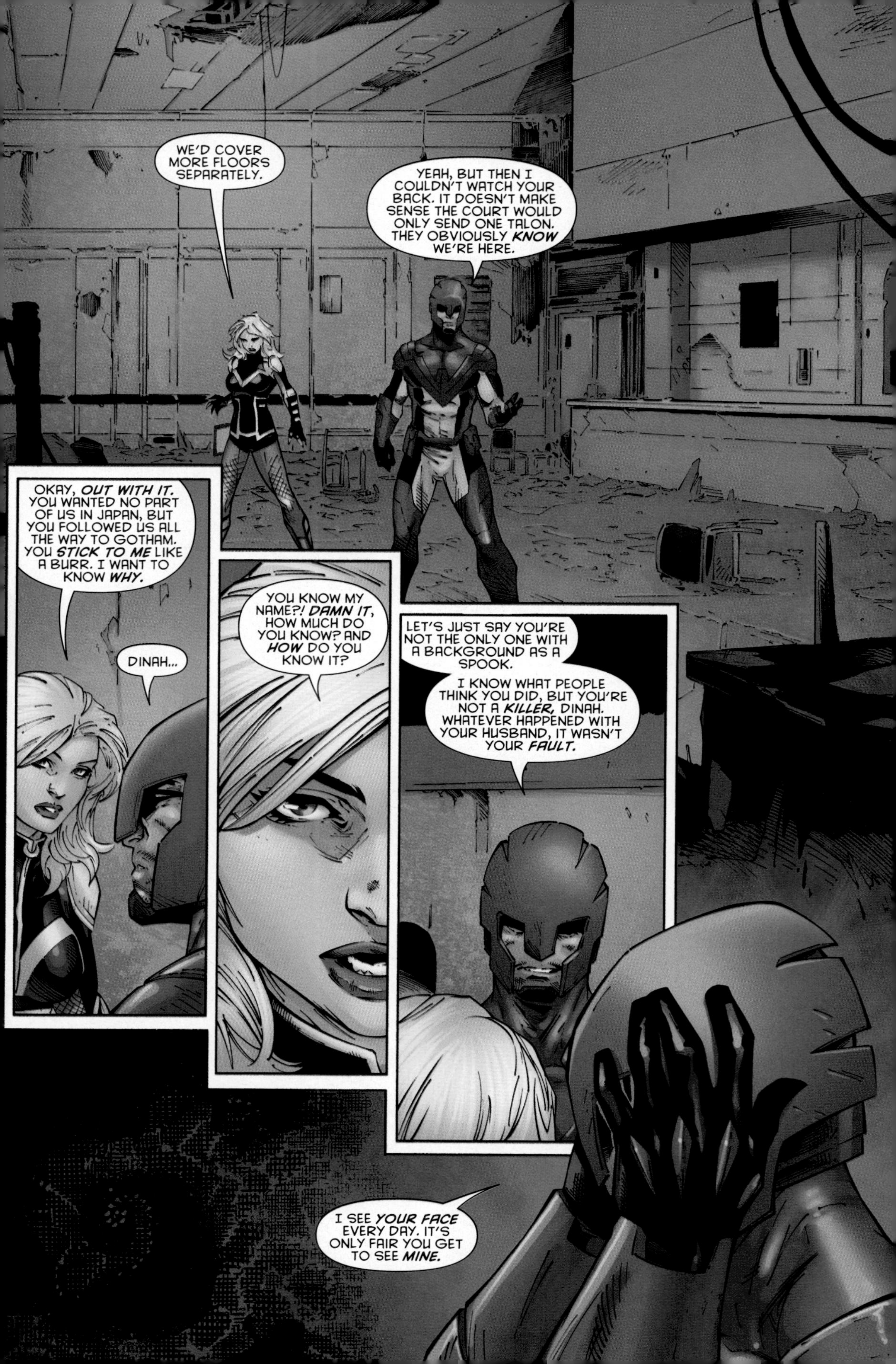
WE'D COVER MORE FLOORS SEPARATELY.
YEAH, BUT THEN I COULDN'T WATCH YOUR BACK. IT DOESN'T MAKE SENSE THE COURT WOULD ONLY SEND ONE TALON. THEY OBVIOUSLY KNOW WE'RE HERE.
OKAY, OUT WITH IT. YOU WANTED NO PART OF US IN JAPAN, BUT YOU FOLLOWED US ALL THE WAY TO GOTHAM. YOU STICK TO ME LIKE A BURR. I WANT TO KNOW WHY.
DINAH...
YOU KNOW MY NAME?! DAMN IT, HOW MUCH DO YOU KNOW? AND HOW DO YOU KNOW IT?
LET'S JUST SAY YOU'RE NOT THE ONLY ONE WITH A BACKGROUND AS A SPOOK.
I KNOW WHAT PEOPLE THINK YOU DID, BUT YOU'RE NOT A KILLER, DINAH. WHATEVER HAPPENED WITH YOUR HUSBAND, IT WASN'T YOUR FAULT.
I SEE YOUR FACE EVERY DAY. IT'S ONLY FAIR YOU GET TO SEE MINE.

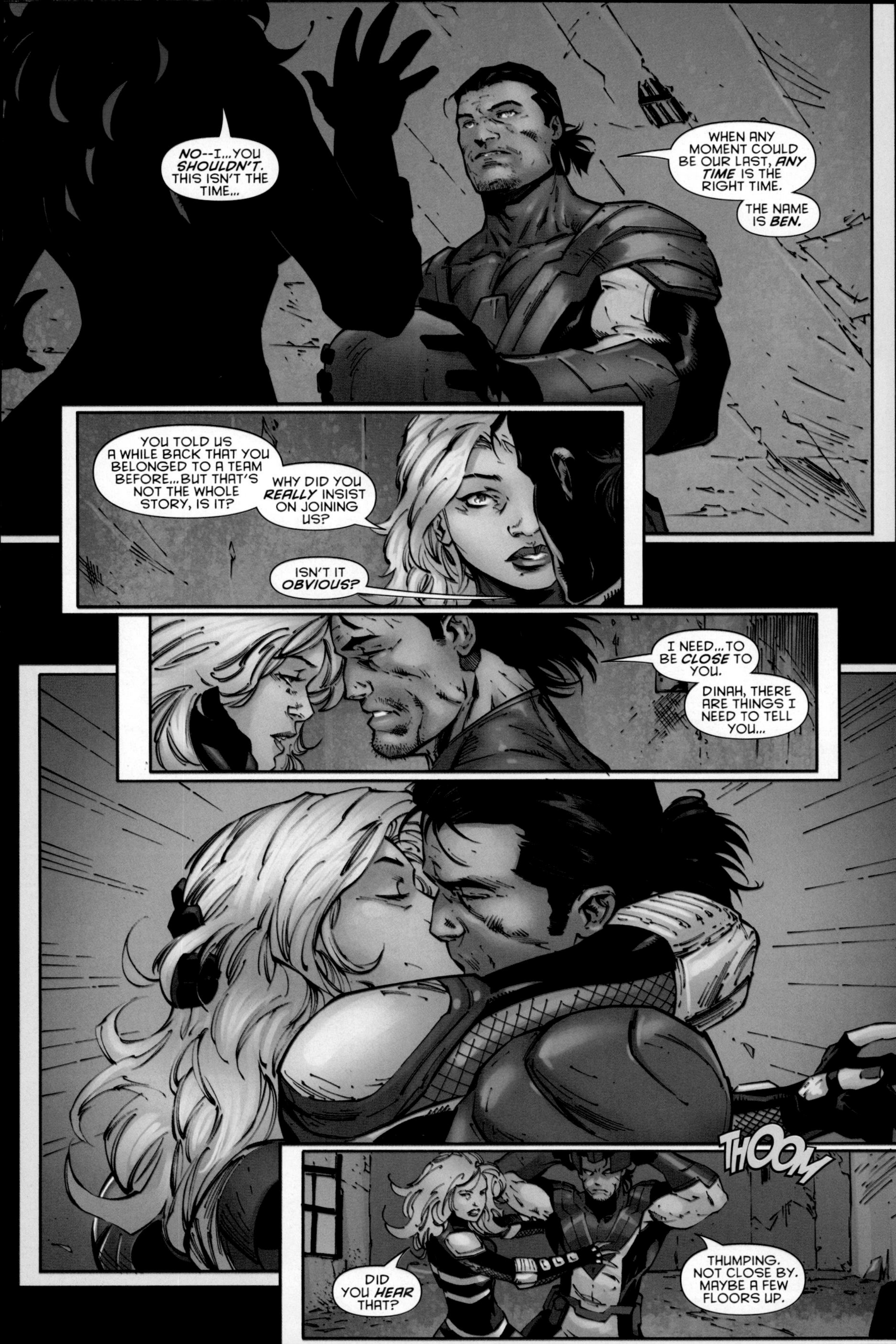
NO--I...YOU SHOULDN'T. THIS ISN'T THE TIME...
WHEN ANY MOMENT COULD BE OUR LAST, ANY TIME IS THE RIGHT TIME.
THE NAME IS BEN.
YOU TOLD US A WHILE BACK THAT YOU BELONGED TO A TEAM BEFORE...BUT THAT'S NOT THE WHOLE STORY, IS IT?
WHY DID YOU REALLY INSIST ON JOINING US?
ISN'T IT OBVIOUS?
I NEED...TO BE CLOSE TO YOU.
DINAH, THERE ARE THINGS I NEED TO TELL YOU...
THOOM
DID YOU HEAR THAT?
THUMPING. NOT CLOSE BY. MAYBE A FEW FLOORS UP.

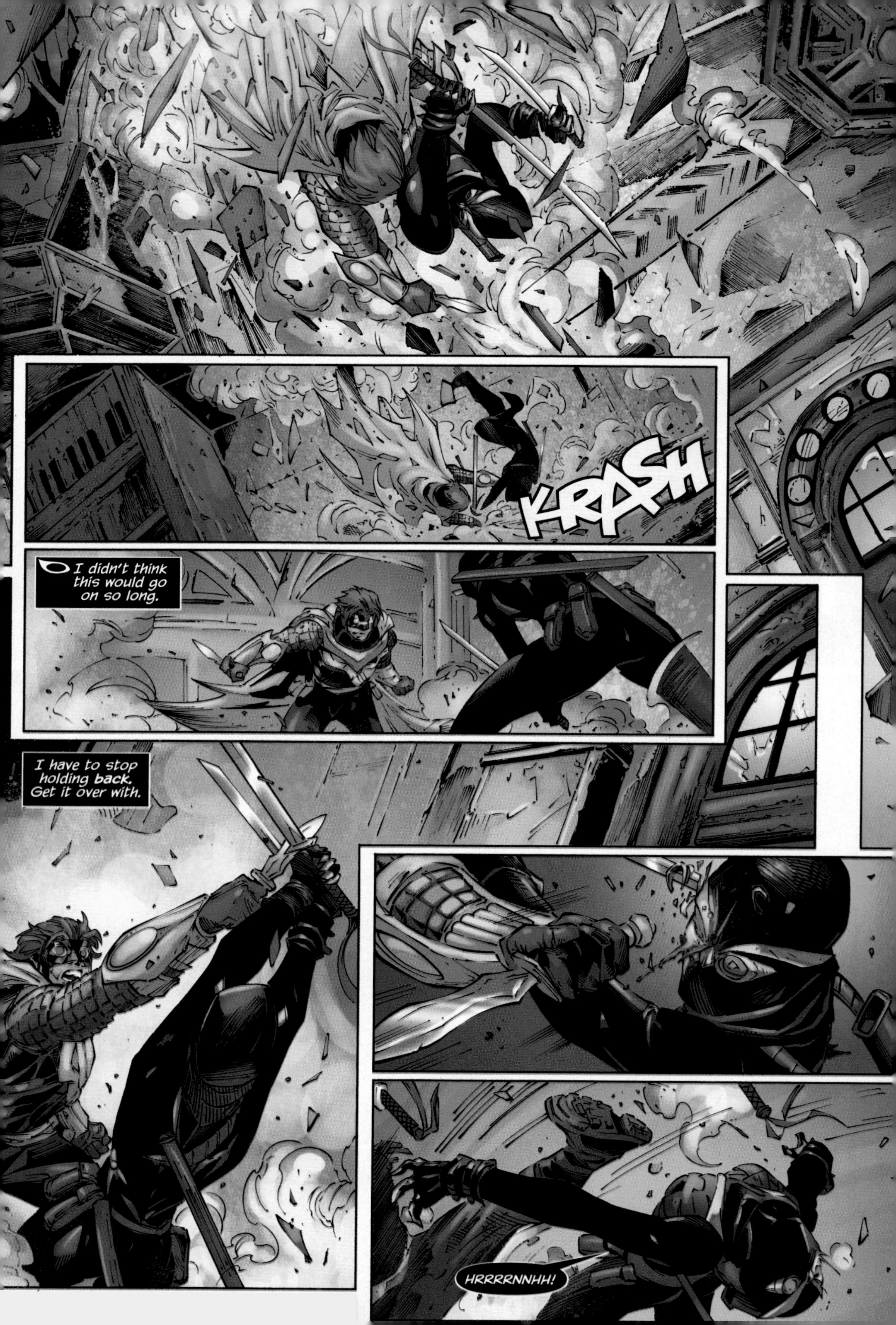
KRASH
I didn't think this would go on so long.
I have to stop holding back. Get it over with.
HRRRRNNHH!

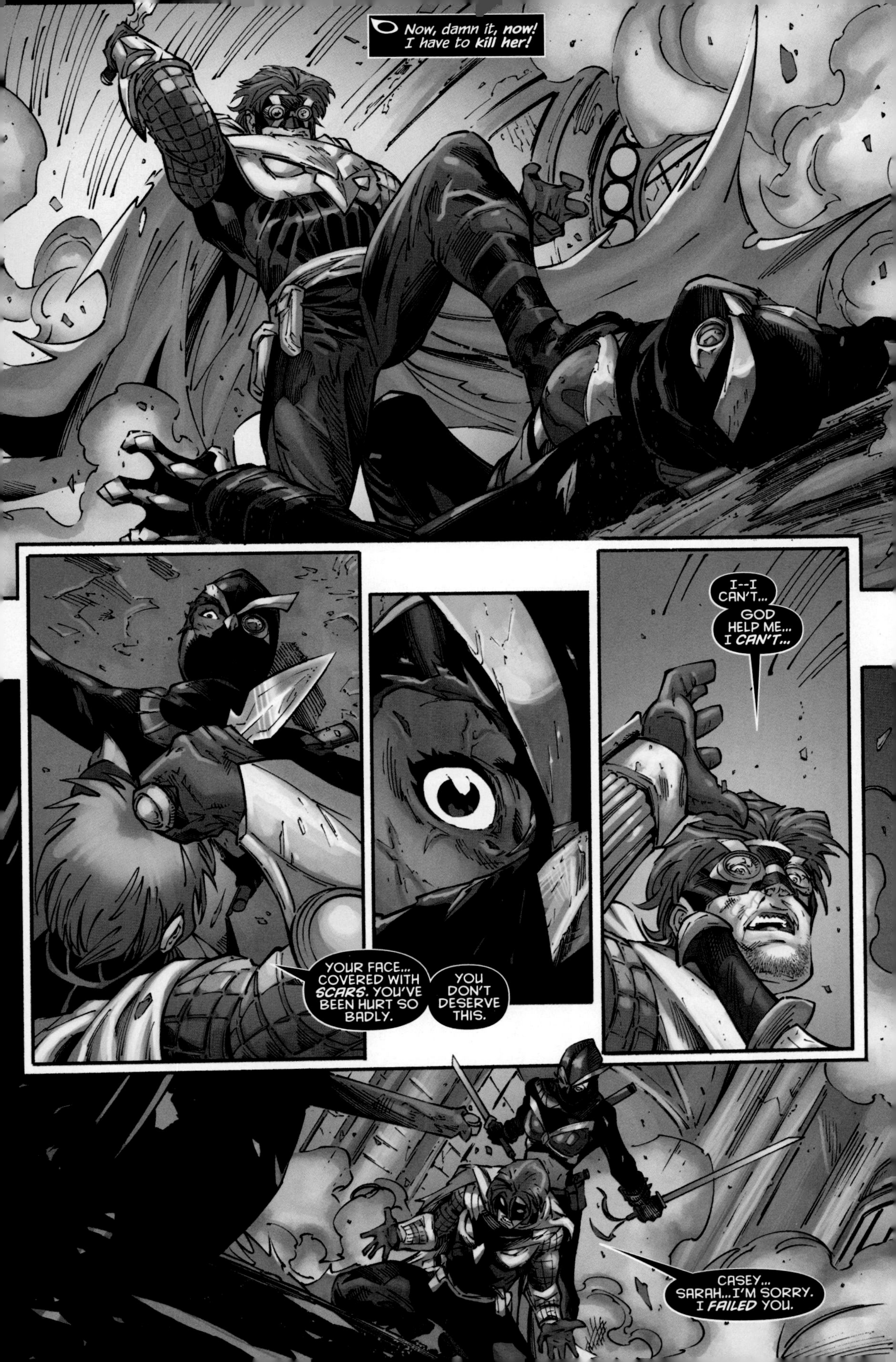
Now, damn it, now! I have to kill her!
YOUR FACE... COVERED WITH SCARS. YOU'VE BEEN HURT SO BADLY.
YOU DON'T DESERVE THIS.
I--I CAN'T... GOD HELP ME... I CAN'T...
CASEY... SARAH... I'M SORRY. I FAILED YOU.

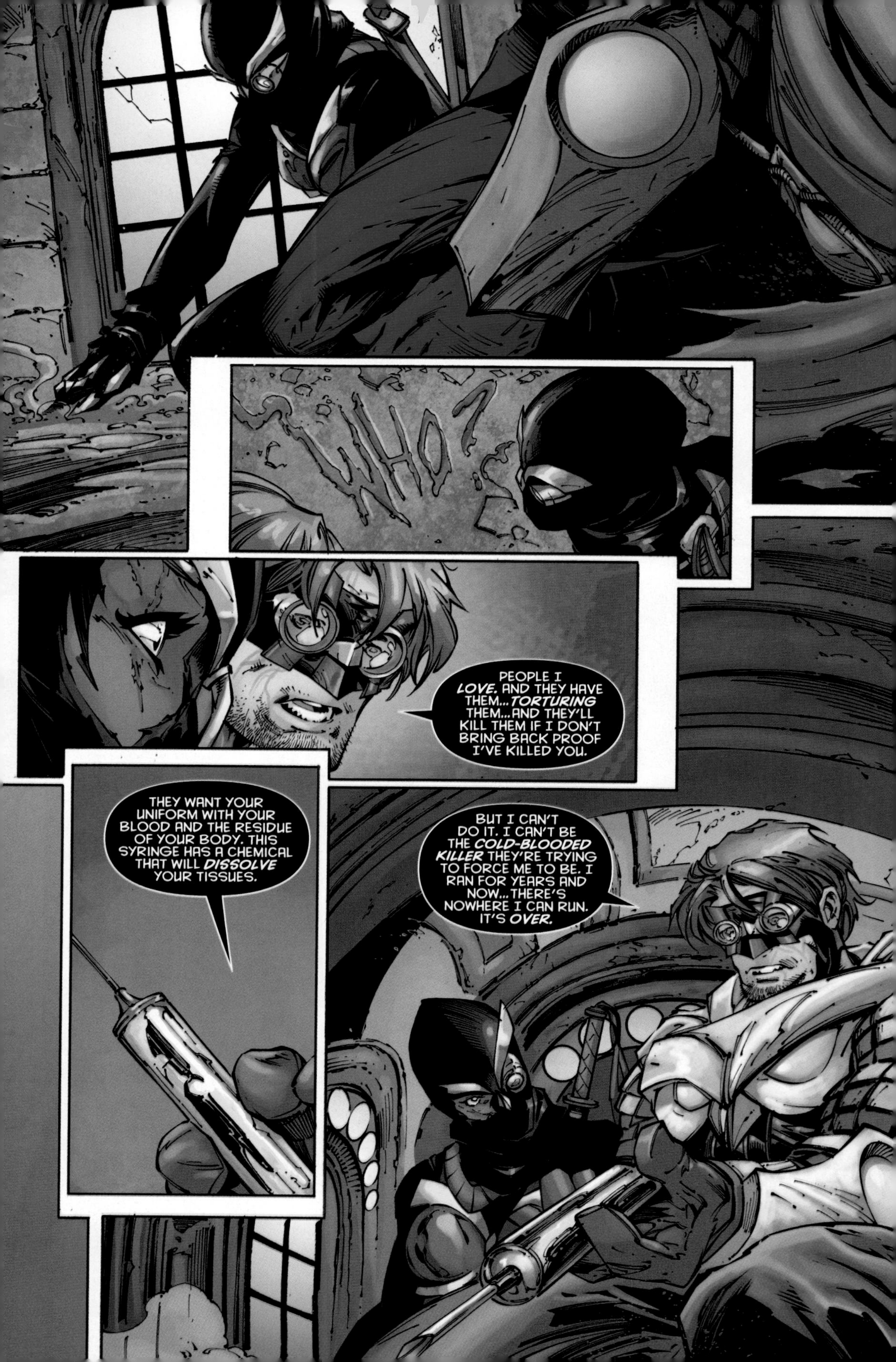
WHO?
PEOPLE I LOVE. AND THEY HAVE THEM...TORTURING THEM...AND THEY'LL KILL THEM IF I DON'T BRING BACK PROOF I'VE KILLED YOU.
THEY WANT YOUR UNIFORM WITH YOUR BLOOD AND THE RESIDUE OF YOUR BODY. THIS SYRINGE HAS A CHEMICAL THAT WILL DISSOLVE YOUR TISSUES.
BUT I CAN'T DO IT. I CAN'T BE THE COLD-BLOODED KILLER THEY'RE TRYING TO FORCE ME TO BE. I RAN FOR YEARS AND NOW...THERE'S NOWHERE I CAN RUN. IT'S OVER.

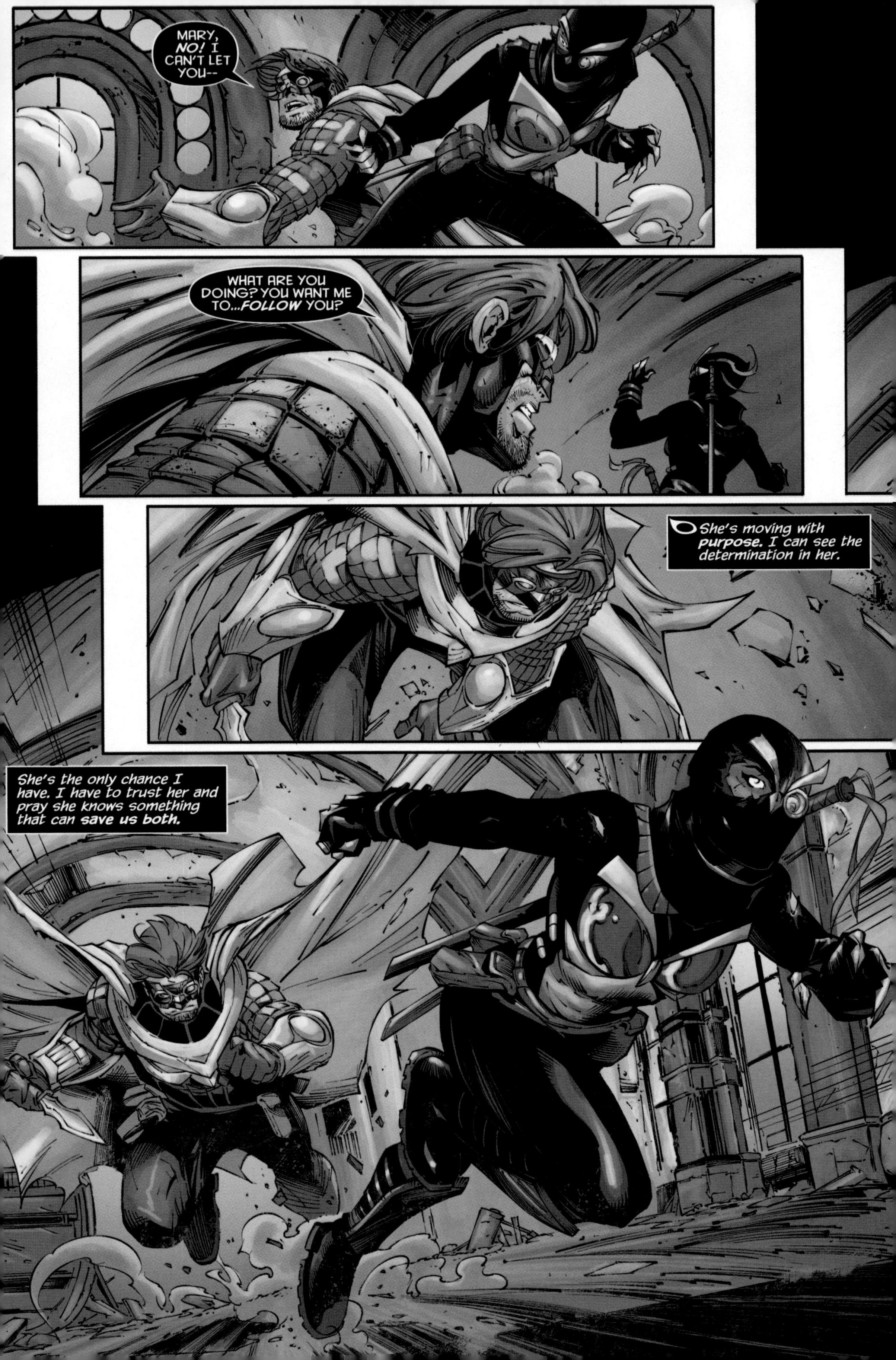
MARY, NO! I CAN'T LET YOU--
WHAT ARE YOU DOING? YOU WANT ME TO...FOLLOW YOU?
She's moving with purpose. I can see the determination in her.
She's the only chance I have. I have to trust her and pray she knows something that can save us both.

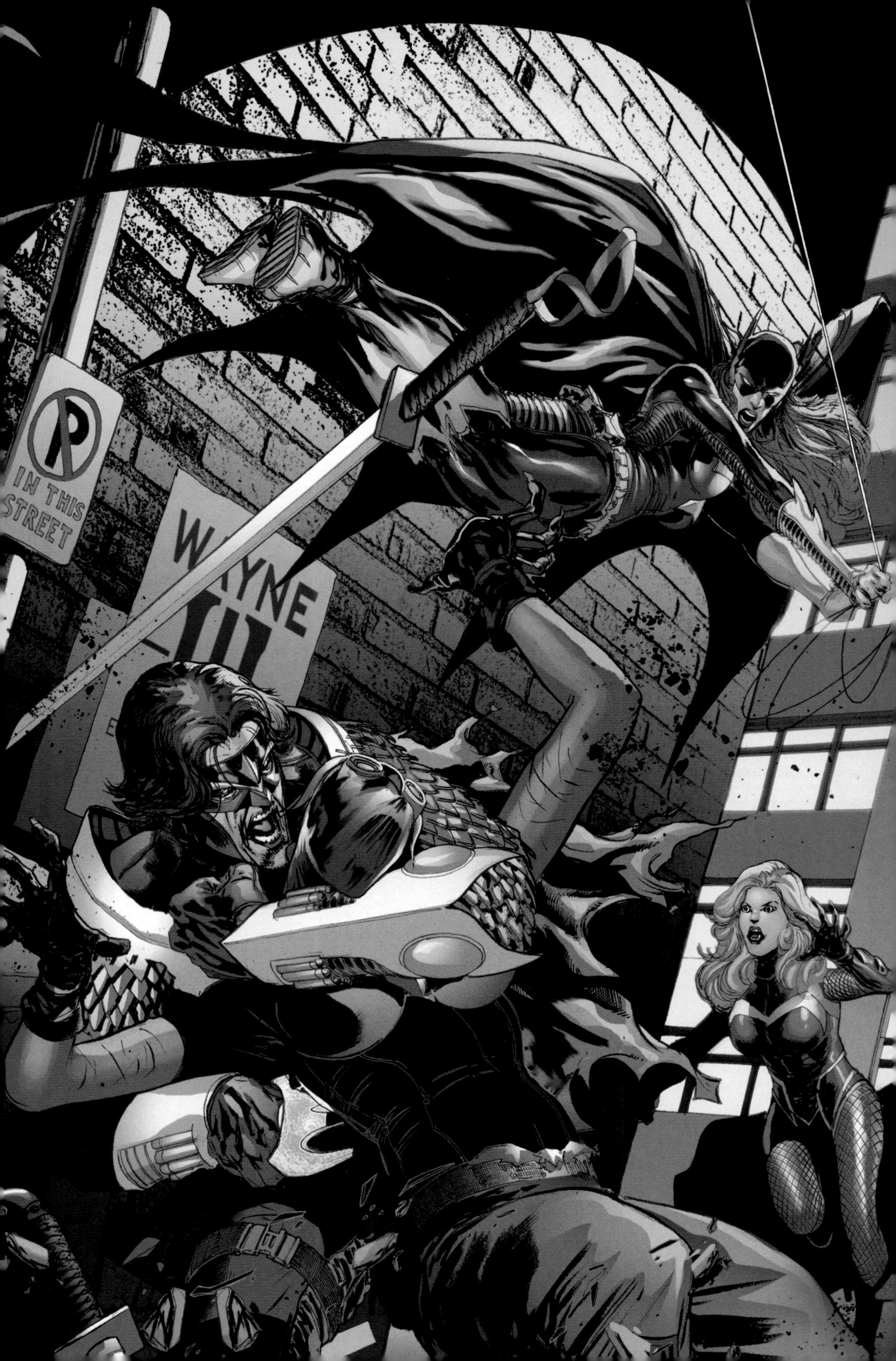
IN THIS STREET

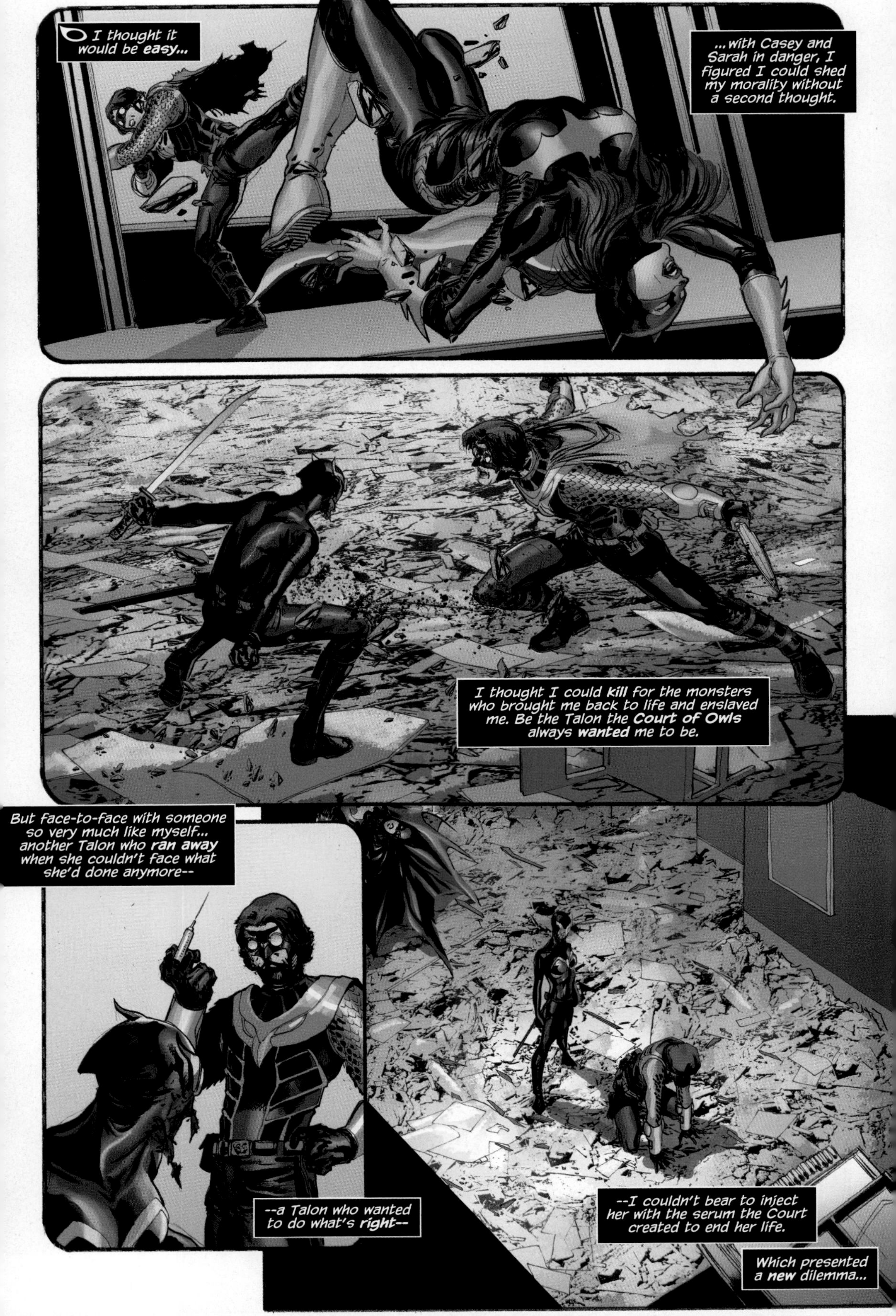
I thought it would be easy...
...with Casey and Sarah in danger, I figured I could shed my morality without a second thought.
I thought I could kill for the monsters who brought me back to life and enslaved me. Be the Talon the Court of Owls always wanted me to be.
But face-to-face with someone so very much like myself... another Talon who ran away when she couldn't face what she'd done anymore--
--a Talon who wanted to do what's right--
--I couldn't bear to inject her with the serum the Court created to end her life.
Which presented a new dilemma...

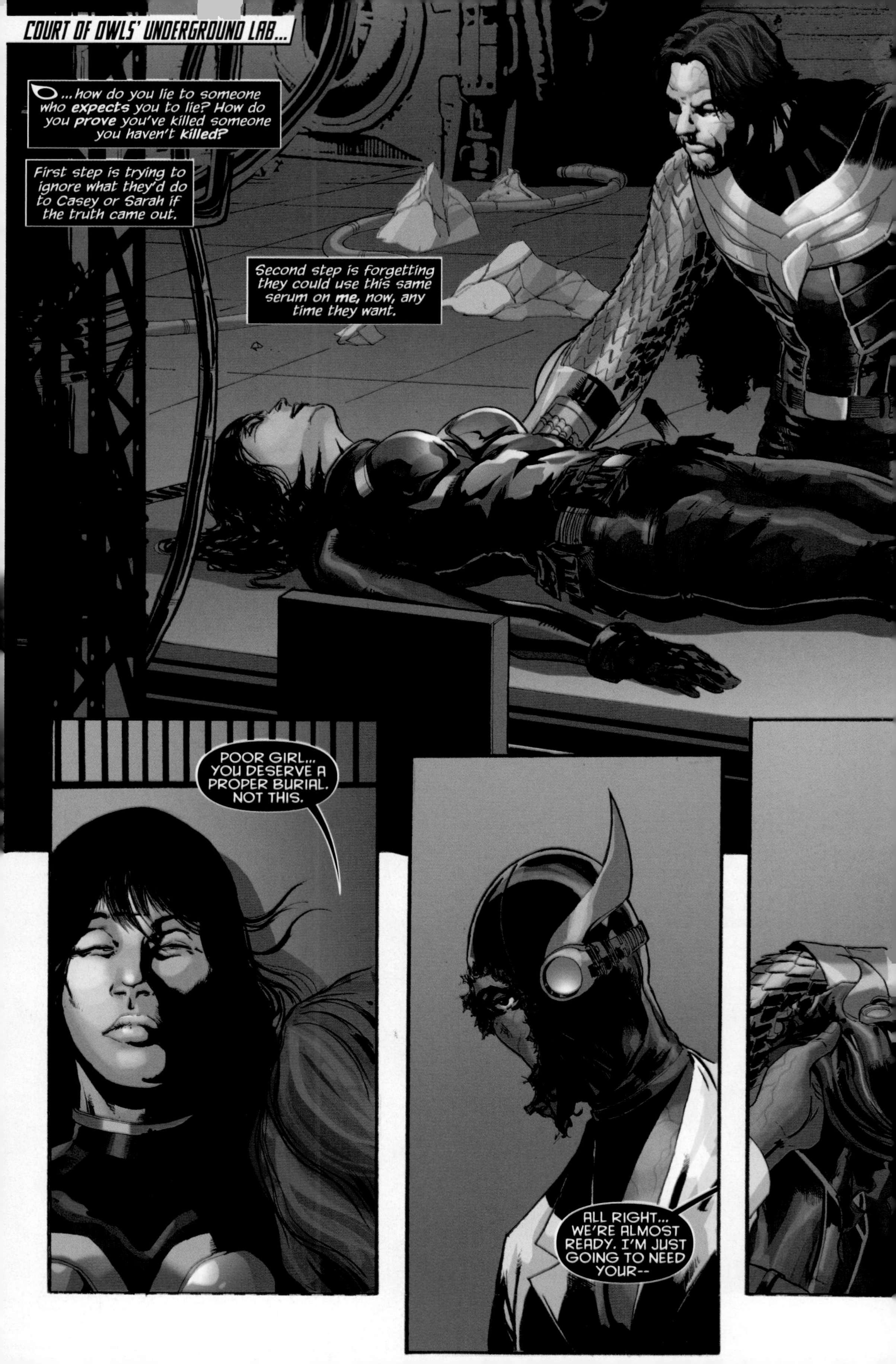
COURT OF OWLS' UNDERGROUND LAB...
...how do you lie to someone who expects you to lie? How do you prove you've killed someone you haven't killed?
First step is trying to ignore what they'd do to Casey or Sarah if the truth came out.
Second step is forgetting they could use this same serum on me, now, any time they want.
POOR GIRL... YOU DESERVE A PROPER BURIAL. NOT THIS.
ALL RIGHT... WE'RE ALMOST READY. I'M JUST GOING TO NEED YOUR--

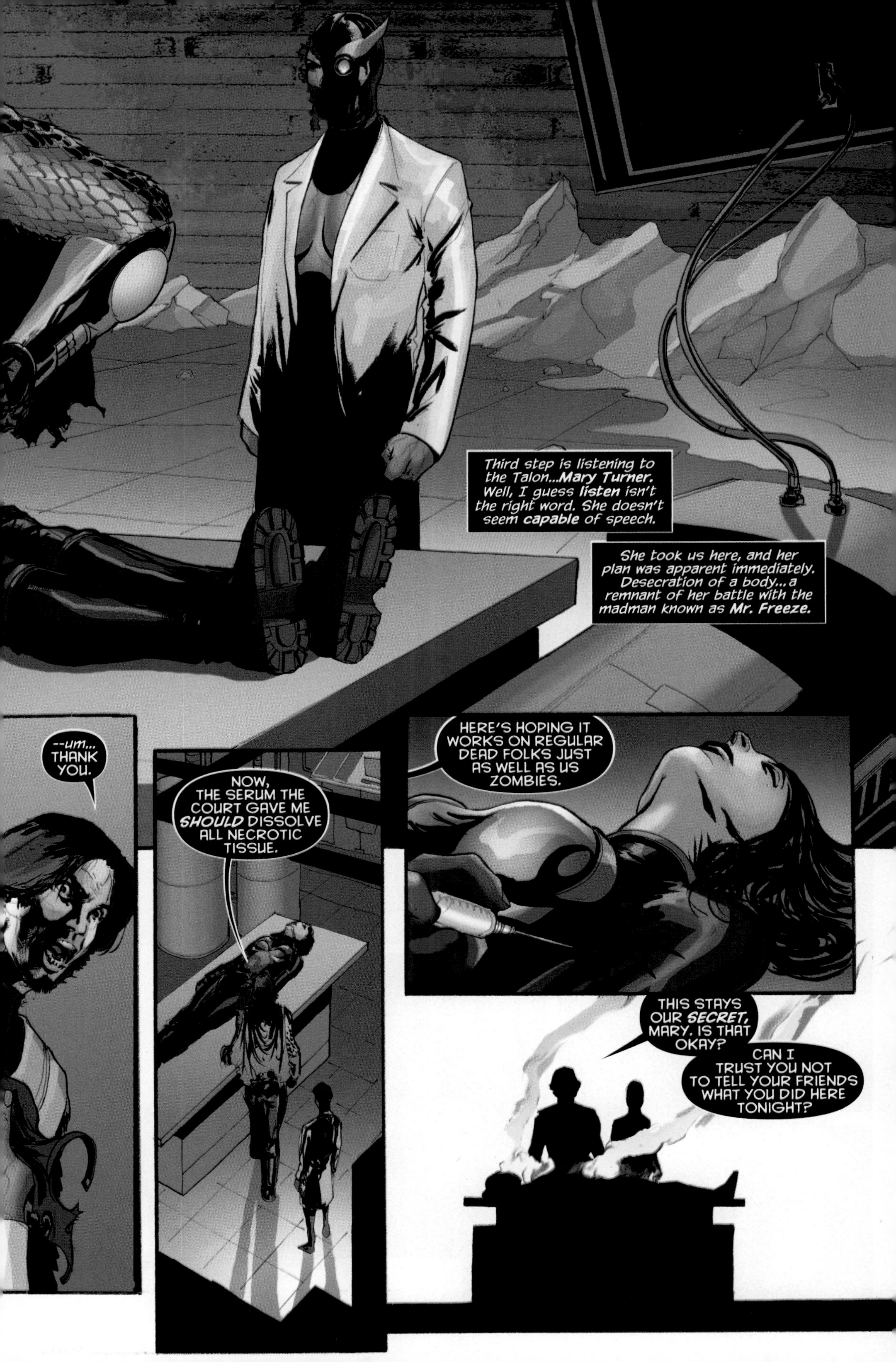
Third step is listening to the Talon...Mary Turner. Well, I guess listen isn't the right word. She doesn't seem capable of speech.
She took us here, and her plan was apparent immediately. Desecration of a body...a remnant of her battle with the madman known as Mr. Freeze.
--um... THANK YOU.
NOW, THE SERUM THE COURT GAVE ME SHOULD DISSOLVE ALL NECROTIC TISSUE.
HERE'S HOPING IT WORKS ON REGULAR DEAD FOLKS JUST AS WELL AS US ZOMBIES.
THIS STAYS OUR SECRET, MARY. IS THAT OKAY?
CAN I TRUST YOU NOT TO TELL YOUR FRIENDS WHAT YOU DID HERE TONIGHT?

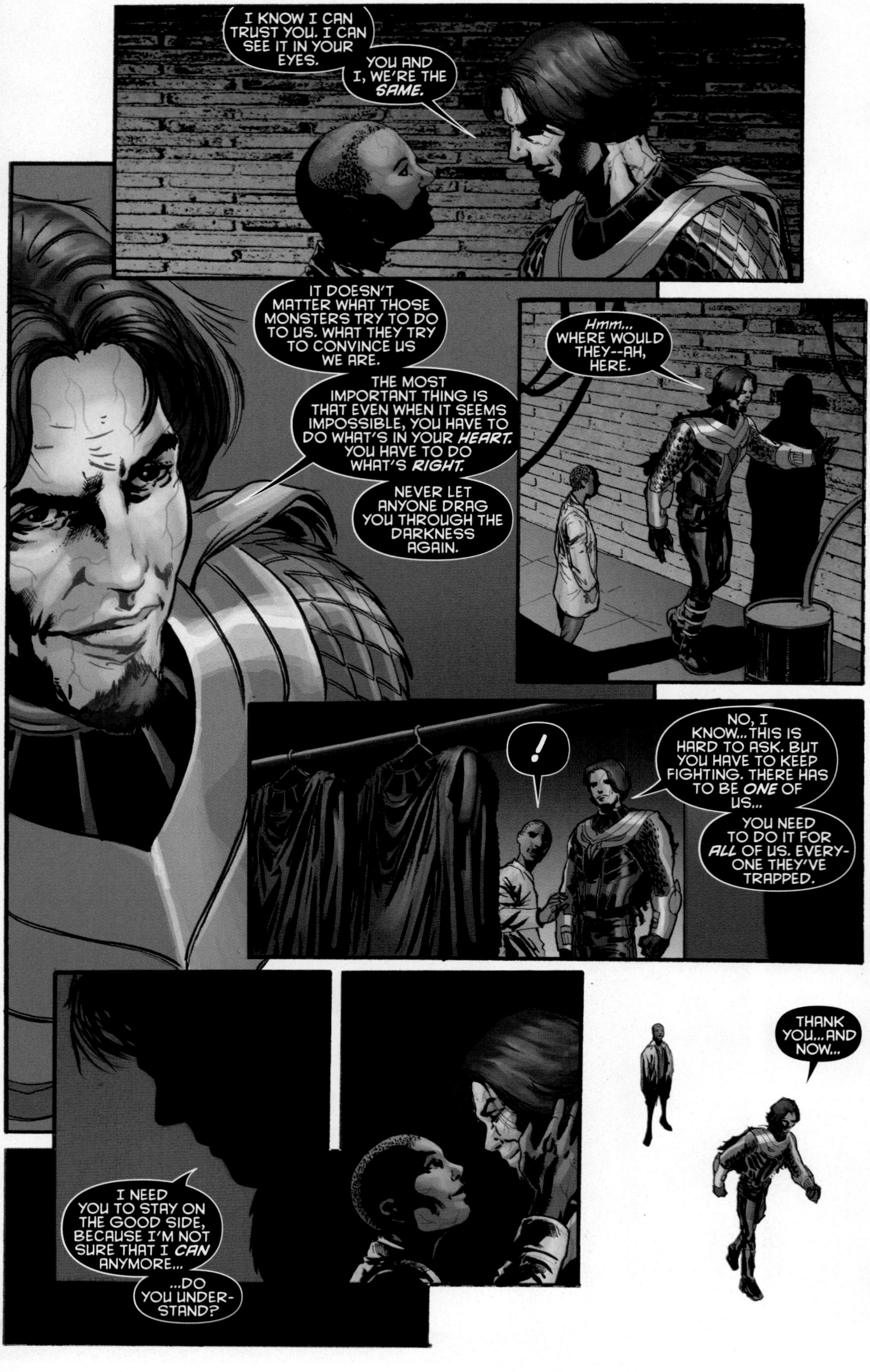
I KNOW I CAN TRUST YOU. I CAN SEE IT IN YOUR EYES.
YOU AND I, WE'RE THE *SAME.*
IT DOESN'T MATTER WHAT THOSE MONSTERS TRY TO DO TO US. WHAT THEY TRY TO CONVINCE US WE ARE.
THE MOST IMPORTANT THING IS THAT EVEN WHEN IT SEEMS IMPOSSIBLE, YOU HAVE TO DO WHAT'S IN YOUR *HEART.* YOU HAVE TO DO WHAT'S *RIGHT.*
NEVER LET ANYONE DRAG YOU THROUGH THE DARKNESS AGAIN.
Hmm... WHERE WOULD THEY--AH, HERE.
!
NO, I KNOW... THIS IS HARD TO ASK. BUT YOU HAVE TO KEEP FIGHTING. THERE HAS TO BE *ONE* OF US...
YOU NEED TO DO IT FOR *ALL* OF US. EVERY-ONE THEY'VE TRAPPED.
I NEED YOU TO STAY ON THE GOOD SIDE, BECAUSE I'M NOT SURE THAT I *CAN* ANYMORE...
...DO YOU UNDER-STAND?
THANK YOU... AND NOW...

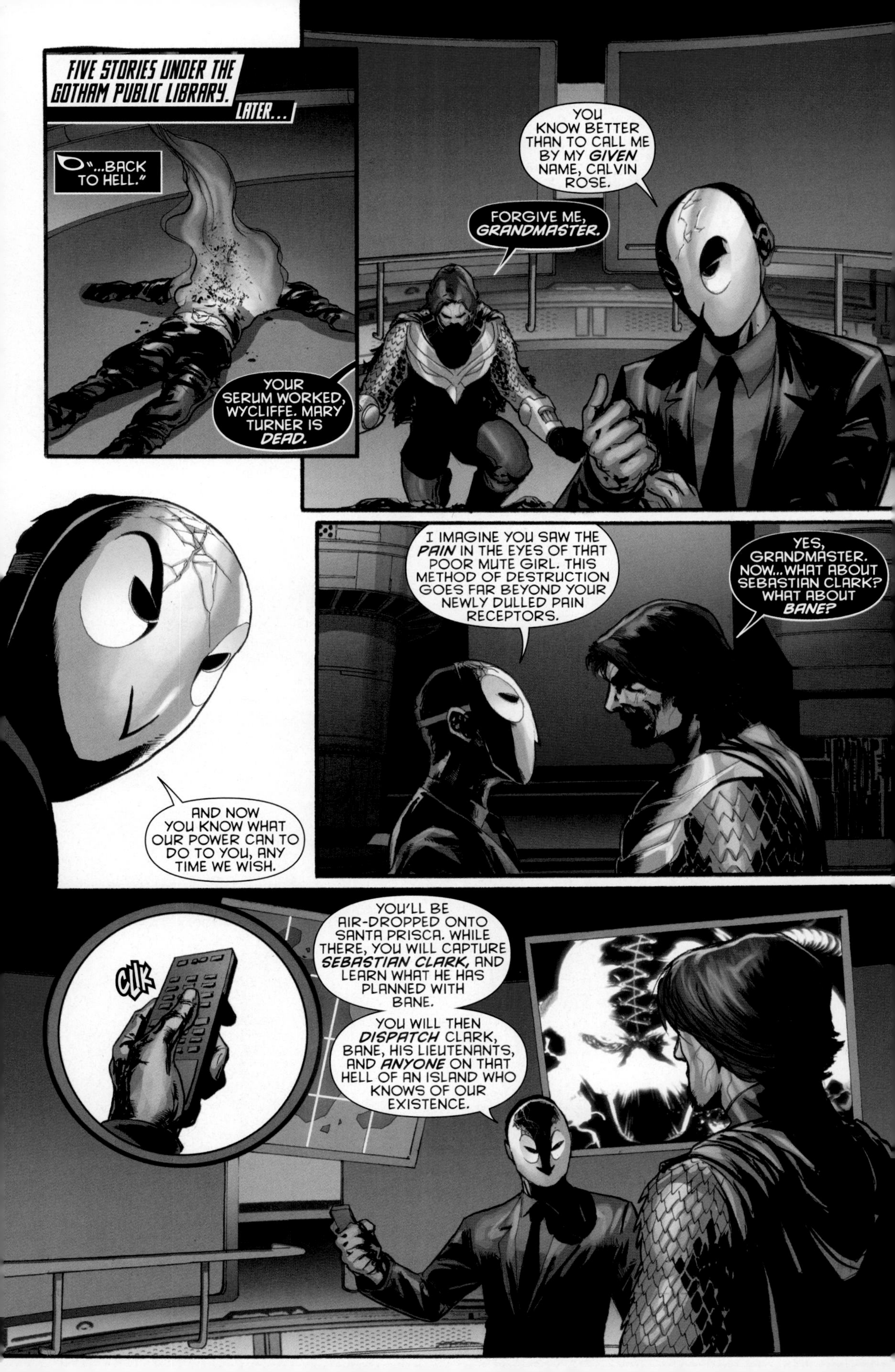
FIVE STORIES UNDER THE GOTHAM PUBLIC LIBRARY.
LATER...
"...BACK TO HELL."
YOUR SERUM WORKED, WYCLIFFE. MARY TURNER IS DEAD.
YOU KNOW BETTER THAN TO CALL ME BY MY GIVEN NAME, CALVIN ROSE.
FORGIVE ME, GRANDMASTER.
AND NOW YOU KNOW WHAT OUR POWER CAN TO DO TO YOU, ANY TIME WE WISH.
I IMAGINE YOU SAW THE PAIN IN THE EYES OF THAT POOR MUTE GIRL. THIS METHOD OF DESTRUCTION GOES FAR BEYOND YOUR NEWLY DULLED PAIN RECEPTORS.
YES, GRANDMASTER. NOW...WHAT ABOUT SEBASTIAN CLARK? WHAT ABOUT BANE?
CLIK
YOU'LL BE AIR-DROPPED ONTO SANTA PRISCA. WHILE THERE, YOU WILL CAPTURE SEBASTIAN CLARK, AND LEARN WHAT HE HAS PLANNED WITH BANE.
YOU WILL THEN DISPATCH CLARK, BANE, HIS LIEUTENANTS, AND ANYONE ON THAT HELL OF AN ISLAND WHO KNOWS OF OUR EXISTENCE.

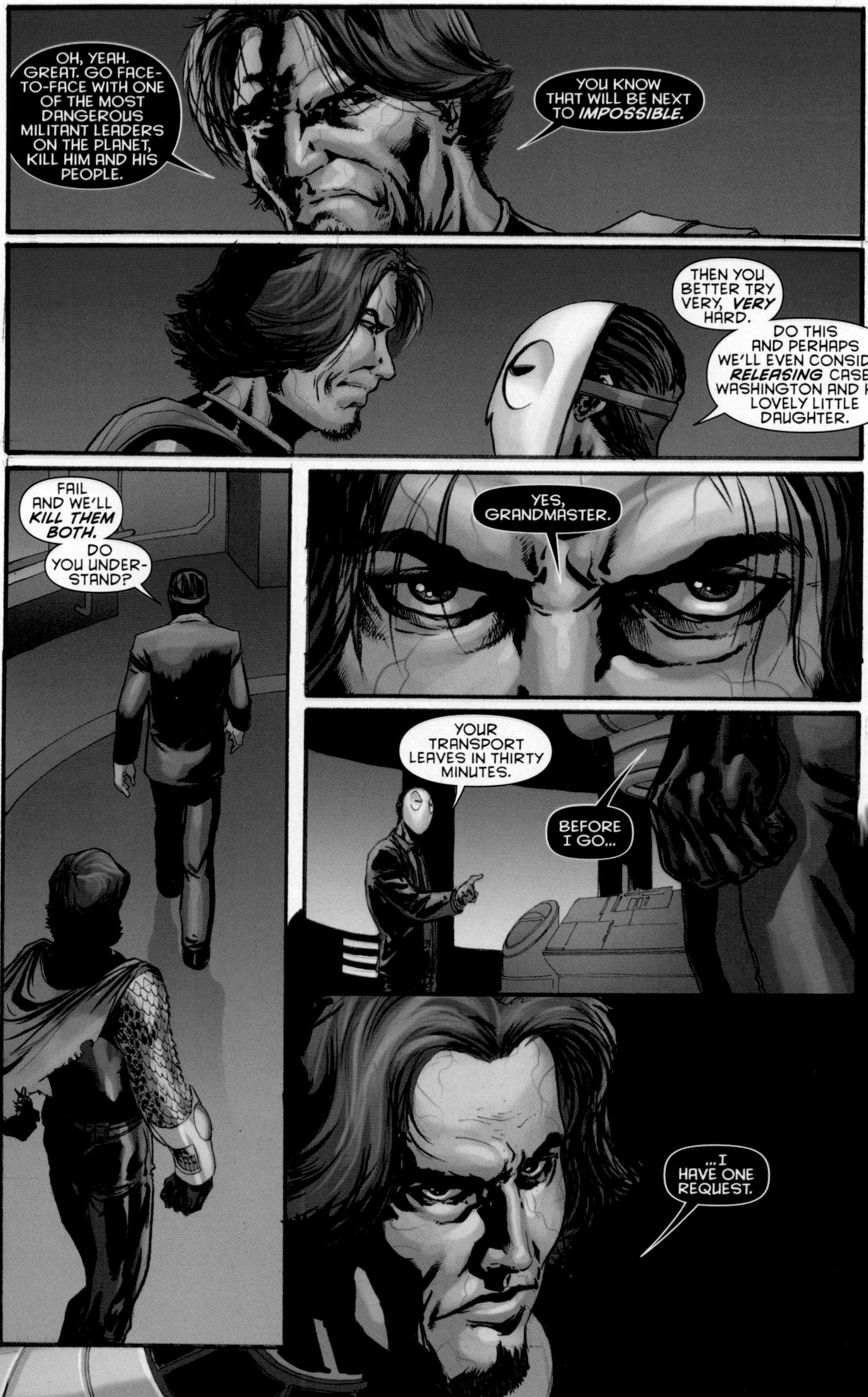
OH, YEAH. GREAT. GO FACE-TO-FACE WITH ONE OF THE MOST DANGEROUS MILITANT LEADERS ON THE PLANET, KILL HIM AND HIS PEOPLE.
YOU KNOW THAT WILL BE NEXT TO *IMPOSSIBLE.*
THEN YOU BETTER TRY VERY, *VERY* HARD.
DO THIS AND PERHAPS WE'LL EVEN CONSIDER *RELEASING* CASEY WASHINGTON AND HER LOVELY LITTLE DAUGHTER.
FAIL AND WE'LL *KILL THEM BOTH.*
DO YOU UNDER-STAND?
YES, GRANDMASTER.
YOUR TRANSPORT LEAVES IN THIRTY MINUTES.
BEFORE I GO...
...I HAVE ONE REQUEST.

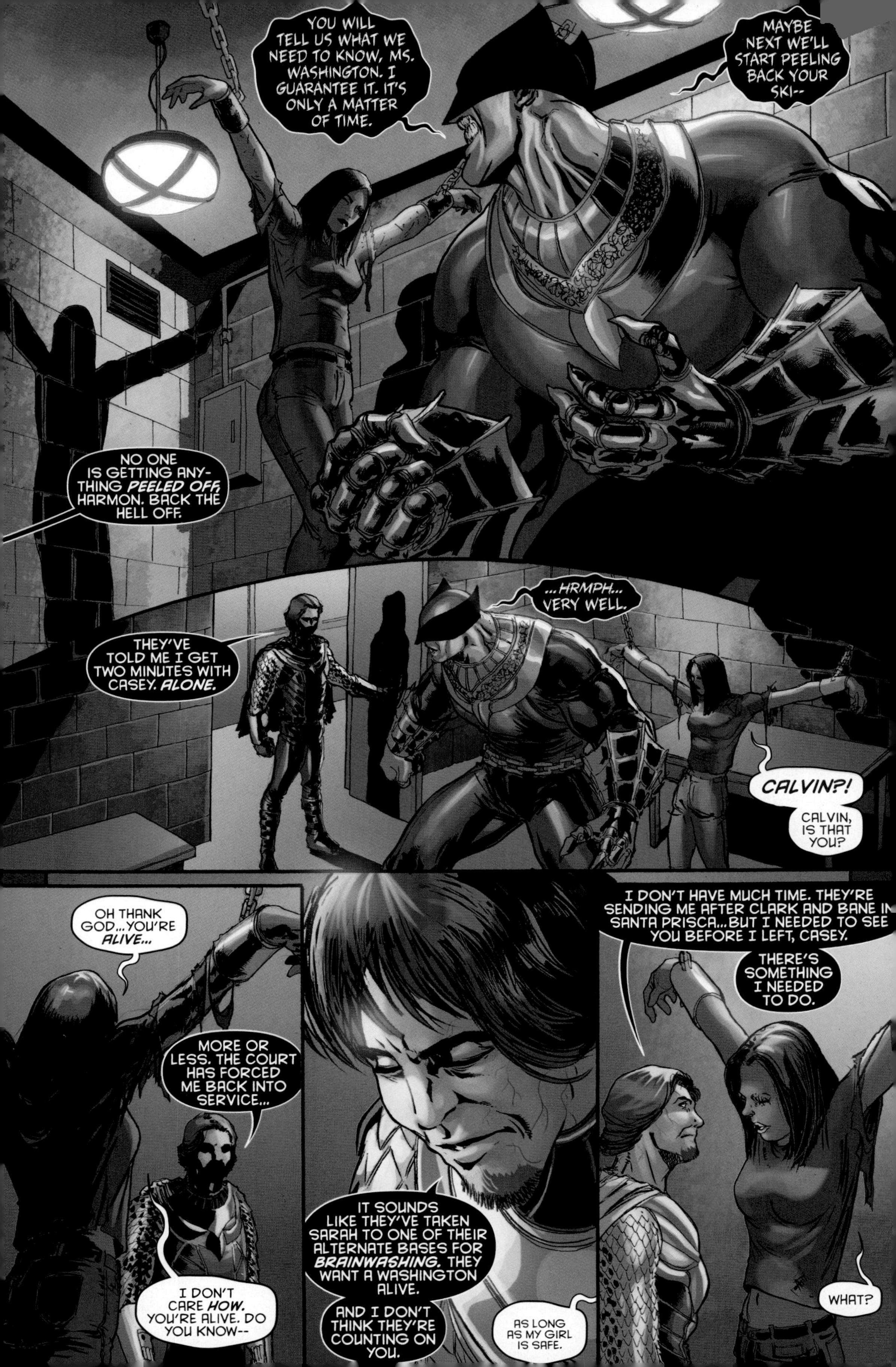
YOU WILL TELL US WHAT WE NEED TO KNOW, MS. WASHINGTON. I GUARANTEE IT. IT'S ONLY A MATTER OF TIME.
MAYBE NEXT WE'LL START PEELING BACK YOUR SKI--
NO ONE IS GETTING ANY-THING *PEELED OFF*, HARMON. BACK THE HELL OFF.
...HRMPH... VERY WELL.
THEY'VE TOLD ME I GET TWO MINUTES WITH CASEY. *ALONE.*
CALVIN?!
CALVIN, IS THAT YOU?
OH THANK GOD...YOU'RE *ALIVE*...
MORE OR LESS. THE COURT HAS FORCED ME BACK INTO SERVICE...
I DON'T CARE *HOW*. YOU'RE ALIVE. DO YOU KNOW--
IT SOUNDS LIKE THEY'VE TAKEN SARAH TO ONE OF THEIR ALTERNATE BASES FOR *BRAINWASHING.* THEY WANT A WASHINGTON ALIVE.
AND I DON'T THINK THEY'RE COUNTING ON YOU.
AS LONG AS MY GIRL IS SAFE.
I DON'T HAVE MUCH TIME. THEY'RE SENDING ME AFTER CLARK AND BANE IN SANTA PRISCA...BUT I NEEDED TO SEE YOU BEFORE I LEFT, CASEY.
THERE'S SOMETHING I NEEDED TO DO.
WHAT?

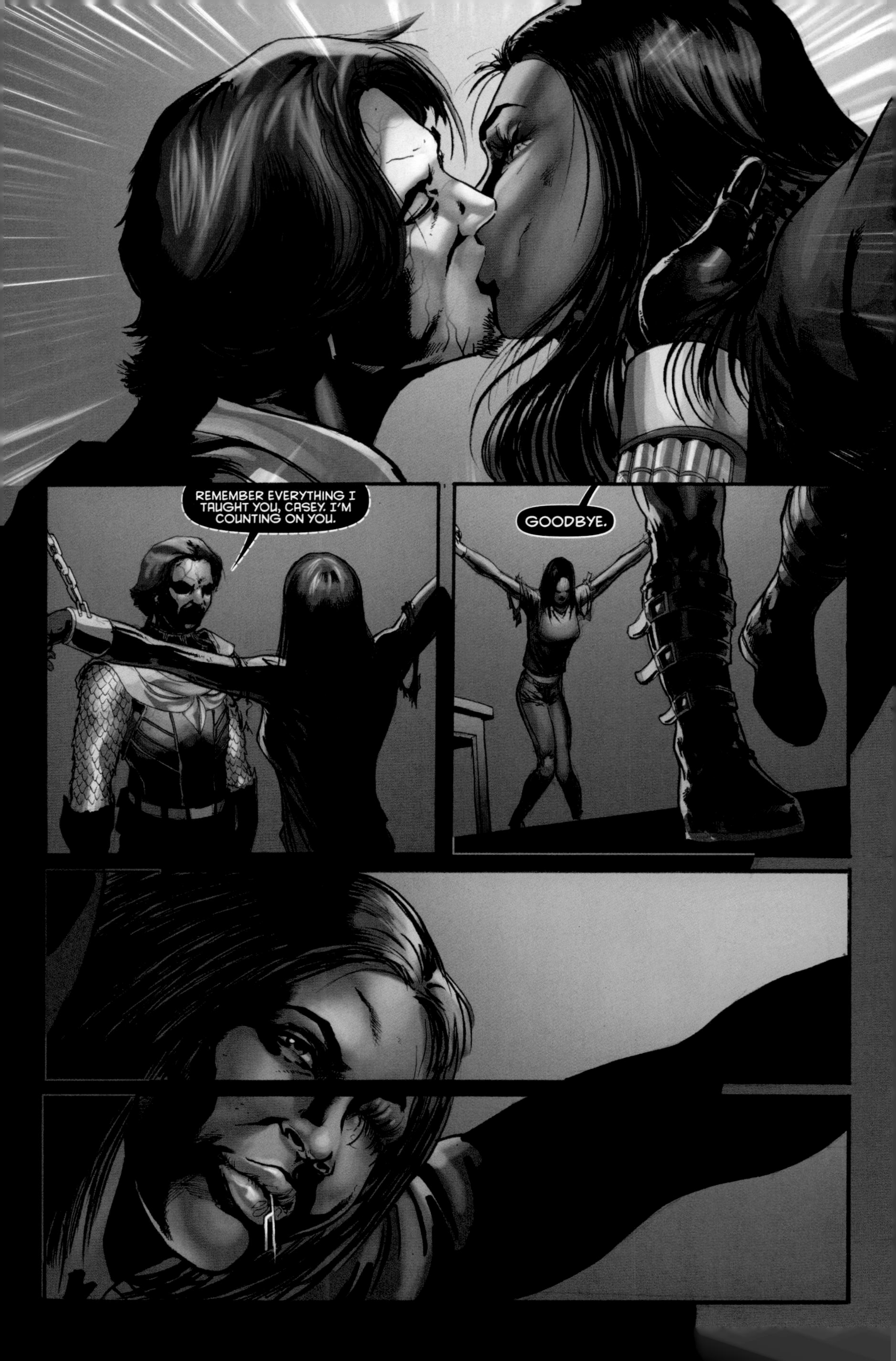
REMEMBER EVERYTHING I TAUGHT YOU, CASEY. I'M COUNTING ON YOU.
GOODBYE.

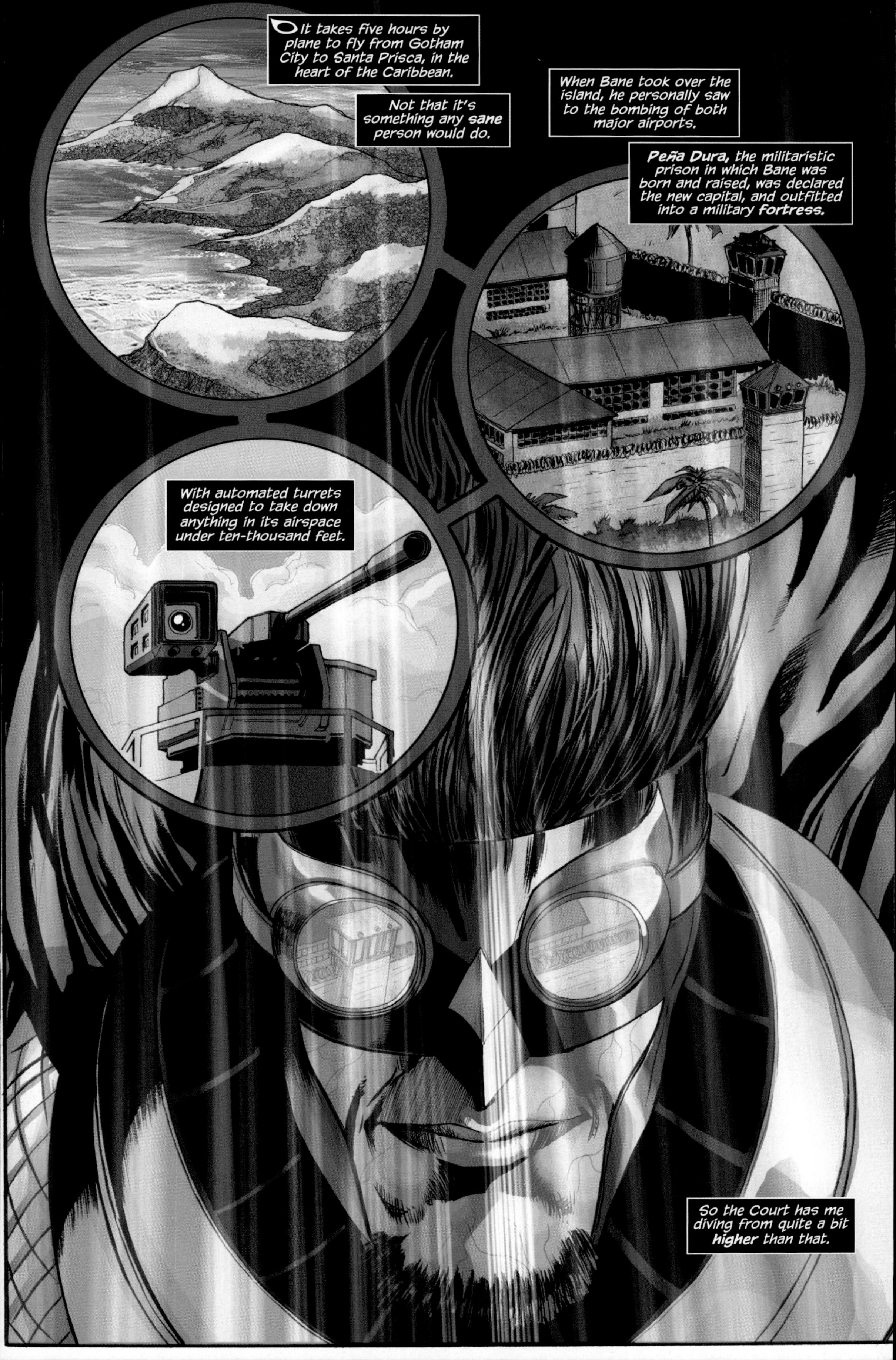
It takes five hours by plane to fly from Gotham City to Santa Prisca, in the heart of the Caribbean.
Not that it's something any **sane** person would do.
When Bane took over the island, he personally saw to the bombing of both major airports.
Peña Dura, the militaristic prison in which Bane was born and raised, was declared the new capital, and outfitted into a military **fortress.**
With automated turrets designed to take down anything in its airspace under ten-thousand feet.
So the Court has me diving from quite a bit **higher** than that.

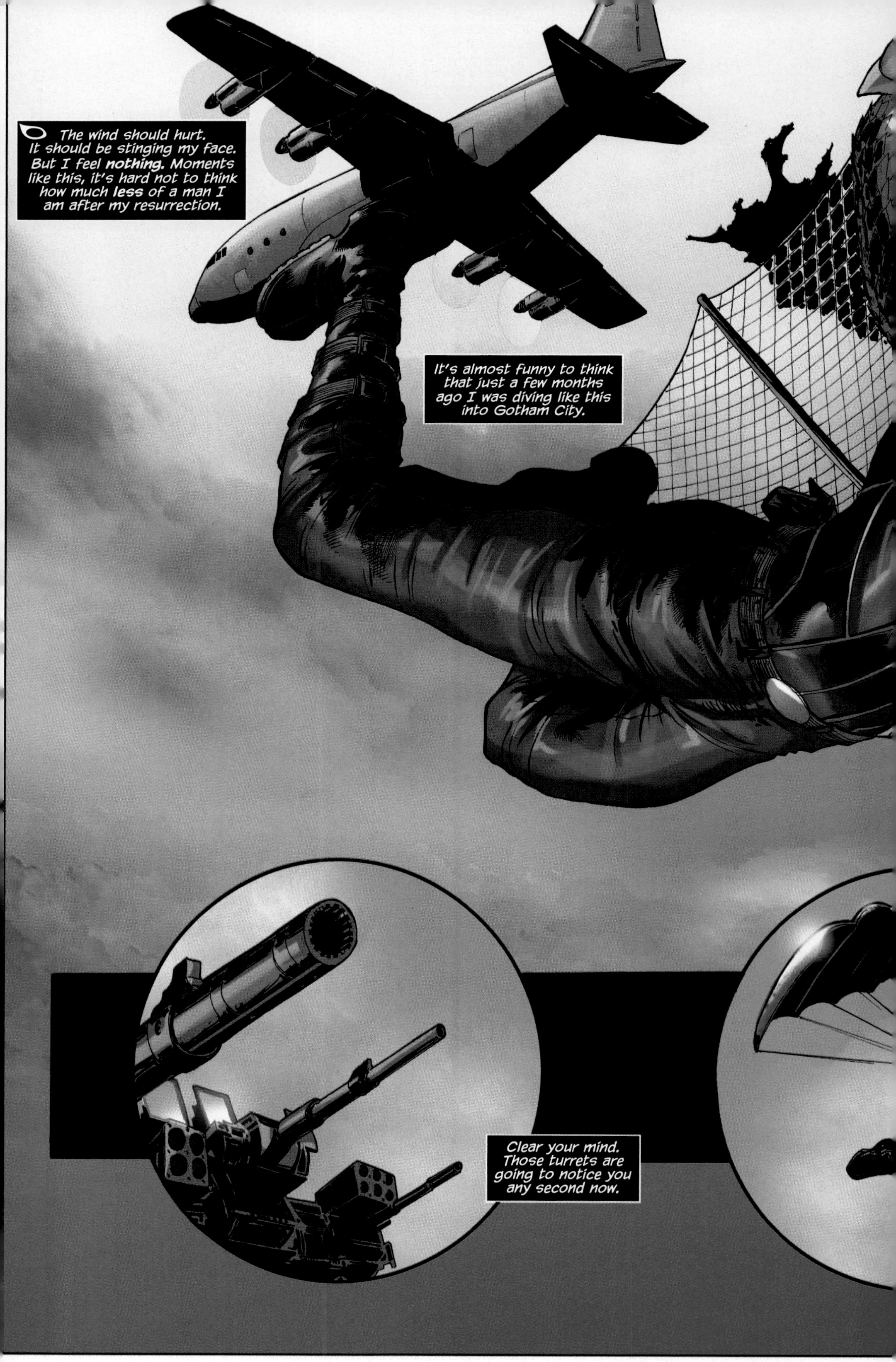
The wind should hurt. It should be stinging my face. But I feel **nothing.** Moments like this, it's hard not to think how much **less** of a man I am after my resurrection.
It's almost funny to think that just a few months ago I was diving like this into Gotham City.
Clear your mind. Those turrets are going to notice you any second now.

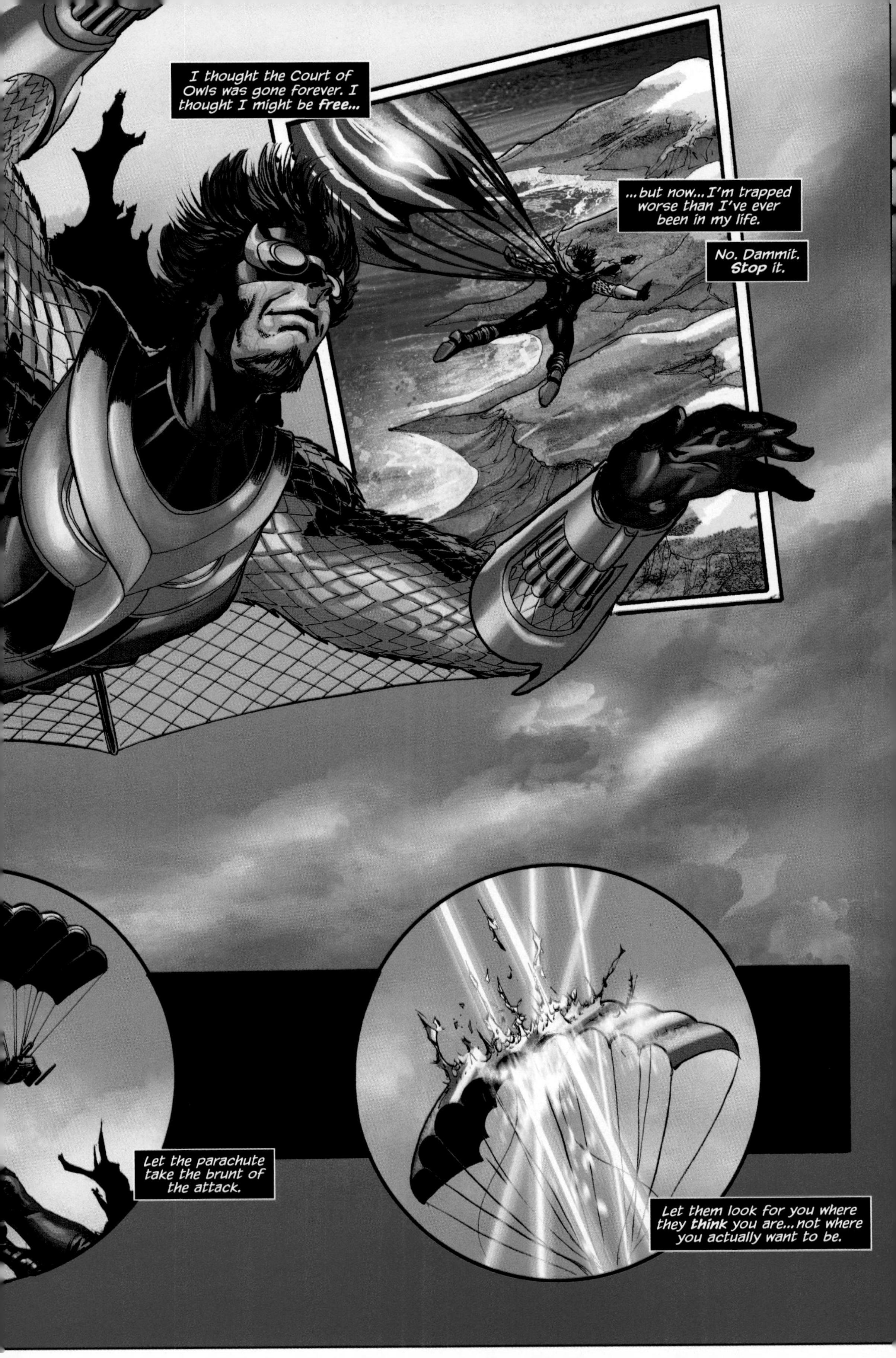
I thought the Court of Owls was gone forever. I thought I might be *free*...
...but now...I'm trapped worse than I've ever been in my life.
No. Dammit. **Stop** it.
Let the parachute take the brunt of the attack.
Let them look for you where they **think** you are...not where you actually want to be.

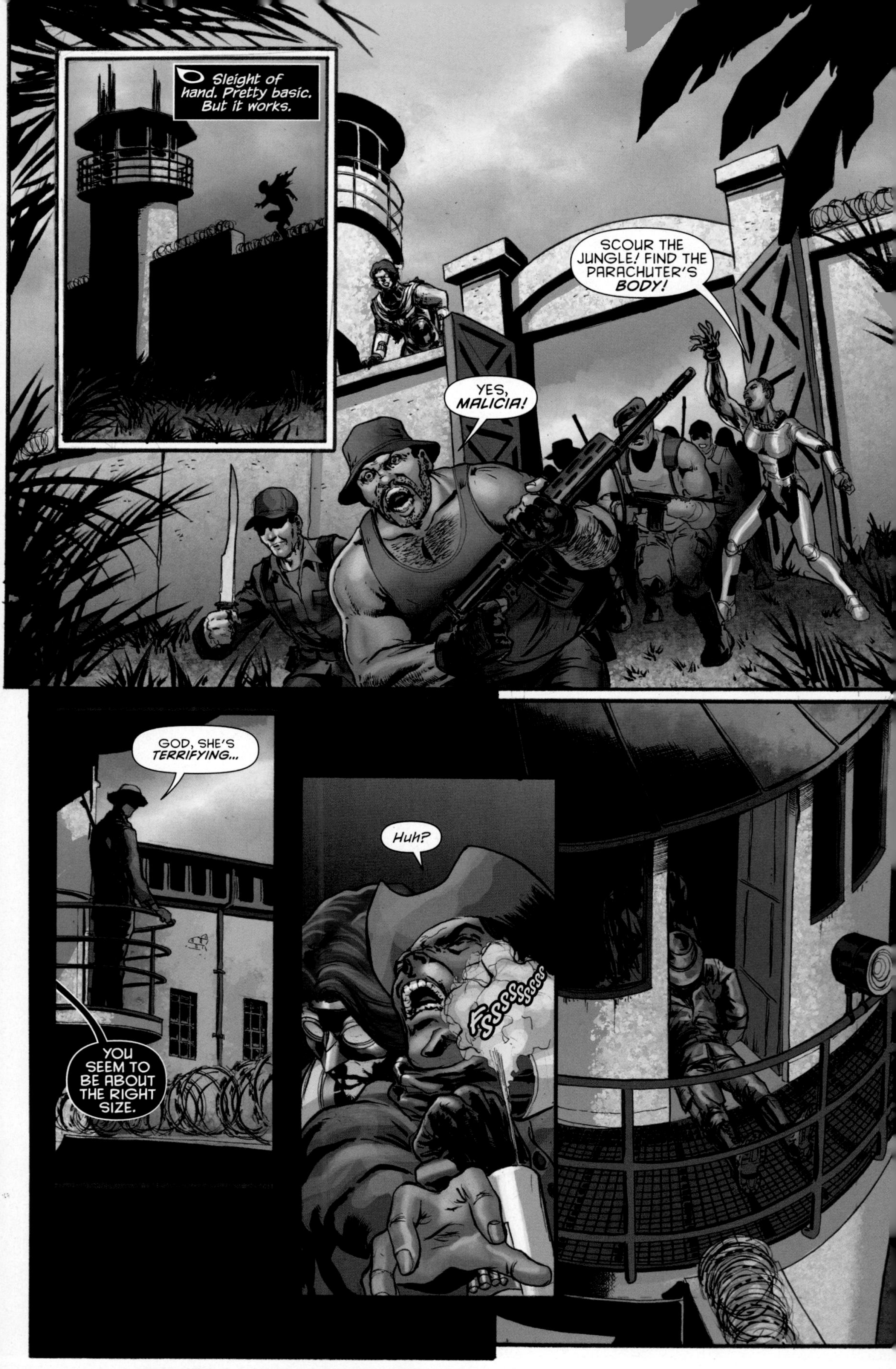

Sleight of hand. Pretty basic. But it works.
SCOUR THE JUNGLE! FIND THE PARACHUTER'S BODY!
YES, MALICIA!
GOD, SHE'S TERRIFYING...
Huh?
YOU SEEM TO BE ABOUT THE RIGHT SIZE.
FSSSSSSSS

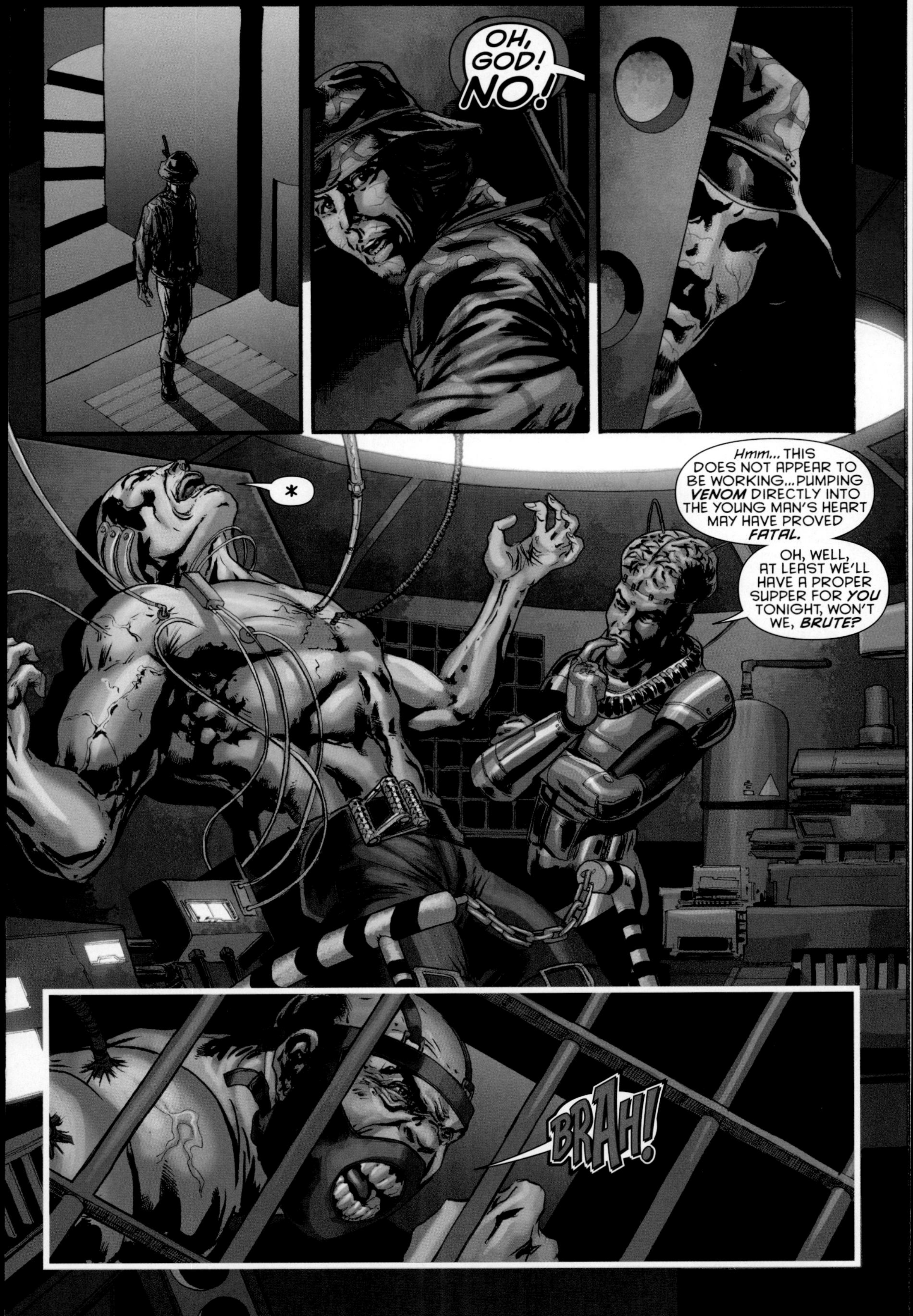
OH, GOD! NO!
*
Hmm... THIS DOES NOT APPEAR TO BE WORKING... PUMPING VENOM DIRECTLY INTO THE YOUNG MAN'S HEART MAY HAVE PROVED FATAL.
OH, WELL, AT LEAST WE'LL HAVE A PROPER SUPPER FOR YOU TONIGHT, WON'T WE, BRUTE?
BRAH!

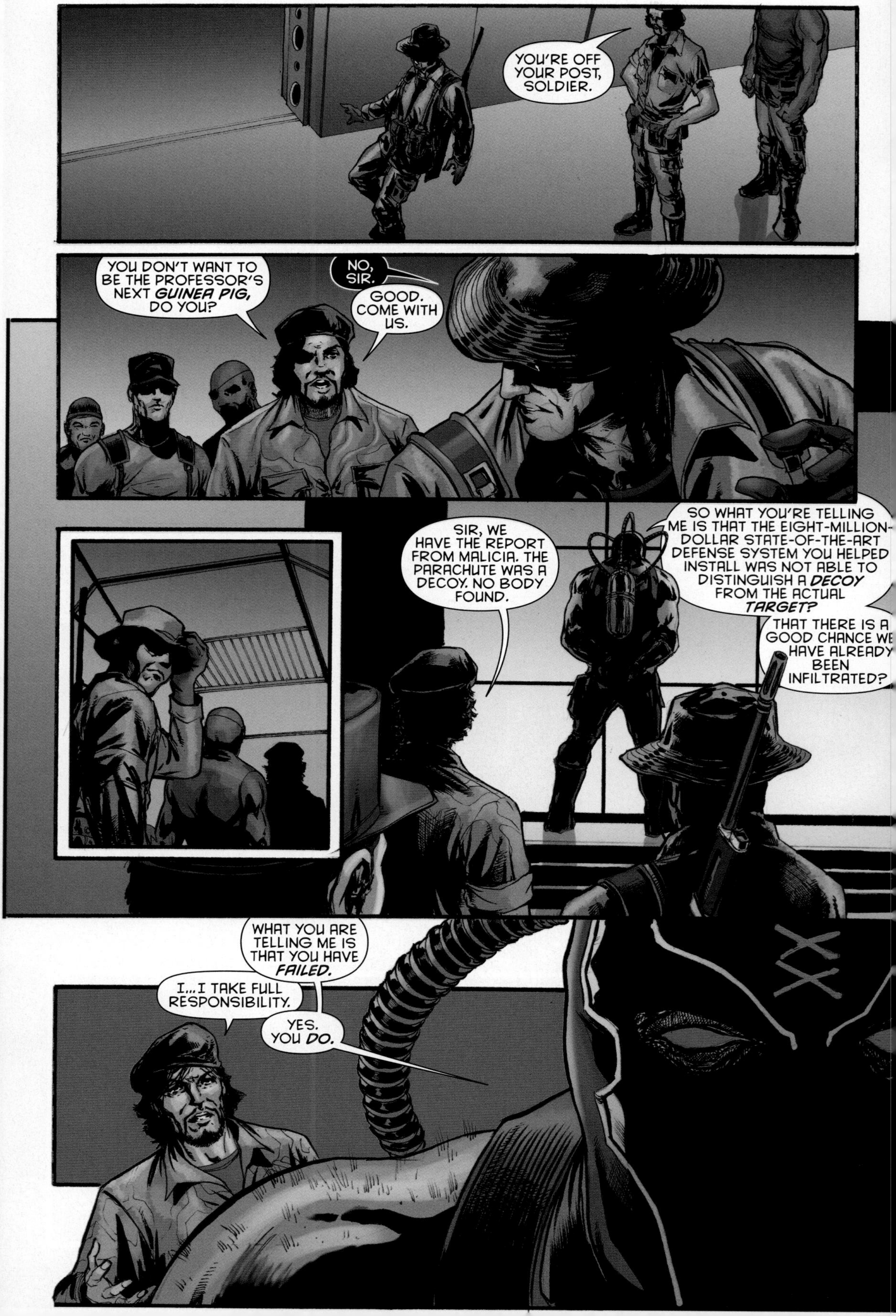
YOU'RE OFF YOUR POST, SOLDIER.
YOU DON'T WANT TO BE THE PROFESSOR'S NEXT *GUINEA PIG,* DO YOU?
NO, SIR.
GOOD. COME WITH US.
SIR, WE HAVE THE REPORT FROM MALICIA. THE PARACHUTE WAS A DECOY. NO BODY FOUND.
SO WHAT YOU'RE TELLING ME IS THAT THE EIGHT-MILLION-DOLLAR STATE-OF-THE-ART DEFENSE SYSTEM YOU HELPED INSTALL WAS NOT ABLE TO DISTINGUISH A *DECOY* FROM THE ACTUAL *TARGET?*
THAT THERE IS A GOOD CHANCE WE HAVE ALREADY BEEN INFILTRATED?
WHAT YOU ARE TELLING ME IS THAT YOU HAVE *FAILED.*
I...I TAKE FULL RESPONSIBILITY.
YES. YOU *DO.*

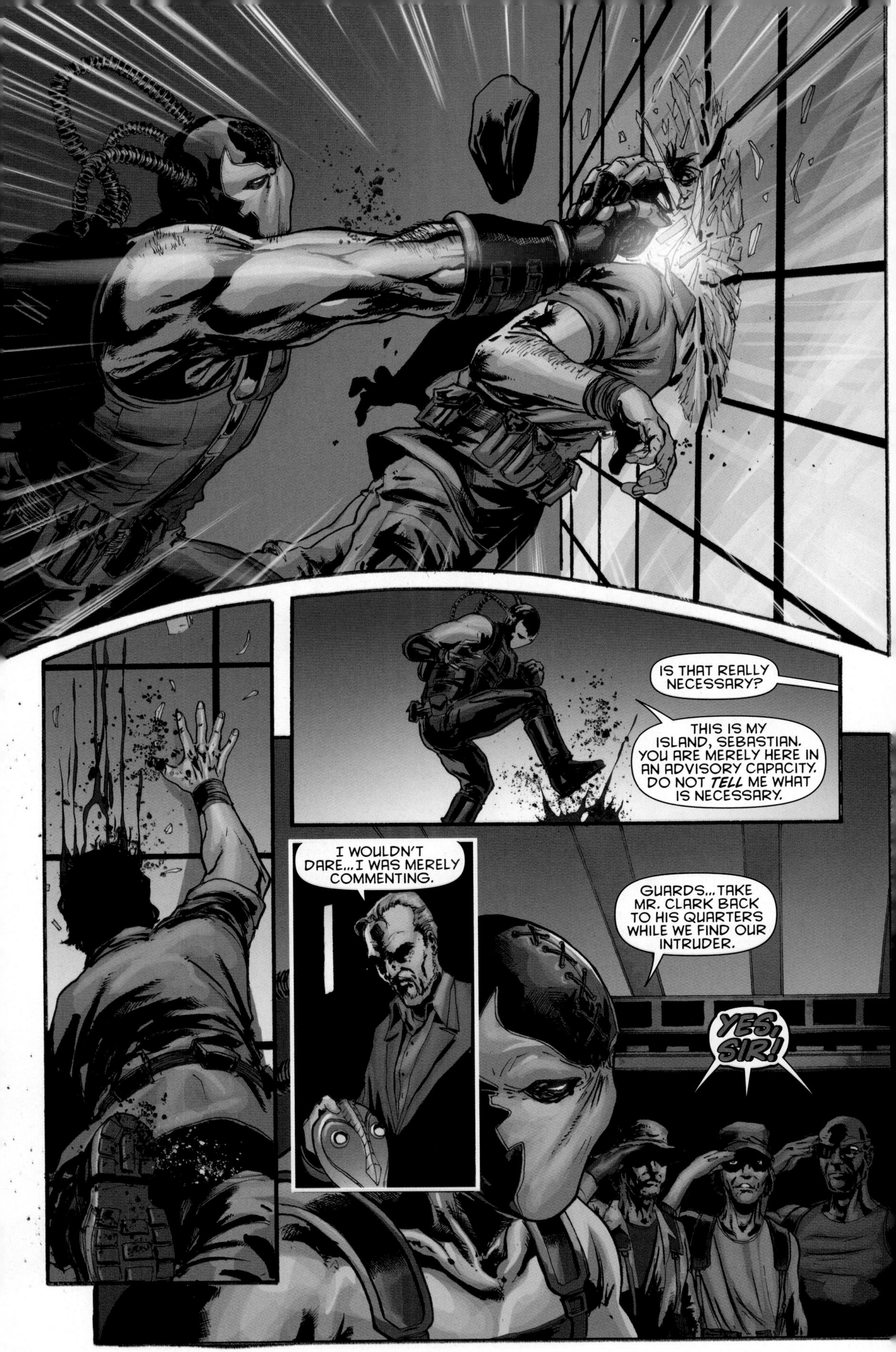
IS THAT REALLY NECESSARY?
THIS IS MY ISLAND, SEBASTIAN. YOU ARE MERELY HERE IN AN ADVISORY CAPACITY. DO NOT *TELL* ME WHAT IS NECESSARY.
I WOULDN'T DARE... I WAS MERELY COMMENTING.
GUARDS... TAKE MR. CLARK BACK TO HIS QUARTERS WHILE WE FIND OUR INTRUDER.
YES, SIR!

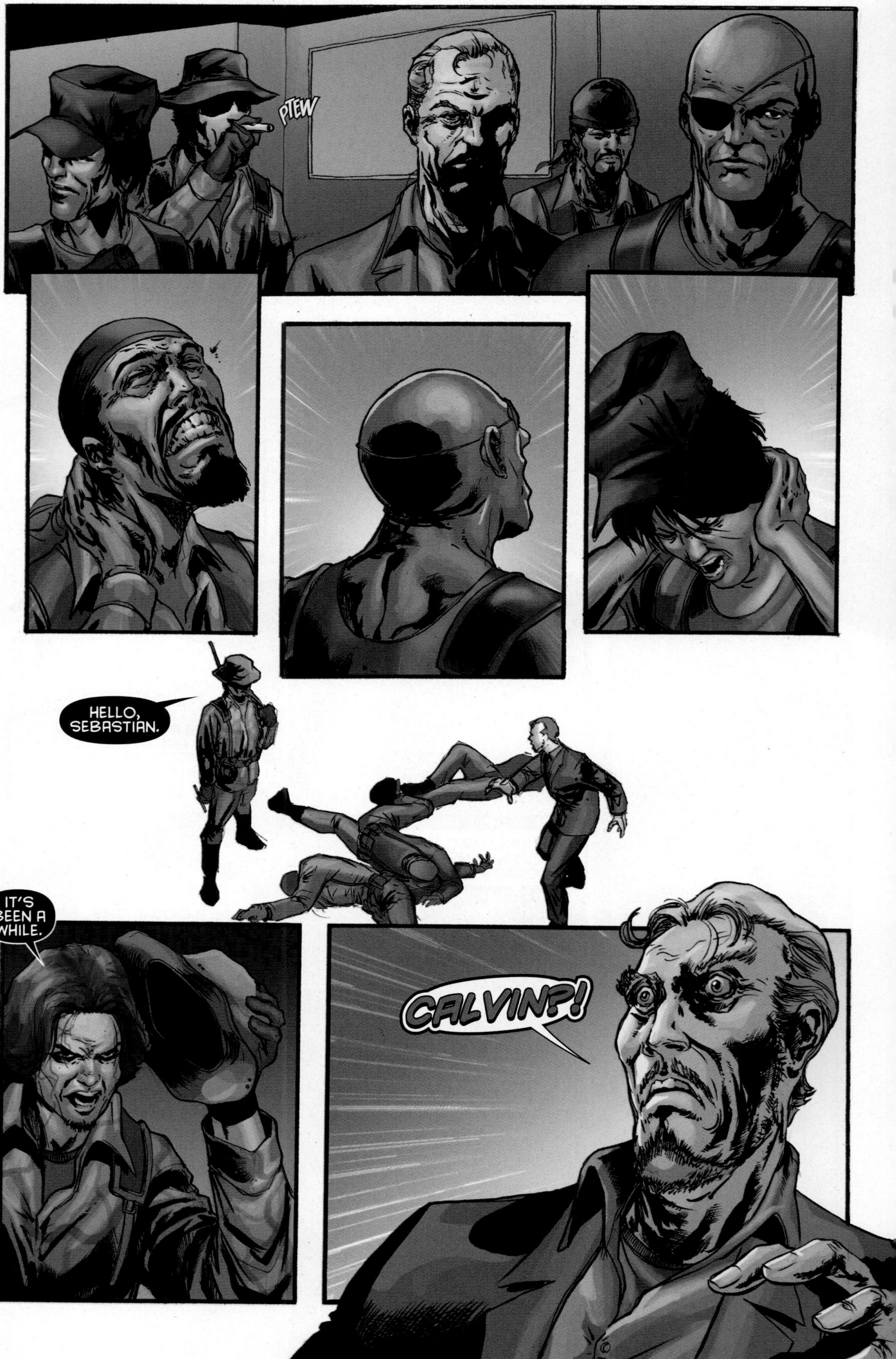
PTEW
HELLO, SEBASTIAN.
IT'S BEEN A WHILE.
CALVIN?!

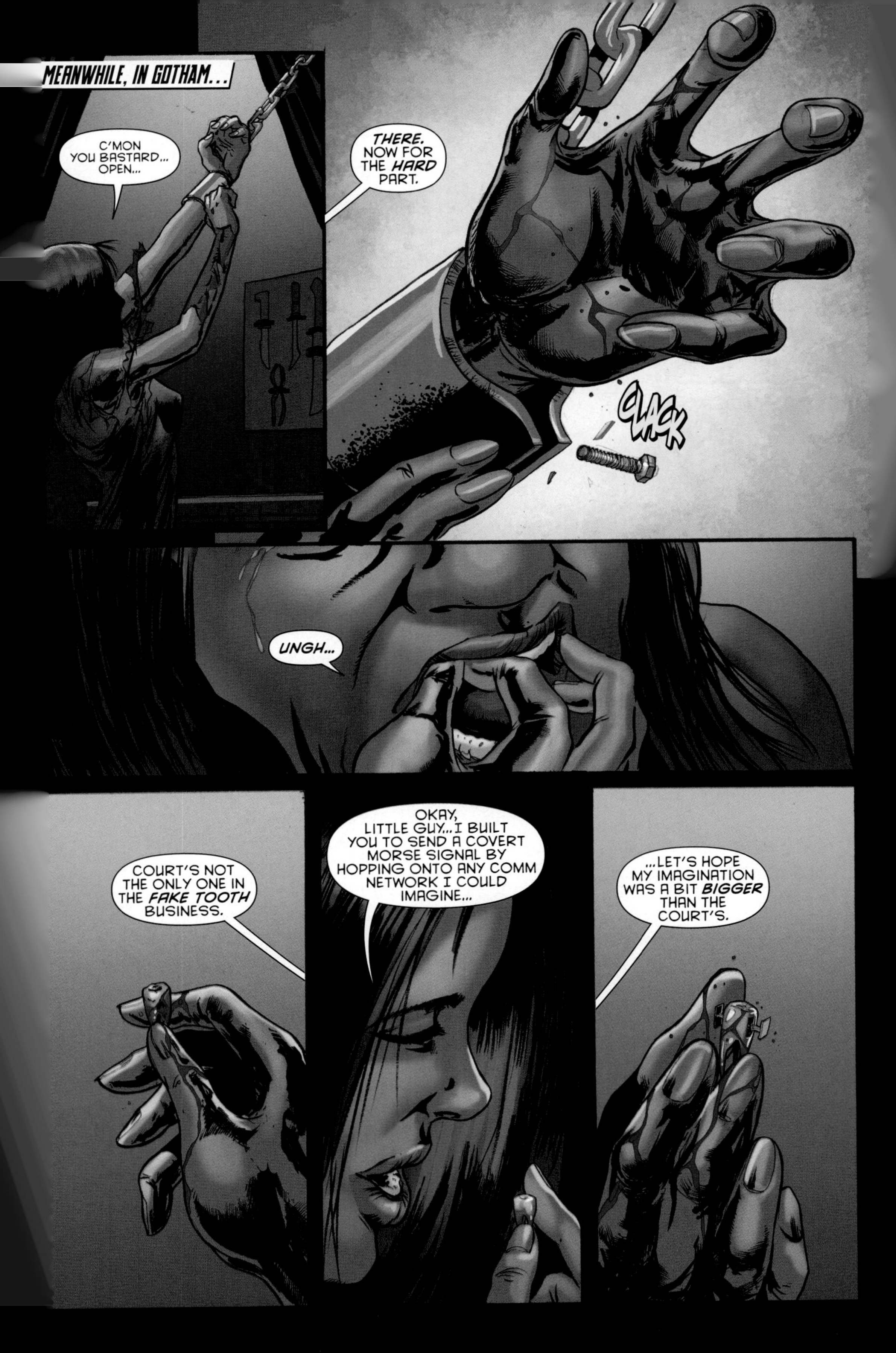
MEANWHILE, IN GOTHAM...
C'MON YOU BASTARD... OPEN...
THERE. NOW FOR THE HARD PART.
CLACK
UNGH...
COURT'S NOT THE ONLY ONE IN THE FAKE TOOTH BUSINESS.
OKAY, LITTLE GUY... I BUILT YOU TO SEND A COVERT MORSE SIGNAL BY HOPPING ONTO ANY COMM NETWORK I COULD IMAGINE...
...LET'S HOPE MY IMAGINATION WAS A BIT BIGGER THAN THE COURT'S.

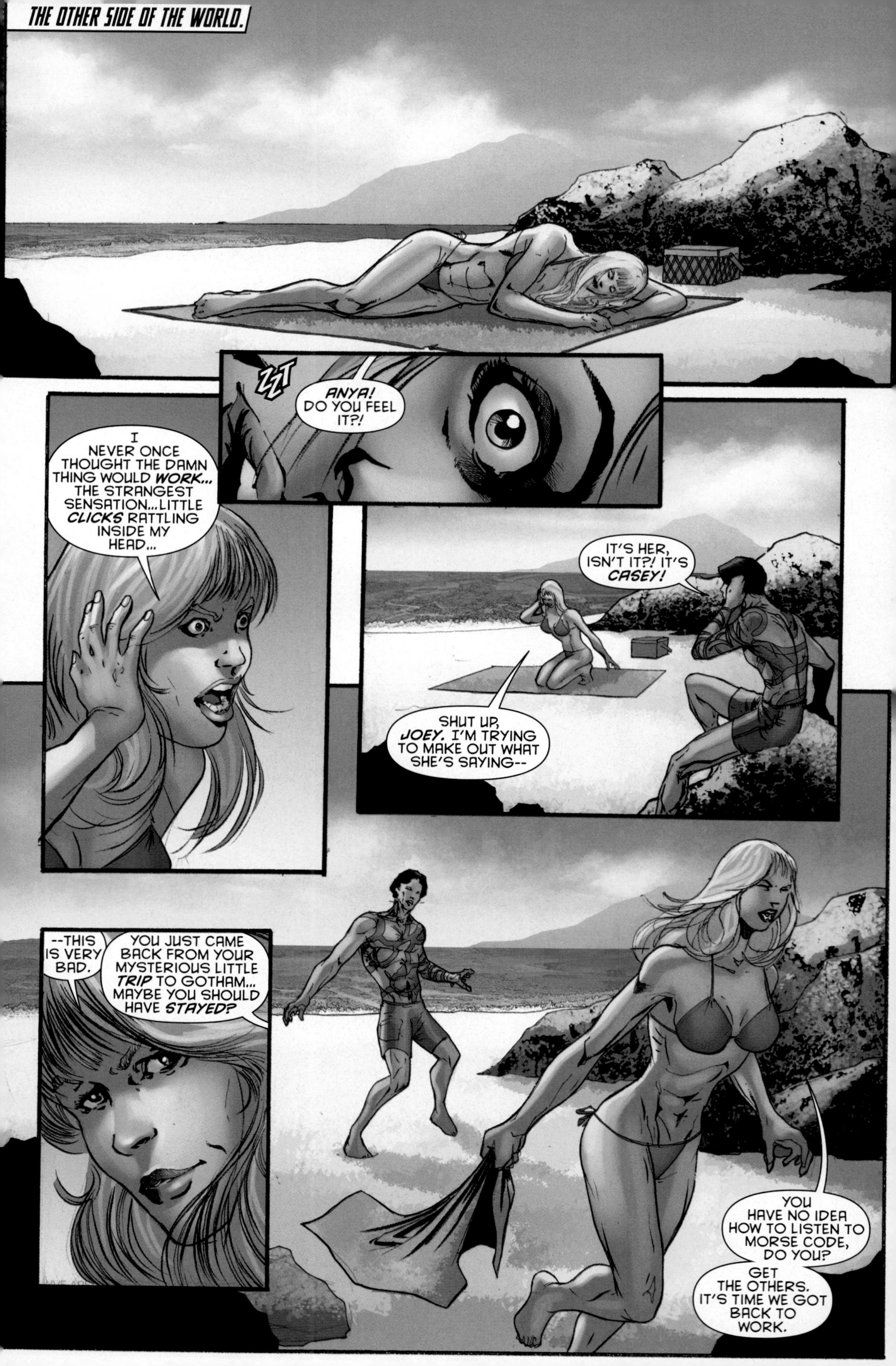
THE OTHER SIDE OF THE WORLD.
ZZZT
ANYA! DO YOU FEEL IT?!
I NEVER ONCE THOUGHT THE DAMN THING WOULD WORK... THE STRANGEST SENSATION...LITTLE CLICKS RATTLING INSIDE MY HEAD...
IT'S HER, ISN'T IT?! IT'S CASEY!
SHUT UP, JOEY. I'M TRYING TO MAKE OUT WHAT SHE'S SAYING--
--THIS IS VERY BAD.
YOU JUST CAME BACK FROM YOUR MYSTERIOUS LITTLE TRIP TO GOTHAM... MAYBE YOU SHOULD HAVE STAYED?
YOU HAVE NO IDEA HOW TO LISTEN TO MORSE CODE, DO YOU?
GET THE OTHERS. IT'S TIME WE GOT BACK TO WORK.

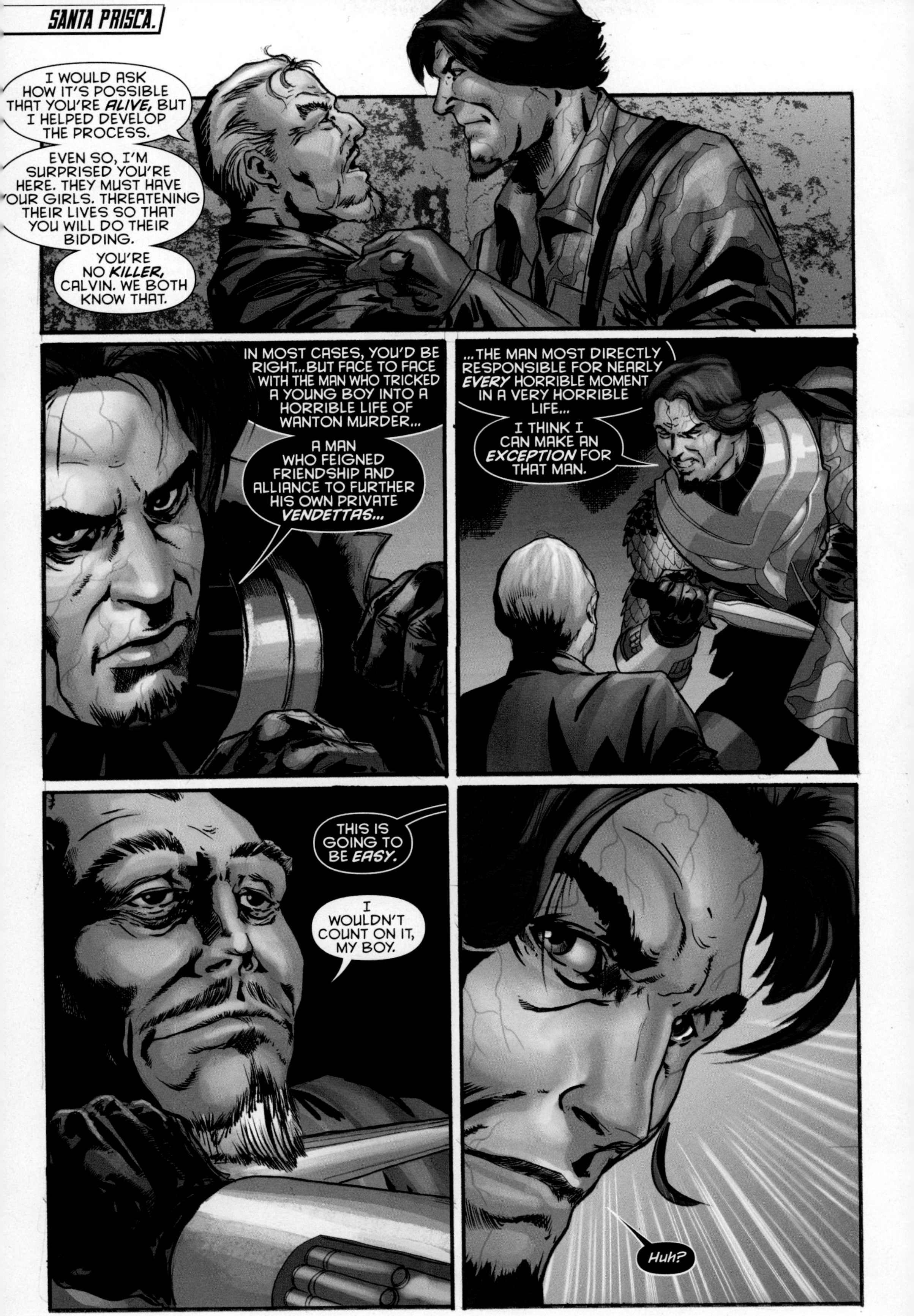
SANTA PRISCA.
I WOULD ASK HOW IT'S POSSIBLE THAT YOU'RE ALIVE, BUT I HELPED DEVELOP THE PROCESS.
EVEN SO, I'M SURPRISED YOU'RE HERE. THEY MUST HAVE YOUR GIRLS. THREATENING THEIR LIVES SO THAT YOU WILL DO THEIR BIDDING.
YOU'RE NO KILLER, CALVIN. WE BOTH KNOW THAT.
IN MOST CASES, YOU'D BE RIGHT...BUT FACE TO FACE WITH THE MAN WHO TRICKED A YOUNG BOY INTO A HORRIBLE LIFE OF WANTON MURDER...
A MAN WHO FEIGNED FRIENDSHIP AND ALLIANCE TO FURTHER HIS OWN PRIVATE VENDETTAS...
...THE MAN MOST DIRECTLY RESPONSIBLE FOR NEARLY EVERY HORRIBLE MOMENT IN A VERY HORRIBLE LIFE...
I THINK I CAN MAKE AN EXCEPTION FOR THAT MAN.
THIS IS GOING TO BE EASY.
I WOULDN'T COUNT ON IT, MY BOY.
Huh?

UNEASY
I'D LIKE YOU TO MEET ONE OF MY NEW ASSOCIATES HERE ON SANTA PRISCA.
WOLF-SPIDER, WOULD YOU DO ME THE HONOR OF RIPPING MR. ROSE APART?
IT WOULD BE MY PLEASURE.
JAMES TYNION IV WRITER GRAHAM NOLAN LAYOUTS MIGUEL SEPULVEDA FINISHES
RAIN BEREDO COLORS TAYLOR ESPOSITO LETTERS SEPULVEDA AND BEREDO COVER
THE STORY CONTINUES IN TALON VOL. 2: FALL OF THE OWLS!

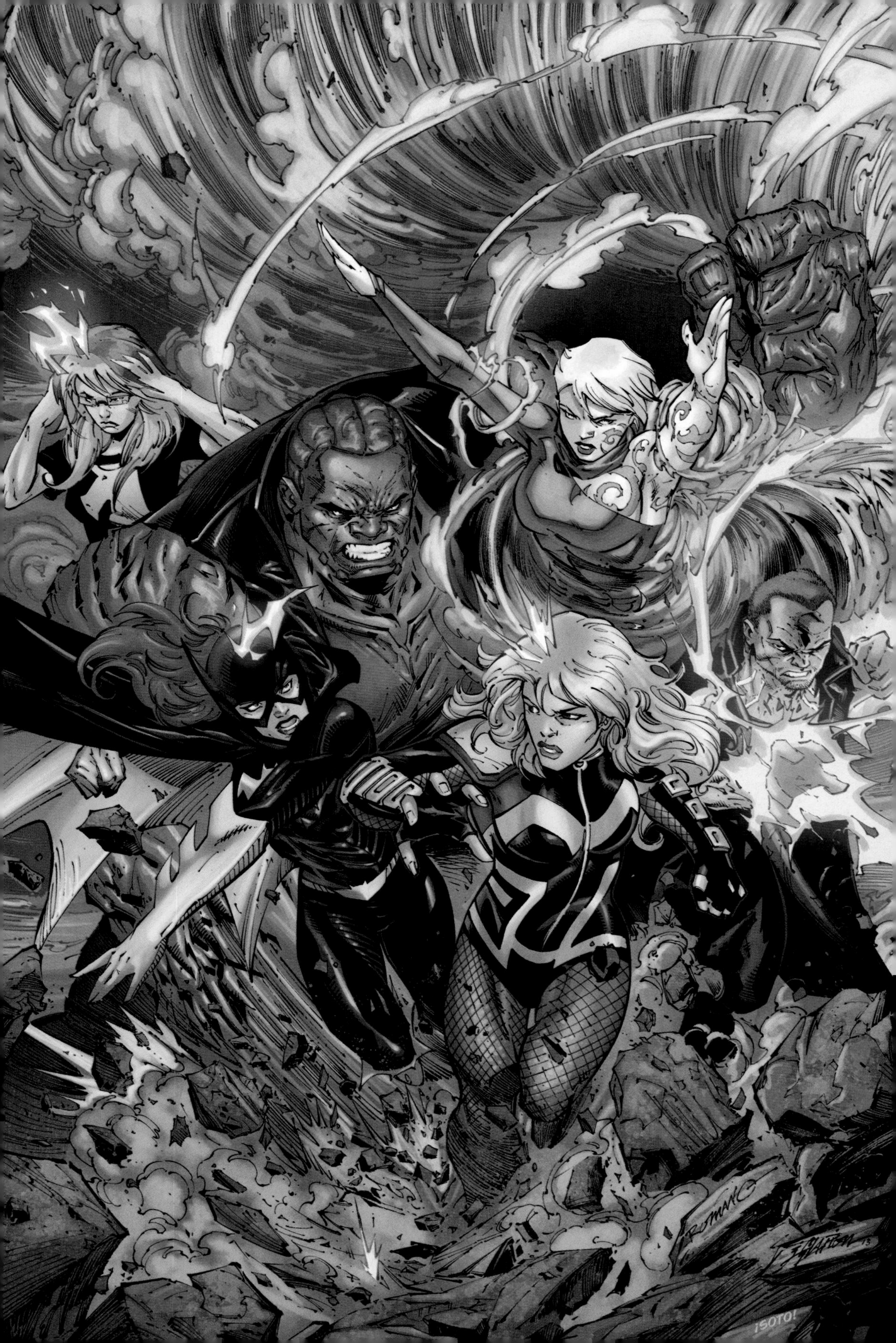
¡SOTO!

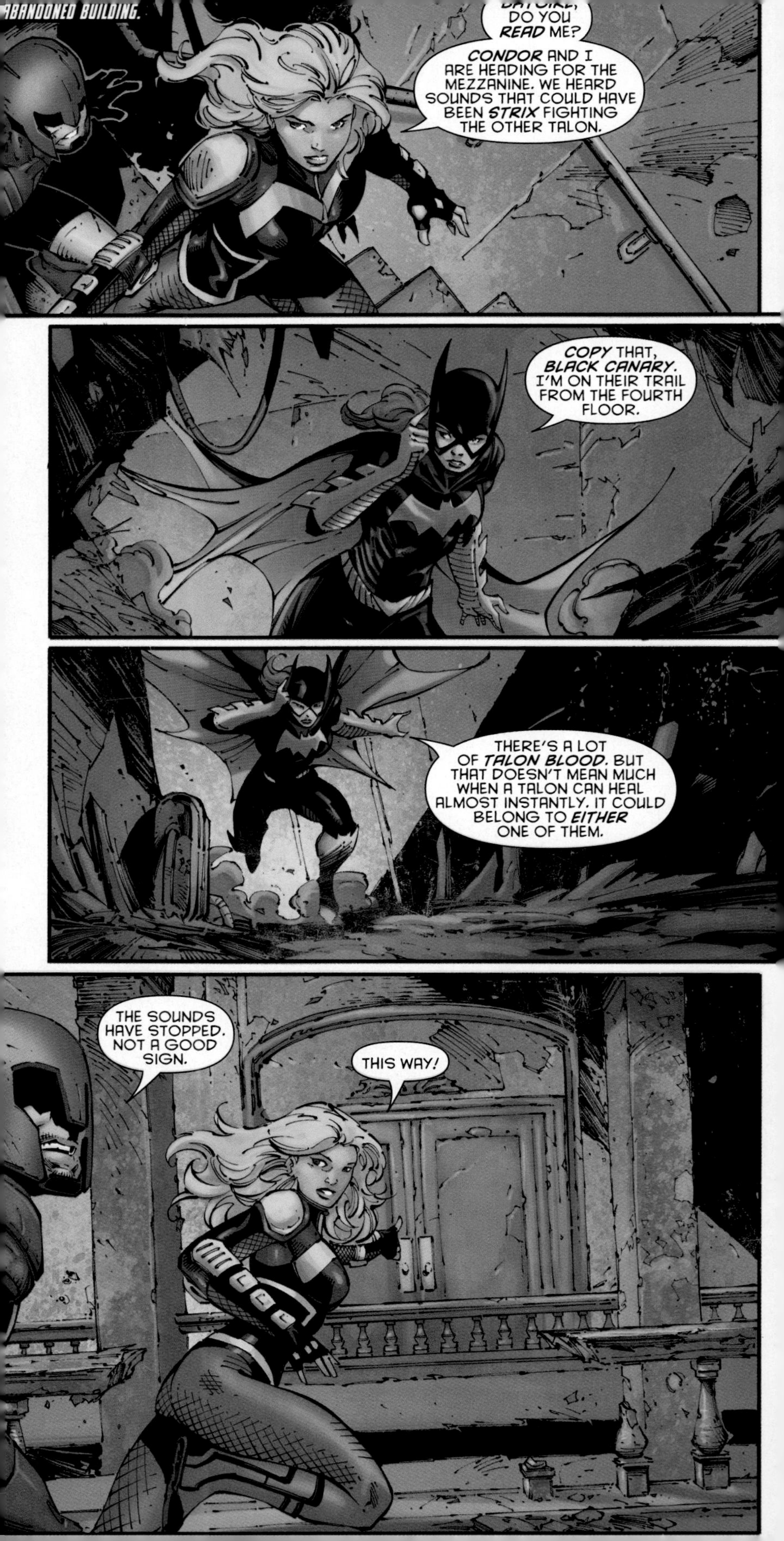
ABANDONED BUILDING.
DO YOU READ ME?
CONDOR AND I ARE HEADING FOR THE MEZZANINE. WE HEARD SOUNDS THAT COULD HAVE BEEN STRIX FIGHTING THE OTHER TALON.
COPY THAT, BLACK CANARY. I'M ON THEIR TRAIL FROM THE FOURTH FLOOR.
THERE'S A LOT OF TALON BLOOD. BUT THAT DOESN'T MEAN MUCH WHEN A TALON CAN HEAL ALMOST INSTANTLY. IT COULD BELONG TO EITHER ONE OF THEM.
THE SOUNDS HAVE STOPPED. NOT A GOOD SIGN.
THIS WAY!

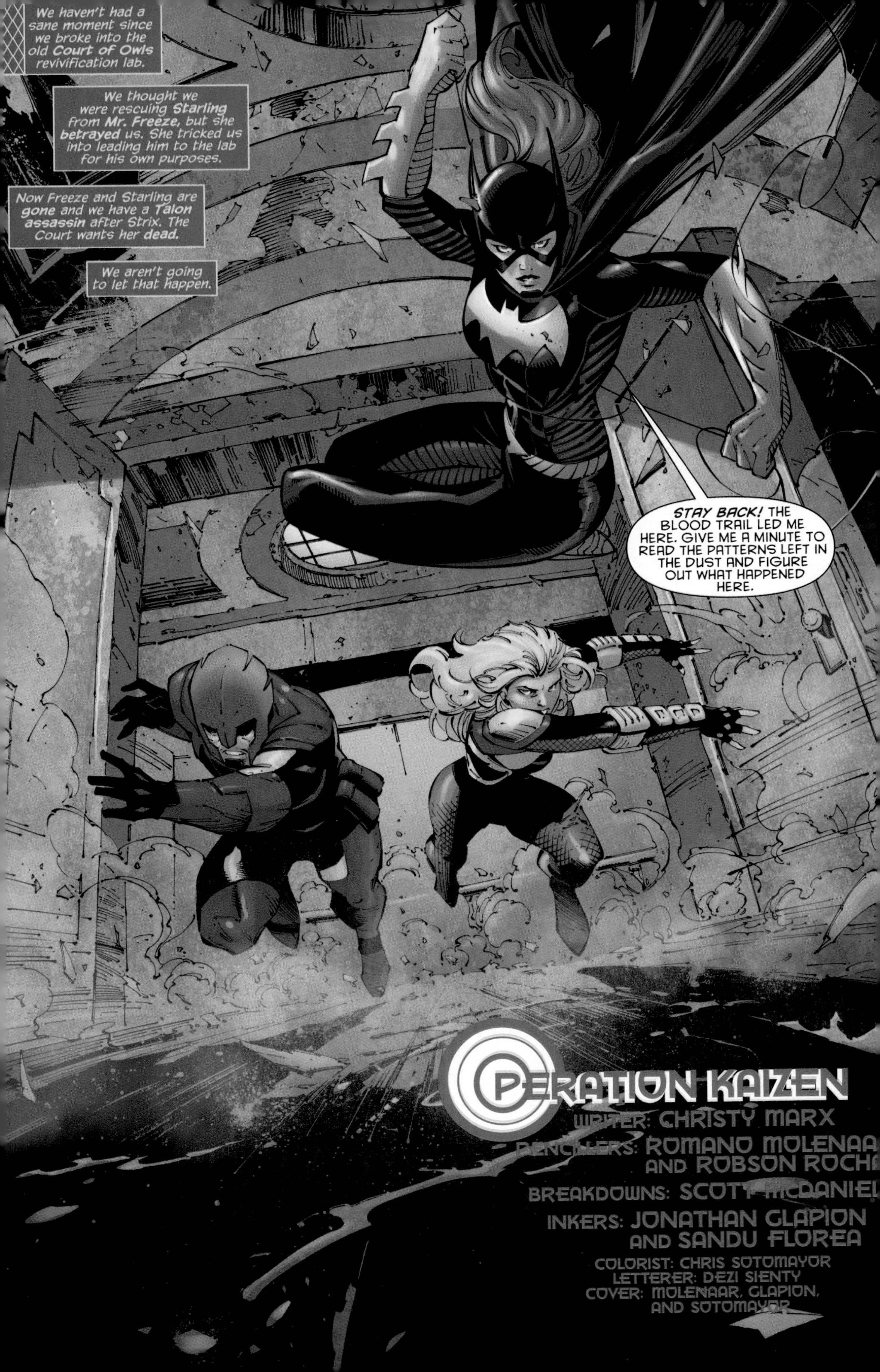
We haven't had a sane moment since we broke into the old Court of Owls revivification lab.
We thought we were rescuing Starling from Mr. Freeze, but she betrayed us. She tricked us into leading him to the lab for his own purposes.
Now Freeze and Starling are gone and we have a Talon assassin after Strix. The Court wants her dead.
We aren't going to let that happen.
STAY BACK! THE BLOOD TRAIL LED ME HERE. GIVE ME A MINUTE TO READ THE PATTERNS LEFT IN THE DUST AND FIGURE OUT WHAT HAPPENED HERE.
OPERATION KAIZEN
WRITER: CHRISTY MARX
PENCILLERS: ROMANO MOLENAAR AND ROBSON ROCHA
BREAKDOWNS: SCOTT MCDANIEL
INKERS: JONATHAN GLAPION AND SANDU FLOREA
COLORIST: CHRIS SOTOMAYOR
LETTERER: DEZI SIENTY
COVER: MOLENAAR, GLAPION, AND SOTOMAYOR

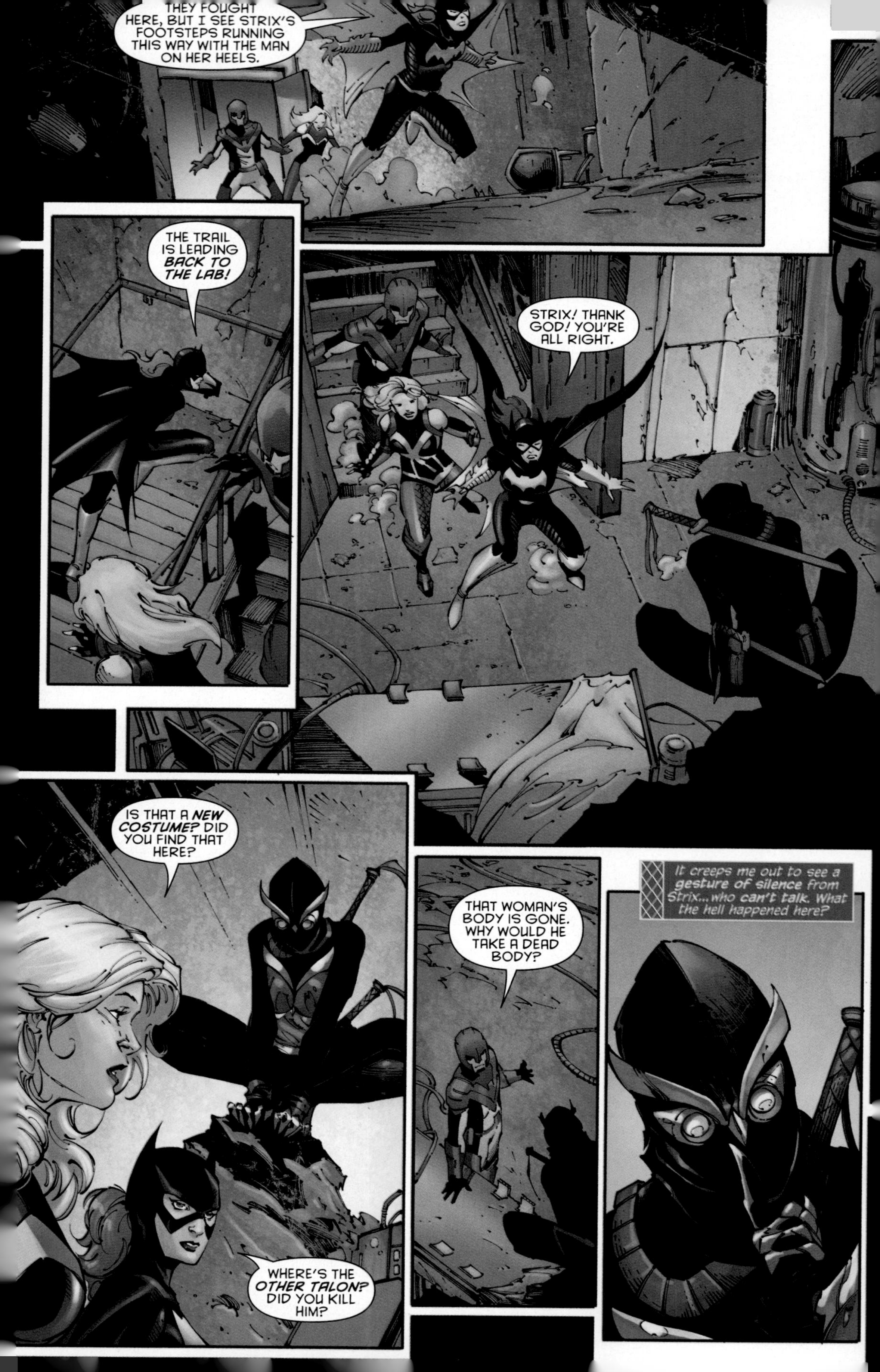

THEY FOUGHT HERE, BUT I SEE STRIX'S FOOTSTEPS RUNNING THIS WAY WITH THE MAN ON HER HEELS.
THE TRAIL IS LEADING BACK TO THE LAB!
STRIX! THANK GOD! YOU'RE ALL RIGHT.
IS THAT A NEW COSTUME? DID YOU FIND THAT HERE?
WHERE'S THE OTHER TALON? DID YOU KILL HIM?
THAT WOMAN'S BODY IS GONE. WHY WOULD HE TAKE A DEAD BODY?
It creeps me out to see a gesture of silence from Strix... who can't talk. What the hell happened here?

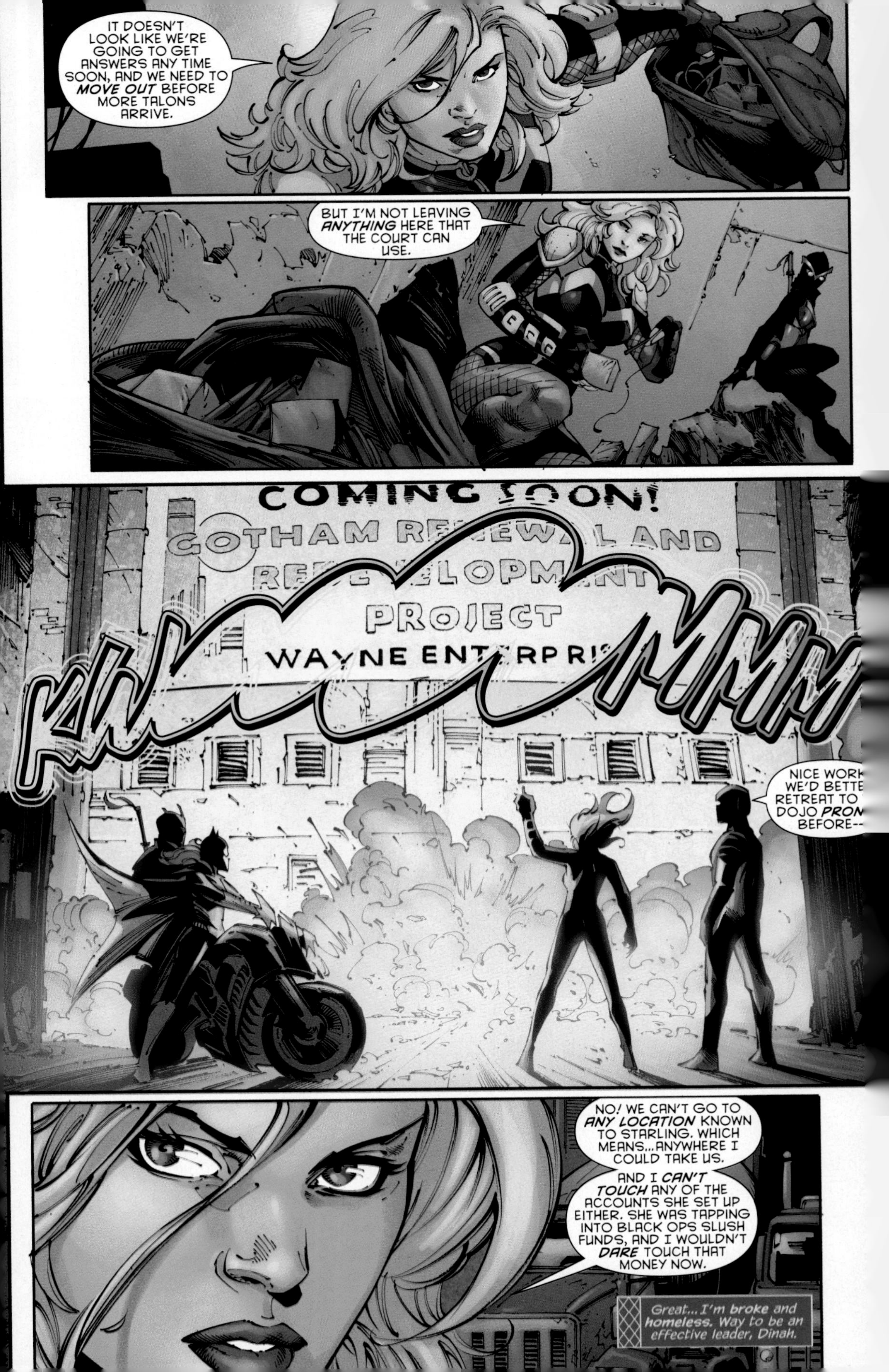
IT DOESN'T LOOK LIKE WE'RE GOING TO GET ANSWERS ANY TIME SOON, AND WE NEED TO *MOVE OUT* BEFORE MORE TALONS ARRIVE.
BUT I'M NOT LEAVING *ANYTHING* HERE THAT THE COURT CAN USE.
COMING SOON!
GOTHAM RENEWAL AND REDEVELOPMENT PROJECT
WAYNE ENTERPRIS
KWHMMMM
NICE WORK WE'D BETTE RETREAT TO DOJO *PRON* BEFORE--
NO! WE CAN'T GO TO *ANY LOCATION* KNOWN TO STARLING. WHICH MEANS...ANYWHERE I COULD TAKE US.
AND I *CAN'T TOUCH* ANY OF THE ACCOUNTS SHE SET UP EITHER. SHE WAS TAPPING INTO BLACK OPS SLUSH FUNDS, AND I WOULDN'T *DARE* TOUCH THAT MONEY NOW.
Great... I'm **broke** and **homeless.** Way to be an effective leader, Dinah.

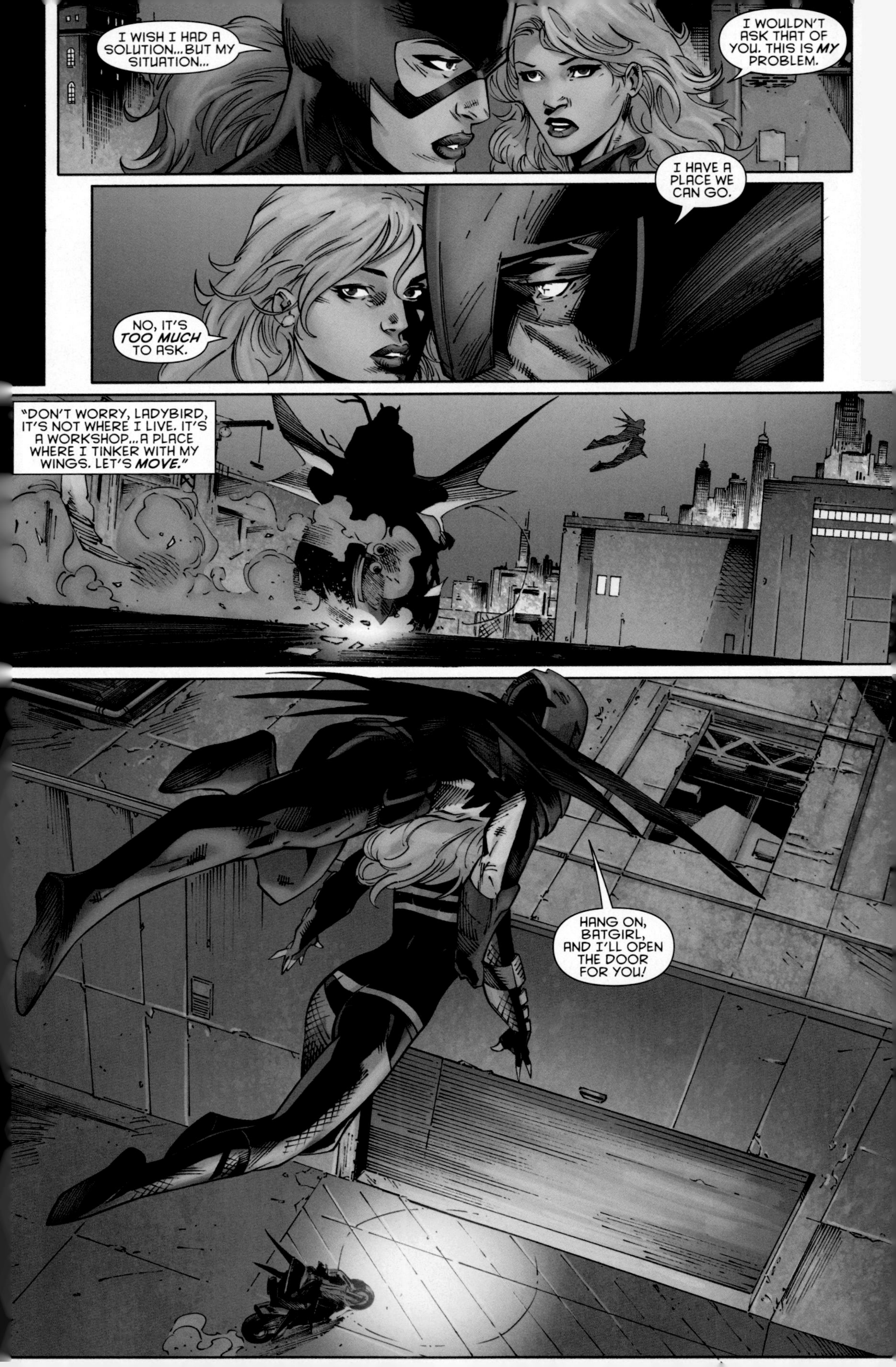

I WISH I HAD A SOLUTION...BUT MY SITUATION...
I WOULDN'T ASK THAT OF YOU. THIS IS MY PROBLEM.
I HAVE A PLACE WE CAN GO.
NO, IT'S TOO MUCH TO ASK.
"DON'T WORRY, LADYBIRD, IT'S NOT WHERE I LIVE. IT'S A WORKSHOP...A PLACE WHERE I TINKER WITH MY WINGS. LET'S MOVE."
HANG ON, BATGIRL, AND I'LL OPEN THE DOOR FOR YOU!

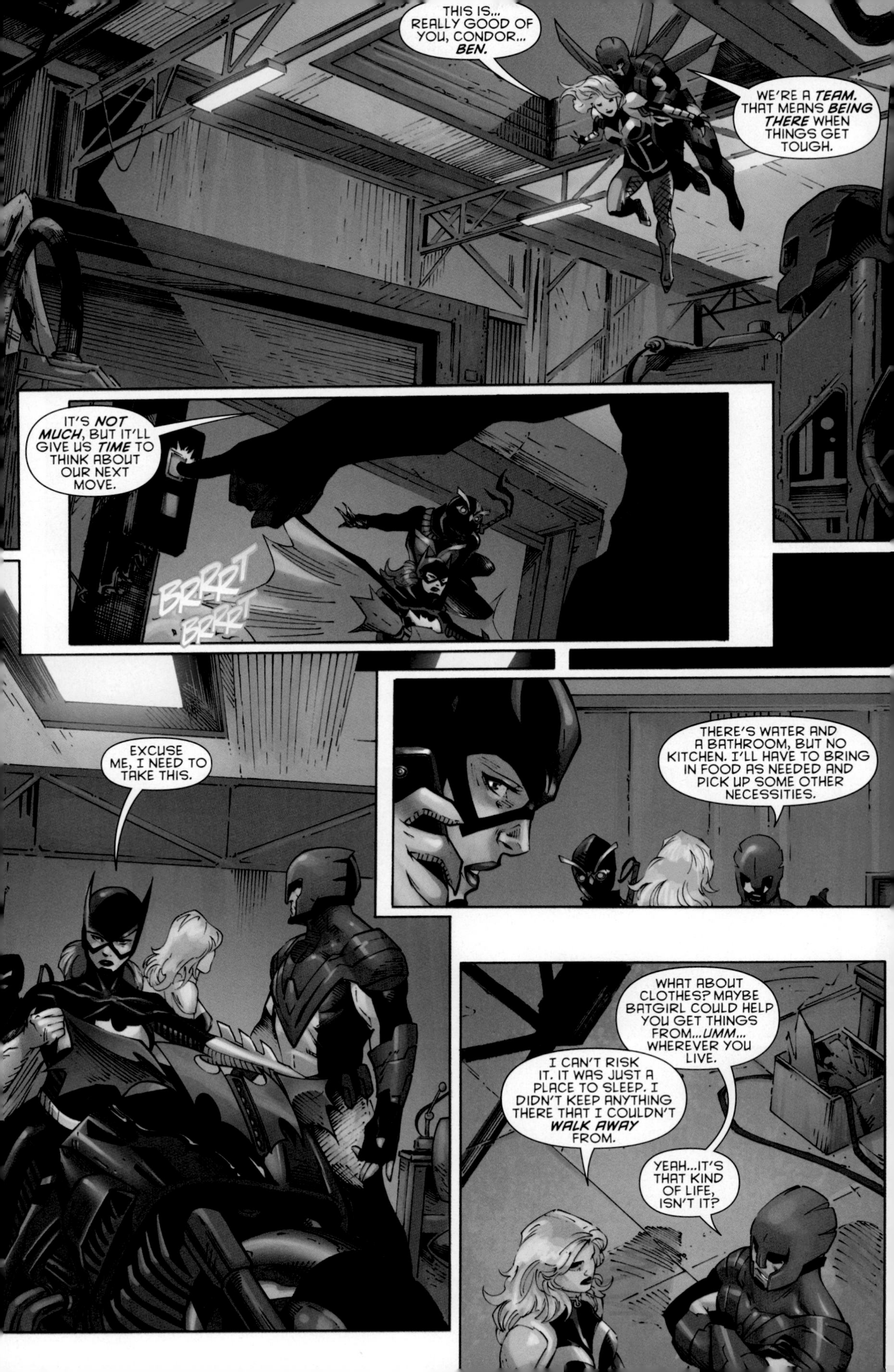
THIS IS... REALLY GOOD OF YOU, CONDOR... BEN.
WE'RE A TEAM. THAT MEANS BEING THERE WHEN THINGS GET TOUGH.
IT'S NOT MUCH, BUT IT'LL GIVE US TIME TO THINK ABOUT OUR NEXT MOVE.
BRRRT BRRRT
THERE'S WATER AND A BATHROOM, BUT NO KITCHEN. I'LL HAVE TO BRING IN FOOD AS NEEDED AND PICK UP SOME OTHER NECESSITIES.
EXCUSE ME, I NEED TO TAKE THIS.
WHAT ABOUT CLOTHES? MAYBE BATGIRL COULD HELP YOU GET THINGS FROM...UMM... WHEREVER YOU LIVE.
I CAN'T RISK IT. IT WAS JUST A PLACE TO SLEEP. I DIDN'T KEEP ANYTHING THERE THAT I COULDN'T WALK AWAY FROM.
YEAH...IT'S THAT KIND OF LIFE, ISN'T IT?

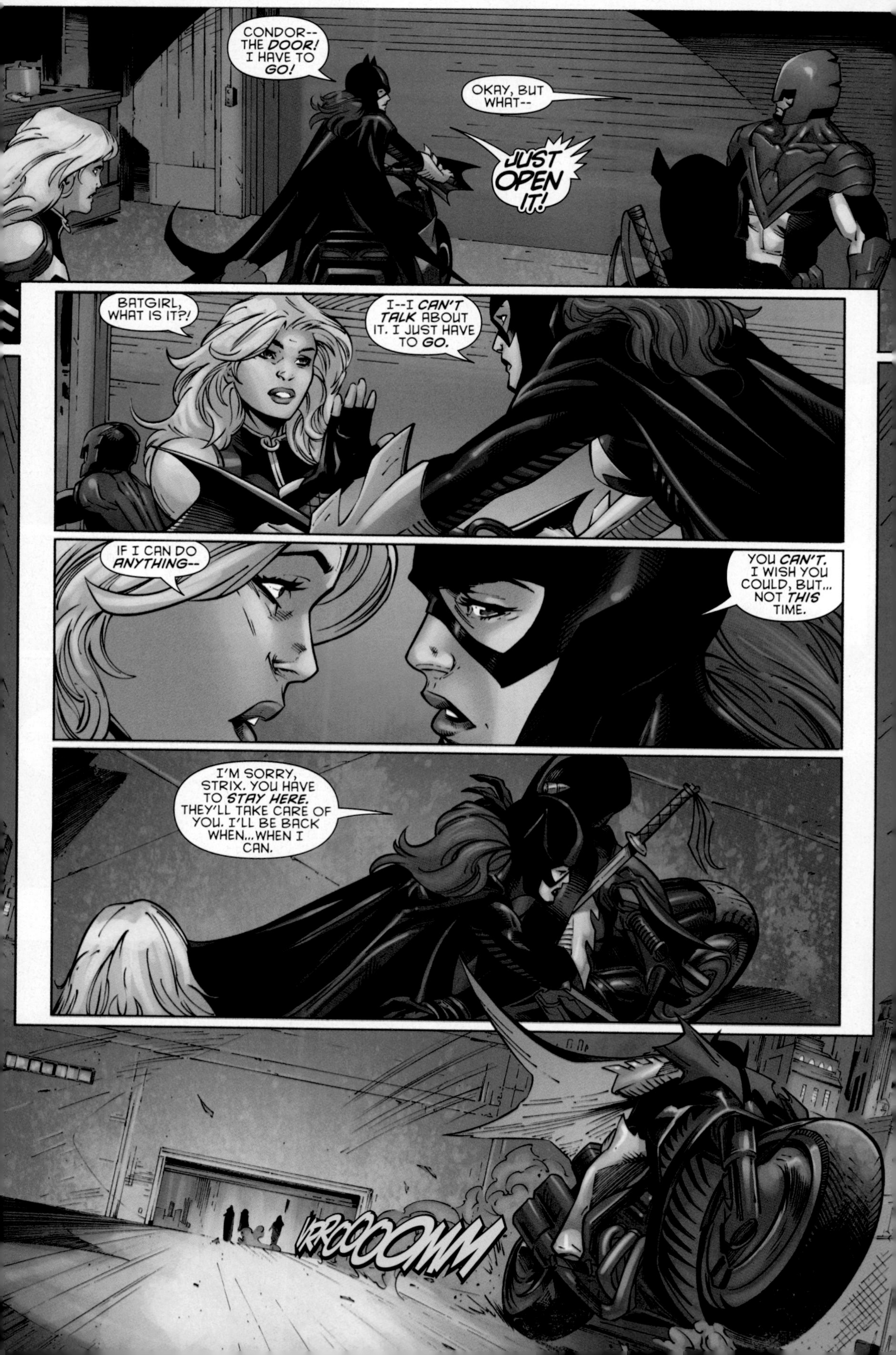
CONDOR-- THE DOOR! I HAVE TO GO!
OKAY, BUT WHAT--
JUST OPEN IT!
BATGIRL, WHAT IS IT?!
I--I CAN'T TALK ABOUT IT. I JUST HAVE TO GO.
IF I CAN DO ANYTHING--
YOU CAN'T. I WISH YOU COULD, BUT... NOT THIS TIME.
I'M SORRY, STRIX. YOU HAVE TO STAY HERE. THEY'LL TAKE CARE OF YOU. I'LL BE BACK WHEN...WHEN I CAN.
VRROOOOOMM

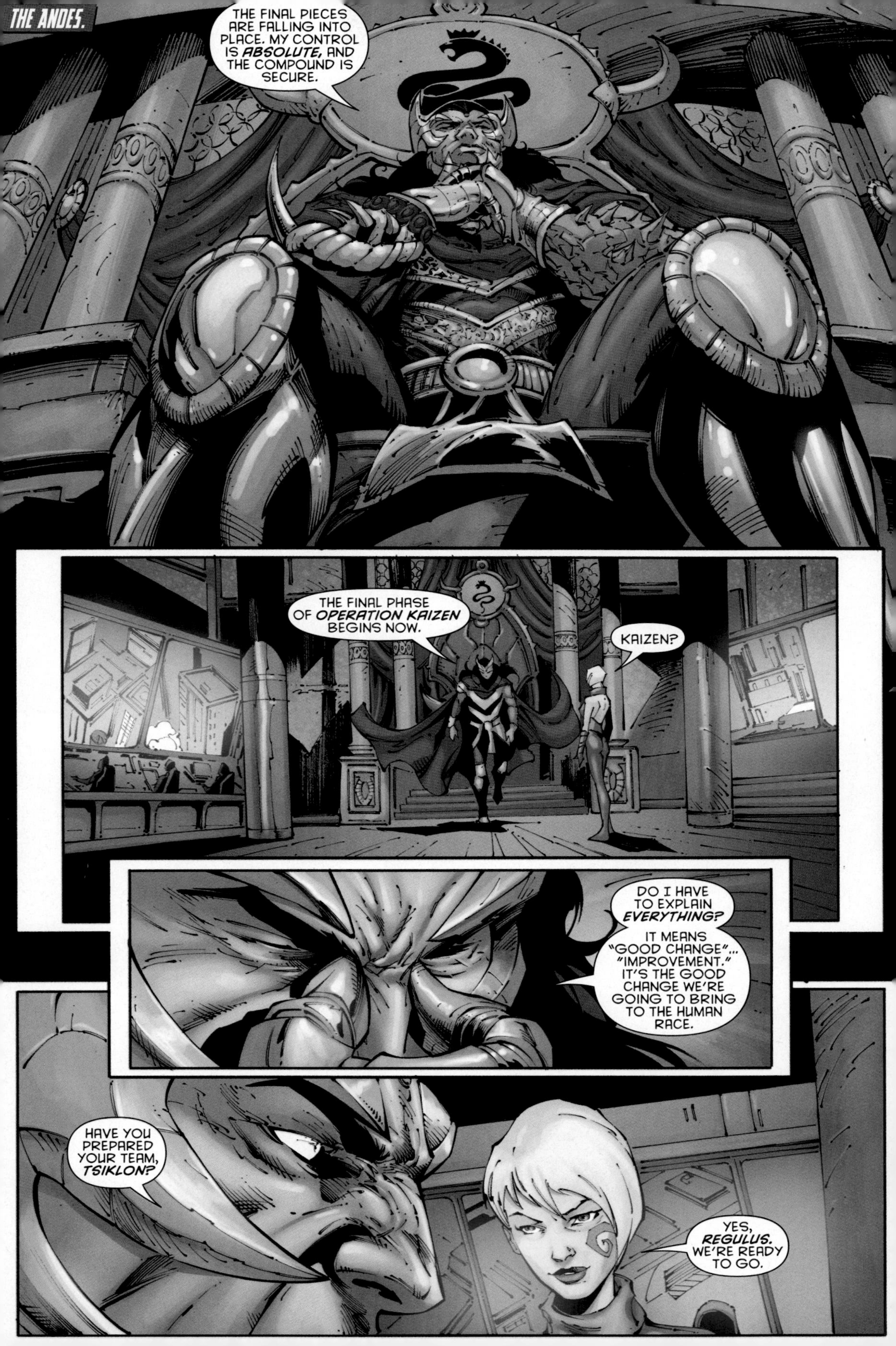
THE ANDES.
THE FINAL PIECES ARE FALLING INTO PLACE. MY CONTROL IS ABSOLUTE, AND THE COMPOUND IS SECURE.
THE FINAL PHASE OF OPERATION KAIZEN BEGINS NOW.
KAIZEN?
DO I HAVE TO EXPLAIN EVERYTHING?
IT MEANS "GOOD CHANGE"... "IMPROVEMENT." IT'S THE GOOD CHANGE WE'RE GOING TO BRING TO THE HUMAN RACE.
HAVE YOU PREPARED YOUR TEAM, TSIKLON?
YES, REGULUS. WE'RE READY TO GO.

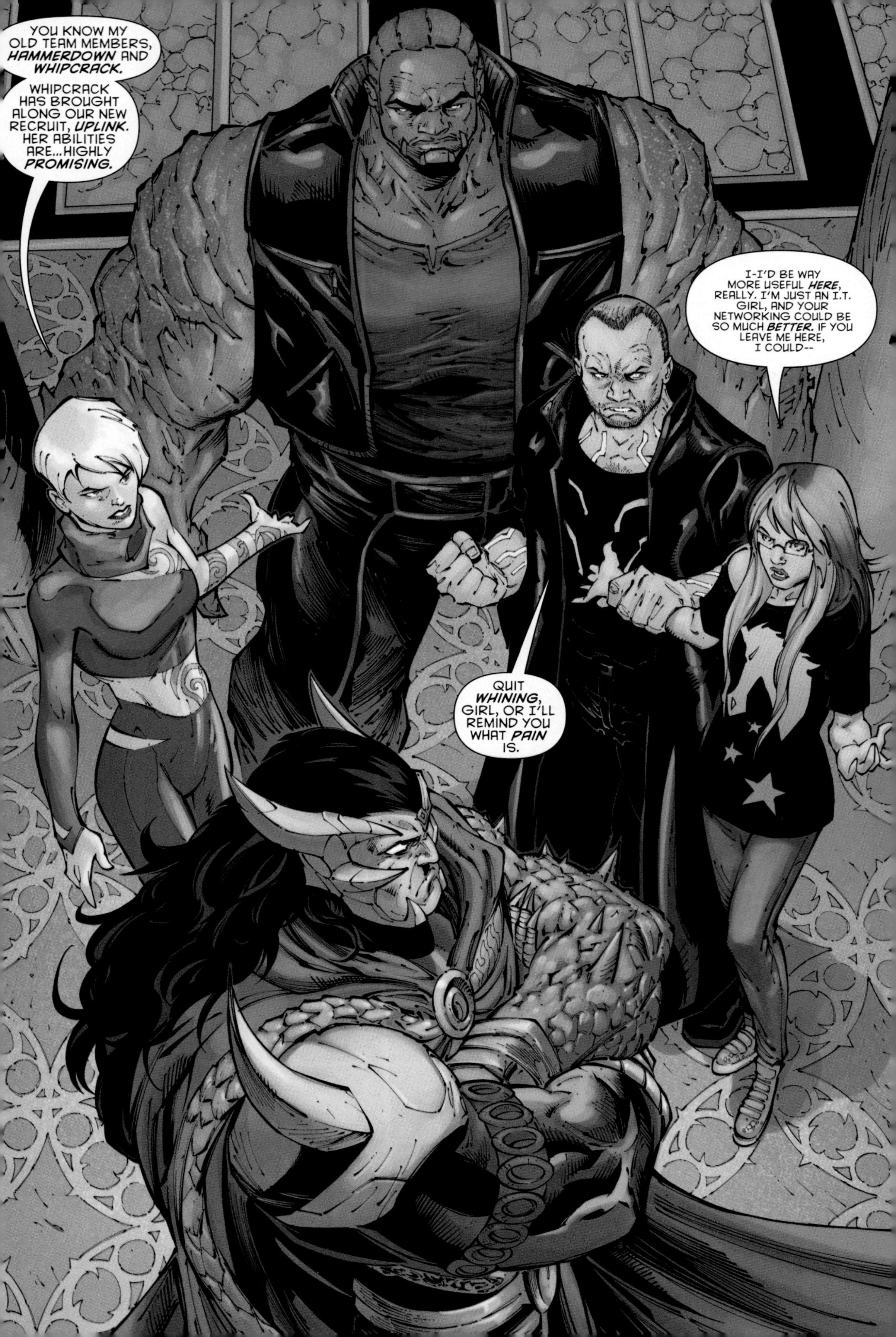
YOU KNOW MY OLD TEAM MEMBERS, HAMMERDOWN AND WHIPCRACK.
WHIPCRACK HAS BROUGHT ALONG OUR NEW RECRUIT, UPLINK. HER ABILITIES ARE...HIGHLY PROMISING.
I-I'D BE WAY MORE USEFUL HERE, REALLY. I'M JUST AN I.T. GIRL, AND YOUR NETWORKING COULD BE SO MUCH BETTER. IF YOU LEAVE ME HERE, I COULD--
QUIT WHINING, GIRL, OR I'LL REMIND YOU WHAT PAIN IS.

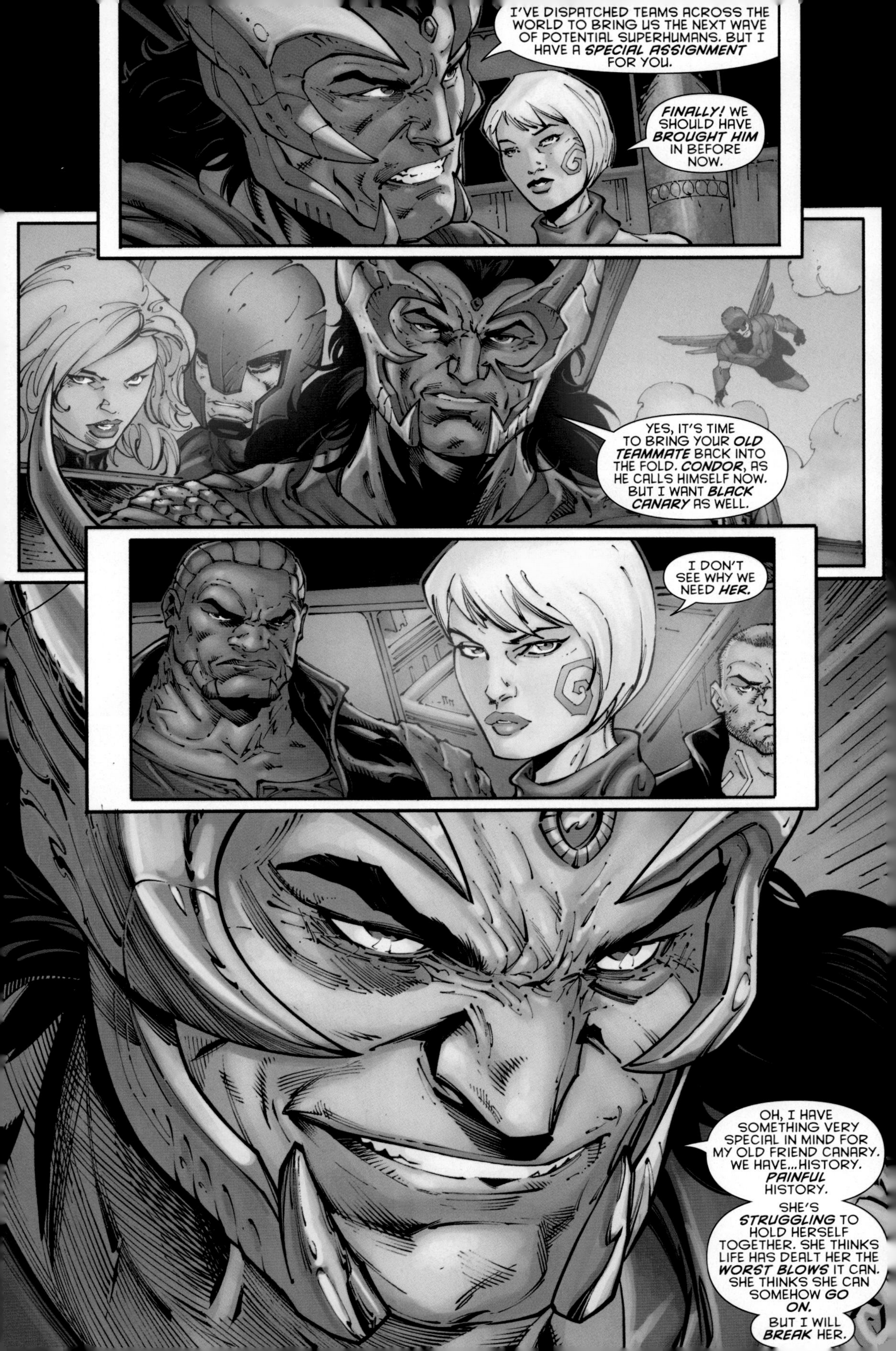
I'VE DISPATCHED TEAMS ACROSS THE WORLD TO BRING US THE NEXT WAVE OF POTENTIAL SUPERHUMANS. BUT I HAVE A SPECIAL ASSIGNMENT FOR YOU.
FINALLY! WE SHOULD HAVE BROUGHT HIM IN BEFORE NOW.
YES, IT'S TIME TO BRING YOUR OLD TEAMMATE BACK INTO THE FOLD. CONDOR, AS HE CALLS HIMSELF NOW. BUT I WANT BLACK CANARY AS WELL.
I DON'T SEE WHY WE NEED HER.
OH, I HAVE SOMETHING VERY SPECIAL IN MIND FOR MY OLD FRIEND CANARY. WE HAVE...HISTORY. PAINFUL HISTORY.
SHE'S STRUGGLING TO HOLD HERSELF TOGETHER. SHE THINKS LIFE HAS DEALT HER THE WORST BLOWS IT CAN. SHE THINKS SHE CAN SOMEHOW GO ON.
BUT I WILL BREAK HER.

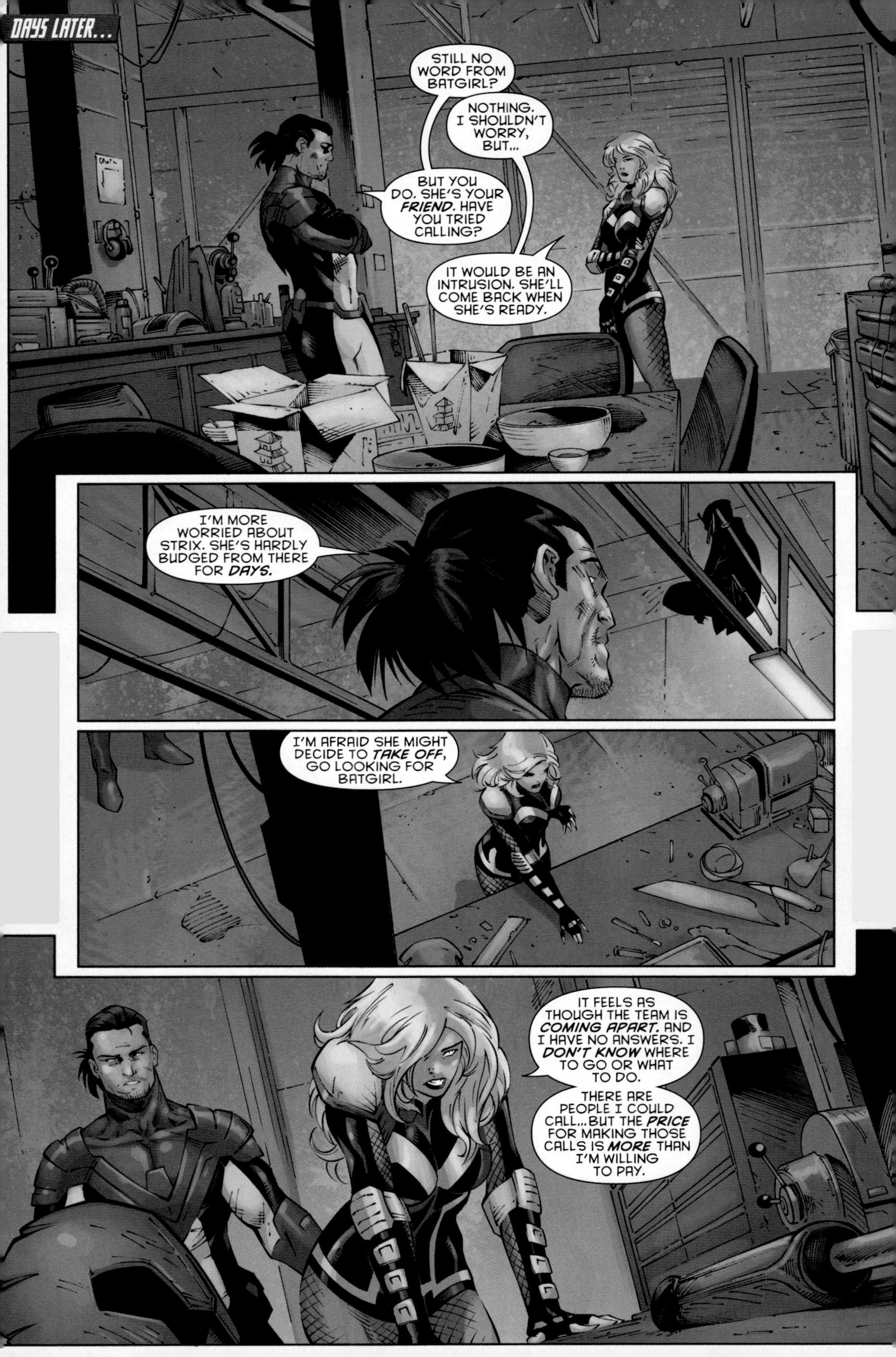
DAYS LATER...
STILL NO WORD FROM BATGIRL?
NOTHING. I SHOULDN'T WORRY, BUT...
BUT YOU DO. SHE'S YOUR *FRIEND.* HAVE YOU TRIED CALLING?
IT WOULD BE AN INTRUSION. SHE'LL COME BACK WHEN SHE'S READY.
I'M MORE WORRIED ABOUT STRIX. SHE'S HARDLY BUDGED FROM THERE FOR *DAYS.*
I'M AFRAID SHE MIGHT DECIDE TO *TAKE OFF,* GO LOOKING FOR BATGIRL.
IT FEELS AS THOUGH THE TEAM IS *COMING APART.* AND I HAVE NO ANSWERS. I *DON'T KNOW* WHERE TO GO OR WHAT TO DO.
THERE ARE PEOPLE I COULD CALL...BUT THE *PRICE* FOR MAKING THOSE CALLS IS *MORE* THAN I'M WILLING TO PAY.

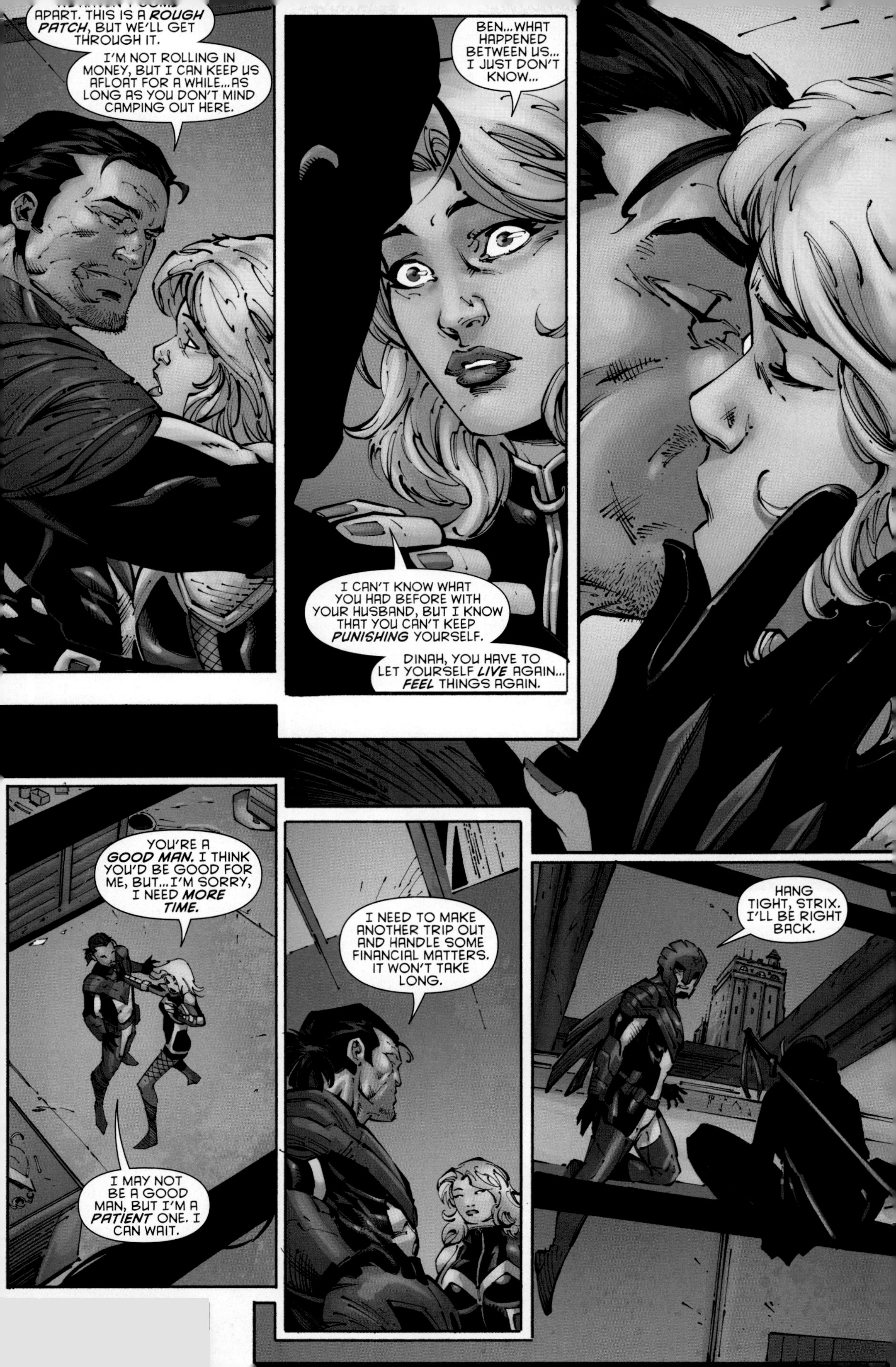

APART. THIS IS A ROUGH PATCH, BUT WE'LL GET THROUGH IT.
I'M NOT ROLLING IN MONEY, BUT I CAN KEEP US AFLOAT FOR A WHILE...AS LONG AS YOU DON'T MIND CAMPING OUT HERE.
BEN...WHAT HAPPENED BETWEEN US... I JUST DON'T KNOW...
I CAN'T KNOW WHAT YOU HAD BEFORE WITH YOUR HUSBAND, BUT I KNOW THAT YOU CAN'T KEEP PUNISHING YOURSELF.
DINAH, YOU HAVE TO LET YOURSELF LIVE AGAIN... FEEL THINGS AGAIN.
YOU'RE A GOOD MAN. I THINK YOU'D BE GOOD FOR ME, BUT...I'M SORRY, I NEED MORE TIME.
I MAY NOT BE A GOOD MAN, BUT I'M A PATIENT ONE. I CAN WAIT.
I NEED TO MAKE ANOTHER TRIP OUT AND HANDLE SOME FINANCIAL MATTERS. IT WON'T TAKE LONG.
HANG TIGHT, STRIX. I'LL BE RIGHT BACK.

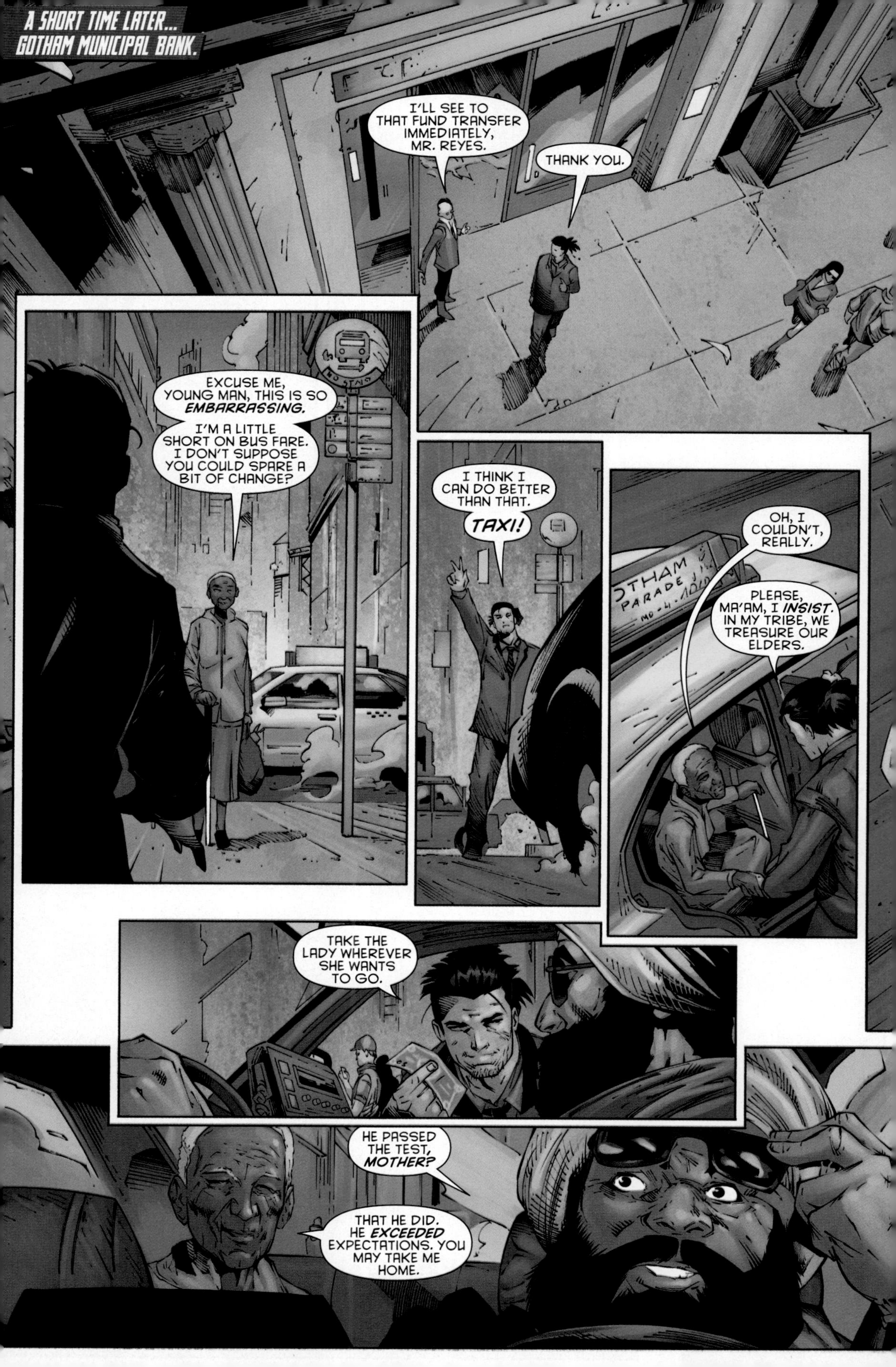
A SHORT TIME LATER...
GOTHAM MUNICIPAL BANK.
I'LL SEE TO THAT FUND TRANSFER IMMEDIATELY, MR. REYES.
THANK YOU.
EXCUSE ME, YOUNG MAN, THIS IS SO *EMBARRASSING.*
I'M A LITTLE SHORT ON BUS FARE. I DON'T SUPPOSE YOU COULD SPARE A BIT OF CHANGE?
I THINK I CAN DO BETTER THAN THAT.
TAXI!
OH, I COULDN'T, REALLY.
PLEASE, MA'AM, I *INSIST*. IN MY TRIBE, WE TREASURE OUR ELDERS.
TAKE THE LADY WHEREVER SHE WANTS TO GO.
HE PASSED THE TEST, *MOTHER?*
THAT HE DID. HE *EXCEEDED* EXPECTATIONS. YOU MAY TAKE ME HOME.

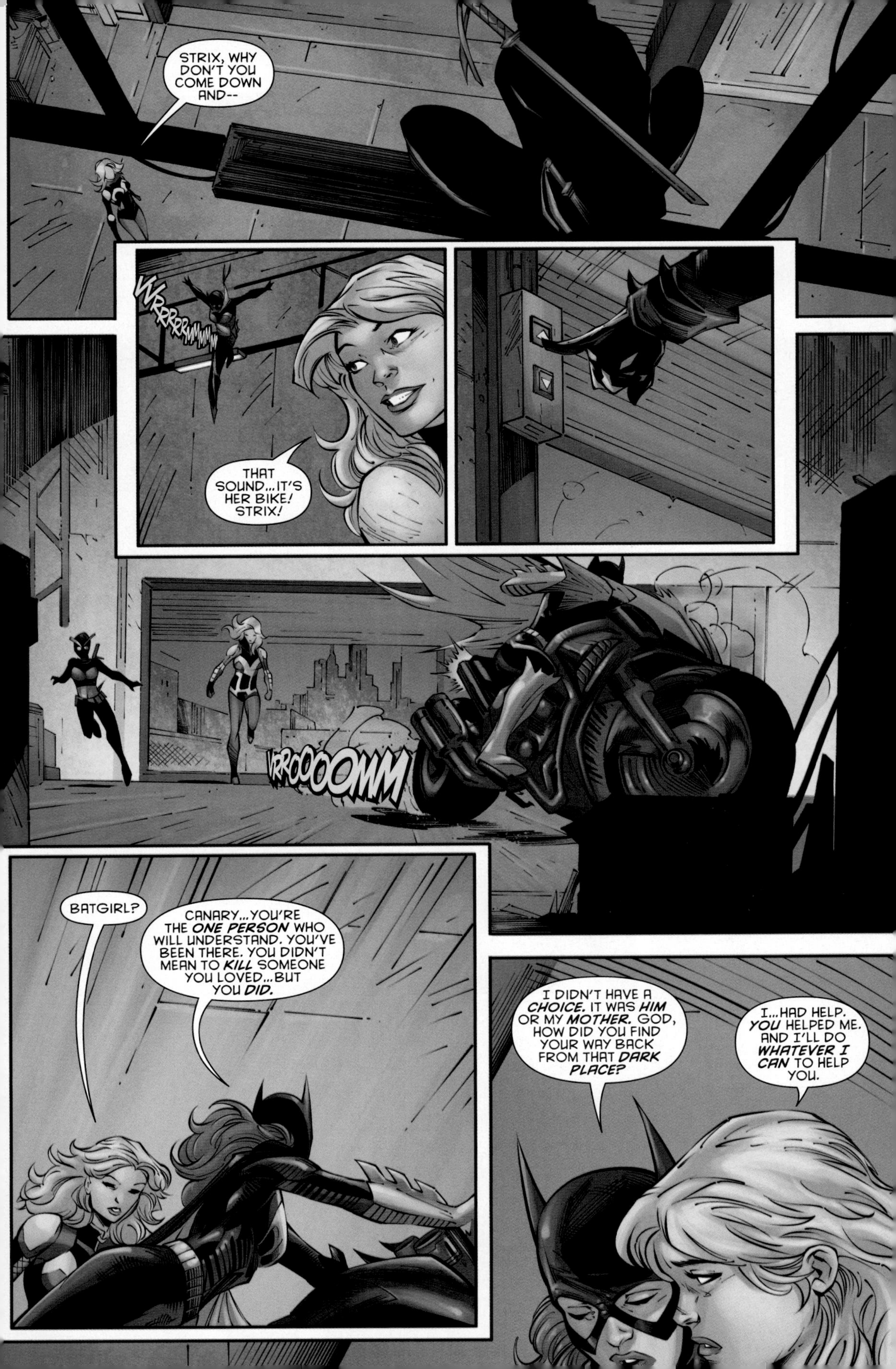
STRIX, WHY DON'T YOU COME DOWN AND--
VVRRRRRMMMM
THAT SOUND...IT'S HER BIKE! STRIX!
VRROOOOOMM
BATGIRL?
CANARY...YOU'RE THE ONE PERSON WHO WILL UNDERSTAND. YOU'VE BEEN THERE. YOU DIDN'T MEAN TO KILL SOMEONE YOU LOVED...BUT YOU DID.
I DIDN'T HAVE A CHOICE. IT WAS HIM OR MY MOTHER. GOD, HOW DID YOU FIND YOUR WAY BACK FROM THAT DARK PLACE?
I...HAD HELP. YOU HELPED ME. AND I'LL DO WHATEVER I CAN TO HELP YOU.

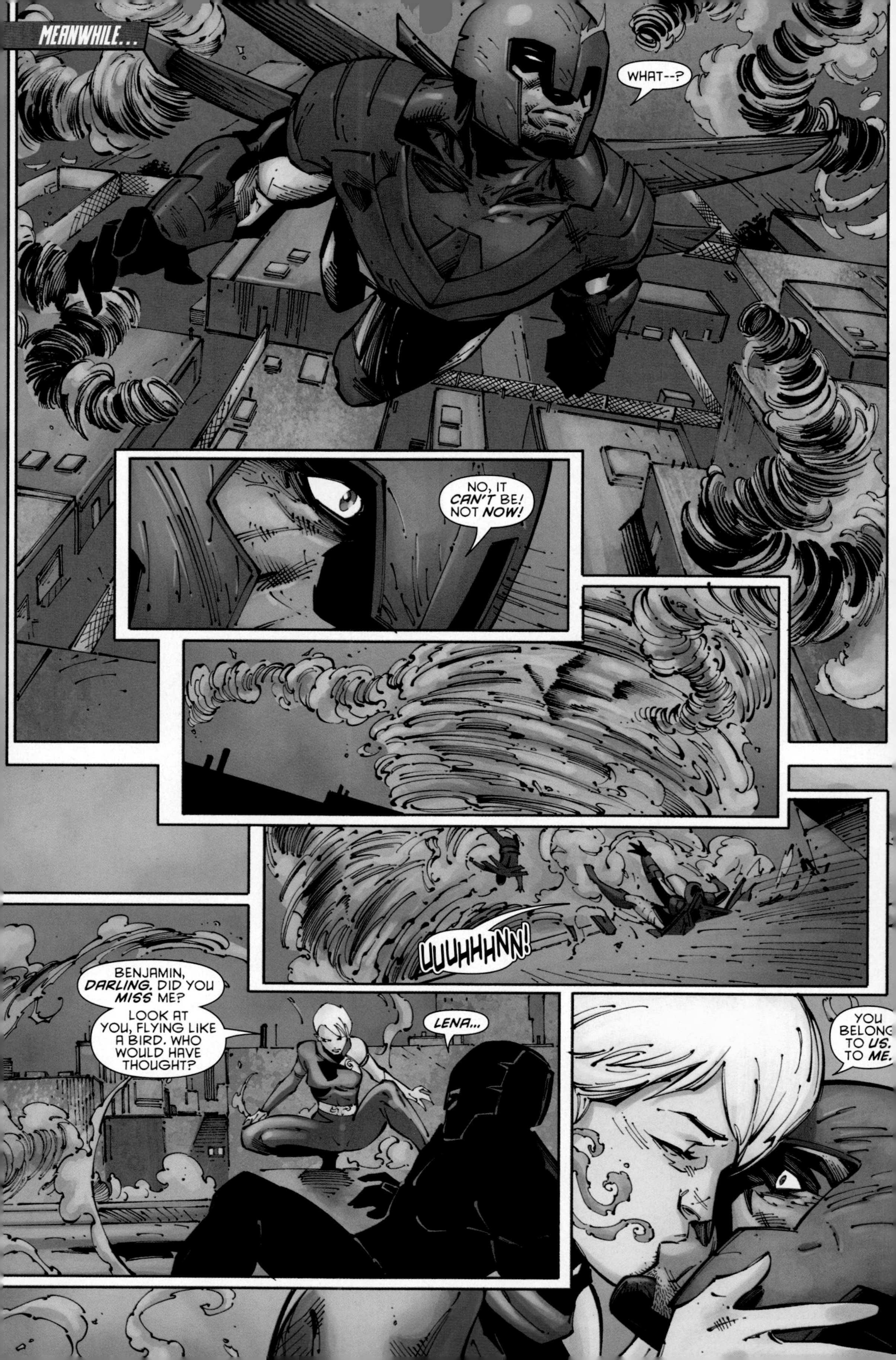
MEANWHILE...
WHAT--?
NO, IT CAN'T BE! NOT NOW!
UUUHHHNN!
BENJAMIN, DARLING. DID YOU MISS ME?
LOOK AT YOU, FLYING LIKE A BIRD. WHO WOULD HAVE THOUGHT?
LENA...
YOU BELONG TO US. TO ME.

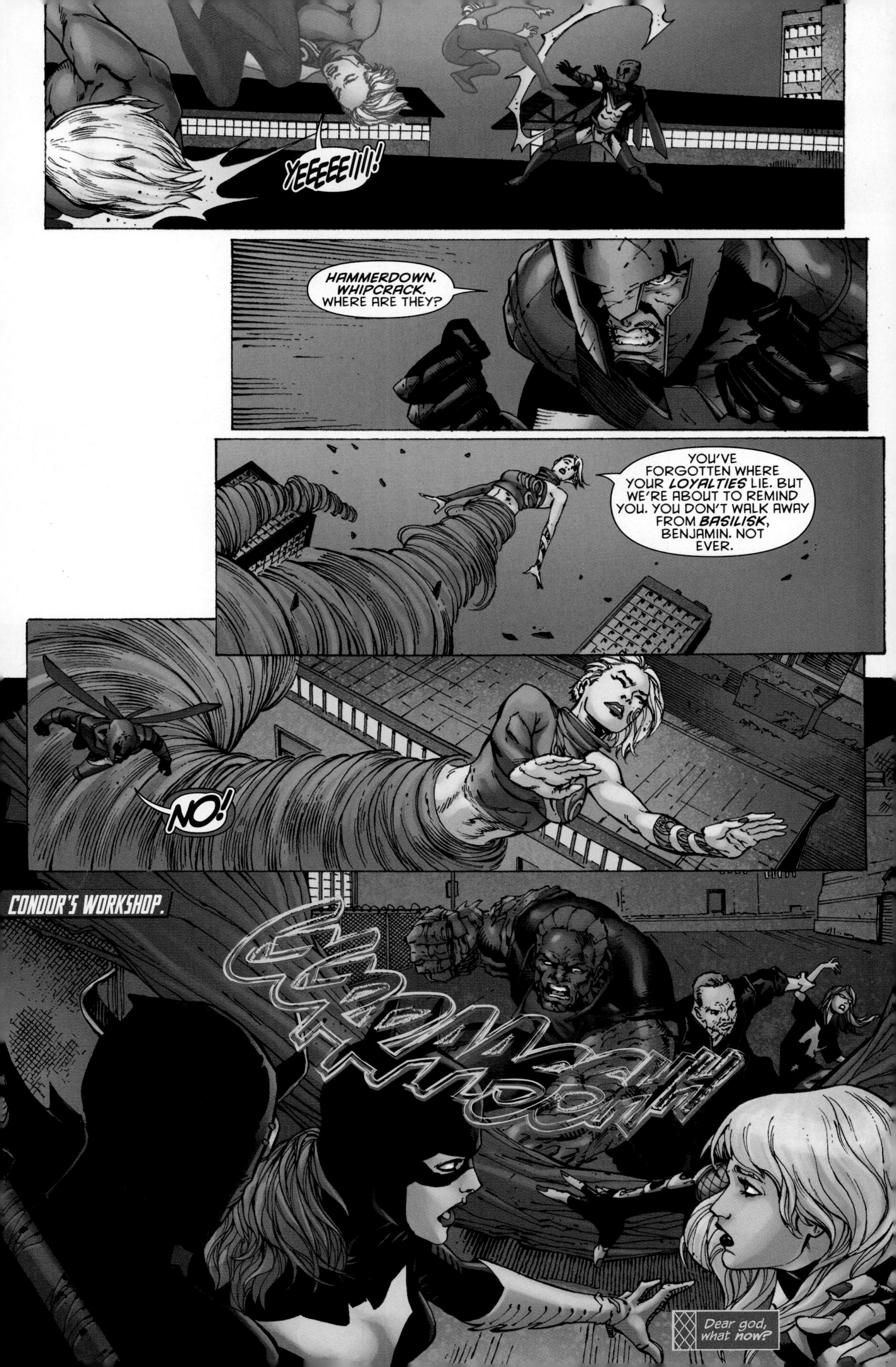
YEEEEE!!!!!
HAMMERDOWN. WHIPCRACK. WHERE ARE THEY?
YOU'VE FORGOTTEN WHERE YOUR LOYALTIES LIE. BUT WE'RE ABOUT TO REMIND YOU. YOU DON'T WALK AWAY FROM BASILISK, BENJAMIN. NOT EVER.
NO!
CONDOR'S WORKSHOP.
Dear god, what now?

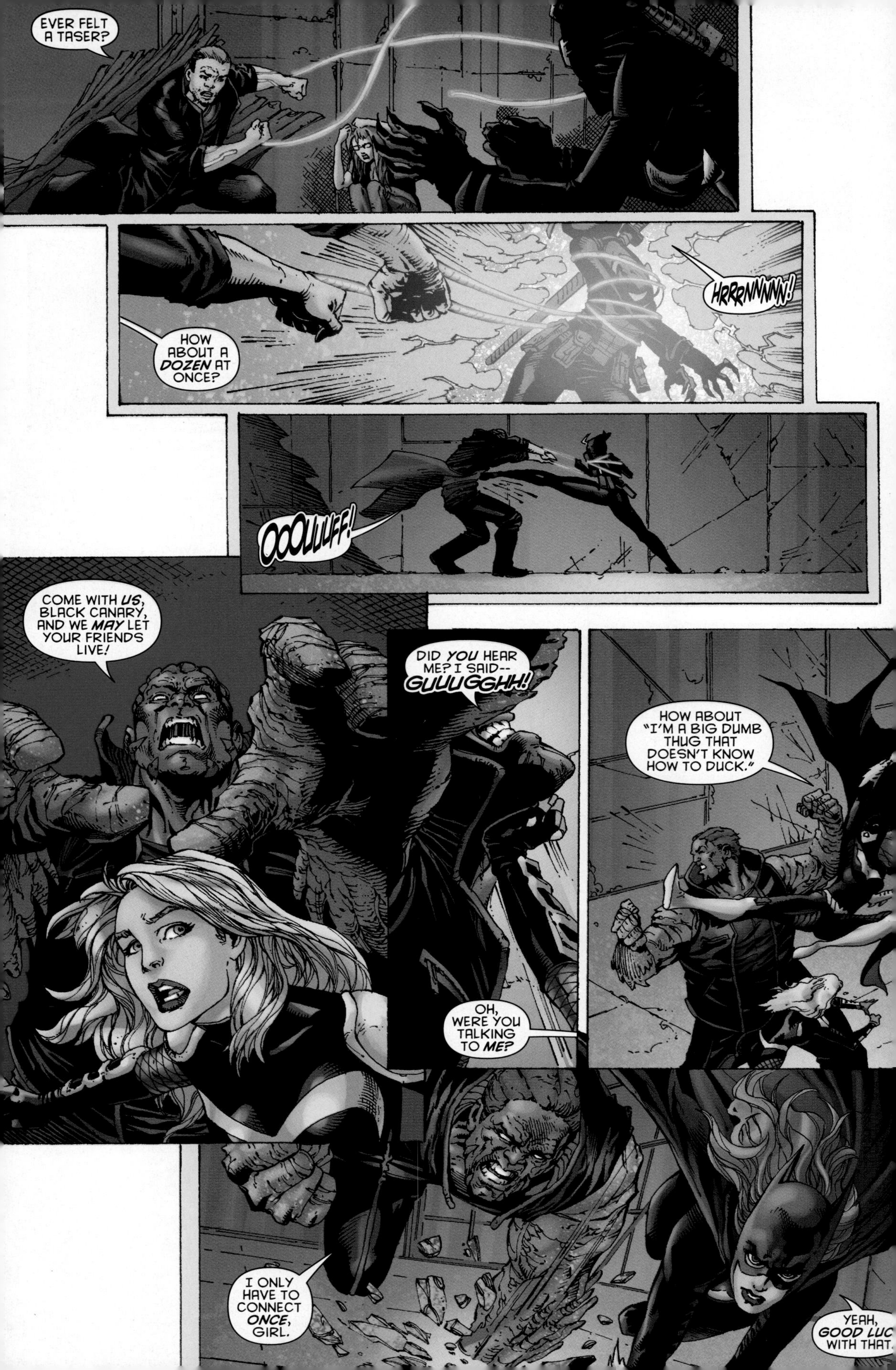
EVER FELT A TASER?
HOW ABOUT A *DOZEN* AT ONCE?
HRRRNNNNN!
OOOLLLUFF!
COME WITH *US*, BLACK CANARY, AND WE *MAY* LET YOUR FRIENDS LIVE!
DID *YOU* HEAR ME? I SAID-- GUUUGGHH!
OH, WERE YOU TALKING TO *ME*?
HOW ABOUT "I'M A BIG DUMB THUG THAT DOESN'T KNOW HOW TO DUCK."
I ONLY HAVE TO CONNECT *ONCE*, GIRL.
YEAH, *GOOD LUC* WITH THAT.

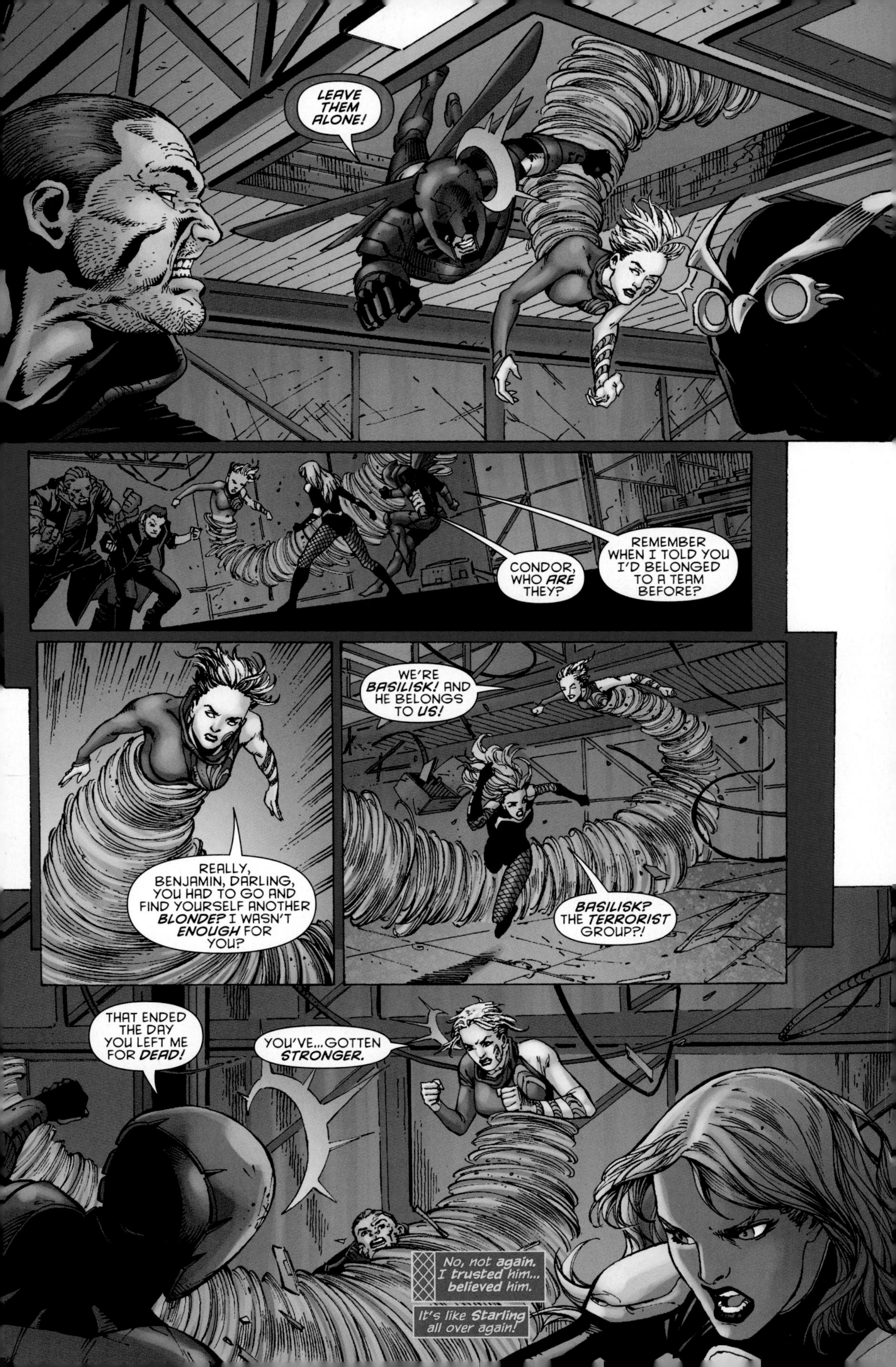
LEAVE THEM ALONE!
CONDOR, WHO *ARE* THEY?
REMEMBER WHEN I TOLD YOU I'D BELONGED TO A TEAM BEFORE?
REALLY, BENJAMIN, DARLING, YOU HAD TO GO AND FIND YOURSELF ANOTHER *BLONDE?* I WASN'T *ENOUGH* FOR YOU?
WE'RE *BASILISK!* AND HE BELONGS TO *US!*
BASILISK? THE *TERRORIST* GROUP?!
THAT ENDED THE DAY YOU LEFT ME FOR *DEAD!*
YOU'VE...GOTTEN *STRONGER.*
No, not *again.* I trusted him... believed him.
It's like *Starling* all over again!

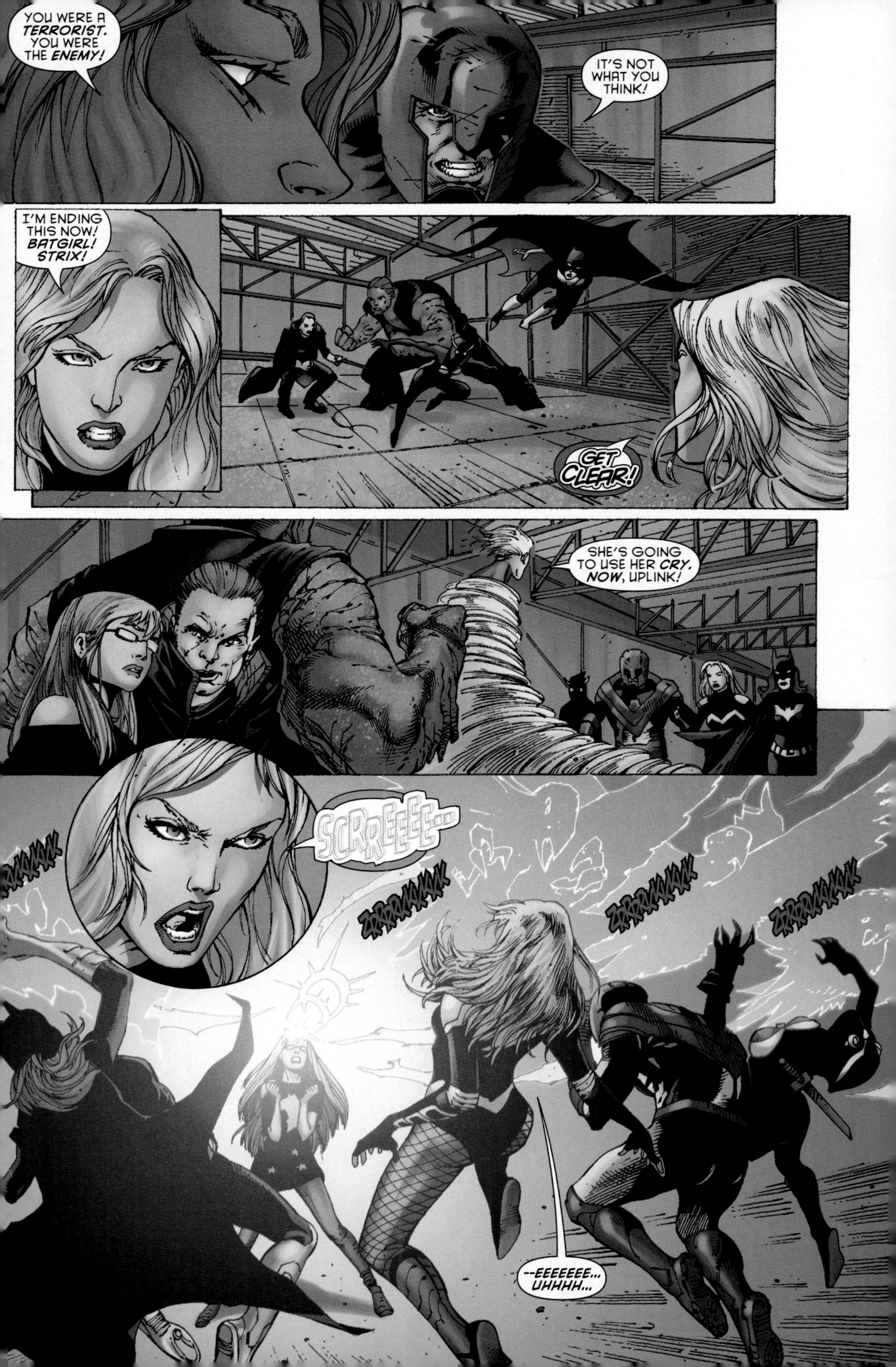
YOU WERE A TERRORIST. YOU WERE THE ENEMY!
IT'S NOT WHAT YOU THINK!
I'M ENDING THIS NOW! BATGIRL! STRIX!
GET CLEAR!
SHE'S GOING TO USE HER CRY. NOW, UPLINK!
SCRREEEEE...
ZRRRAKAKAKK
ZRRRAKAKAKK
ZRRRAKAKAKK
--EEEEEEE... UHHHH...

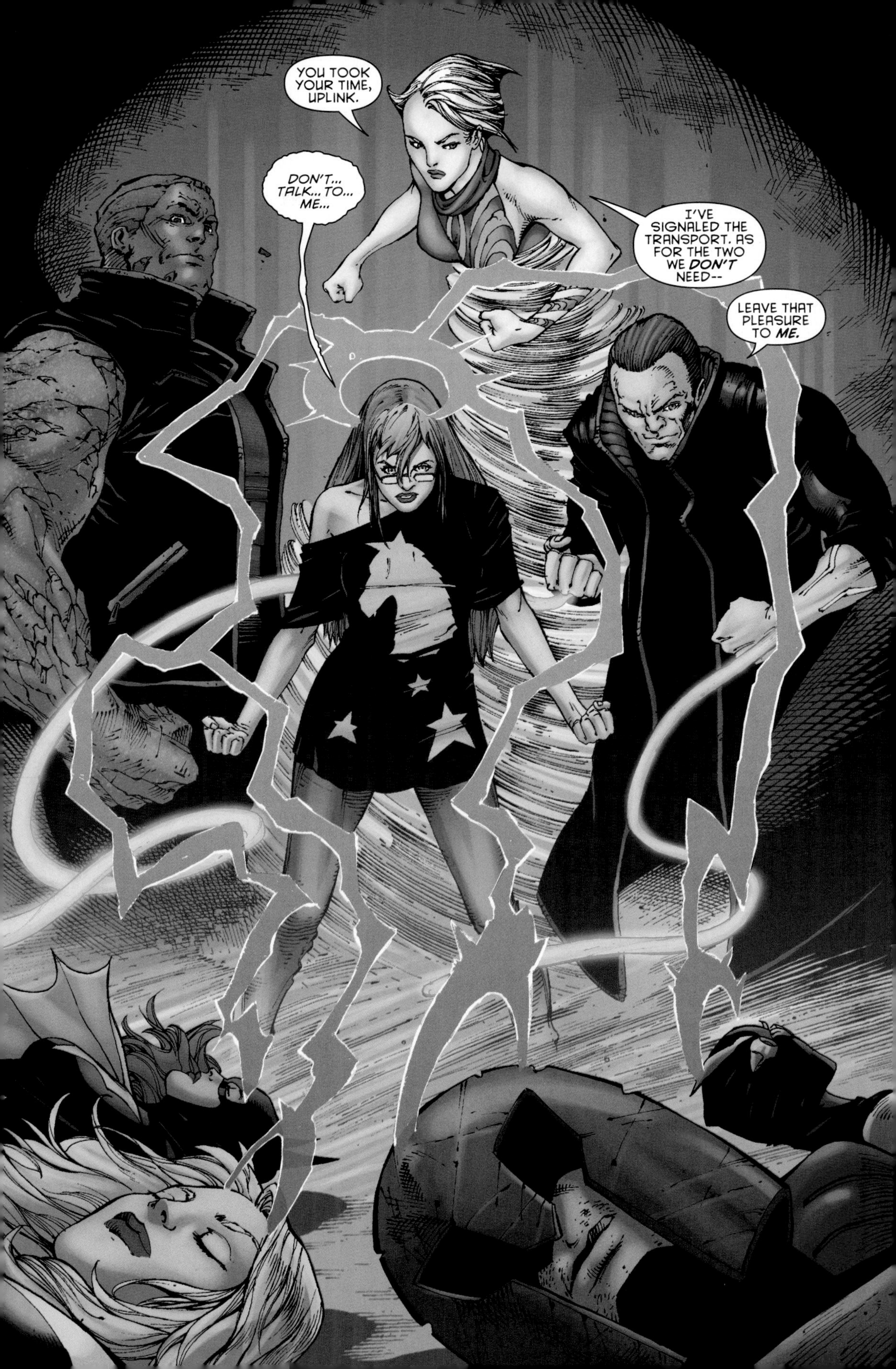
YOU TOOK YOUR TIME, UPLINK.
DON'T... TALK... TO... ME...
I'VE SIGNALED THE TRANSPORT. AS FOR THE TWO WE DON'T NEED--
LEAVE THAT PLEASURE TO ME.

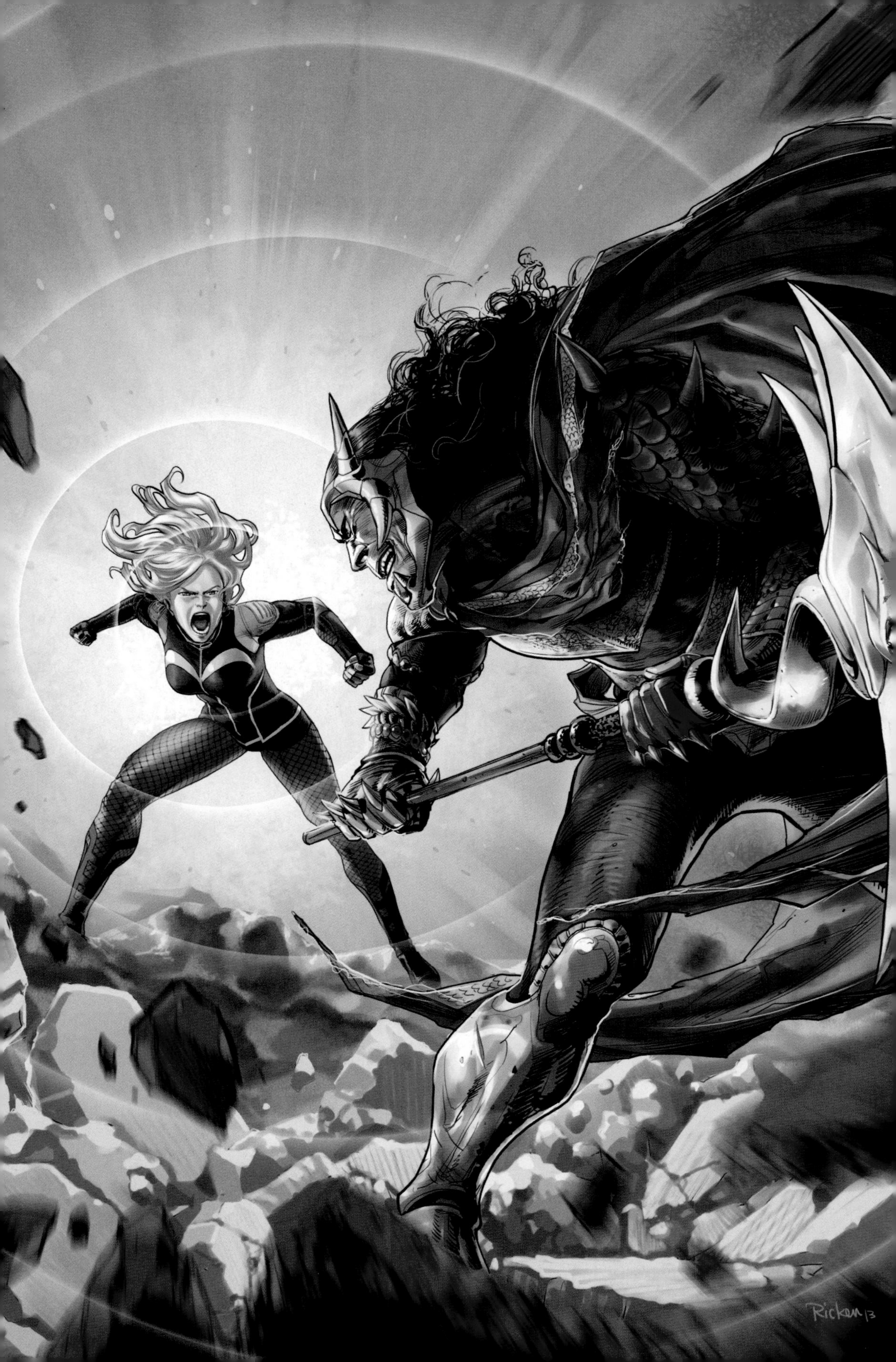
Rickon 13

DREAMS THAT NEVER WERE

CHRISTY MARX WRITER
ROMANO MOLENAAR PENCILS
SCOTT McDANIEL BREAKDOWNS
JONATHAN GLAPION INKS
CHRIS SOTOMAYOR COLORS
DEZI SIENTY LETTERS
RICKEN COVER

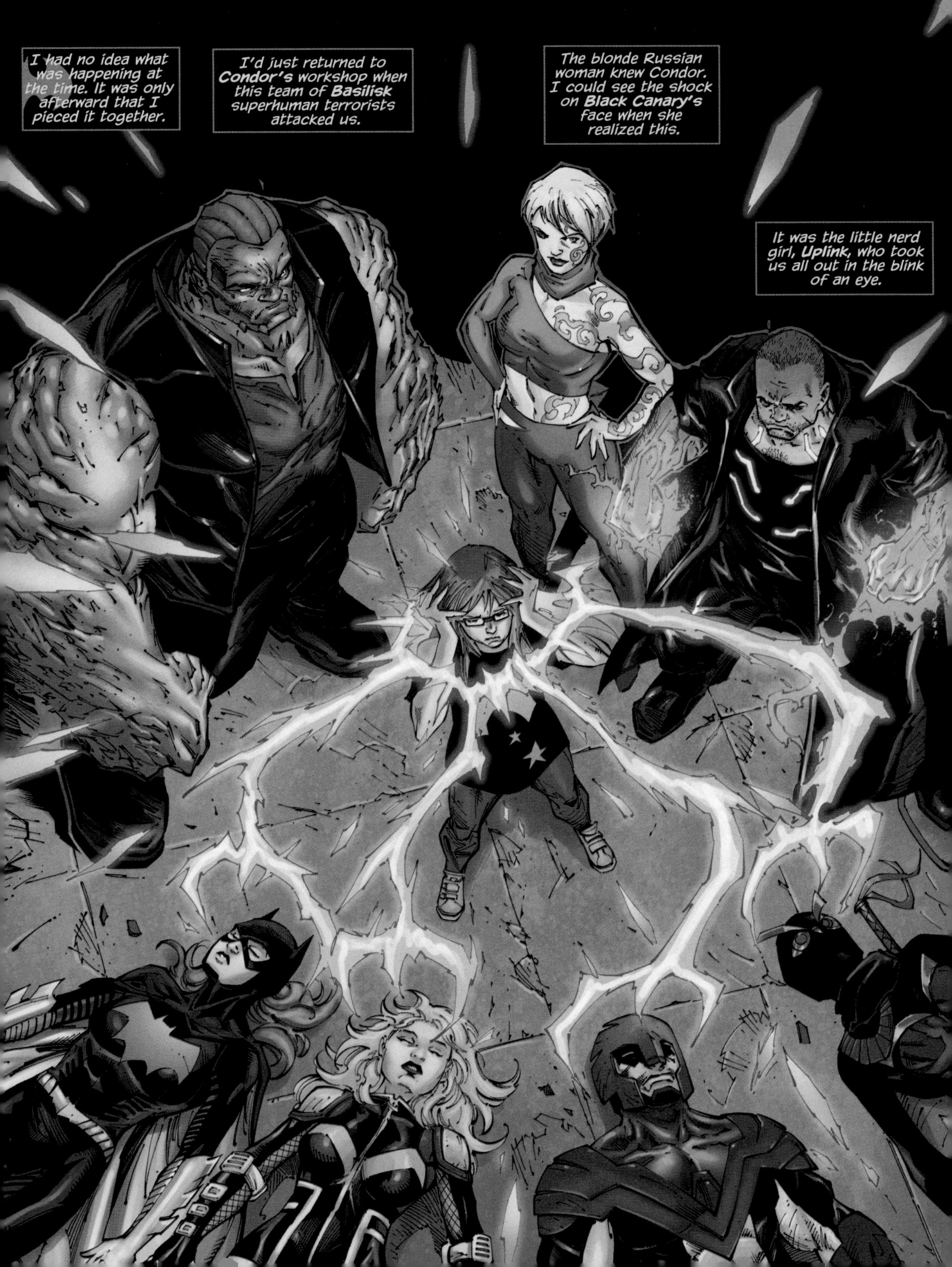

I had no idea what was happening at the time. It was only afterward that I pieced it together.
I'd just returned to Condor's workshop when this team of Basilisk superhuman terrorists attacked us.
The blonde Russian woman knew Condor. I could see the shock on Black Canary's face when she realized this.
It was the little nerd girl, Uplink, who took us all out in the blink of an eye.

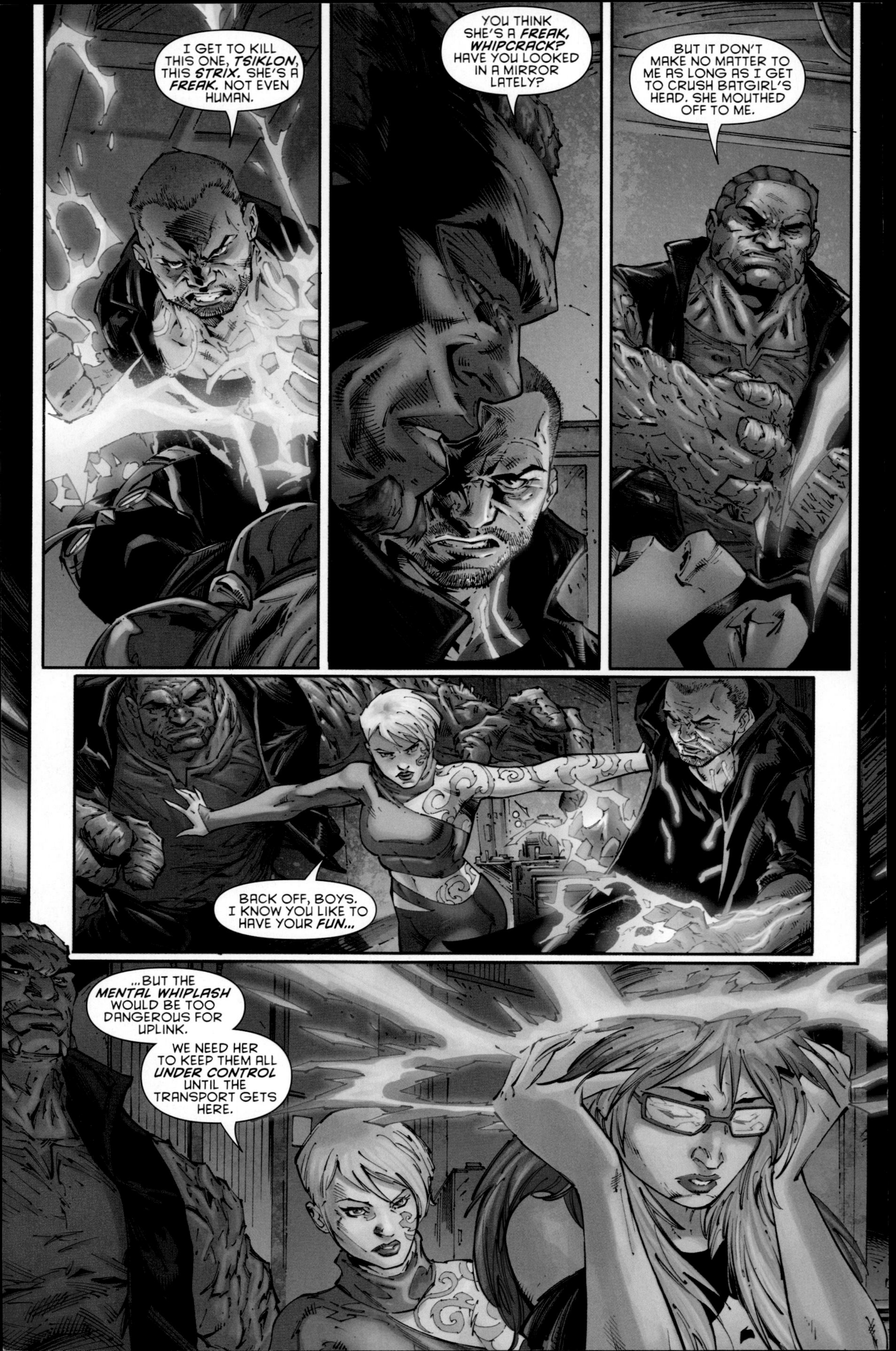
I GET TO KILL THIS ONE, TSIKLON, THIS STRIX. SHE'S A FREAK. NOT EVEN HUMAN.
YOU THINK SHE'S A FREAK, WHIPCRACK? HAVE YOU LOOKED IN A MIRROR LATELY?
BUT IT DON'T MAKE NO MATTER TO ME AS LONG AS I GET TO CRUSH BATGIRL'S HEAD. SHE MOUTHED OFF TO ME.
BACK OFF, BOYS. I KNOW YOU LIKE TO HAVE YOUR FUN...
...BUT THE MENTAL WHIPLASH WOULD BE TOO DANGEROUS FOR UPLINK.
WE NEED HER TO KEEP THEM ALL UNDER CONTROL UNTIL THE TRANSPORT GETS HERE.

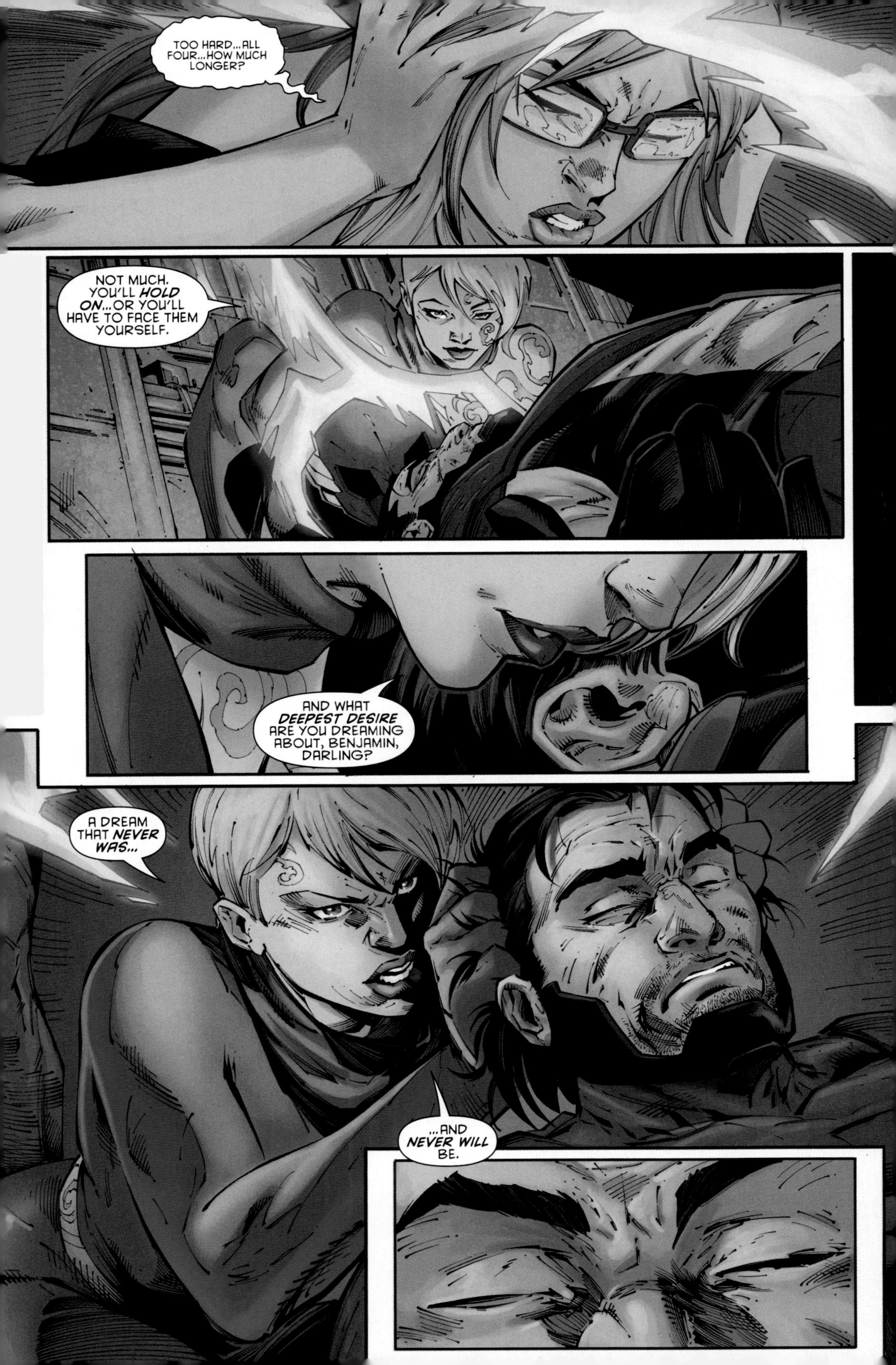
TOO HARD...ALL FOUR...HOW MUCH LONGER?
NOT MUCH. YOU'LL HOLD ON...OR YOU'LL HAVE TO FACE THEM YOURSELF.
AND WHAT DEEPEST DESIRE ARE YOU DREAMING ABOUT, BENJAMIN, DARLING?
A DREAM THAT NEVER WAS...
...AND NEVER WILL BE.

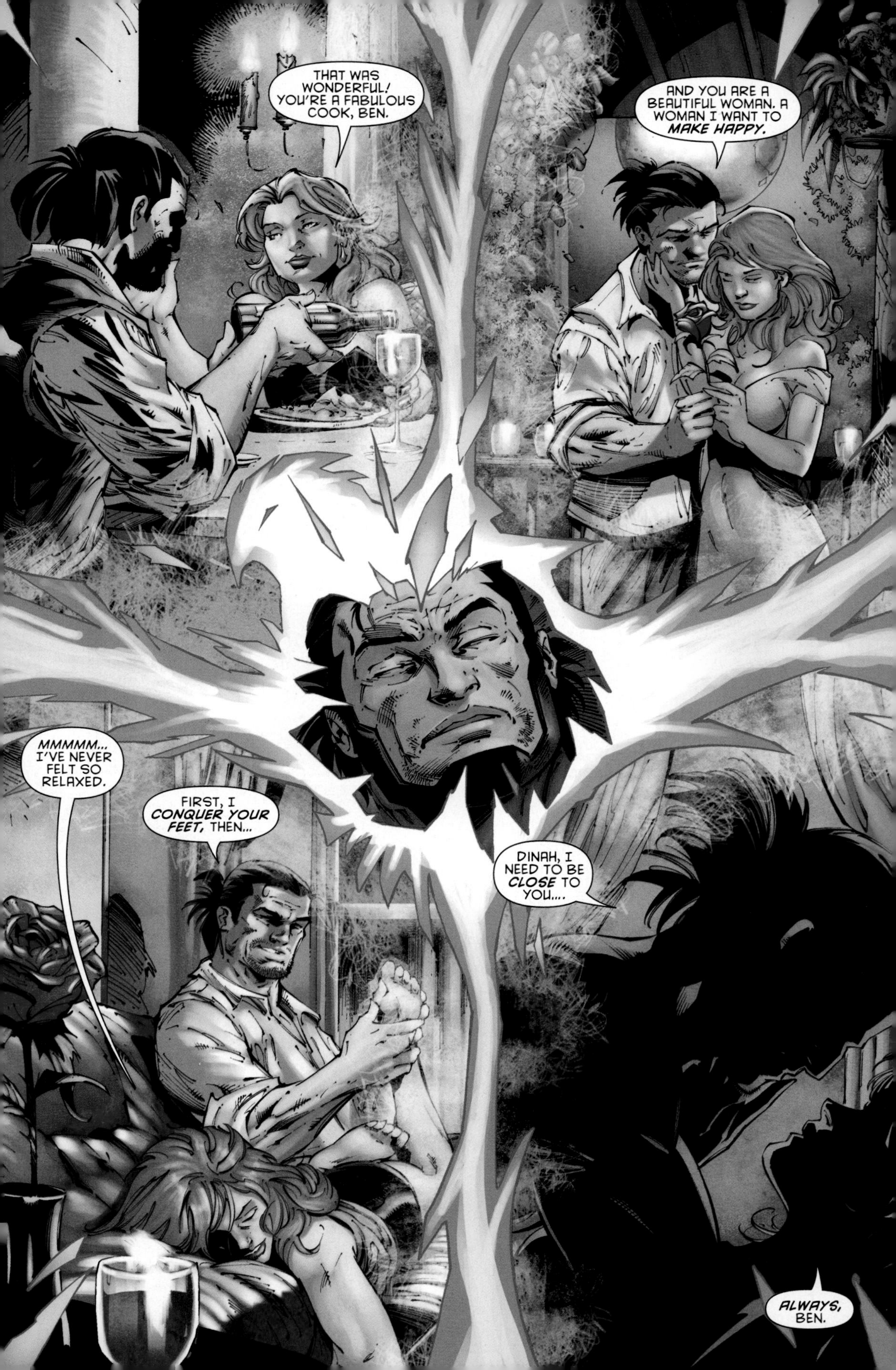
THAT WAS WONDERFUL! YOU'RE A FABULOUS COOK, BEN.
AND YOU ARE A BEAUTIFUL WOMAN. A WOMAN I WANT TO MAKE HAPPY.
MMMMM... I'VE NEVER FELT SO RELAXED.
FIRST, I CONQUER YOUR FEET, THEN...
DINAH, I NEED TO BE CLOSE TO YOU....
ALWAYS, BEN.

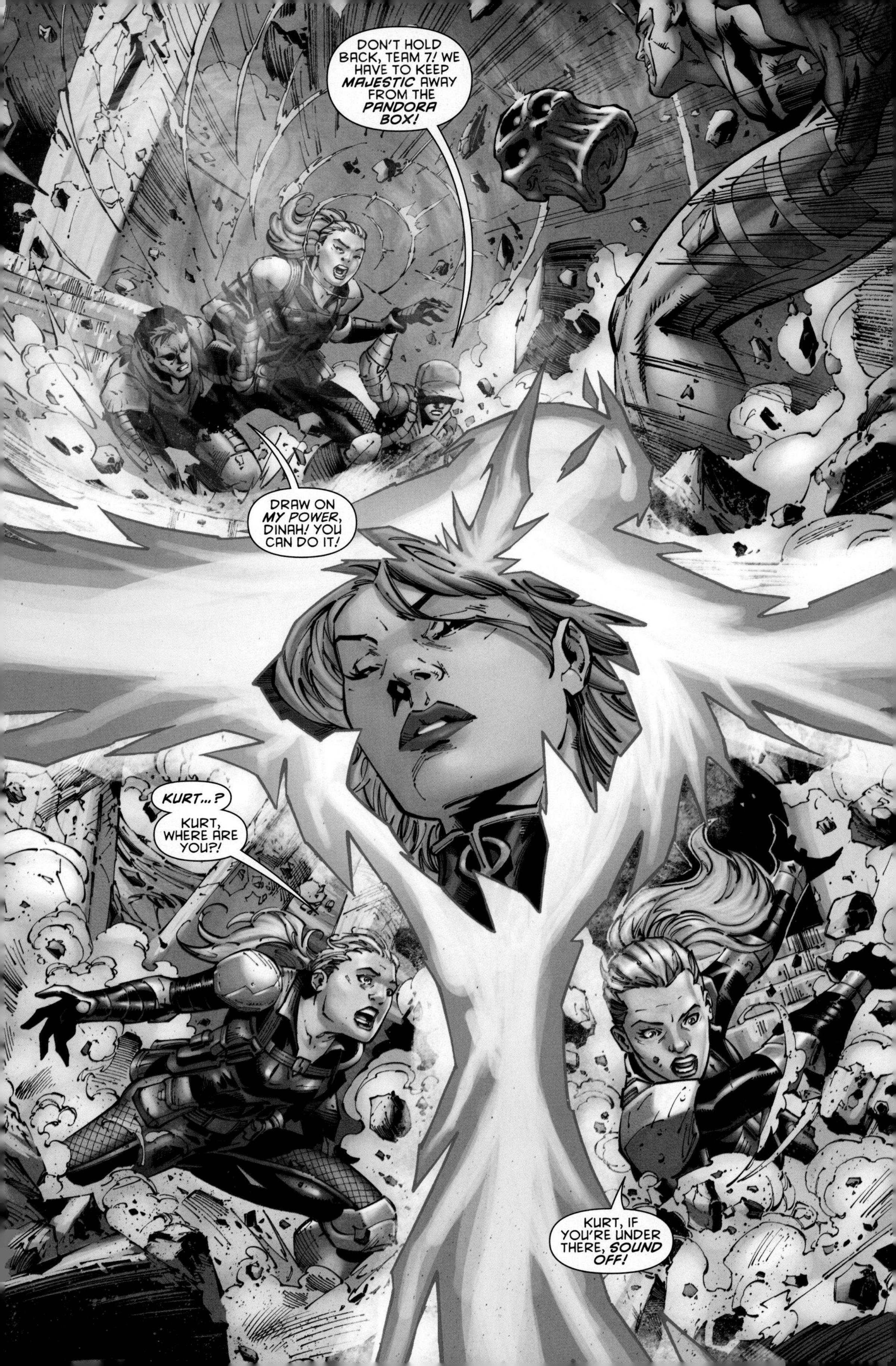
DON'T HOLD BACK, TEAM 7! WE HAVE TO KEEP MAJESTIC AWAY FROM THE PANDORA BOX!
DRAW ON MY POWER, DINAH! YOU CAN DO IT!
KURT...?
KURT, WHERE ARE YOU?!
KURT, IF YOU'RE UNDER THERE, SOUND OFF!

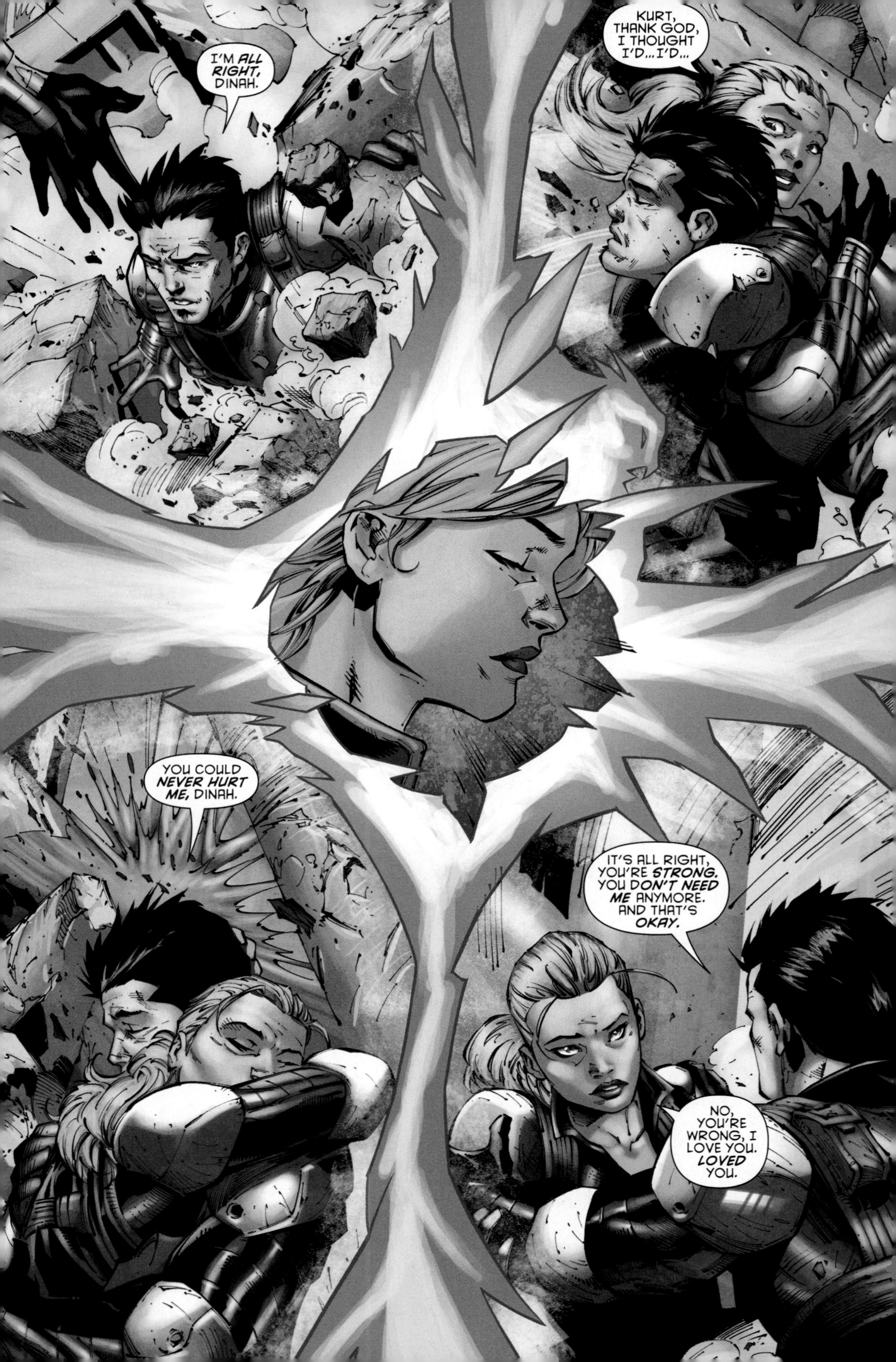
I'M ALL RIGHT, DINAH.
KURT, THANK GOD, I THOUGHT I'D...I'D...
YOU COULD NEVER HURT ME, DINAH.
IT'S ALL RIGHT, YOU'RE STRONG. YOU DON'T NEED ME ANYMORE. AND THAT'S OKAY.
NO, YOU'RE WRONG, I LOVE YOU. LOVED YOU.

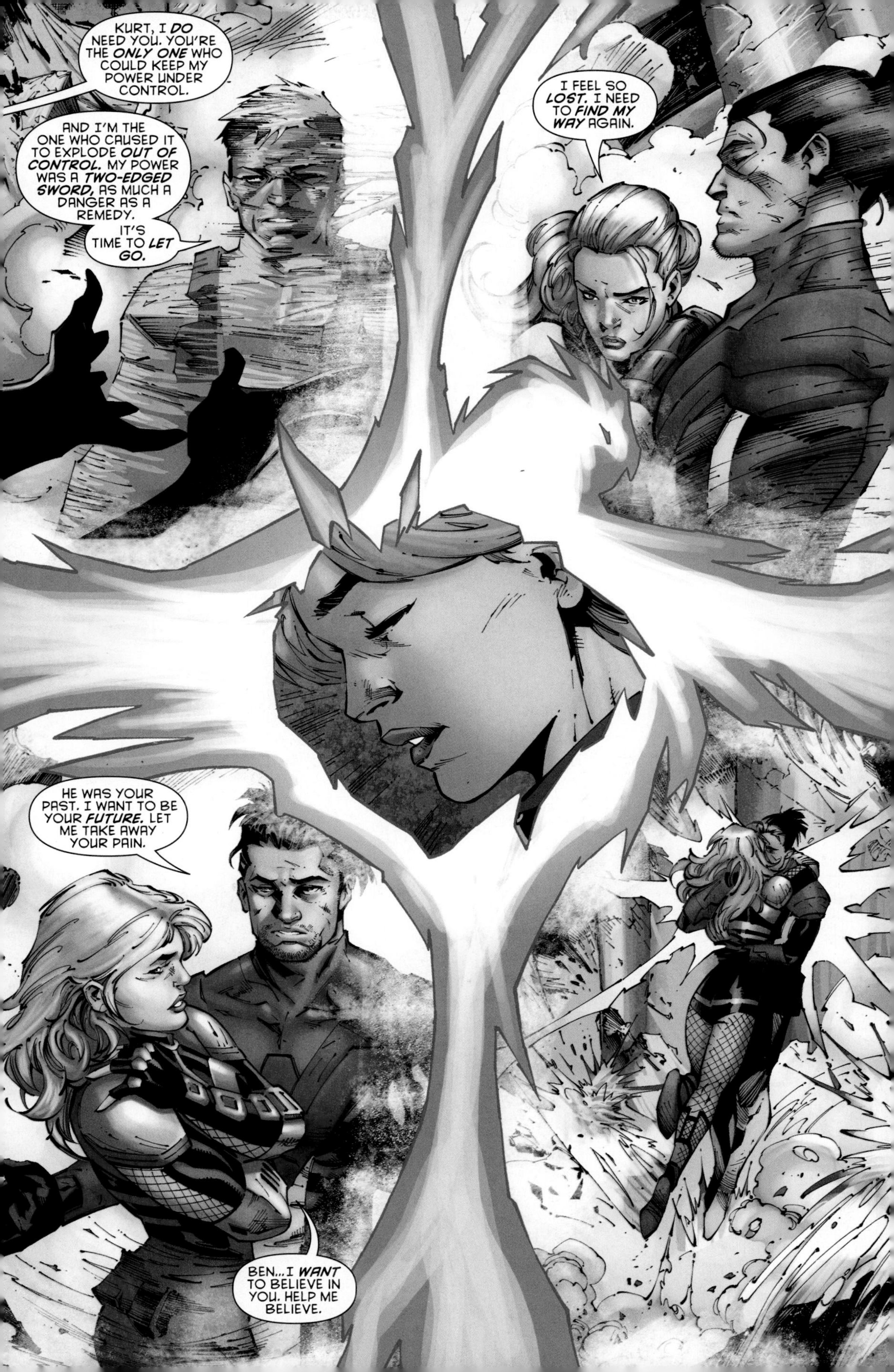

KURT, I DO NEED YOU. YOU'RE THE ONLY ONE WHO COULD KEEP MY POWER UNDER CONTROL.
AND I'M THE ONE WHO CAUSED IT TO EXPLODE OUT OF CONTROL. MY POWER WAS A TWO-EDGED SWORD, AS MUCH A DANGER AS A REMEDY.
IT'S TIME TO LET GO.
I FEEL SO LOST. I NEED TO FIND MY WAY AGAIN.
HE WAS YOUR PAST. I WANT TO BE YOUR FUTURE. LET ME TAKE AWAY YOUR PAIN.
BEN... I WANT TO BELIEVE IN YOU. HELP ME BELIEVE.

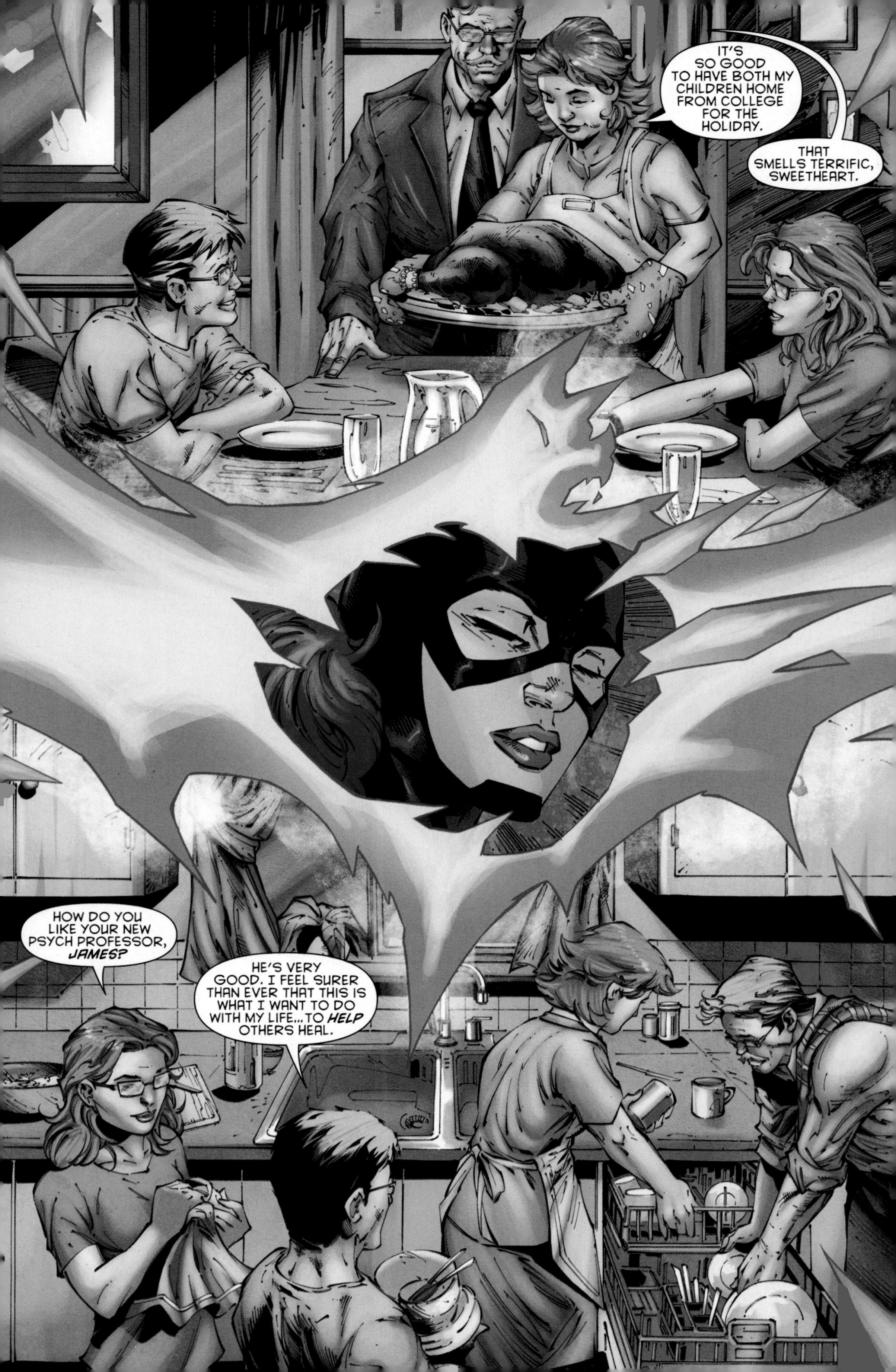
IT'S SO GOOD TO HAVE BOTH MY CHILDREN HOME FROM COLLEGE FOR THE HOLIDAY.
THAT SMELLS TERRIFIC, SWEETHEART.
HOW DO YOU LIKE YOUR NEW PSYCH PROFESSOR, JAMES?
HE'S VERY GOOD. I FEEL SURER THAN EVER THAT THIS IS WHAT I WANT TO DO WITH MY LIFE...TO HELP OTHERS HEAL.

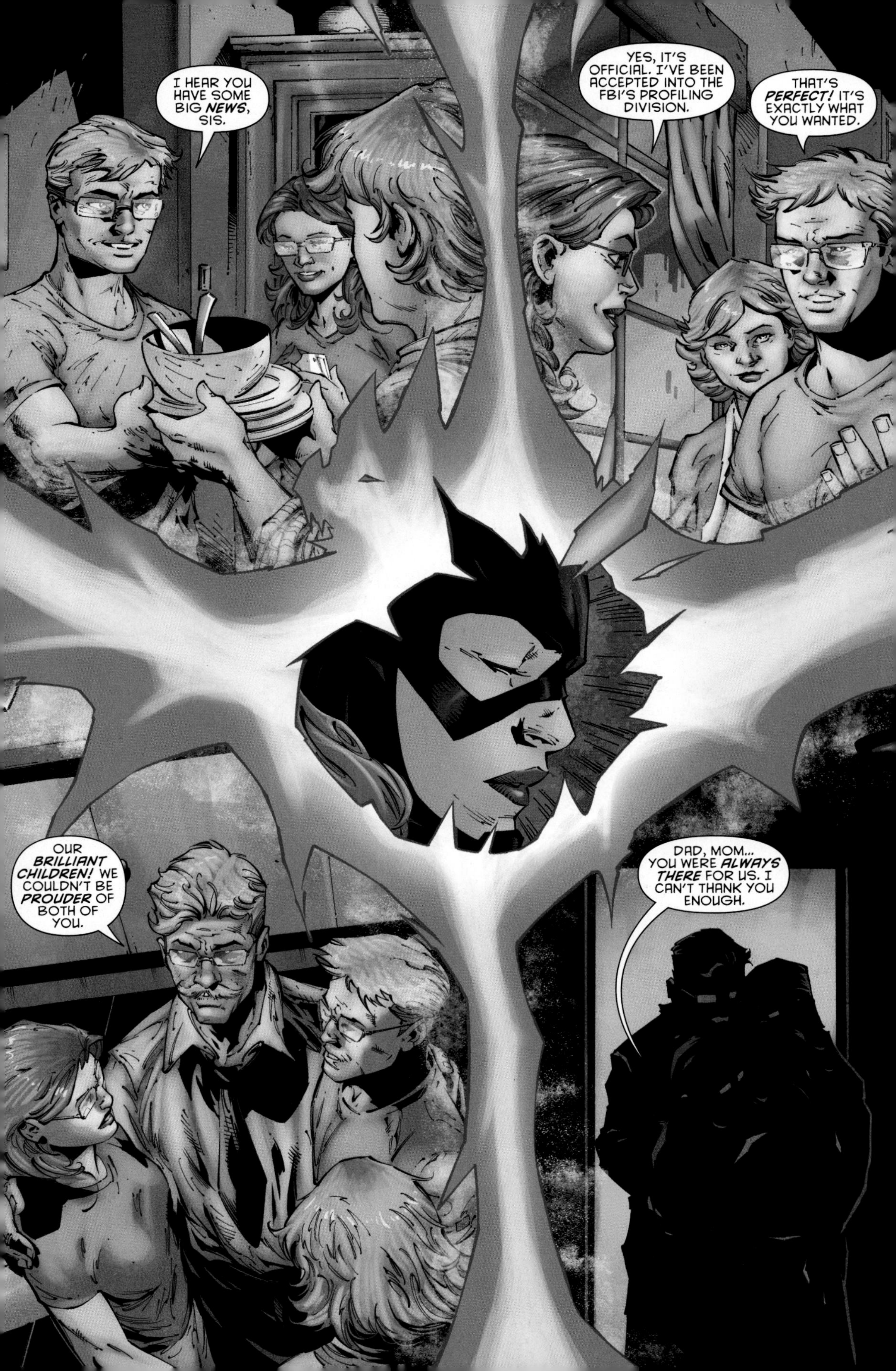
I HEAR YOU HAVE SOME BIG NEWS, SIS.
YES, IT'S OFFICIAL. I'VE BEEN ACCEPTED INTO THE FBI'S PROFILING DIVISION.
THAT'S PERFECT! IT'S EXACTLY WHAT YOU WANTED.
OUR BRILLIANT CHILDREN! WE COULDN'T BE PROUDER OF BOTH OF YOU.
DAD, MOM... YOU WERE ALWAYS THERE FOR US. I CAN'T THANK YOU ENOUGH.

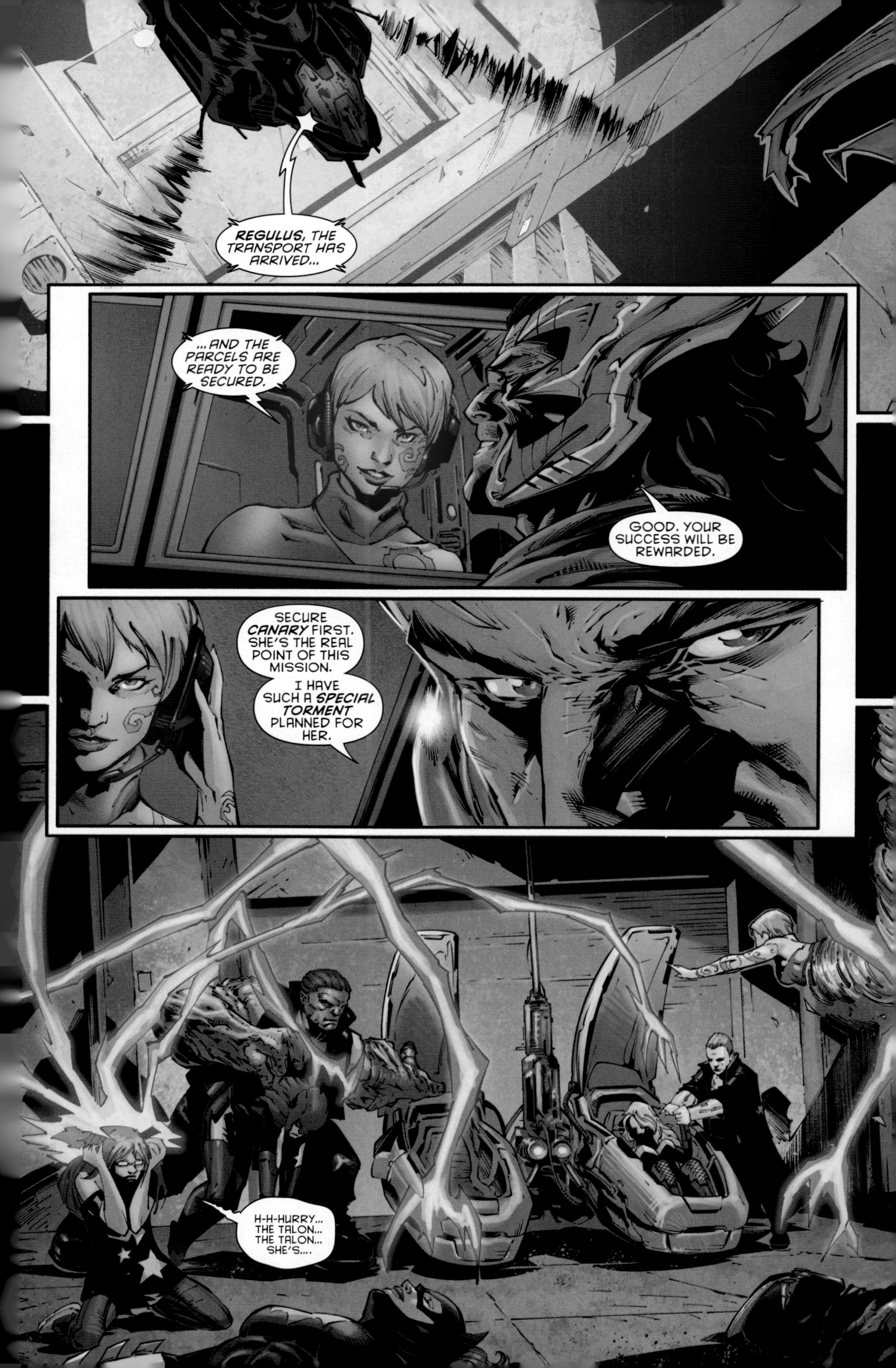
REGULUS, THE TRANSPORT HAS ARRIVED...
...AND THE PARCELS ARE READY TO BE SECURED.
GOOD. YOUR SUCCESS WILL BE REWARDED.
SECURE CANARY FIRST. SHE'S THE REAL POINT OF THIS MISSION.
I HAVE SUCH A SPECIAL TORMENT PLANNED FOR HER.
H-H-HURRY... THE TALON... THE TALON... SHE'S....

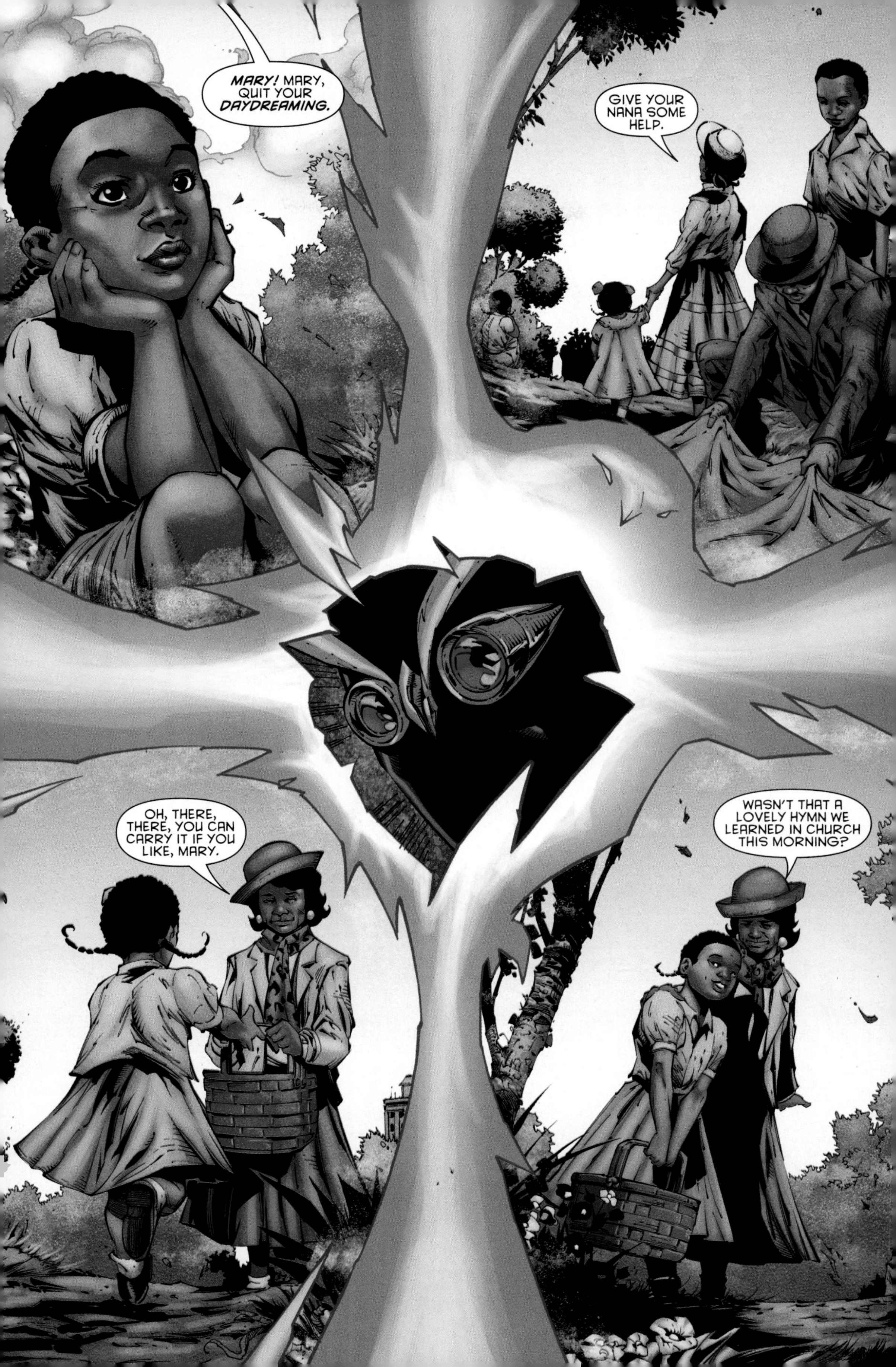

MARY! MARY, QUIT YOUR DAYDREAMING.
GIVE YOUR NANA SOME HELP.
OH, THERE, THERE, YOU CAN CARRY IT IF YOU LIKE, MARY.
WASN'T THAT A LOVELY HYMN WE LEARNED IN CHURCH THIS MORNING?

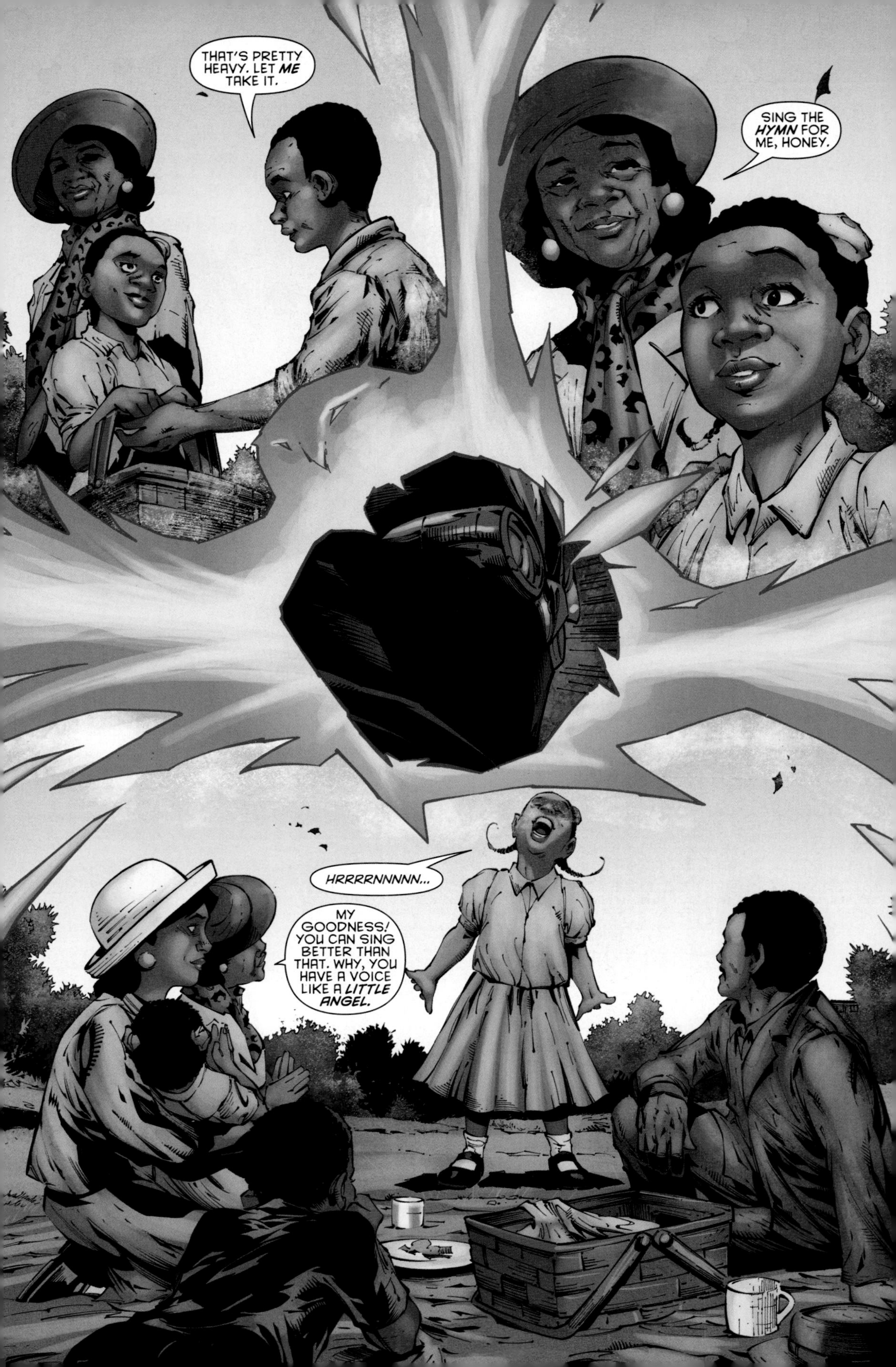

THAT'S PRETTY HEAVY. LET ME TAKE IT.
SING THE HYMN FOR ME, HONEY.
HRRRRNNNNN...
MY GOODNESS! YOU CAN SING BETTER THAN THAT. WHY, YOU HAVE A VOICE LIKE A LITTLE ANGEL.

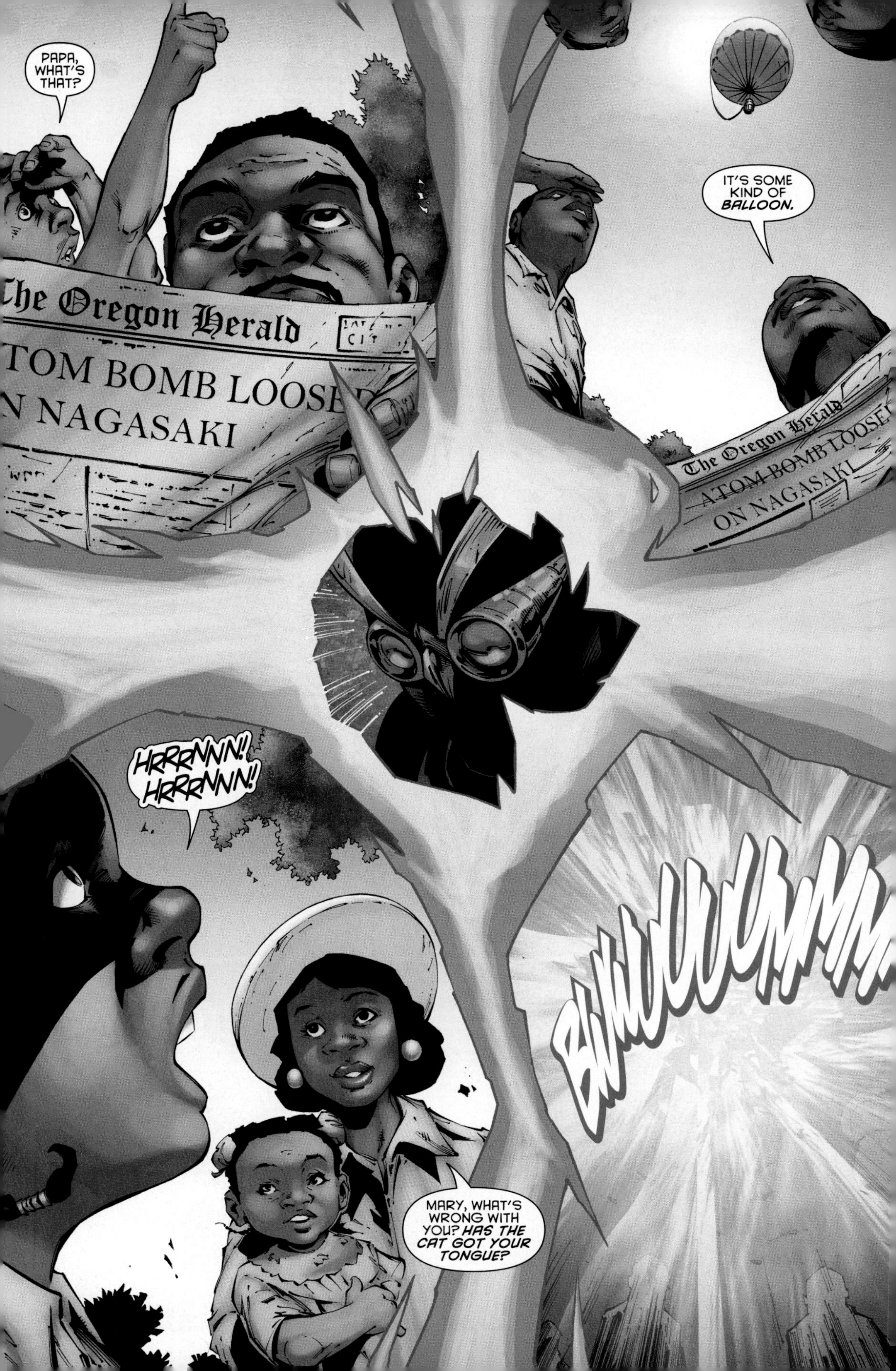
PAPA, WHAT'S THAT?
The Oregon Herald
ATOM BOMB LOOSED ON NAGASAKI
IT'S SOME KIND OF BALLOON.
The Oregon Herald
ATOM BOMB LOOSED ON NAGASAKI
HRRRNNN! HRRRNNN!
BWUUUUMMM
MARY, WHAT'S WRONG WITH YOU? HAS THE CAT GOT YOUR TONGUE?

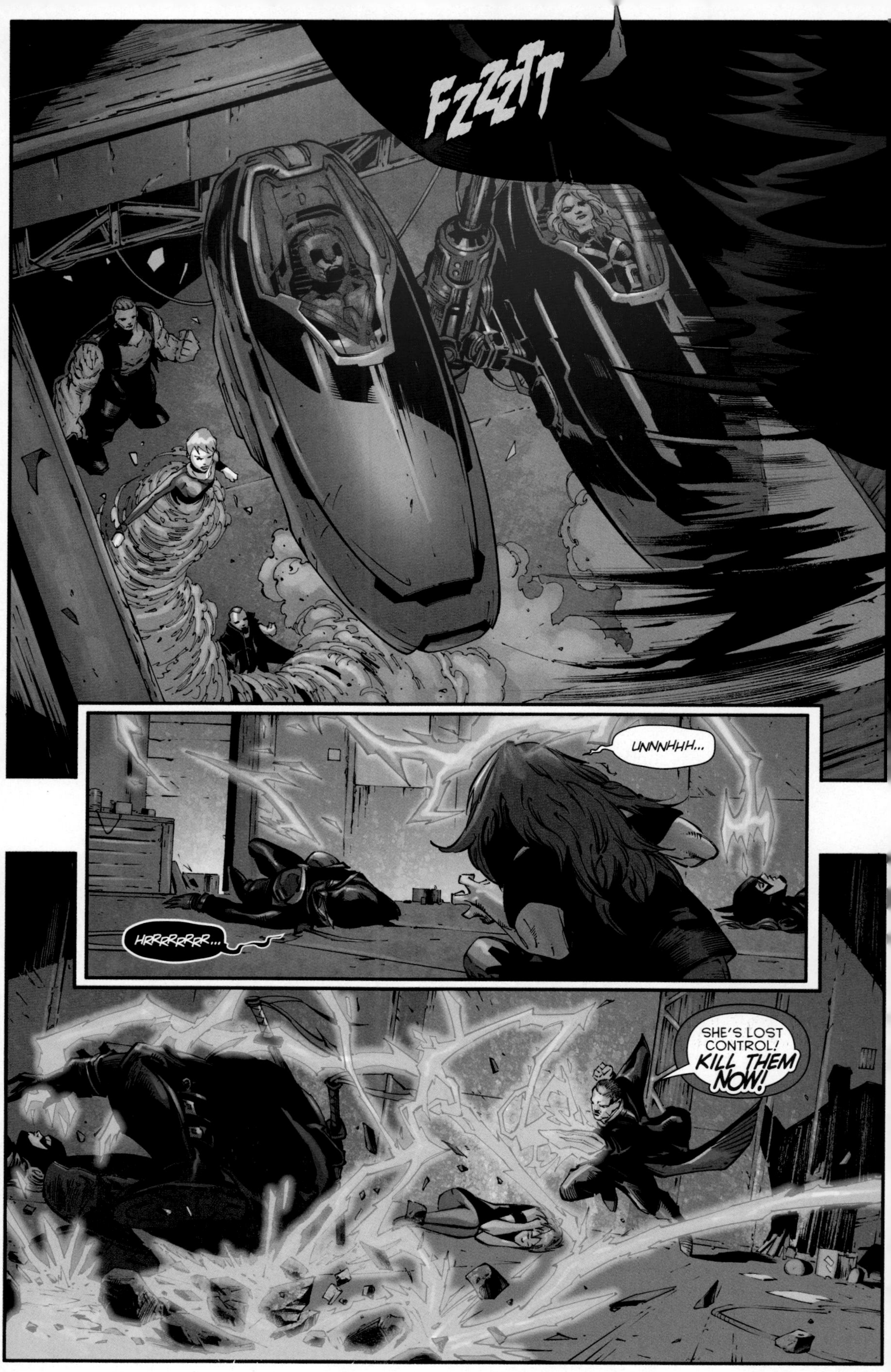
FZZZTT
UNNHHH...
HRRRRRRRR...
SHE'S LOST CONTROL! KILL THEM NOW!

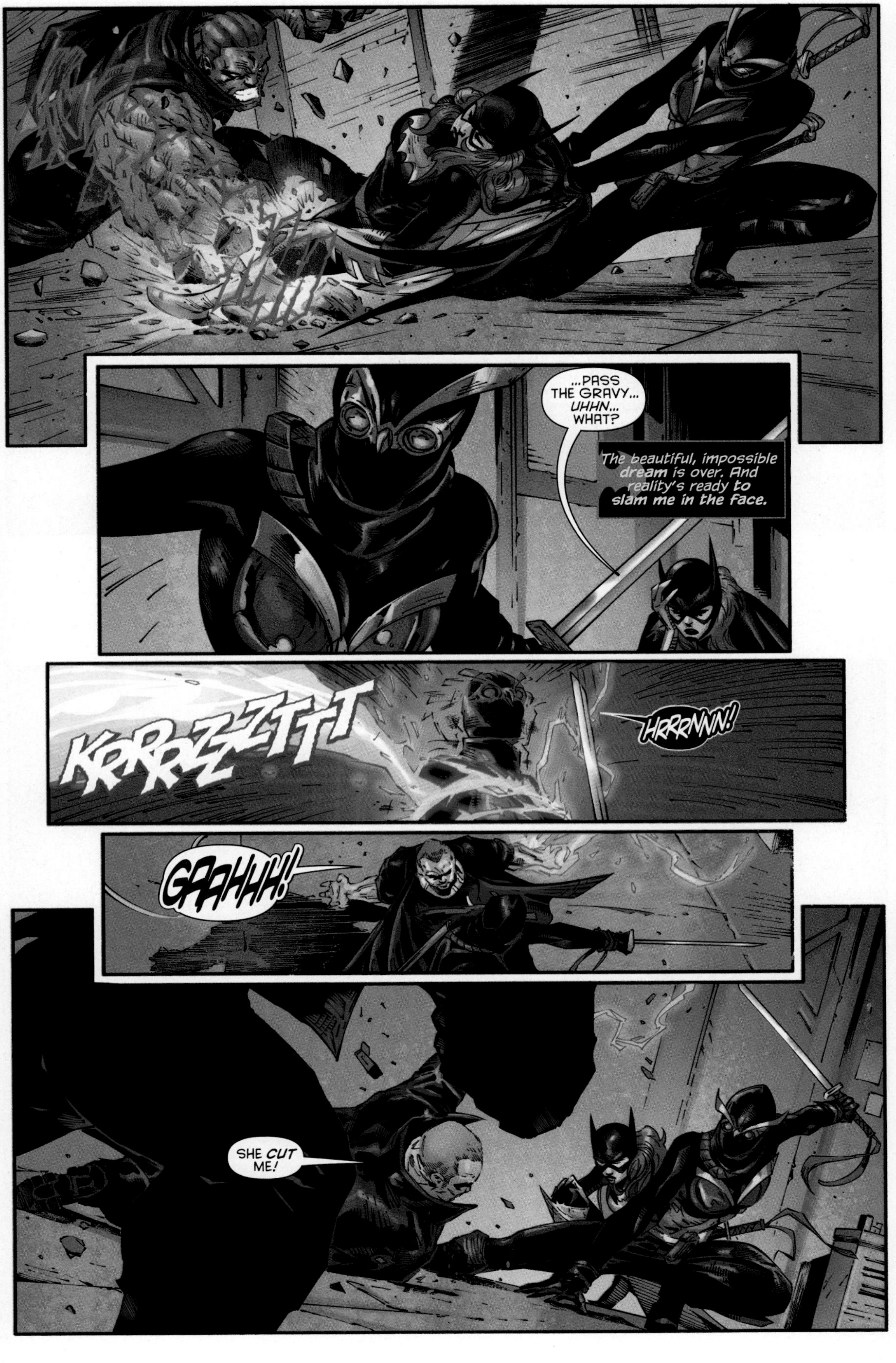
...PASS THE GRAVY... UHHN... WHAT?
The beautiful, impossible dream is over. And reality's ready to slam me in the face.
KRRRZZZTTTT
HRRRNNN!
GAAHHH!
SHE CUT ME!

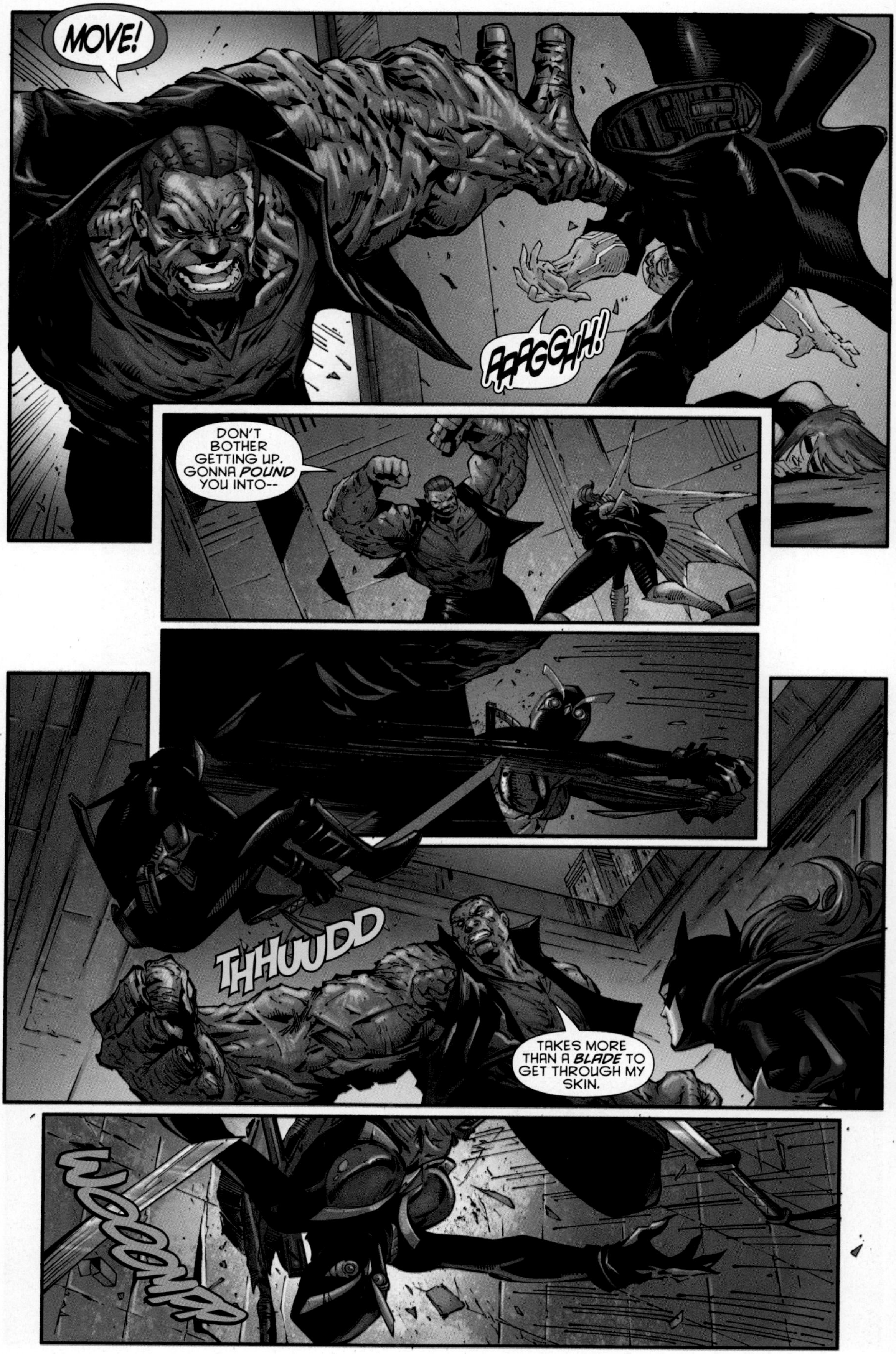
MOVE!
AAAGGHH!
DON'T BOTHER GETTING UP. GONNA POUND YOU INTO--
THHUUDD
TAKES MORE THAN A BLADE TO GET THROUGH MY SKIN.
WOOMP

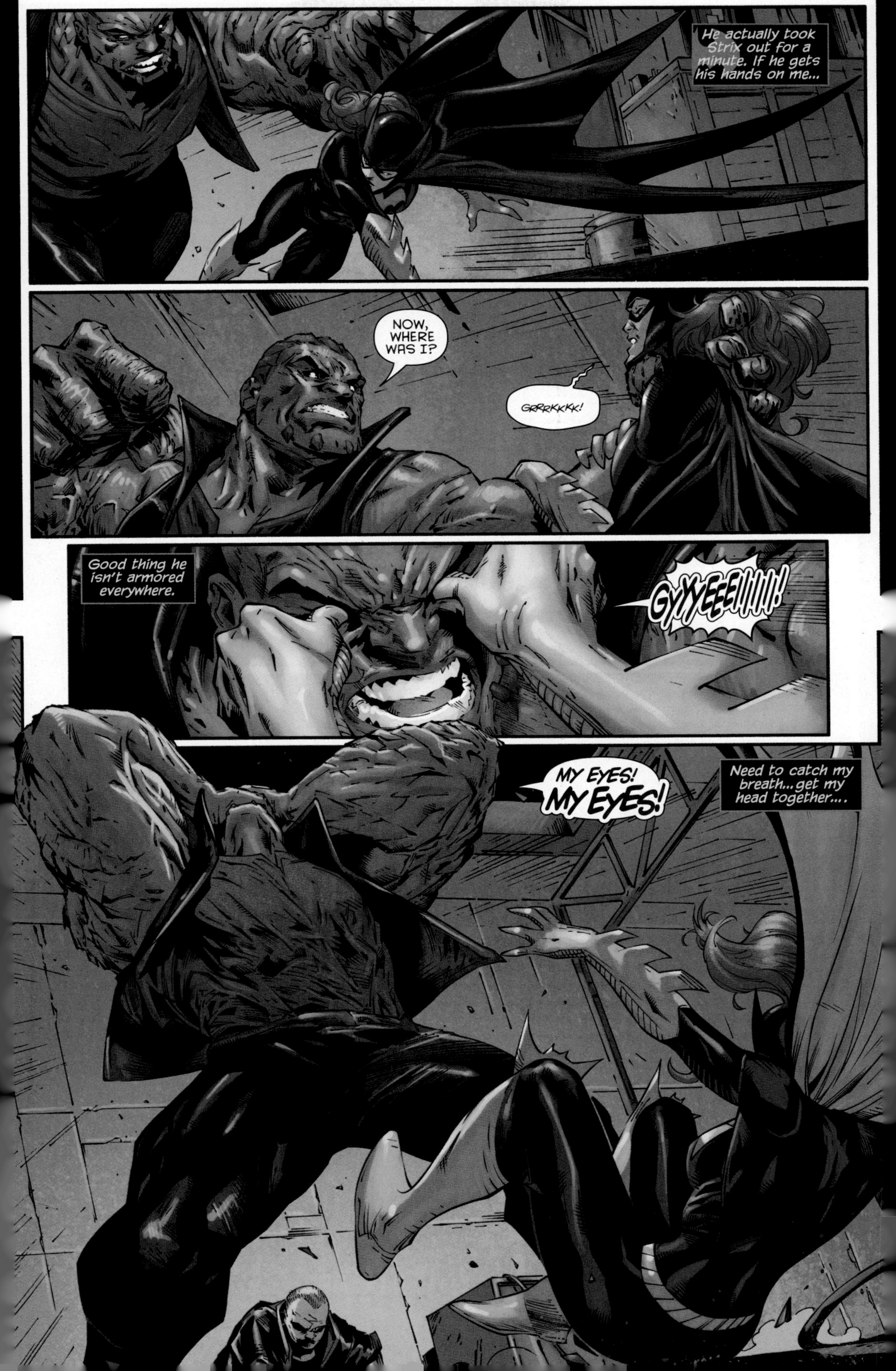
He actually took Strix out for a minute. If he gets his hands on me...
NOW, WHERE WAS I?
GRRRKKKK!
Good thing he isn't armored everywhere.
GYYYEEE!!!!!!!
MY EYES! MY EYES!
Need to catch my breath...get my head together....

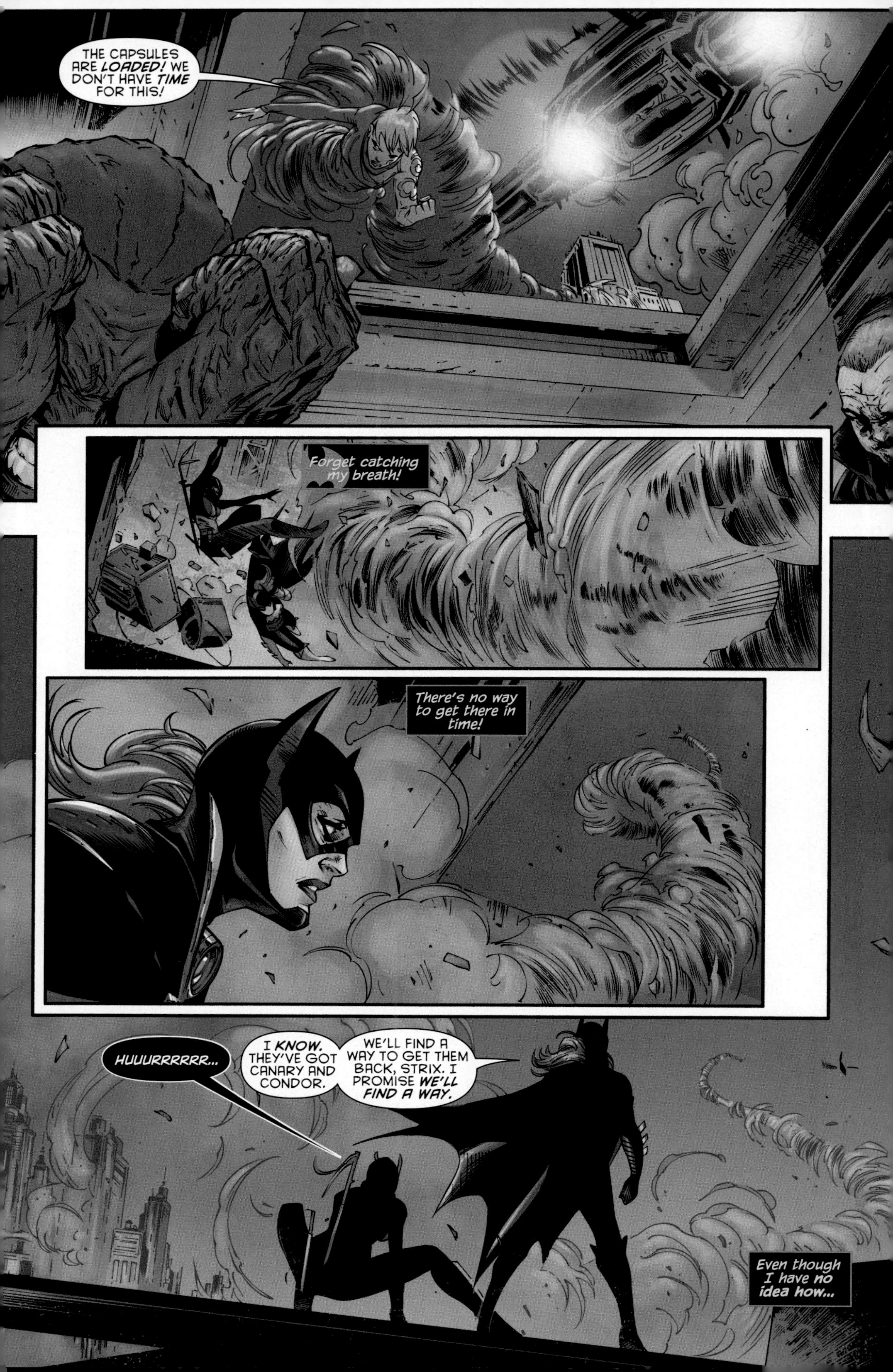
THE CAPSULES ARE LOADED! WE DON'T HAVE TIME FOR THIS!
Forget catching my breath!
There's no way to get there in time!
HUUURRRRRR...
I KNOW. THEY'VE GOT CANARY AND CONDOR.
WE'LL FIND A WAY TO GET THEM BACK, STRIX. I PROMISE WE'LL FIND A WAY.
Even though I have no idea how...

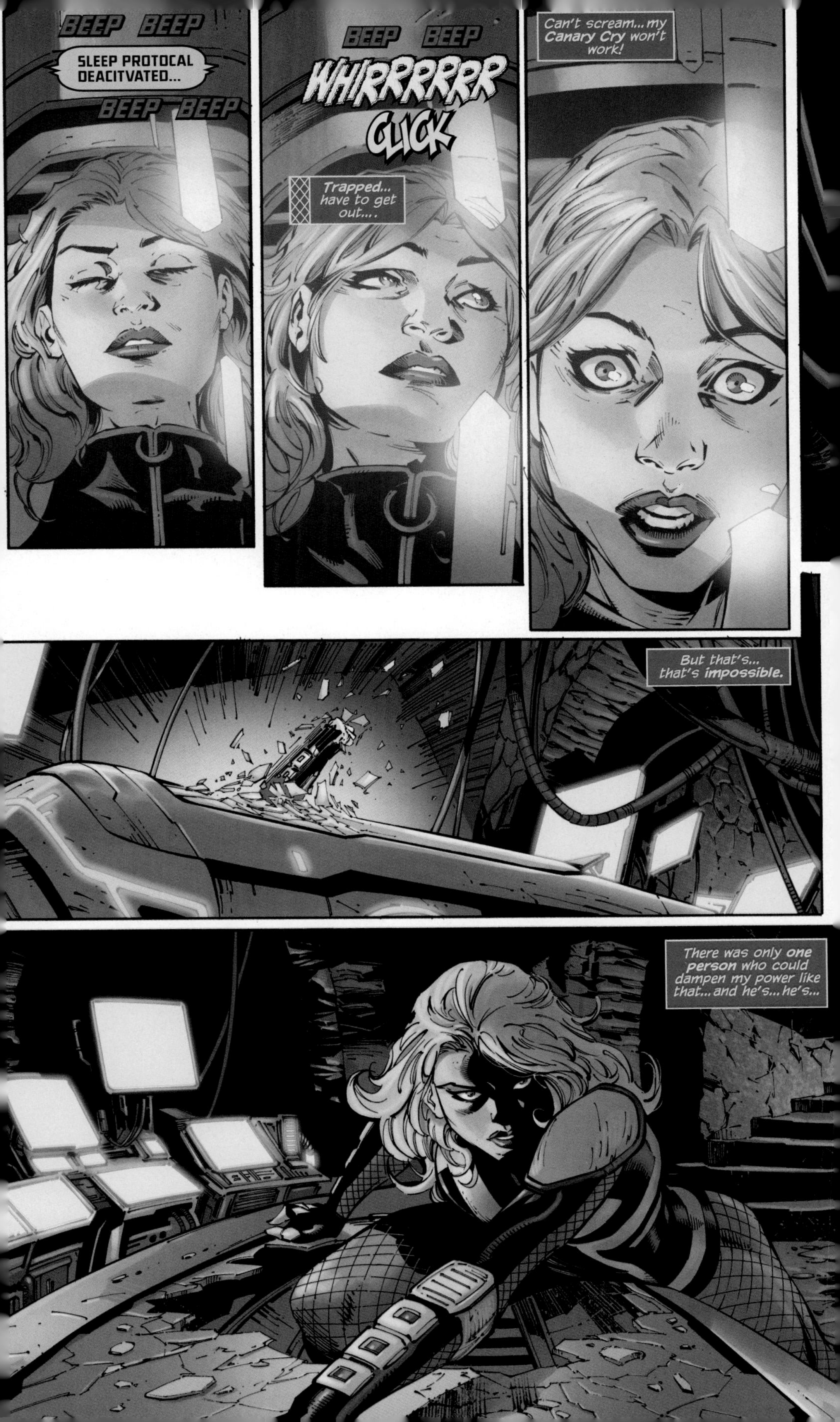
BEEP BEEP
SLEEP PROTOCAL DEACITVATED...
BEEP BEEP
BEEP BEEP
WHIRRRRRR
CLICK
Trapped... have to get out....
Can't scream... my Canary Cry won't work!
But that's... that's impossible.
There was only one person who could dampen my power like that... and he's... he's...

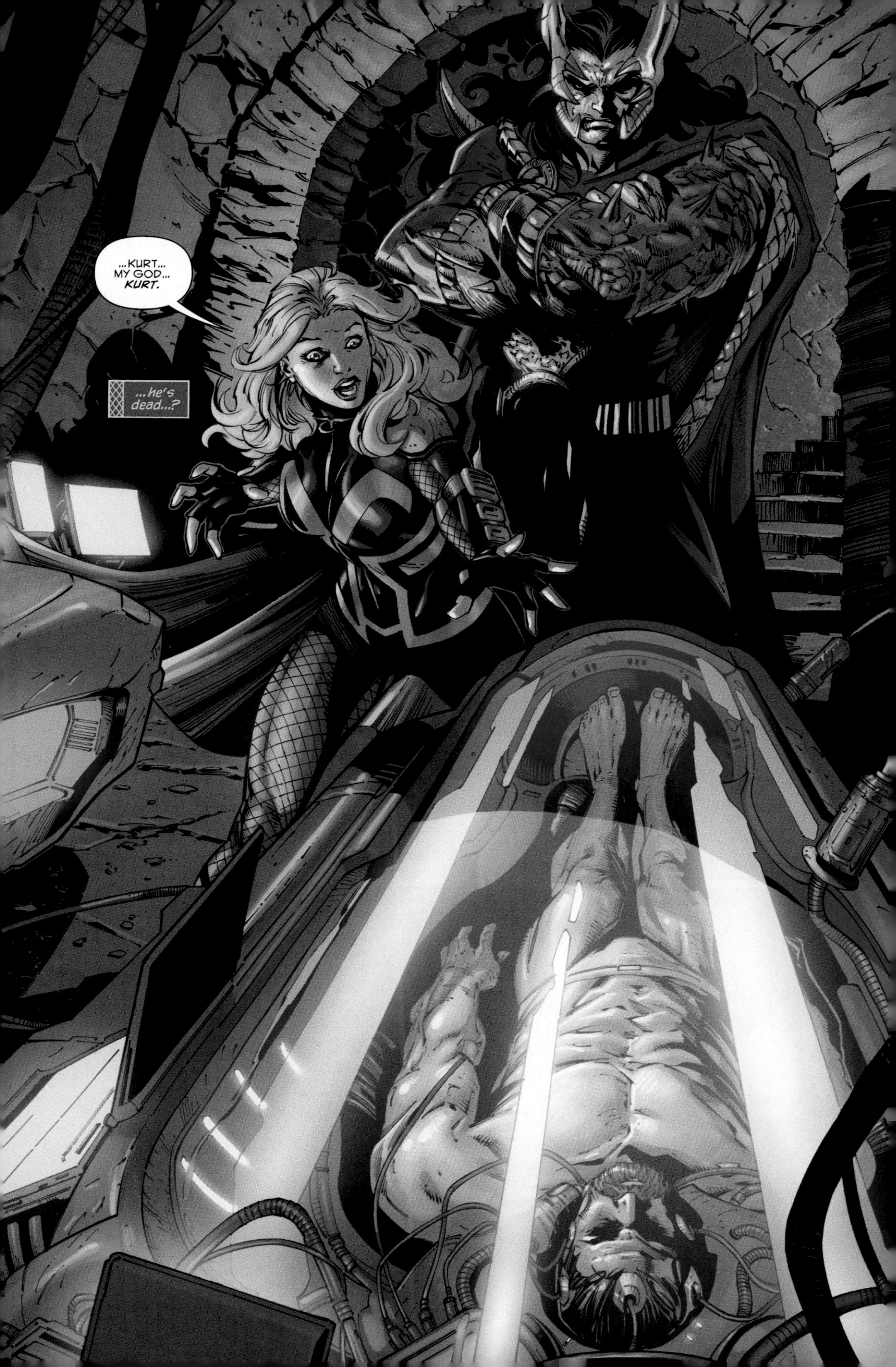
...KURT... MY GOD... KURT.
...he's dead...?

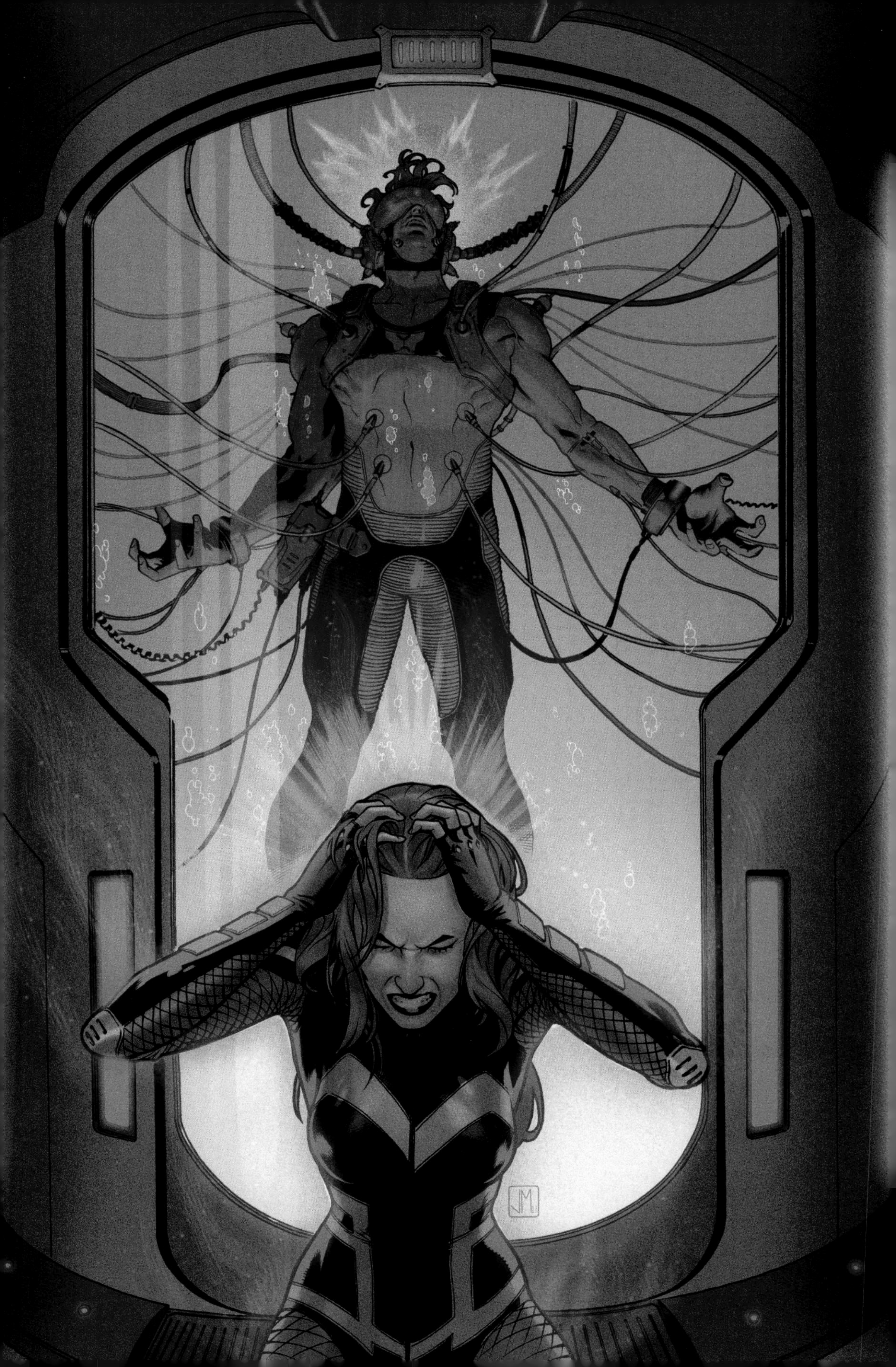

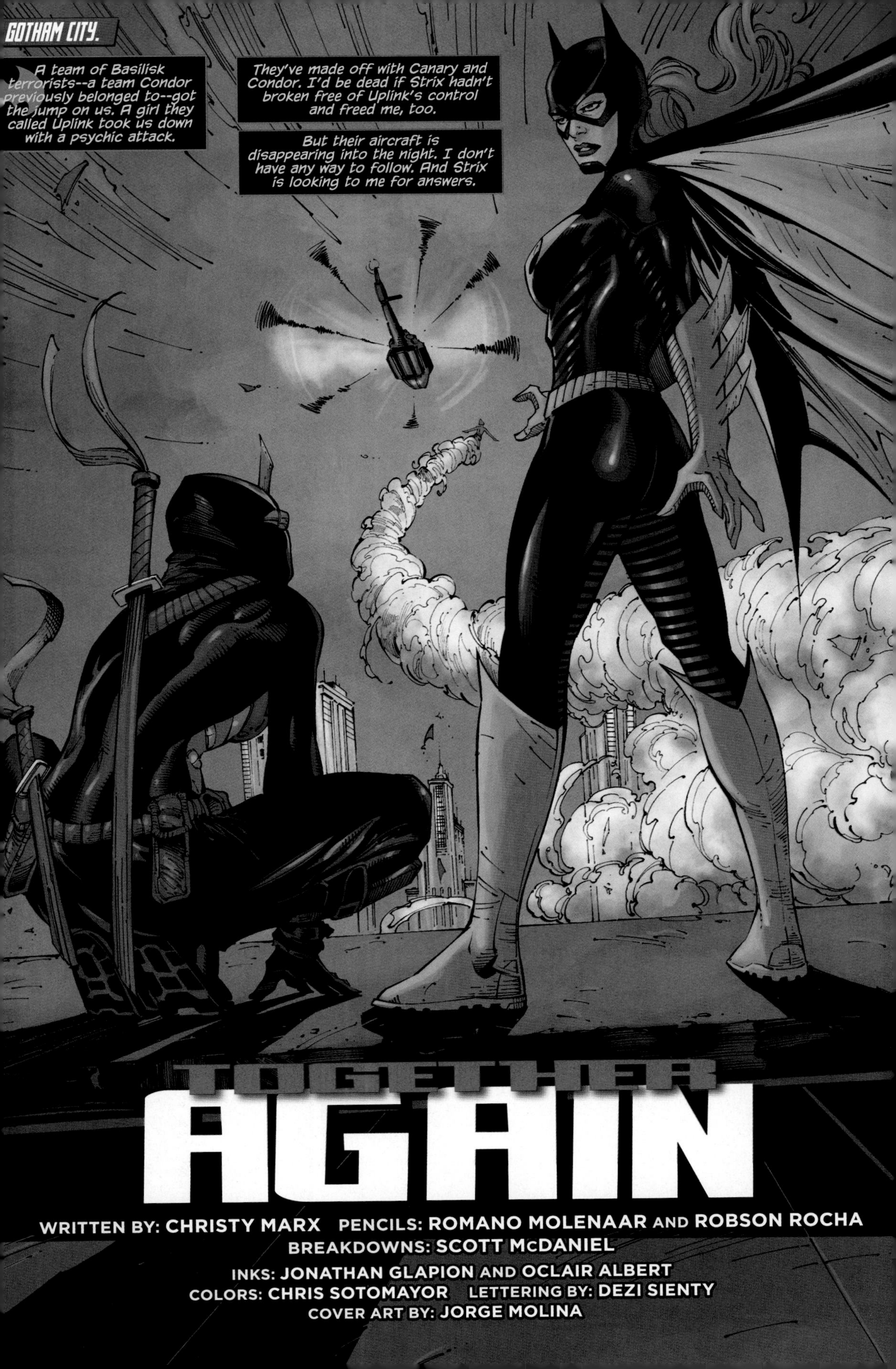

GOTHAM CITY.
A team of Basilisk terrorists--a team Condor previously belonged to--got the jump on us. A girl they called Uplink took us down with a psychic attack.
They've made off with Canary and Condor. I'd be dead if Strix hadn't broken free of Uplink's control and freed me, too.
But their aircraft is disappearing into the night. I don't have any way to follow. And Strix is looking to me for answers.
TOGETHER AGAIN
WRITTEN BY: CHRISTY MARX PENCILS: ROMANO MOLENAAR AND ROBSON ROCHA
BREAKDOWNS: SCOTT McDANIEL
INKS: JONATHAN GLAPION AND OCLAIR ALBERT
COLORS: CHRIS SOTOMAYOR LETTERING BY: DEZI SIENTY
COVER ART BY: JORGE MOLINA

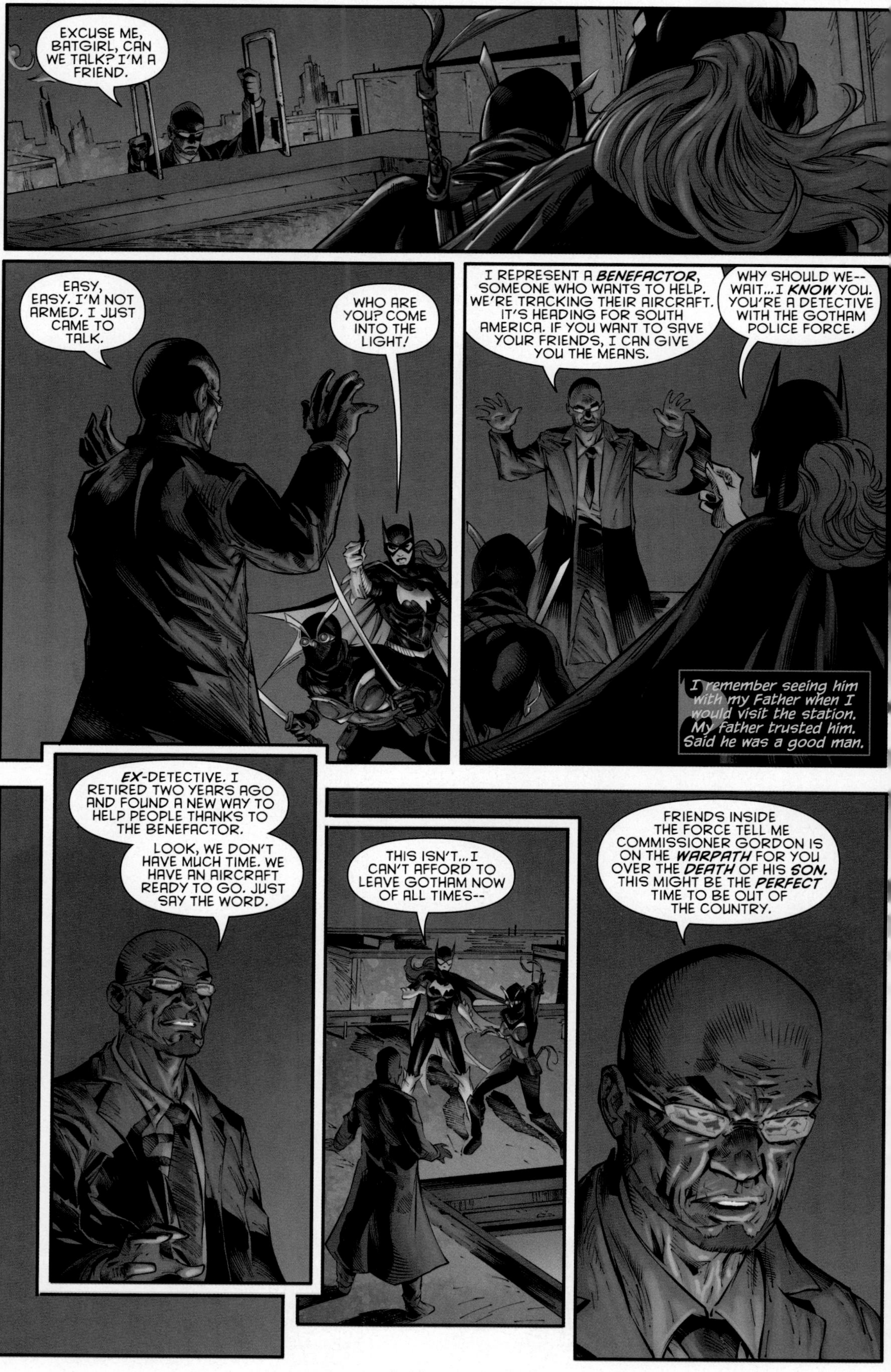
EXCUSE ME, BATGIRL, CAN WE TALK? I'M A FRIEND.
EASY, EASY. I'M NOT ARMED. I JUST CAME TO TALK.
WHO ARE YOU? COME INTO THE LIGHT!
I REPRESENT A BENEFACTOR, SOMEONE WHO WANTS TO HELP. WE'RE TRACKING THEIR AIRCRAFT. IT'S HEADING FOR SOUTH AMERICA. IF YOU WANT TO SAVE YOUR FRIENDS, I CAN GIVE YOU THE MEANS.
WHY SHOULD WE-- WAIT...I KNOW YOU. YOU'RE A DETECTIVE WITH THE GOTHAM POLICE FORCE.
I remember seeing him with my Father when I would visit the station. My father trusted him. Said he was a good man.
EX-DETECTIVE. I RETIRED TWO YEARS AGO AND FOUND A NEW WAY TO HELP PEOPLE THANKS TO THE BENEFACTOR.
LOOK, WE DON'T HAVE MUCH TIME. WE HAVE AN AIRCRAFT READY TO GO. JUST SAY THE WORD.
THIS ISN'T...I CAN'T AFFORD TO LEAVE GOTHAM NOW OF ALL TIMES--
FRIENDS INSIDE THE FORCE TELL ME COMMISSIONER GORDON IS ON THE WARPATH FOR YOU OVER THE DEATH OF HIS SON. THIS MIGHT BE THE PERFECT TIME TO BE OUT OF THE COUNTRY.

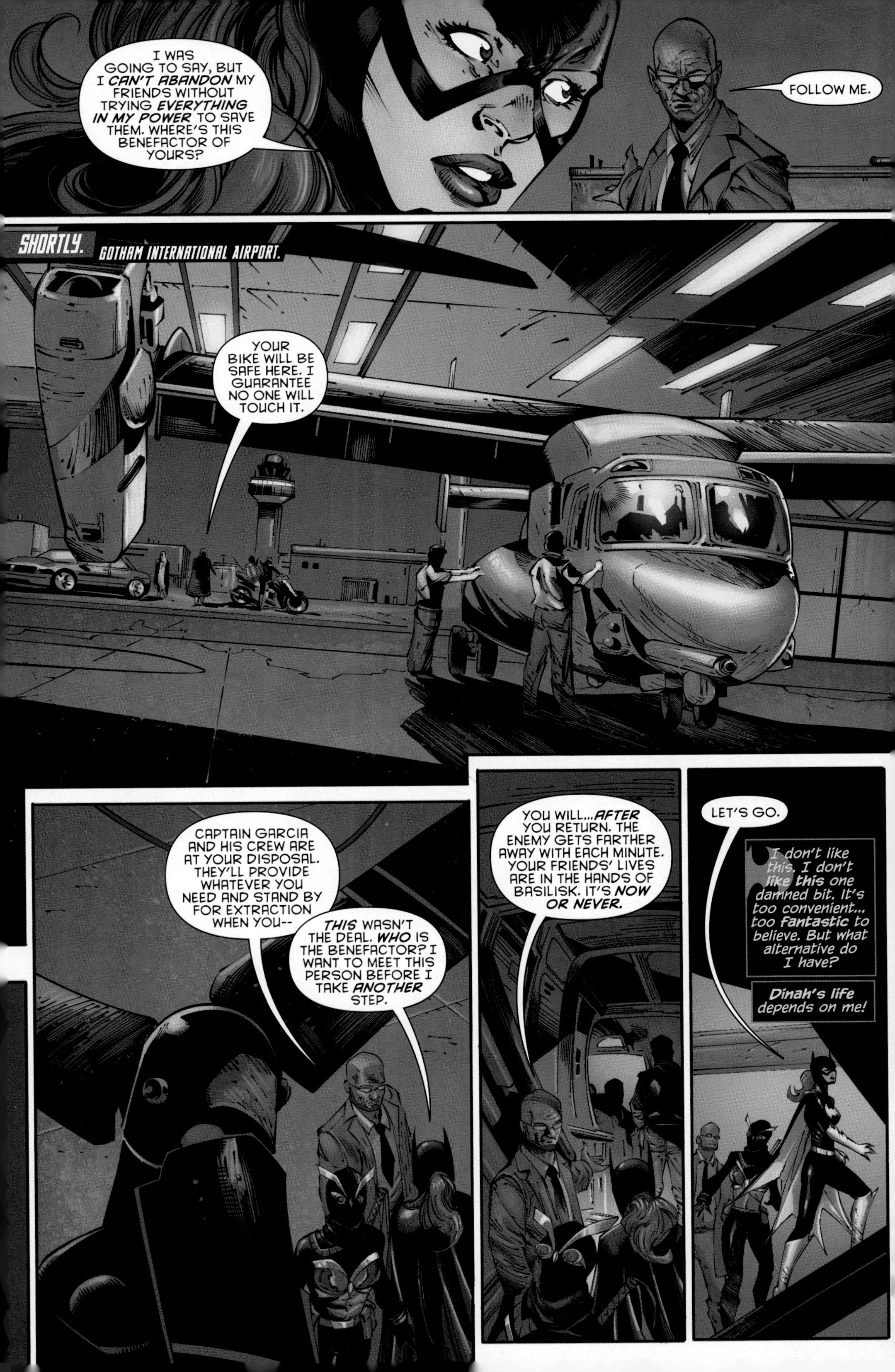

I WAS GOING TO SAY, BUT I CAN'T ABANDON MY FRIENDS WITHOUT TRYING EVERYTHING IN MY POWER TO SAVE THEM. WHERE'S THIS BENEFACTOR OF YOURS?
FOLLOW ME.
SHORTLY.
GOTHAM INTERNATIONAL AIRPORT.
YOUR BIKE WILL BE SAFE HERE. I GUARANTEE NO ONE WILL TOUCH IT.
CAPTAIN GARCIA AND HIS CREW ARE AT YOUR DISPOSAL. THEY'LL PROVIDE WHATEVER YOU NEED AND STAND BY FOR EXTRACTION WHEN YOU--
THIS WASN'T THE DEAL. WHO IS THE BENEFACTOR? I WANT TO MEET THIS PERSON BEFORE I TAKE ANOTHER STEP.
YOU WILL...AFTER YOU RETURN. THE ENEMY GETS FARTHER AWAY WITH EACH MINUTE. YOUR FRIENDS' LIVES ARE IN THE HANDS OF BASILISK. IT'S NOW OR NEVER.
LET'S GO.
I don't like this. I don't like this one damned bit. It's too convenient... too fantastic to believe. But what alternative do I have?
Dinah's life depends on me!

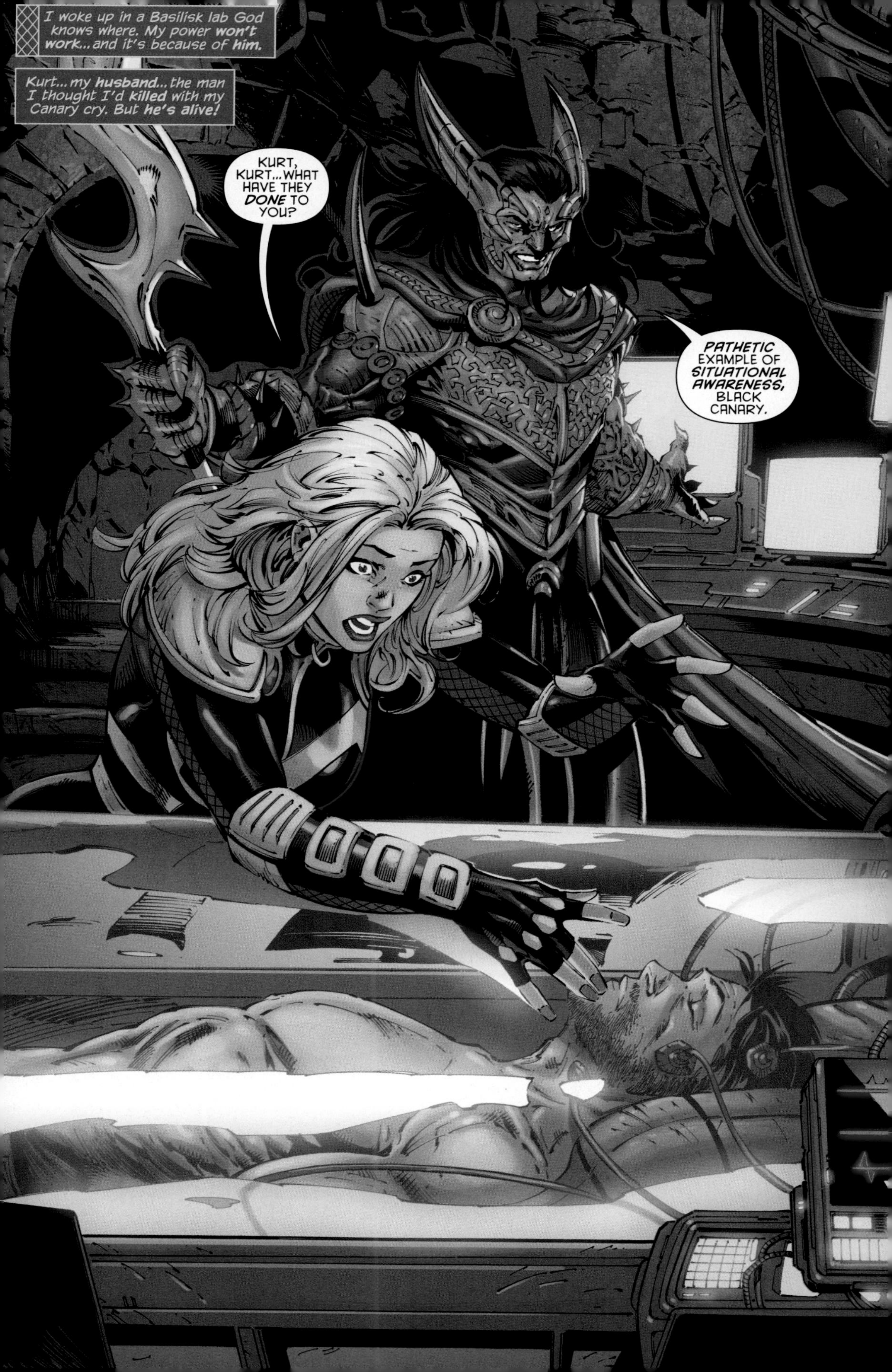
I woke up in a Basilisk lab God knows where. My power won't work... and it's because of him.
Kurt... my husband... the man I thought I'd killed with my Canary cry. But he's alive!
KURT, KURT... WHAT HAVE THEY DONE TO YOU?
PATHETIC EXAMPLE OF SITUATIONAL AWARENESS, BLACK CANARY.

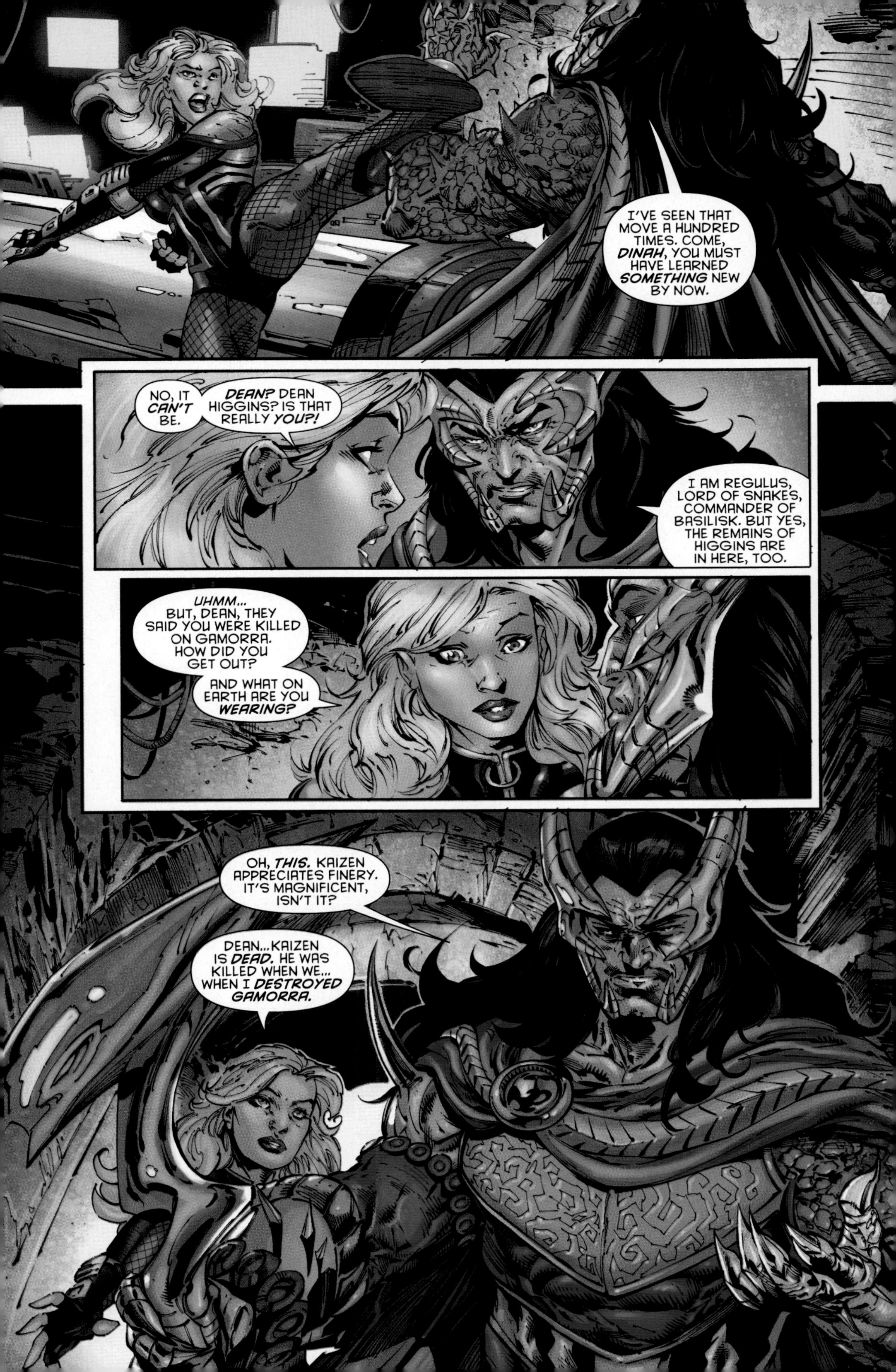

I'VE SEEN THAT MOVE A HUNDRED TIMES. COME, DINAH, YOU MUST HAVE LEARNED SOMETHING NEW BY NOW.
NO, IT CAN'T BE.
DEAN? DEAN HIGGINS? IS THAT REALLY YOU?!
I AM REGULUS, LORD OF SNAKES, COMMANDER OF BASILISK. BUT YES, THE REMAINS OF HIGGINS ARE IN HERE, TOO.
UHMM... BUT, DEAN, THEY SAID YOU WERE KILLED ON GAMORRA. HOW DID YOU GET OUT?
AND WHAT ON EARTH ARE YOU WEARING?
OH, THIS. KAIZEN APPRECIATES FINERY. IT'S MAGNIFICENT, ISN'T IT?
DEAN...KAIZEN IS DEAD. HE WAS KILLED WHEN WE... WHEN I DESTROYED GAMORRA.

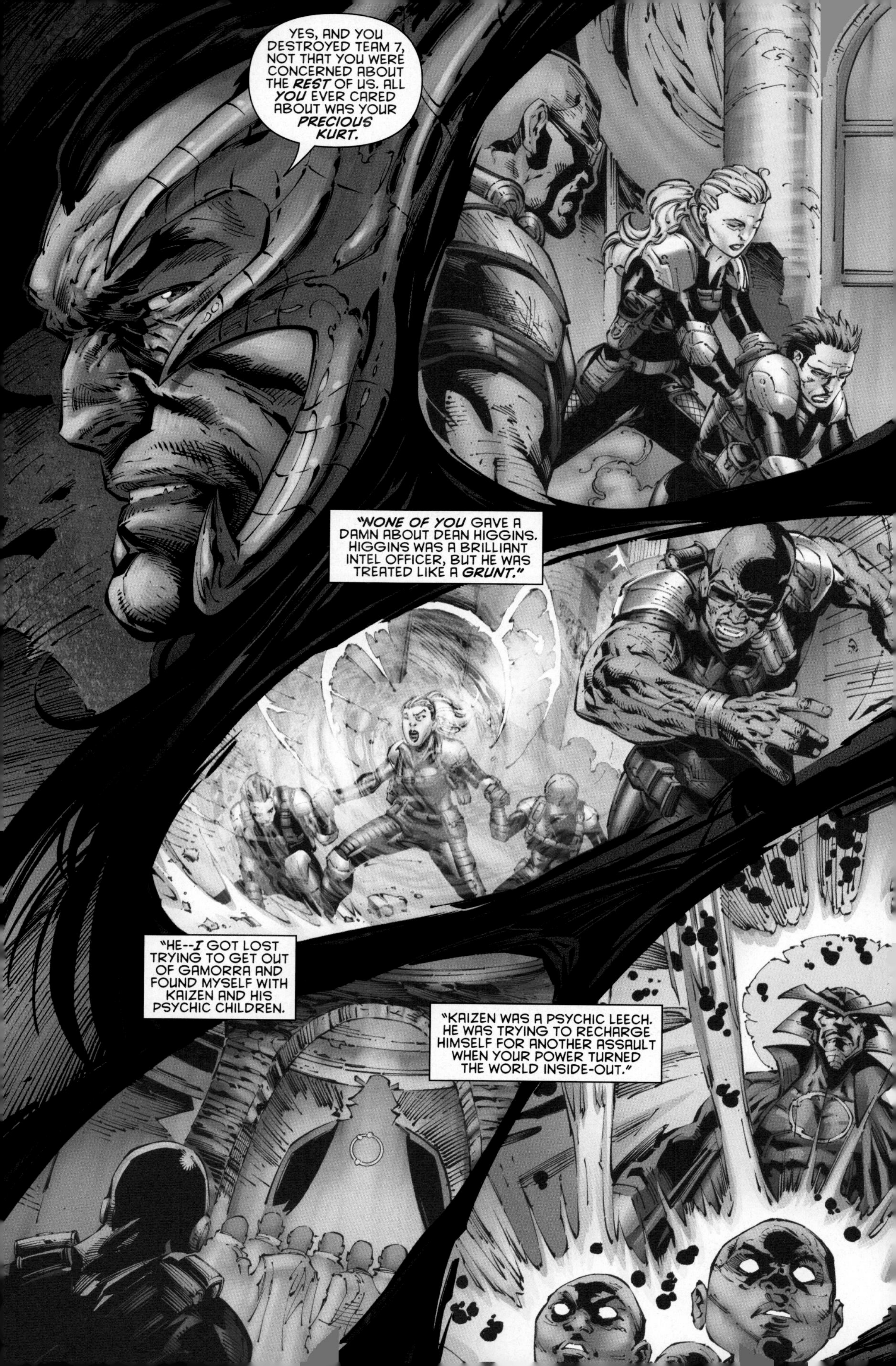
YES, AND YOU DESTROYED TEAM 7, NOT THAT YOU WERE CONCERNED ABOUT THE REST OF US. ALL YOU EVER CARED ABOUT WAS YOUR PRECIOUS KURT.
"NONE OF YOU GAVE A DAMN ABOUT DEAN HIGGINS. HIGGINS WAS A BRILLIANT INTEL OFFICER, BUT HE WAS TREATED LIKE A GRUNT."
"HE--I GOT LOST TRYING TO GET OUT OF GAMORRA AND FOUND MYSELF WITH KAIZEN AND HIS PSYCHIC CHILDREN.
"KAIZEN WAS A PSYCHIC LEECH. HE WAS TRYING TO RECHARGE HIMSELF FOR ANOTHER ASSAULT WHEN YOUR POWER TURNED THE WORLD INSIDE-OUT."

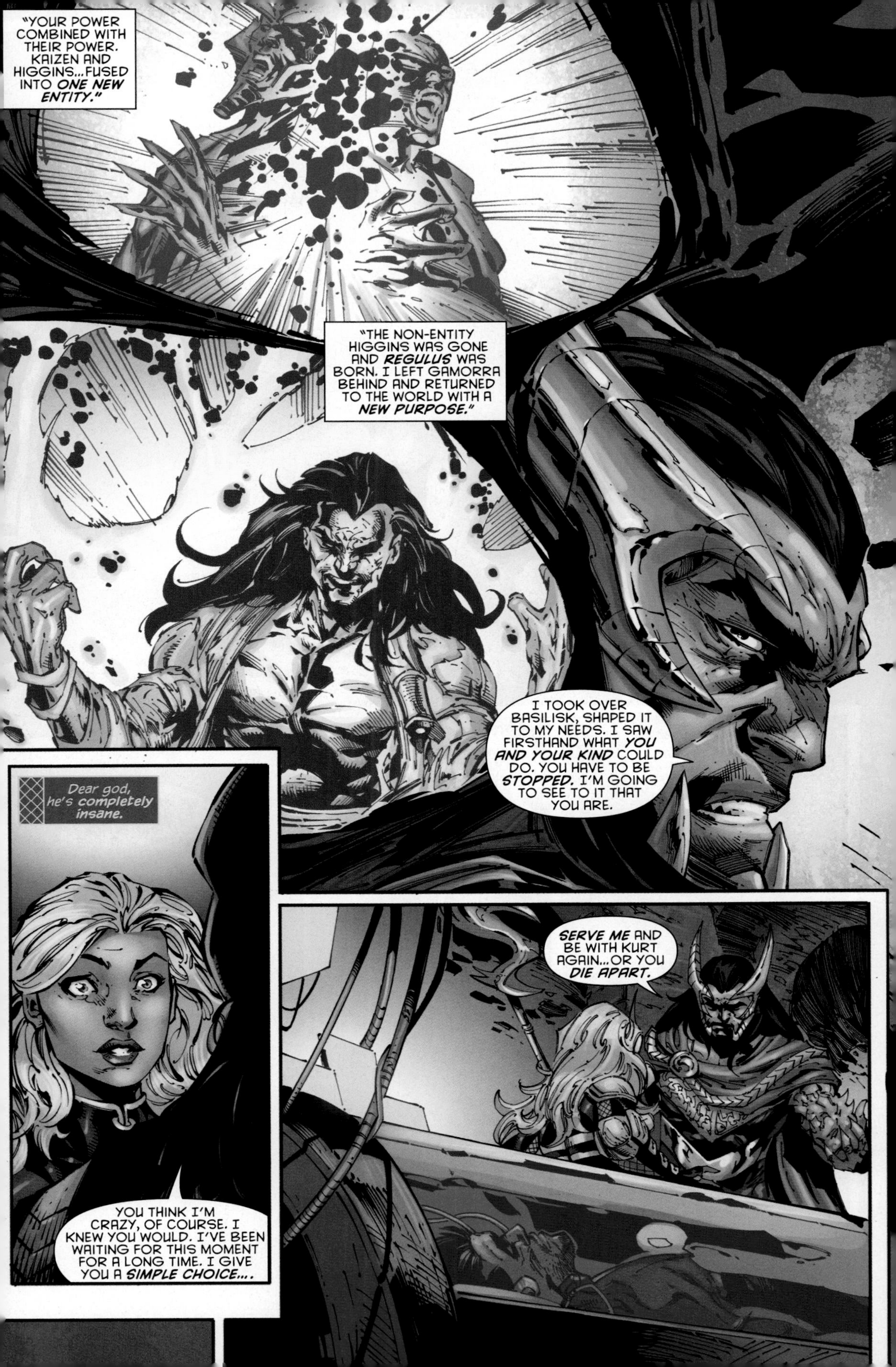
"YOUR POWER COMBINED WITH THEIR POWER. KAIZEN AND HIGGINS...FUSED INTO ONE NEW ENTITY."
"THE NON-ENTITY HIGGINS WAS GONE AND REGULUS WAS BORN. I LEFT GAMORRA BEHIND AND RETURNED TO THE WORLD WITH A NEW PURPOSE."
I TOOK OVER BASILISK, SHAPED IT TO MY NEEDS. I SAW FIRSTHAND WHAT YOU AND YOUR KIND COULD DO. YOU HAVE TO BE STOPPED. I'M GOING TO SEE TO IT THAT YOU ARE.
Dear god, he's completely insane.
YOU THINK I'M CRAZY, OF COURSE. I KNEW YOU WOULD. I'VE BEEN WAITING FOR THIS MOMENT FOR A LONG TIME. I GIVE YOU A SIMPLE CHOICE....
SERVE ME AND BE WITH KURT AGAIN...OR YOU DIE APART.

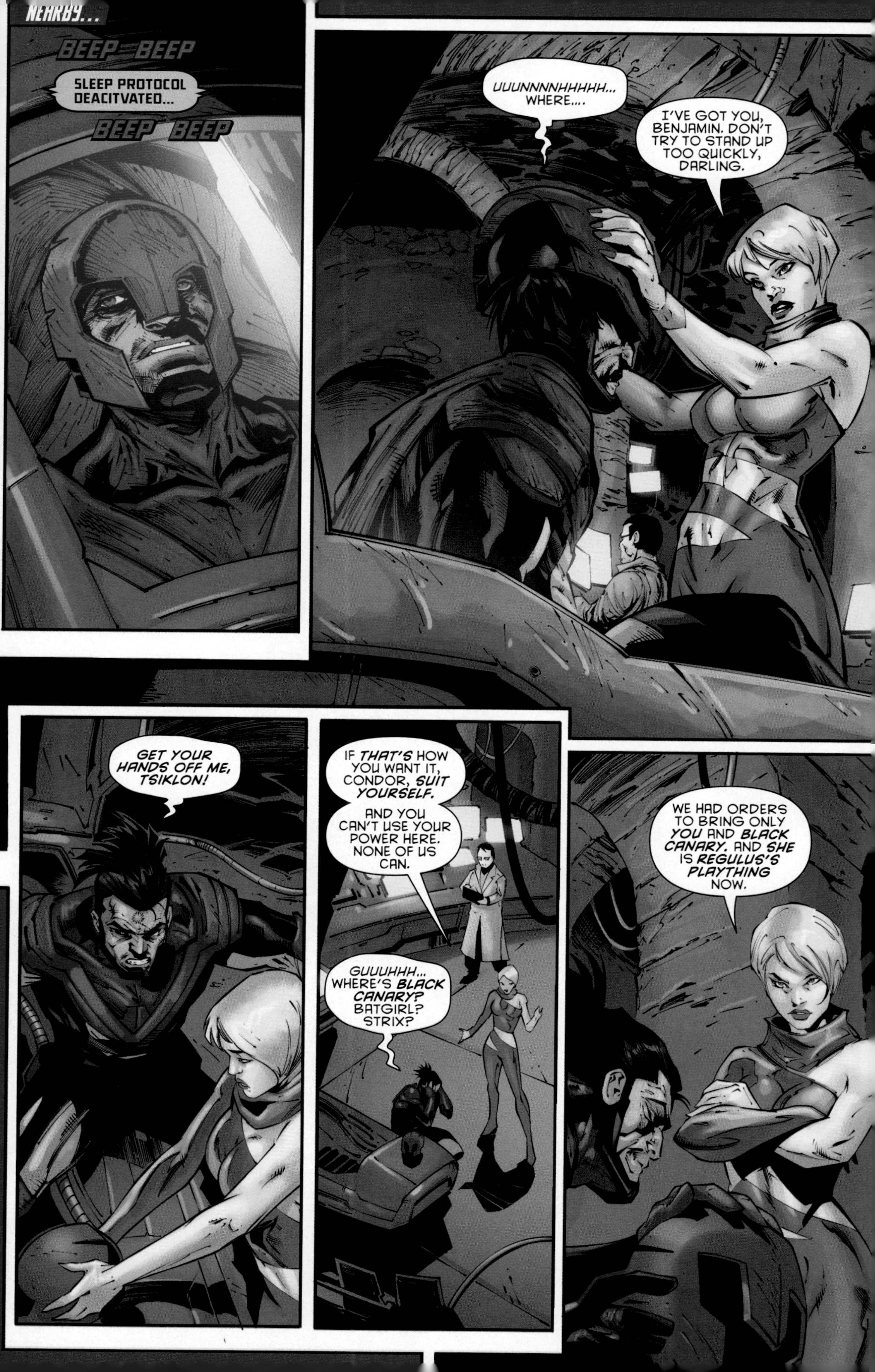
NEARBY...
BEEP BEEP
SLEEP PROTOCOL DEACITVATED...
BEEP BEEP
UUUNNNNHHHHH... WHERE....
I'VE GOT YOU, BENJAMIN. DON'T TRY TO STAND UP TOO QUICKLY, DARLING.
GET YOUR HANDS OFF ME, TSIKLON!
IF THAT'S HOW YOU WANT IT, CONDOR, SUIT YOURSELF.
AND YOU CAN'T USE YOUR POWER HERE. NONE OF US CAN.
GUUUHHH... WHERE'S BLACK CANARY? BATGIRL? STRIX?
WE HAD ORDERS TO BRING ONLY YOU AND BLACK CANARY. AND SHE IS REGULUS'S PLAYTHING NOW.

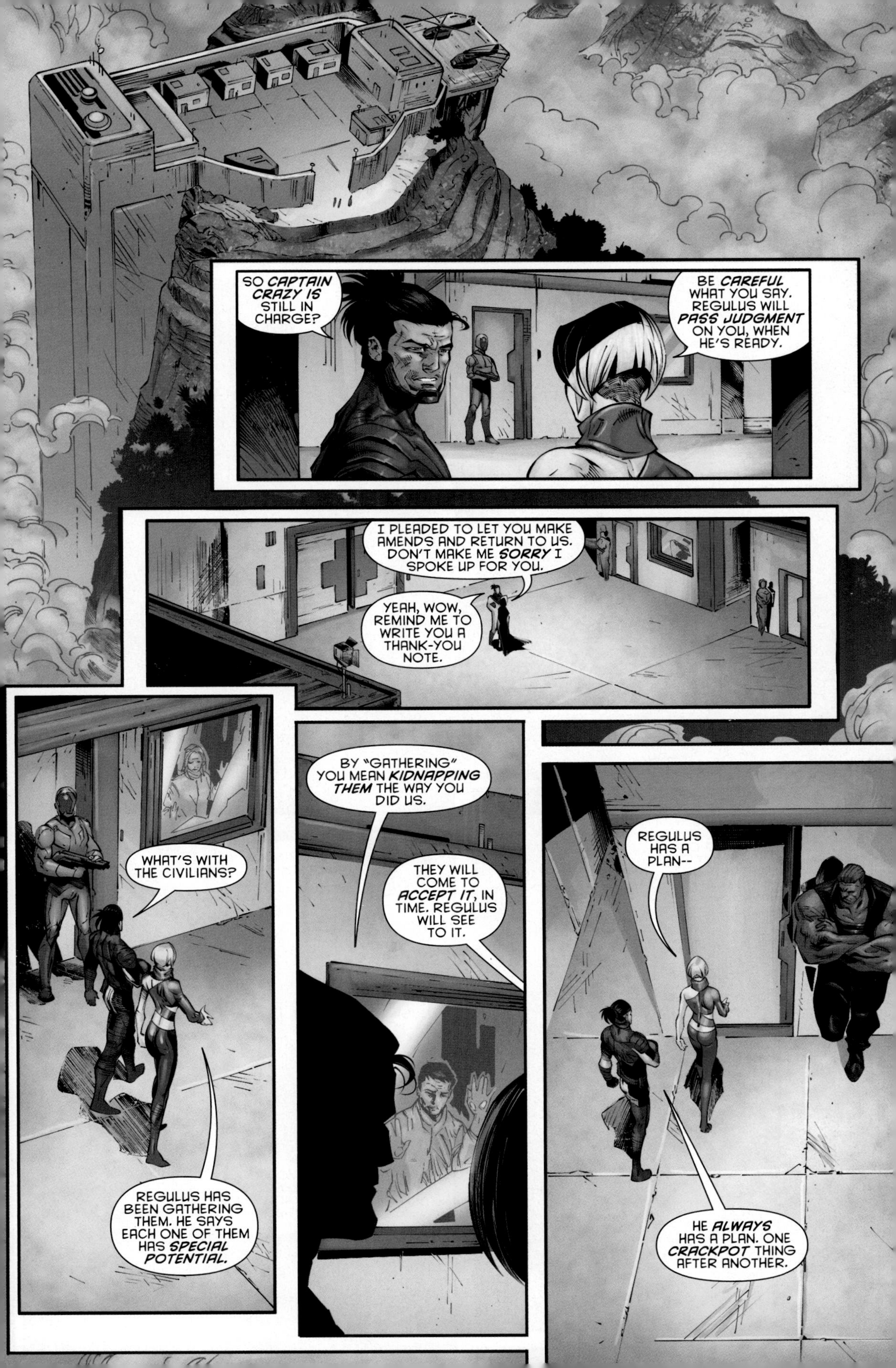
SO CAPTAIN CRAZY IS STILL IN CHARGE?
BE CAREFUL WHAT YOU SAY. REGULUS WILL PASS JUDGMENT ON YOU, WHEN HE'S READY.
I PLEADED TO LET YOU MAKE AMENDS AND RETURN TO US. DON'T MAKE ME SORRY I SPOKE UP FOR YOU.
YEAH, WOW, REMIND ME TO WRITE YOU A THANK-YOU NOTE.
WHAT'S WITH THE CIVILIANS?
REGULUS HAS BEEN GATHERING THEM. HE SAYS EACH ONE OF THEM HAS SPECIAL POTENTIAL.
BY "GATHERING" YOU MEAN KIDNAPPING THEM THE WAY YOU DID US.
THEY WILL COME TO ACCEPT IT, IN TIME. REGULUS WILL SEE TO IT.
REGULUS HAS A PLAN--
HE ALWAYS HAS A PLAN. ONE CRACKPOT THING AFTER ANOTHER.

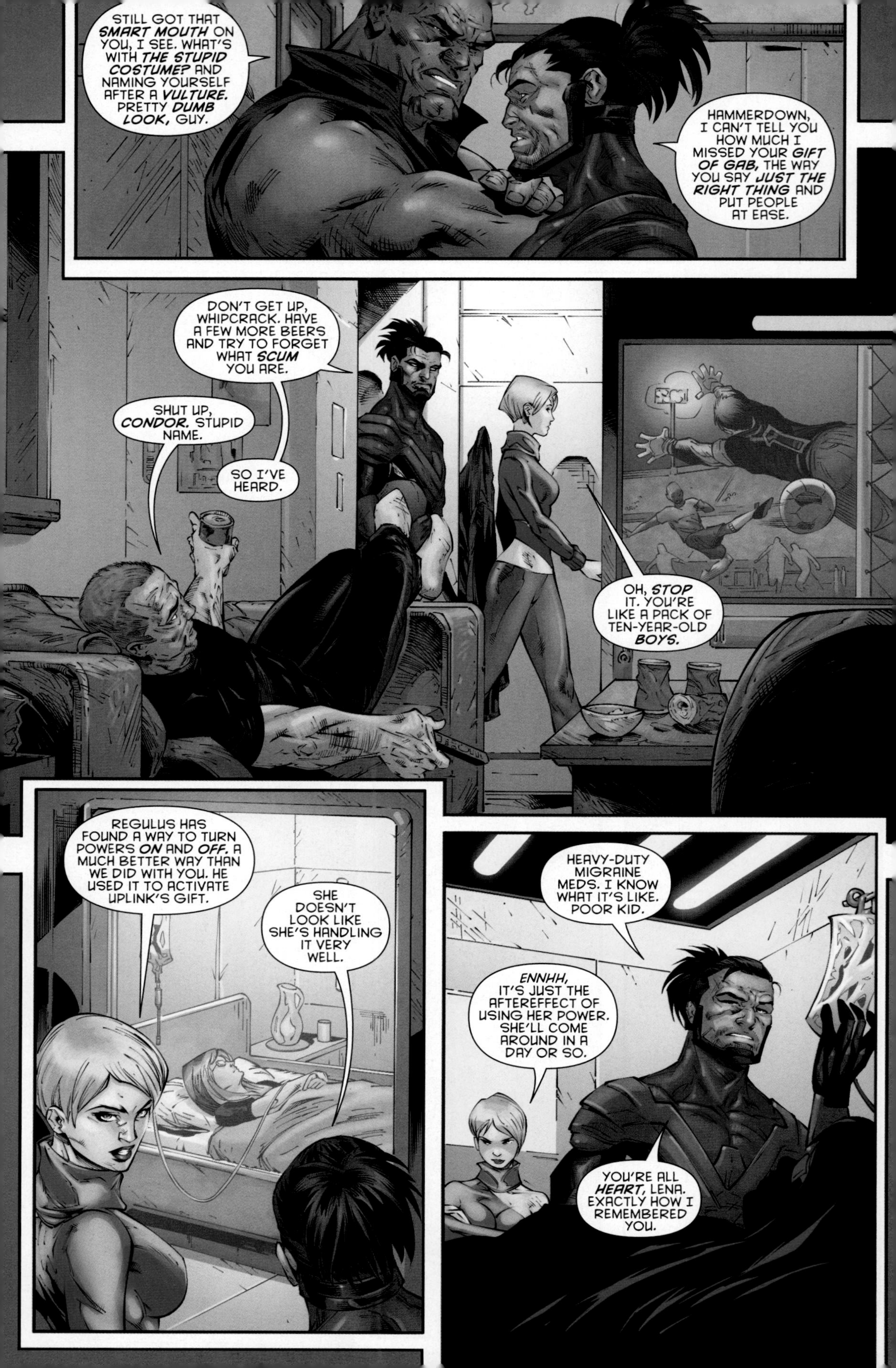
STILL GOT THAT SMART MOUTH ON YOU, I SEE. WHAT'S WITH THE STUPID COSTUME? AND NAMING YOURSELF AFTER A VULTURE. PRETTY DUMB LOOK, GUY.
HAMMERDOWN, I CAN'T TELL YOU HOW MUCH I MISSED YOUR GIFT OF GAB, THE WAY YOU SAY JUST THE RIGHT THING AND PUT PEOPLE AT EASE.
DON'T GET UP, WHIPCRACK. HAVE A FEW MORE BEERS AND TRY TO FORGET WHAT SCUM YOU ARE.
SHUT UP, CONDOR. STUPID NAME.
SO I'VE HEARD.
OH, STOP IT. YOU'RE LIKE A PACK OF TEN-YEAR-OLD BOYS.
REGULUS HAS FOUND A WAY TO TURN POWERS ON AND OFF. A MUCH BETTER WAY THAN WE DID WITH YOU. HE USED IT TO ACTIVATE UPLINK'S GIFT.
SHE DOESN'T LOOK LIKE SHE'S HANDLING IT VERY WELL.
HEAVY-DUTY MIGRAINE MEDS. I KNOW WHAT IT'S LIKE. POOR KID.
ENNHH, IT'S JUST THE AFTEREFFECT OF USING HER POWER. SHE'LL COME AROUND IN A DAY OR SO.
YOU'RE ALL HEART, LENA. EXACTLY HOW I REMEMBERED YOU.

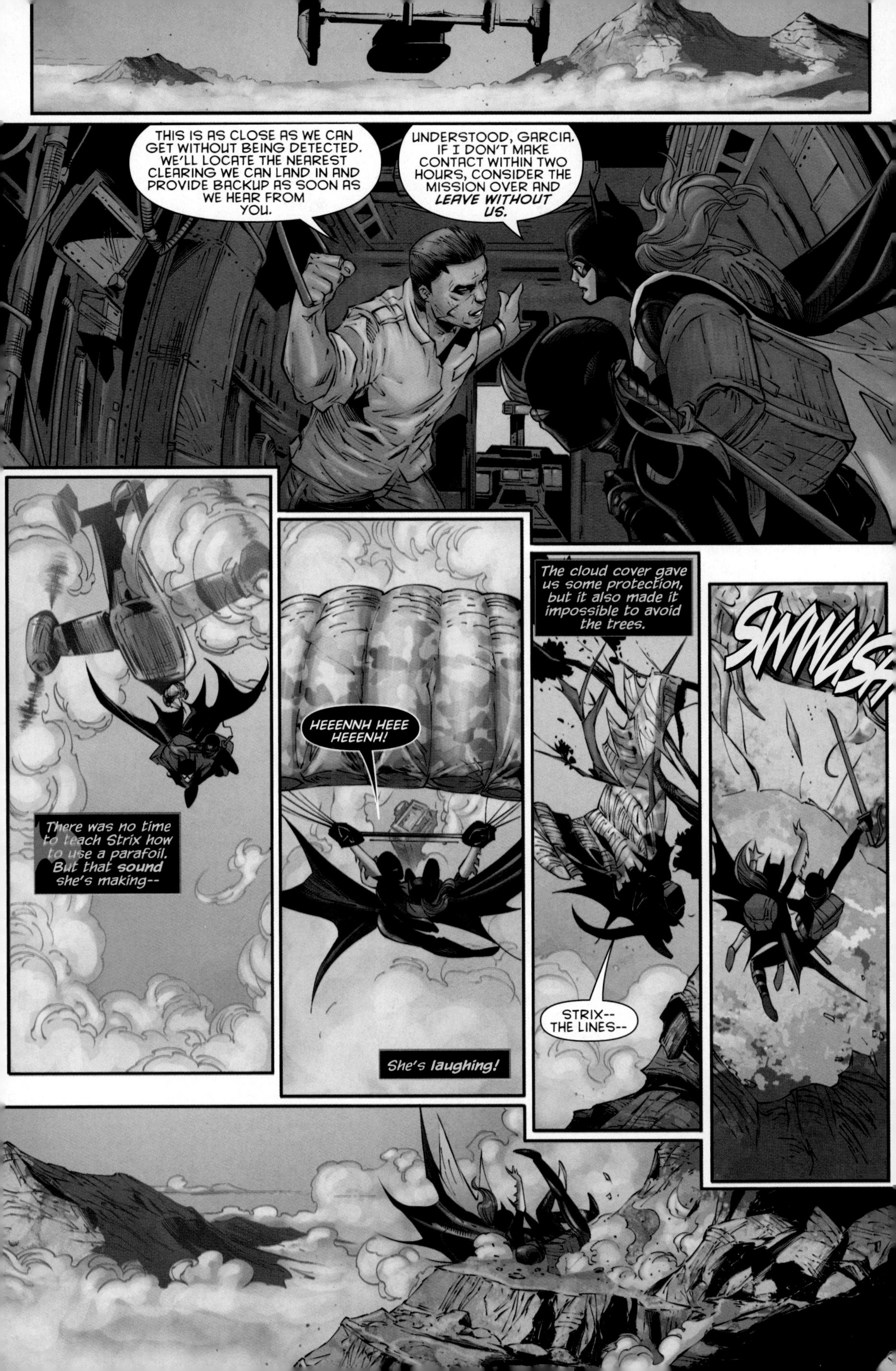
THIS IS AS CLOSE AS WE CAN GET WITHOUT BEING DETECTED. WE'LL LOCATE THE NEAREST CLEARING WE CAN LAND IN AND PROVIDE BACKUP AS SOON AS WE HEAR FROM YOU.
UNDERSTOOD, GARCIA. IF I DON'T MAKE CONTACT WITHIN TWO HOURS, CONSIDER THE MISSION OVER AND *LEAVE WITHOUT US.*
There was no time to teach Strix how to use a parafoil. But that **sound** she's making--
HEEENNH HEEE HEEENH!
She's **laughing!**
The cloud cover gave us some protection, but it also made it impossible to avoid the trees.
STRIX-- THE LINES--
SWWUSH

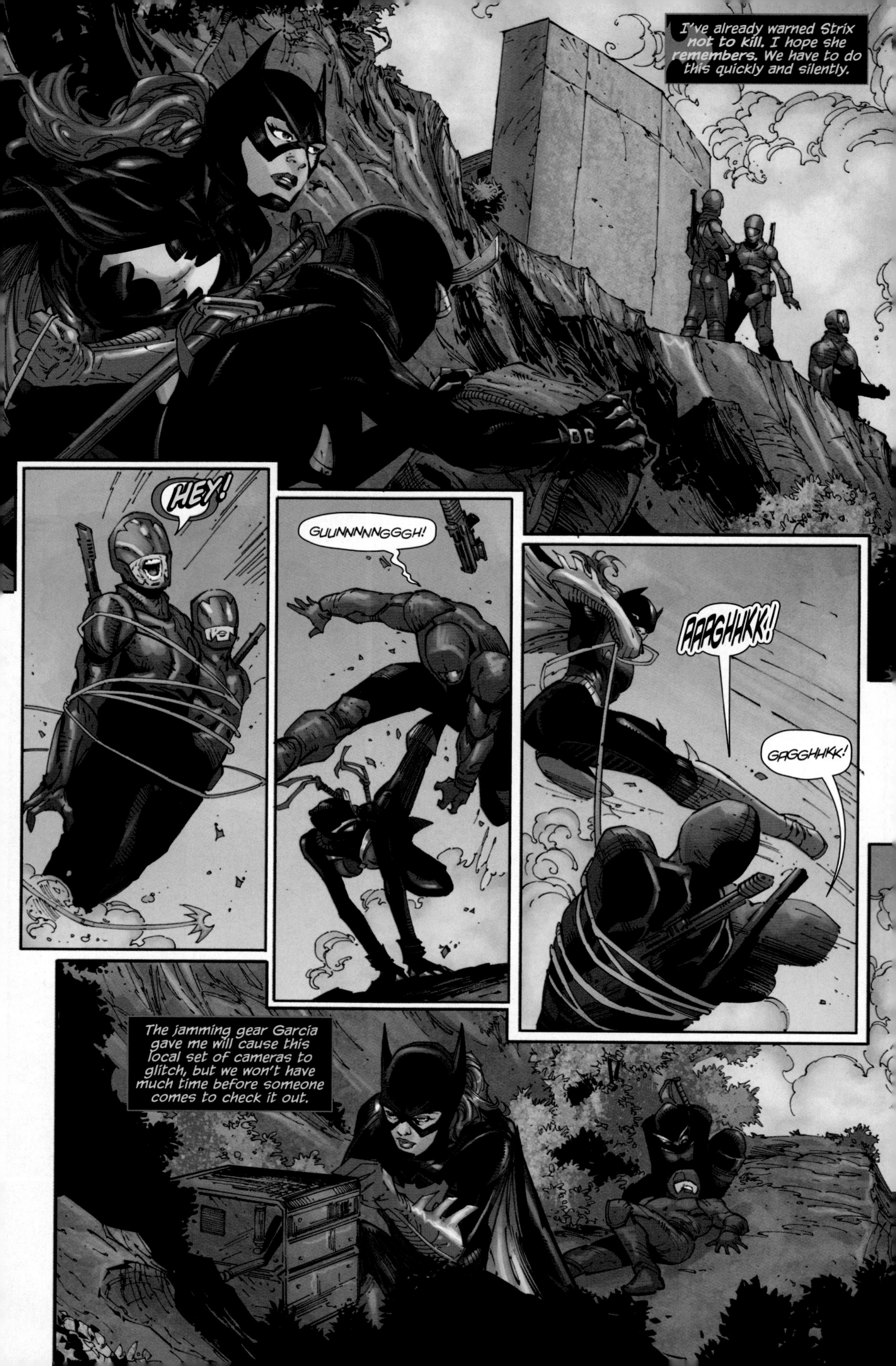
I've already warned Strix not to kill. I hope she remembers. We have to do this quickly and silently.
HEY!
GUUNNNNNGGGH!
AAAGHHKK!
GAGGHHKK!
The jamming gear Garcia gave me will cause this local set of cameras to glitch, but we won't have much time before someone comes to check it out.

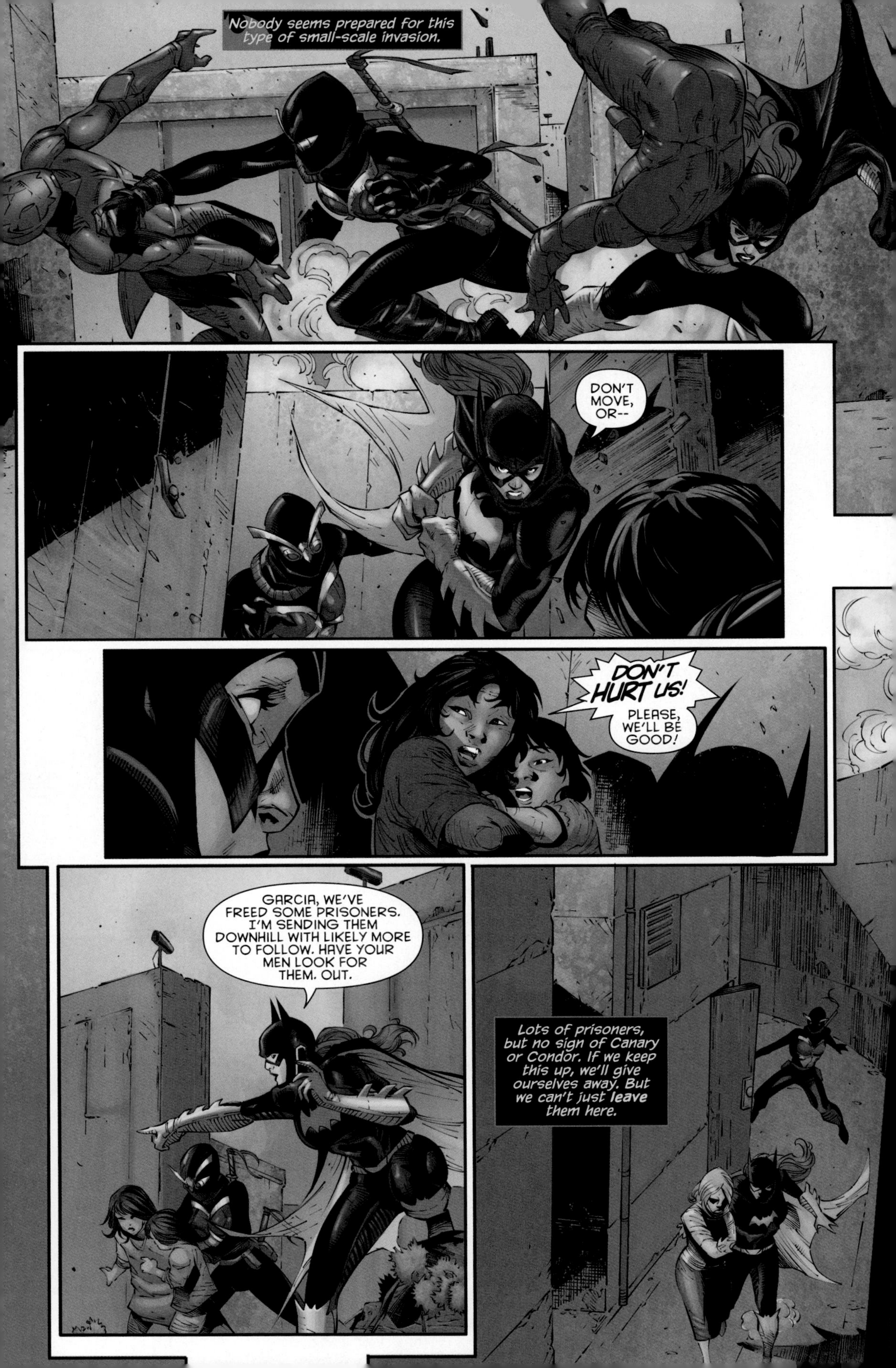
Nobody seems prepared for this type of small-scale invasion.
DON'T MOVE, OR--
DON'T HURT US!
PLEASE, WE'LL BE GOOD!
GARCIA, WE'VE FREED SOME PRISONERS. I'M SENDING THEM DOWNHILL WITH LIKELY MORE TO FOLLOW. HAVE YOUR MEN LOOK FOR THEM. OUT.
Lots of prisoners, but no sign of Canary or Condor. If we keep this up, we'll give ourselves away. But we can't just leave them here.

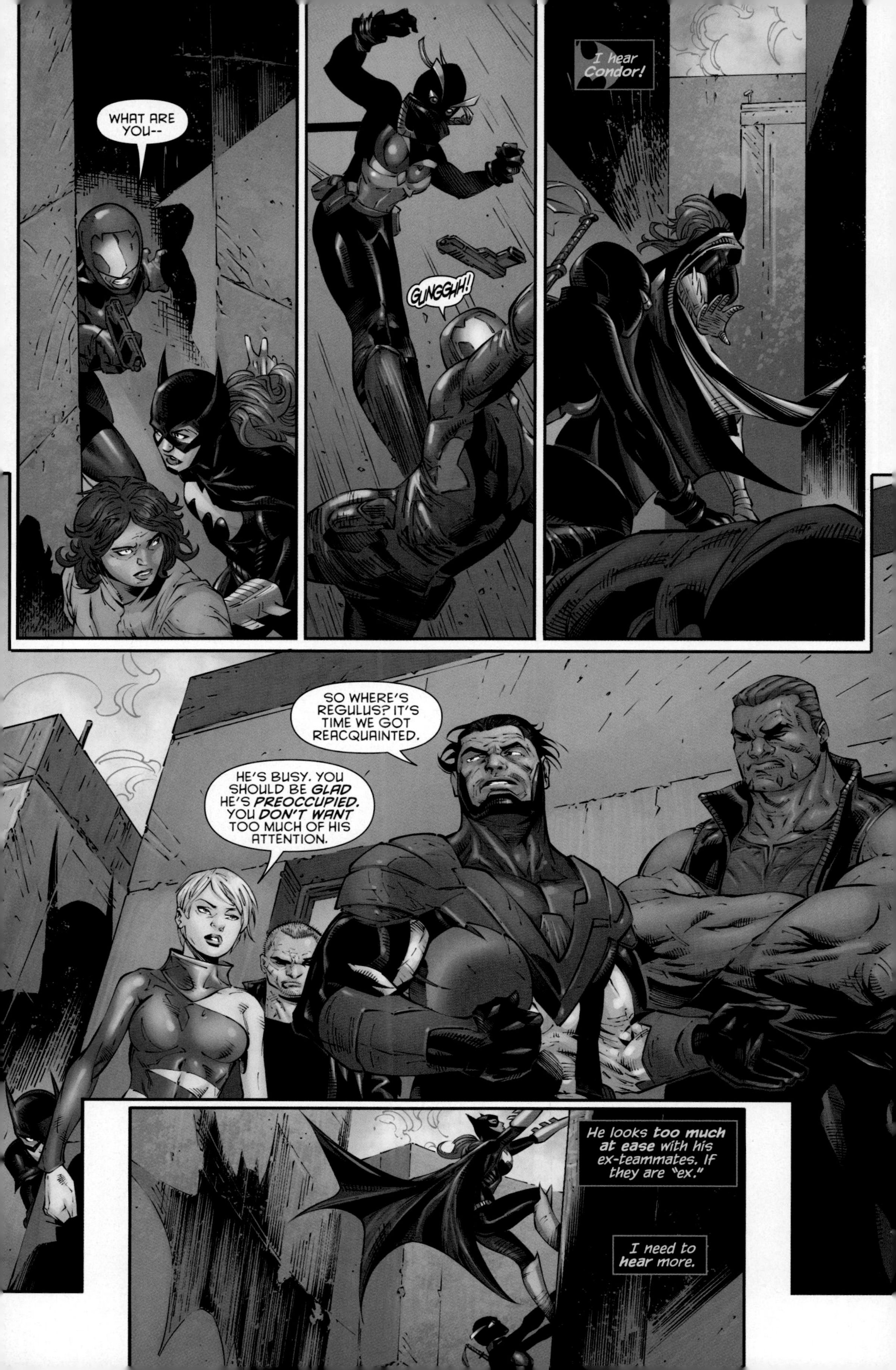

WHAT ARE YOU--
GUNGGHH!
I hear Condor!
SO WHERE'S REGULUS? IT'S TIME WE GOT REACQUAINTED.
HE'S BUSY. YOU SHOULD BE GLAD HE'S PREOCCUPIED. YOU DON'T WANT TOO MUCH OF HIS ATTENTION.
He looks too much at ease with his ex-teammates. If they are "ex."
I need to hear more.

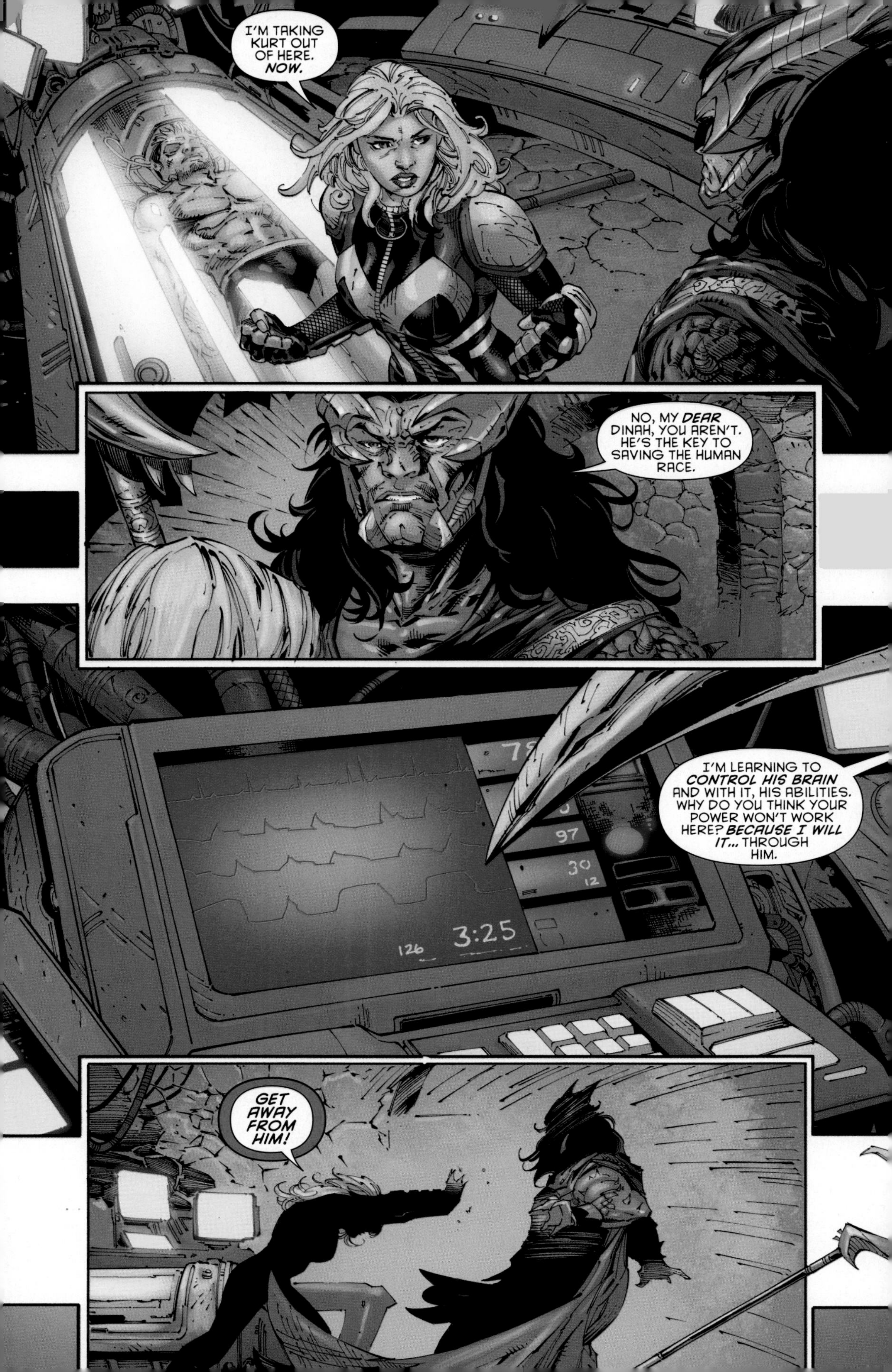
I'M TAKING KURT OUT OF HERE. *NOW.*
NO, MY *DEAR* DINAH, YOU AREN'T. HE'S THE KEY TO SAVING THE HUMAN RACE.
I'M LEARNING TO **CONTROL HIS BRAIN** AND WITH IT, HIS ABILITIES. WHY DO YOU THINK YOUR POWER WON'T WORK HERE? ***BECAUSE I WILL IT...*** THROUGH HIM.
GET AWAY FROM HIM!

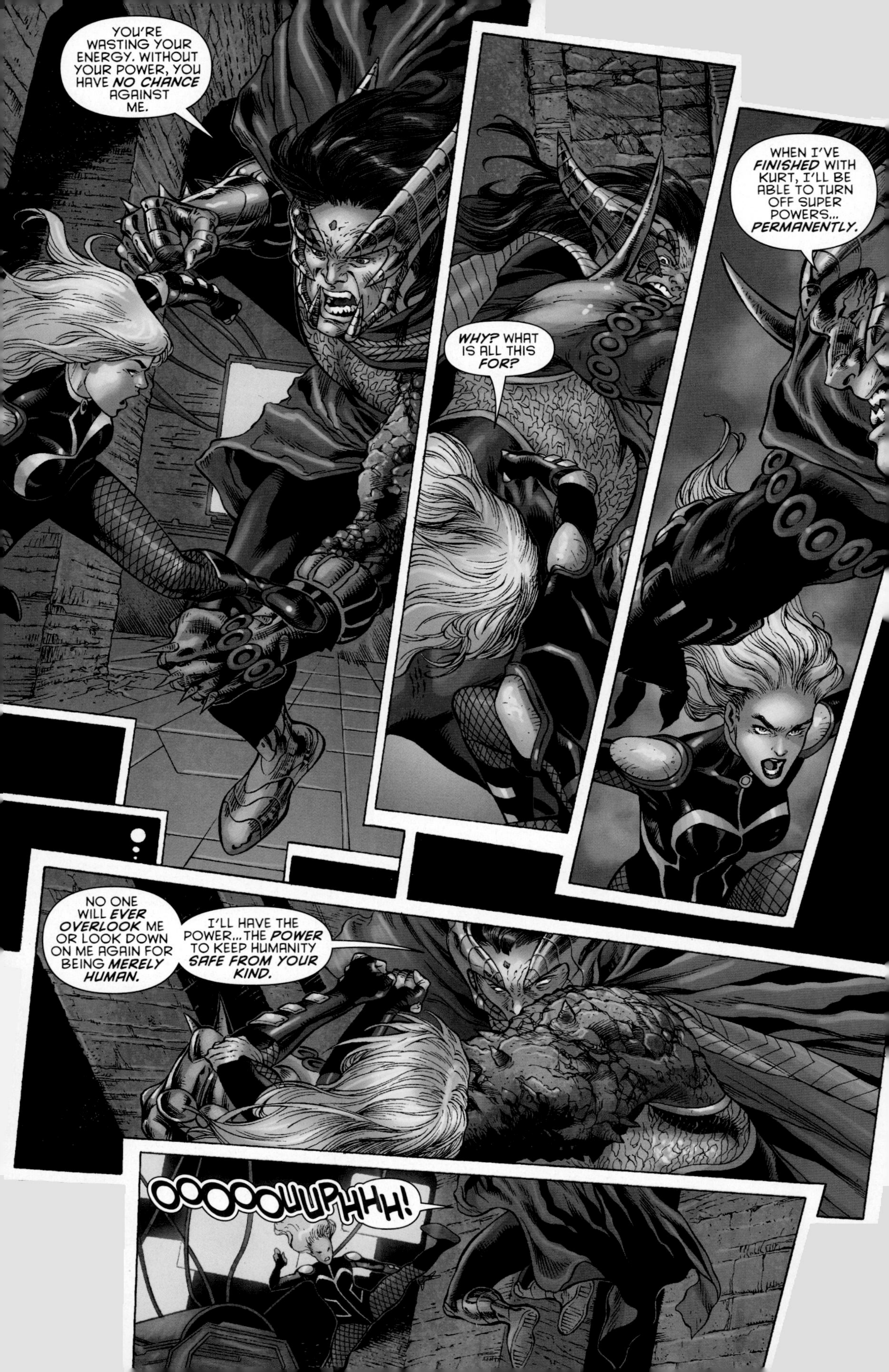
YOU'RE WASTING YOUR ENERGY. WITHOUT YOUR POWER, YOU HAVE NO CHANCE AGAINST ME.
WHY? WHAT IS ALL THIS FOR?
WHEN I'VE FINISHED WITH KURT, I'LL BE ABLE TO TURN OFF SUPER POWERS... PERMANENTLY.
NO ONE WILL EVER OVERLOOK ME OR LOOK DOWN ON ME AGAIN FOR BEING MERELY HUMAN.
I'LL HAVE THE POWER... THE POWER TO KEEP HUMANITY SAFE FROM YOUR KIND.
OOOOOOUUPHHH!

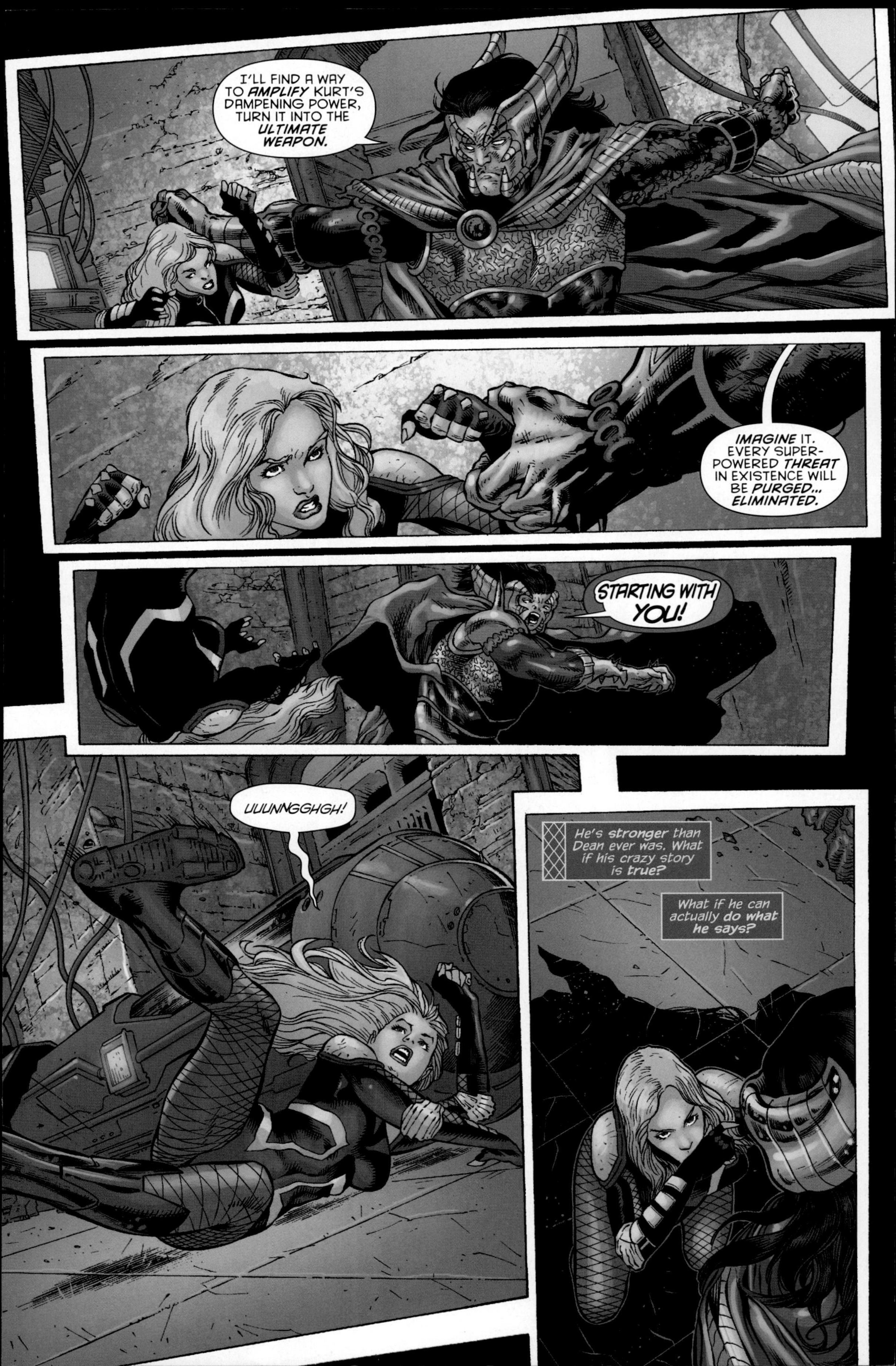
I'LL FIND A WAY TO AMPLIFY KURT'S DAMPENING POWER, TURN IT INTO THE ULTIMATE WEAPON.
IMAGINE IT. EVERY SUPER-POWERED THREAT IN EXISTENCE WILL BE PURGED... ELIMINATED.
STARTING WITH YOU!
UUUNNGGHGH!
He's stronger than Dean ever was. What if his crazy story is true?
What if he can actually do what he says?

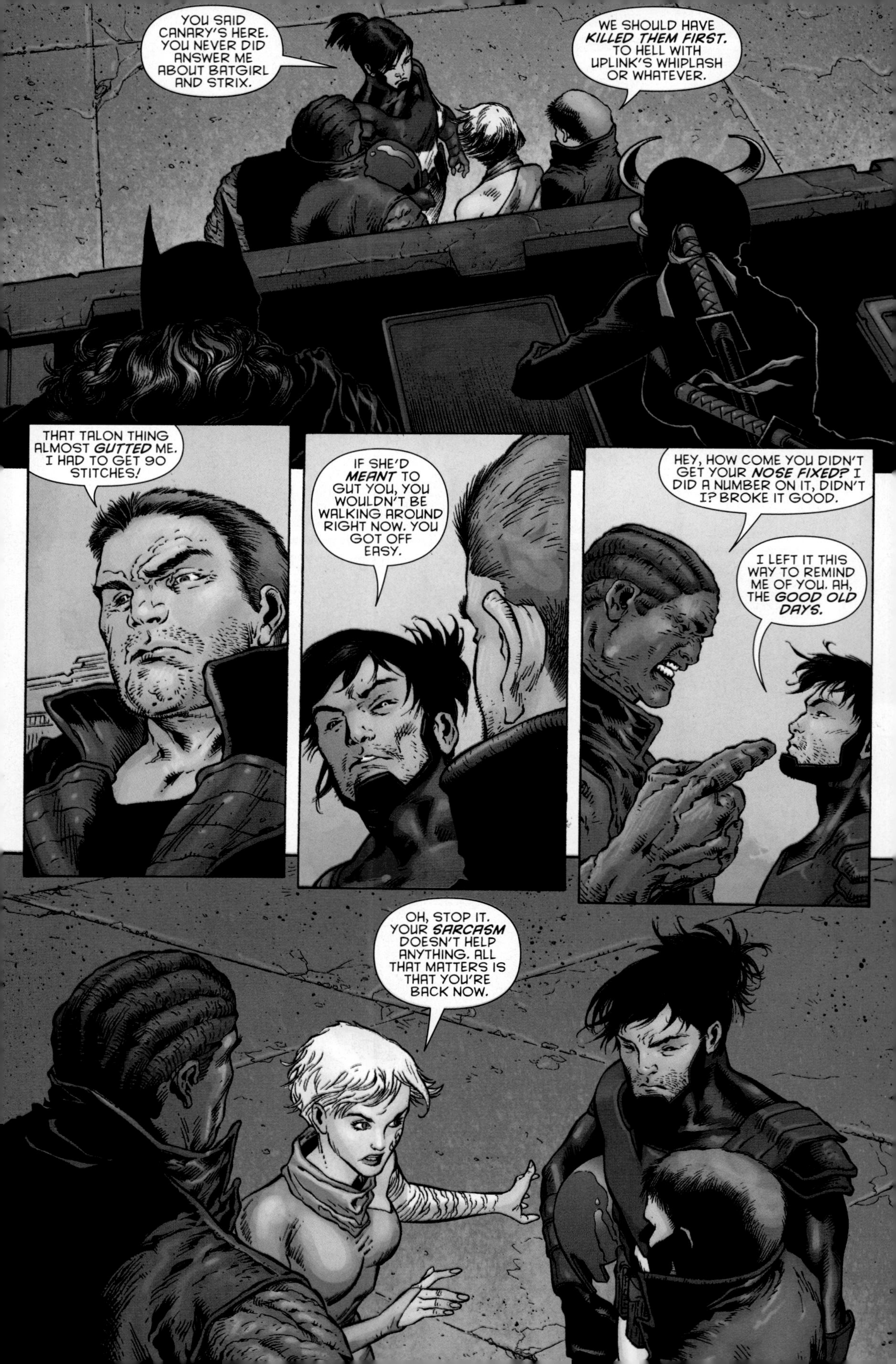
YOU SAID CANARY'S HERE. YOU NEVER DID ANSWER ME ABOUT BATGIRL AND STRIX.
WE SHOULD HAVE KILLED THEM FIRST. TO HELL WITH UPLINK'S WHIPLASH OR WHATEVER.
THAT TALON THING ALMOST GUTTED ME. I HAD TO GET 90 STITCHES!
IF SHE'D MEANT TO GUT YOU, YOU WOULDN'T BE WALKING AROUND RIGHT NOW. YOU GOT OFF EASY.
HEY, HOW COME YOU DIDN'T GET YOUR NOSE FIXED? I DID A NUMBER ON IT, DIDN'T I? BROKE IT GOOD.
I LEFT IT THIS WAY TO REMIND ME OF YOU. AH, THE GOOD OLD DAYS.
OH, STOP IT. YOUR SARCASM DOESN'T HELP ANYTHING. ALL THAT MATTERS IS THAT YOU'RE BACK NOW.

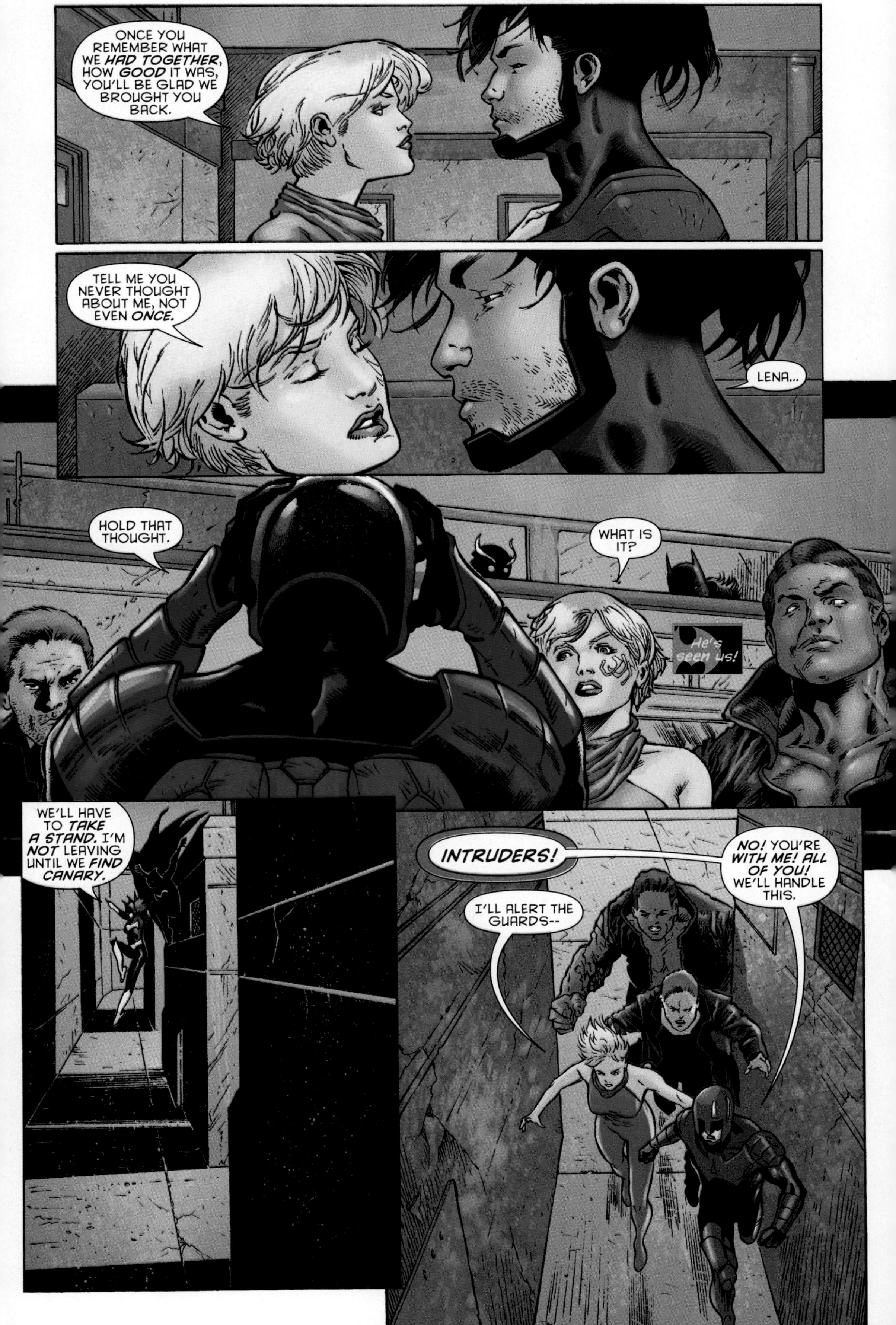

ONCE YOU REMEMBER WHAT WE HAD TOGETHER, HOW GOOD IT WAS, YOU'LL BE GLAD WE BROUGHT YOU BACK.
TELL ME YOU NEVER THOUGHT ABOUT ME, NOT EVEN ONCE.
LENA...
HOLD THAT THOUGHT.
WHAT IS IT?
He's seen us!
WE'LL HAVE TO TAKE A STAND. I'M NOT LEAVING UNTIL WE FIND CANARY.
INTRUDERS!
I'LL ALERT THE GUARDS--
NO! YOU'RE WITH ME! ALL OF YOU! WE'LL HANDLE THIS.

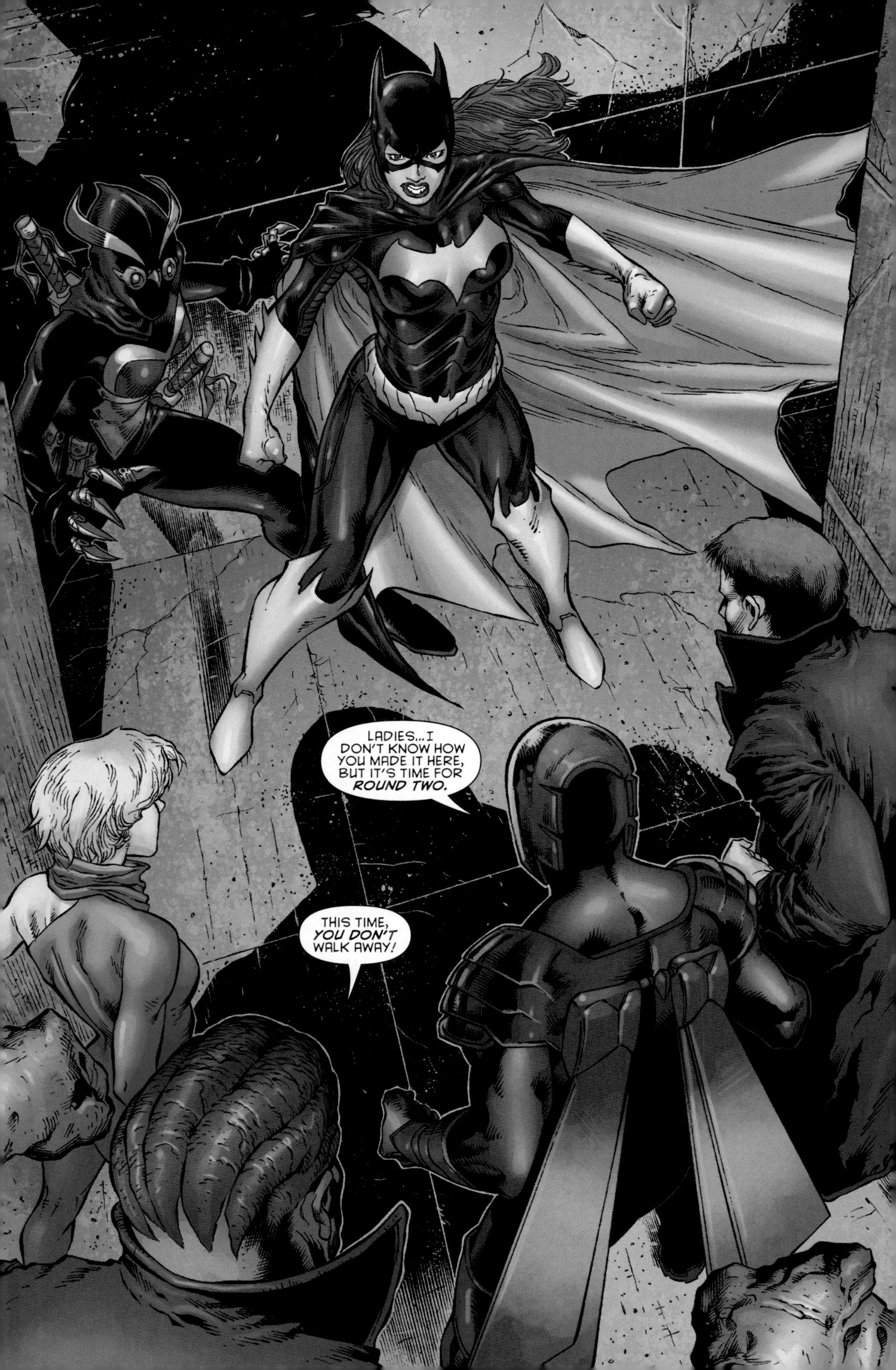

LADIES... I DON'T KNOW HOW YOU MADE IT HERE, BUT IT'S TIME FOR ROUND TWO.
THIS TIME, YOU DON'T WALK AWAY!

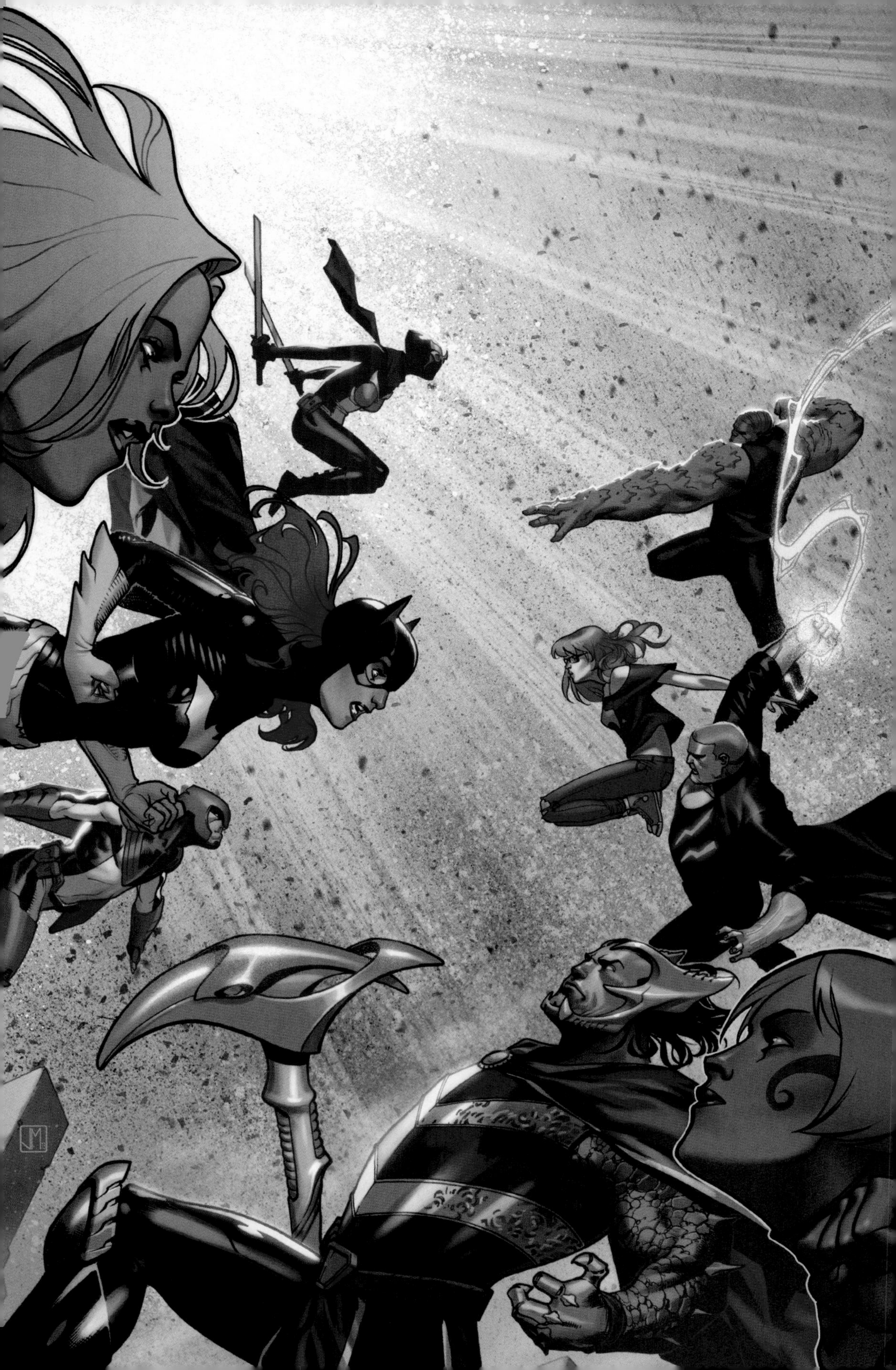

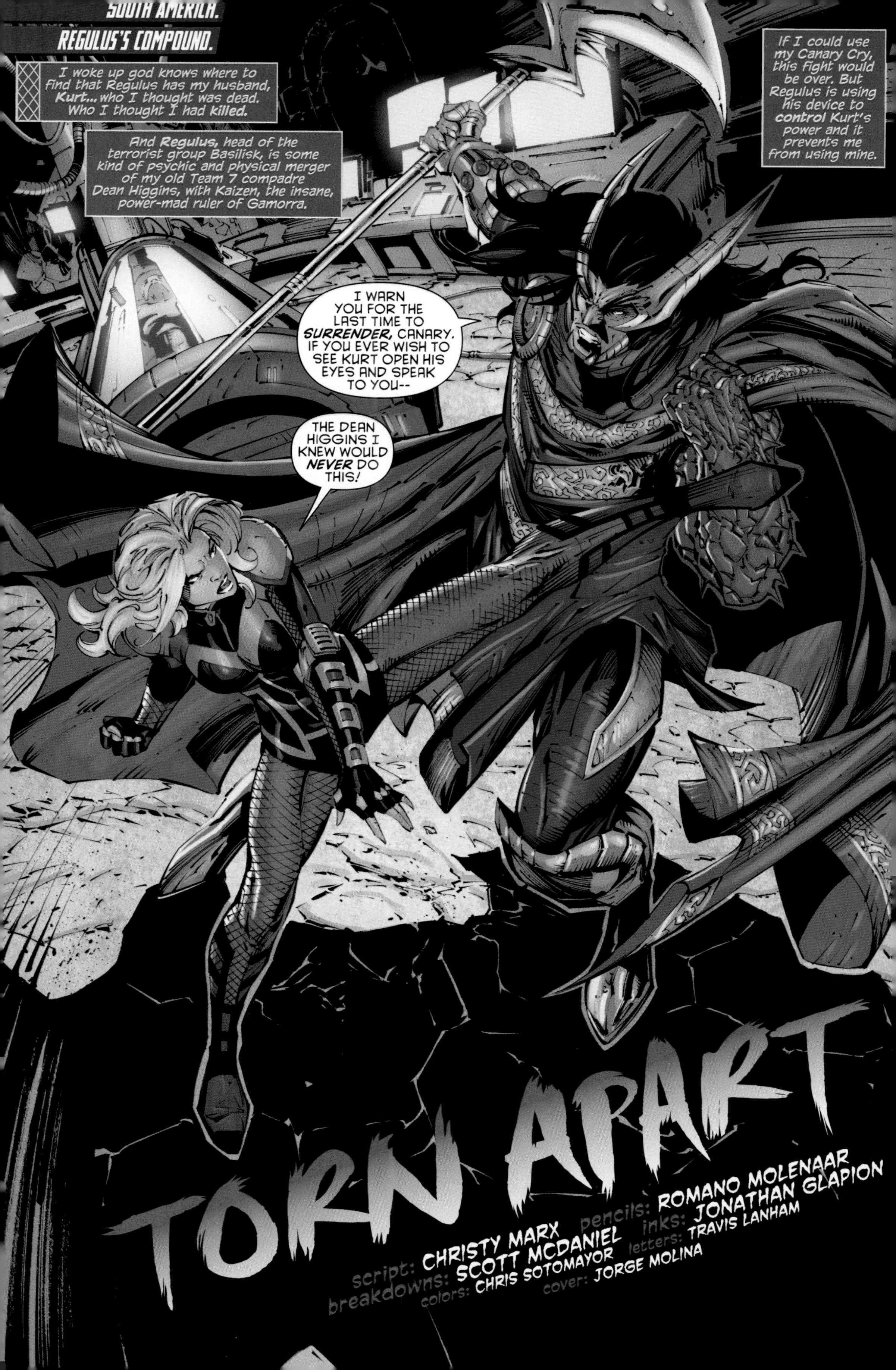
SOUTH AMERICA.
REGULUS'S COMPOUND.
I woke up god knows where to find that Regulus has my husband, Kurt...who I thought was dead. Who I thought I had killed.
And Regulus, head of the terrorist group Basilisk, is some kind of psychic and physical merger of my old Team 7 compadre Dean Higgins, with Kaizen, the insane, power-mad ruler of Gamorra.
If I could use my Canary Cry, this fight would be over. But Regulus is using his device to control Kurt's power and it prevents me from using mine.
I WARN YOU FOR THE LAST TIME TO SURRENDER, CANARY. IF YOU EVER WISH TO SEE KURT OPEN HIS EYES AND SPEAK TO YOU--
THE DEAN HIGGINS I KNEW WOULD NEVER DO THIS!
TORN APART
script: CHRISTY MARX pencils: ROMANO MOLENAAR
breakdowns: SCOTT McDANIEL inks: JONATHAN GLAPION
colors: CHRIS SOTOMAYOR letters: TRAVIS LANHAM
cover: JORGE MOLINA

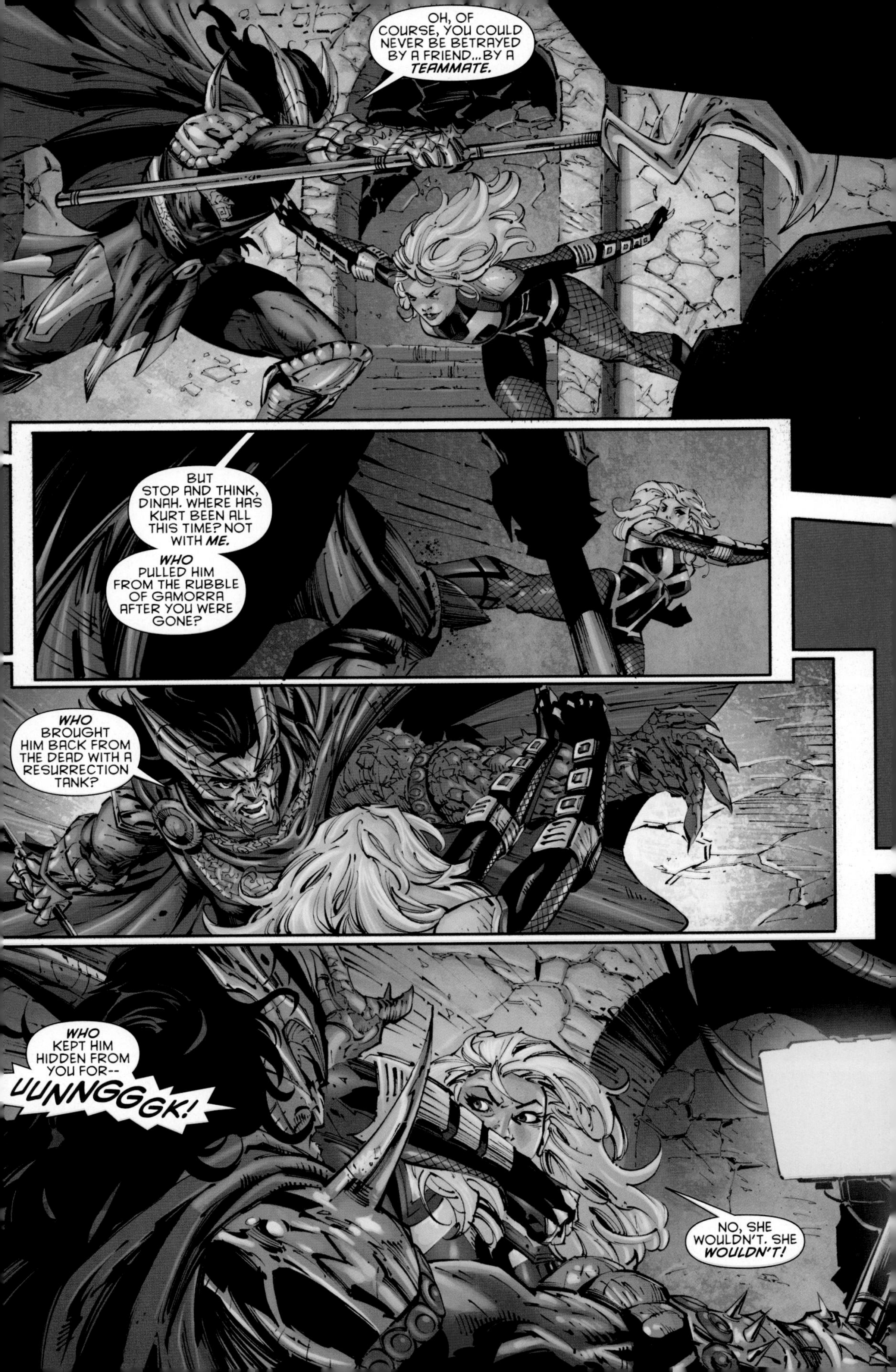
OH, OF COURSE, YOU COULD NEVER BE BETRAYED BY A FRIEND...BY A TEAMMATE.
BUT STOP AND THINK, DINAH. WHERE HAS KURT BEEN ALL THIS TIME? NOT WITH ME.
WHO PULLED HIM FROM THE RUBBLE OF GAMORRA AFTER YOU WERE GONE?
WHO BROUGHT HIM BACK FROM THE DEAD WITH A RESURRECTION TANK?
WHO KEPT HIM HIDDEN FROM YOU FOR--
UUNNGGGK!
NO, SHE WOULDN'T. SHE WOULDN'T!

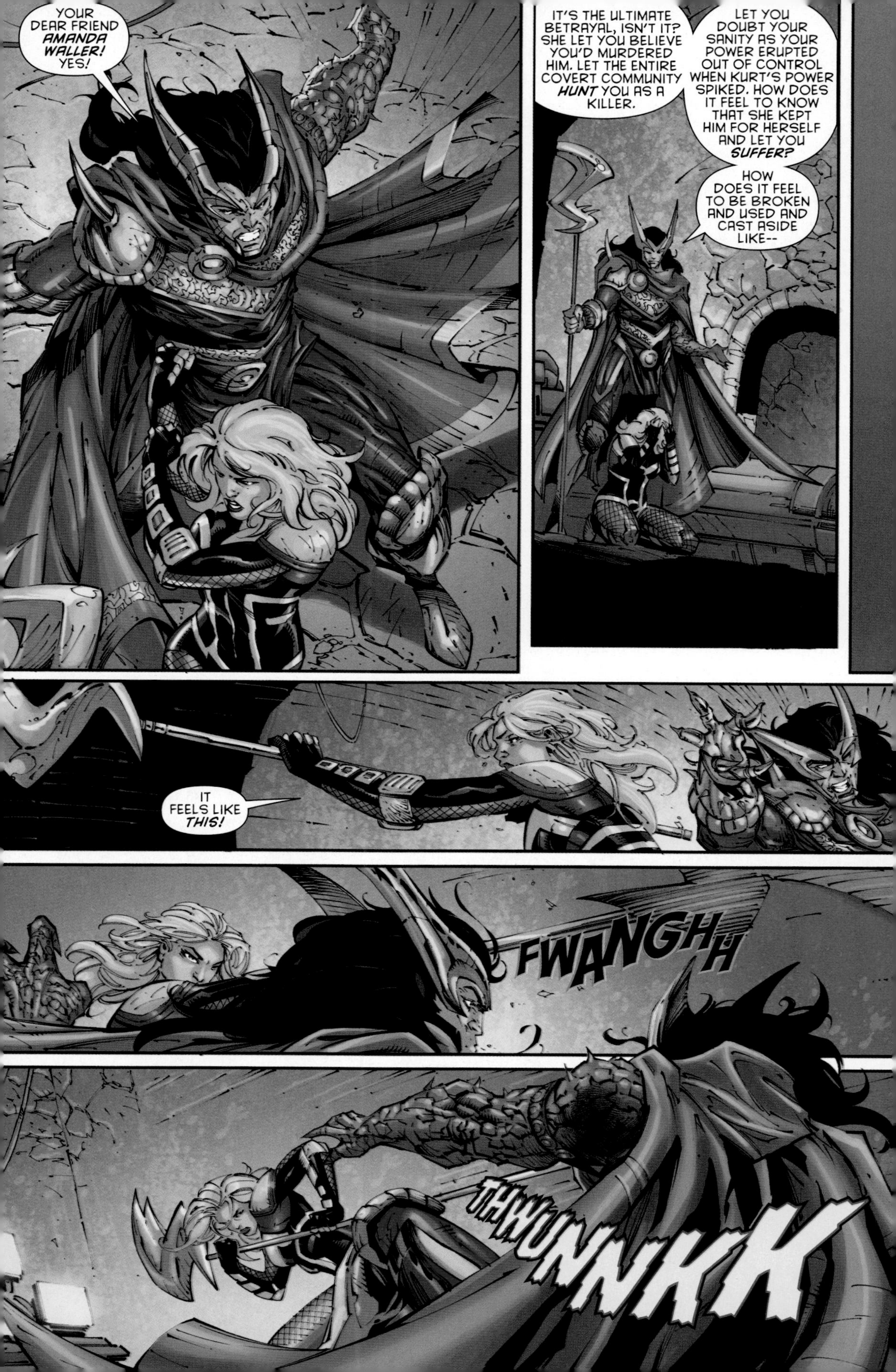

YOUR DEAR FRIEND AMANDA WALLER! YES!
IT'S THE ULTIMATE BETRAYAL, ISN'T IT? SHE LET YOU BELIEVE YOU'D MURDERED HIM. LET THE ENTIRE COVERT COMMUNITY HUNT YOU AS A KILLER.
LET YOU DOUBT YOUR SANITY AS YOUR POWER ERUPTED OUT OF CONTROL WHEN KURT'S POWER SPIKED. HOW DOES IT FEEL TO KNOW THAT SHE KEPT HIM FOR HERSELF AND LET YOU SUFFER?
HOW DOES IT FEEL TO BE BROKEN AND USED AND CAST ASIDE LIKE--
IT FEELS LIKE THIS!
FWANGHH
THWUNNKK

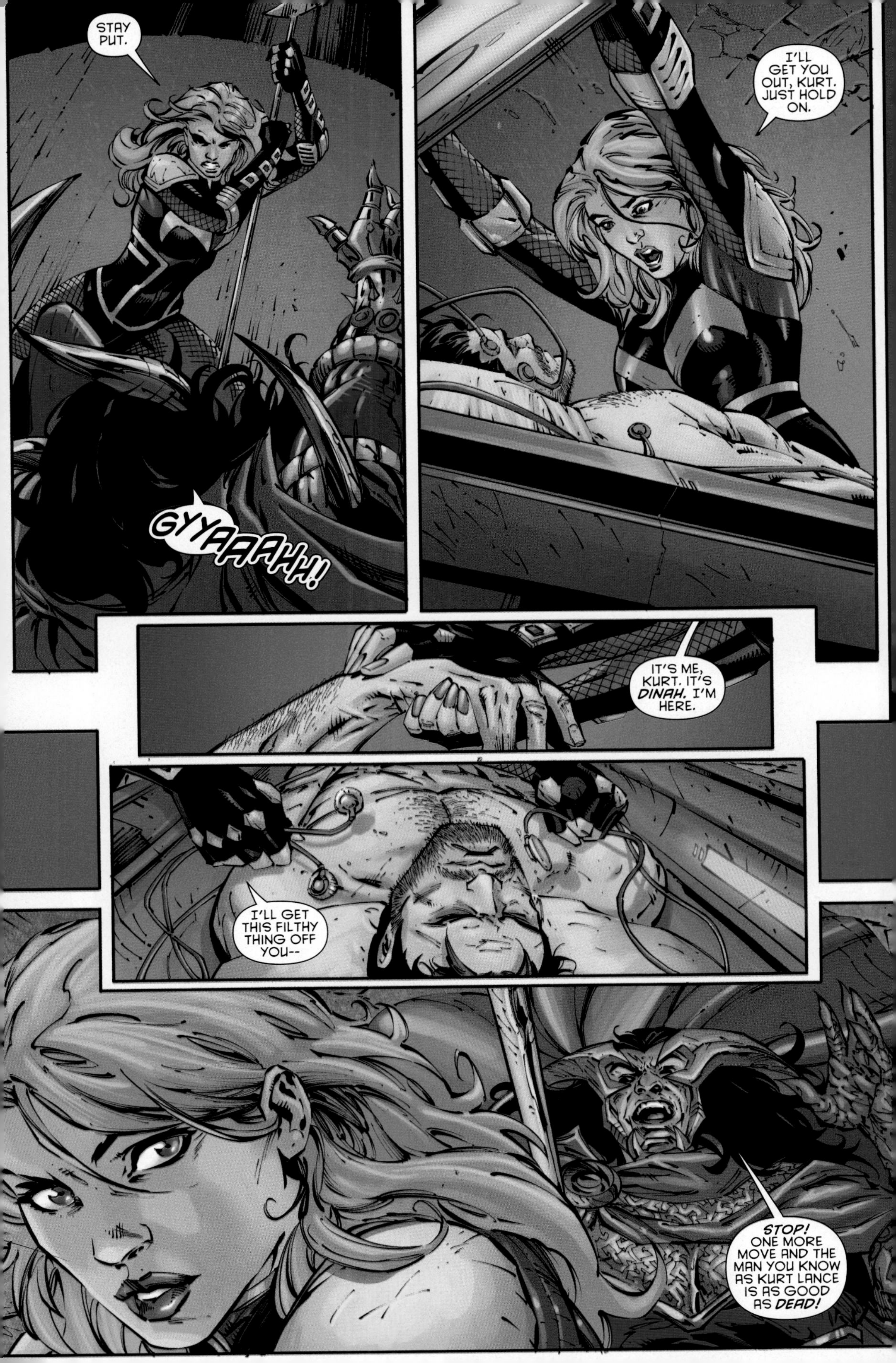
STAY PUT.
GYYAAAAHH!
I'LL GET YOU OUT, KURT. JUST HOLD ON.
IT'S ME, KURT. IT'S *DINAH.* I'M HERE.
I'LL GET THIS FILTHY THING OFF YOU--
STOP! ONE MORE MOVE AND THE MAN YOU KNOW AS KURT LANCE IS AS GOOD AS *DEAD!*

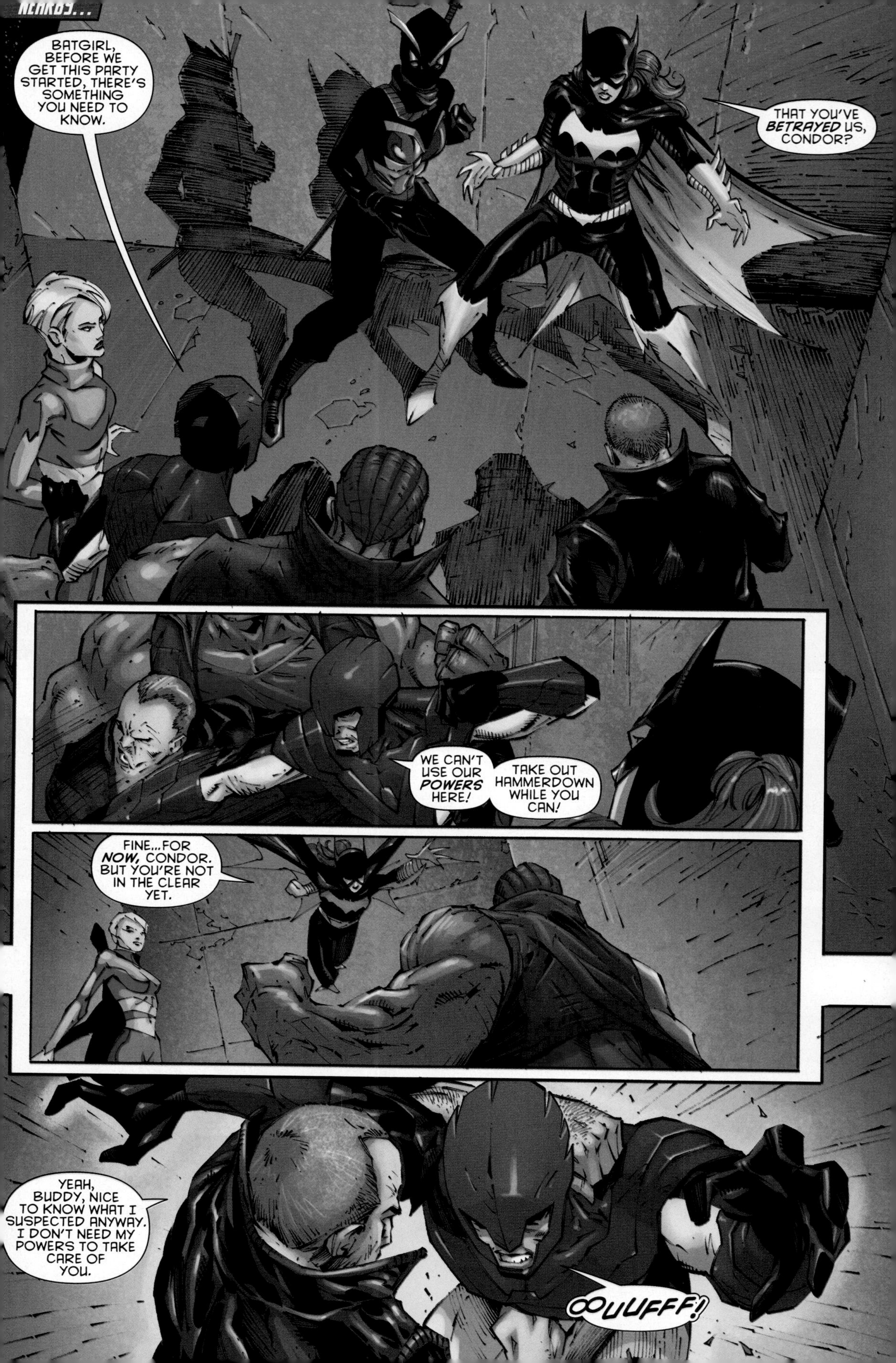

NEARBY...
BATGIRL, BEFORE WE GET THIS PARTY STARTED, THERE'S SOMETHING YOU NEED TO KNOW.
THAT YOU'VE BETRAYED US, CONDOR?
WE CAN'T USE OUR POWERS HERE!
TAKE OUT HAMMERDOWN WHILE YOU CAN!
FINE...FOR NOW, CONDOR. BUT YOU'RE NOT IN THE CLEAR YET.
YEAH, BUDDY, NICE TO KNOW WHAT I SUSPECTED ANYWAY. I DON'T NEED MY POWERS TO TAKE CARE OF YOU.
OOUUFFF!

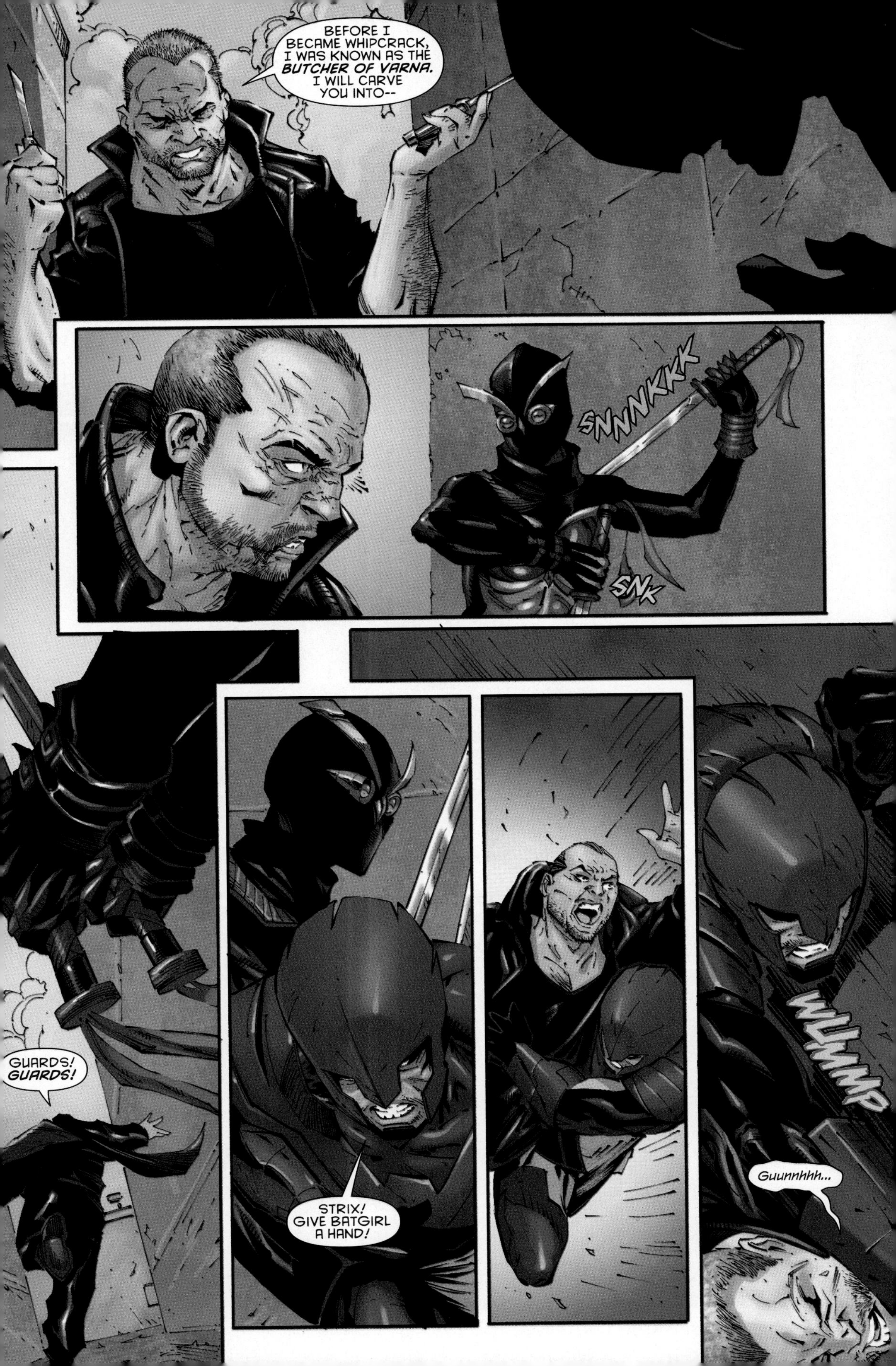
BEFORE I BECAME WHIPCRACK, I WAS KNOWN AS THE *BUTCHER OF VARNA.* I WILL CARVE YOU INTO--
SNNNKKK
SNK
GUARDS! *GUARDS!*
STRIX! GIVE BATGIRL A HAND!
WUMMP
Guunnhhh...

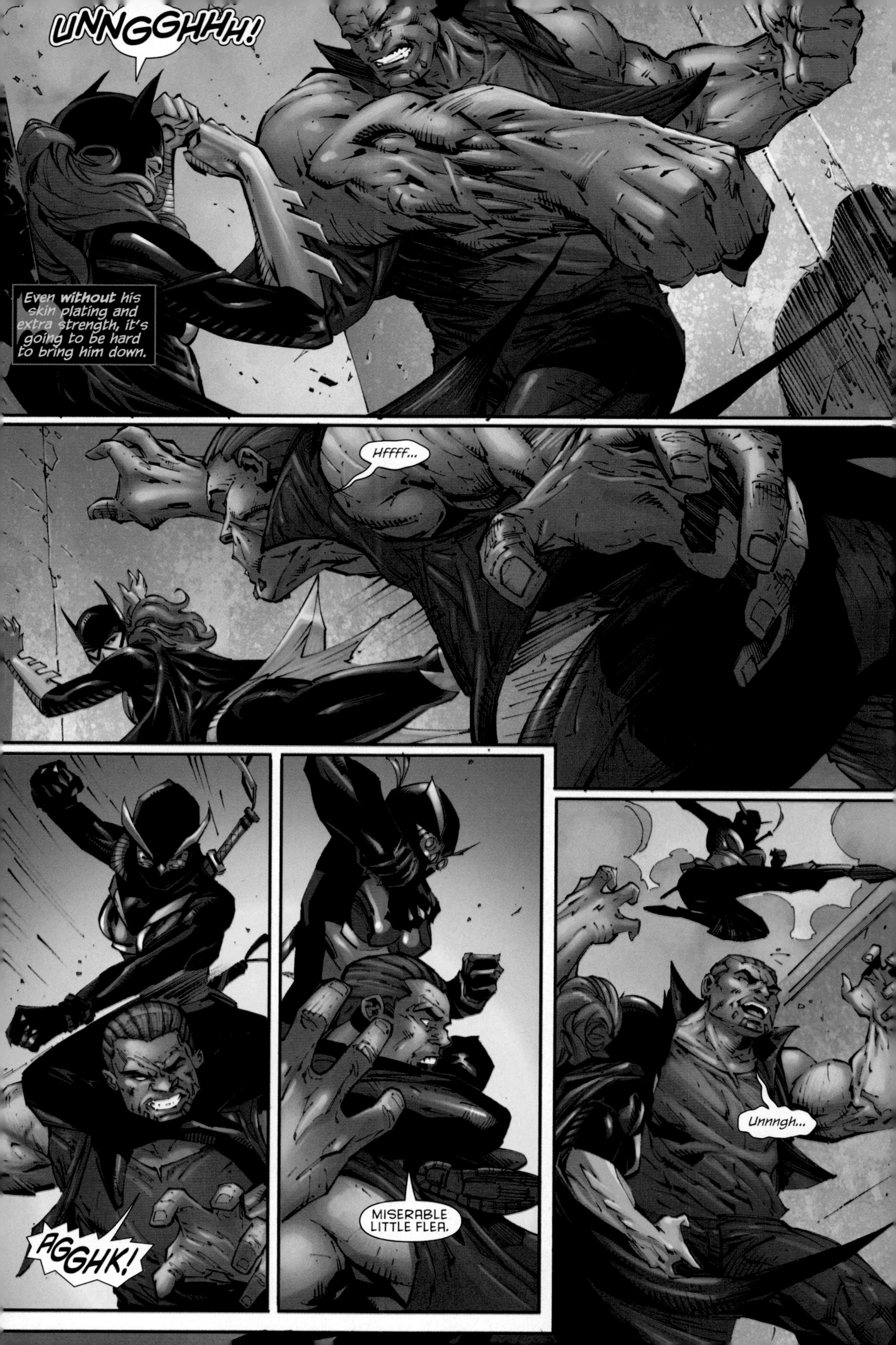
UNNGGHHH!
Even without his skin plating and extra strength, it's going to be hard to bring him down.
Hffff...
AGGHK!
MISERABLE LITTLE FLEA.
Unnngh...

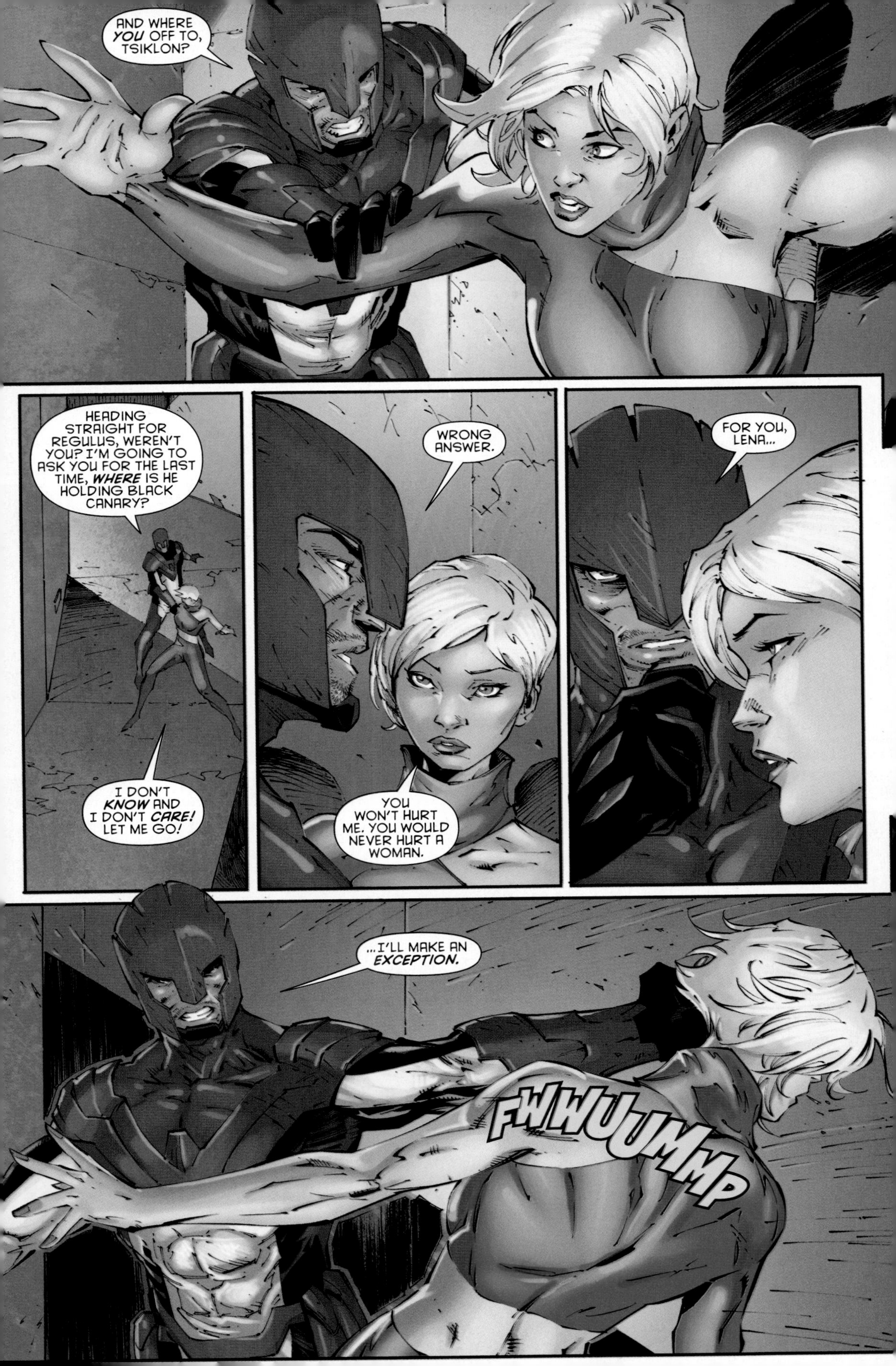
AND WHERE *YOU* OFF TO, TSIKLON?
HEADING STRAIGHT FOR REGULUS, WEREN'T YOU? I'M GOING TO ASK YOU FOR THE LAST TIME, *WHERE* IS HE HOLDING BLACK CANARY?
I DON'T *KNOW* AND I DON'T *CARE!* LET ME GO!
WRONG ANSWER.
YOU WON'T HURT ME. YOU WOULD NEVER HURT A WOMAN.
FOR YOU, LENA...
...I'LL MAKE AN *EXCEPTION.*
FWWUUMMP

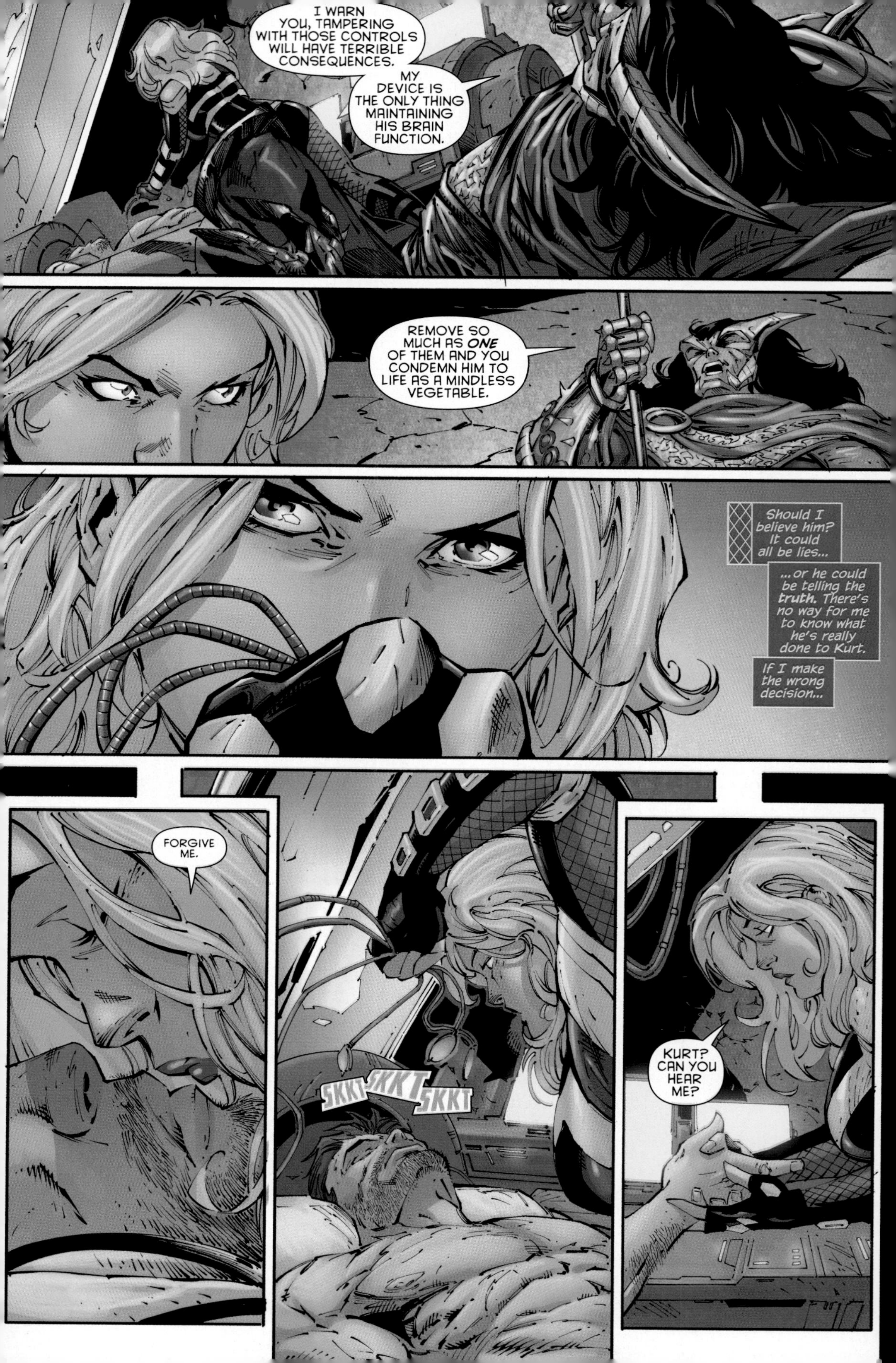
I WARN YOU, TAMPERING WITH THOSE CONTROLS WILL HAVE TERRIBLE CONSEQUENCES.
MY DEVICE IS THE ONLY THING MAINTAINING HIS BRAIN FUNCTION.
REMOVE SO MUCH AS *ONE* OF THEM AND YOU CONDEMN HIM TO LIFE AS A MINDLESS VEGETABLE.
Should I believe him? It could all be lies...
...or he could be telling the **truth**. There's no way for me to know what he's really done to Kurt.
If I make the wrong decision...
FORGIVE ME.
SKKT SKKT SKKT
KURT? CAN YOU HEAR ME?

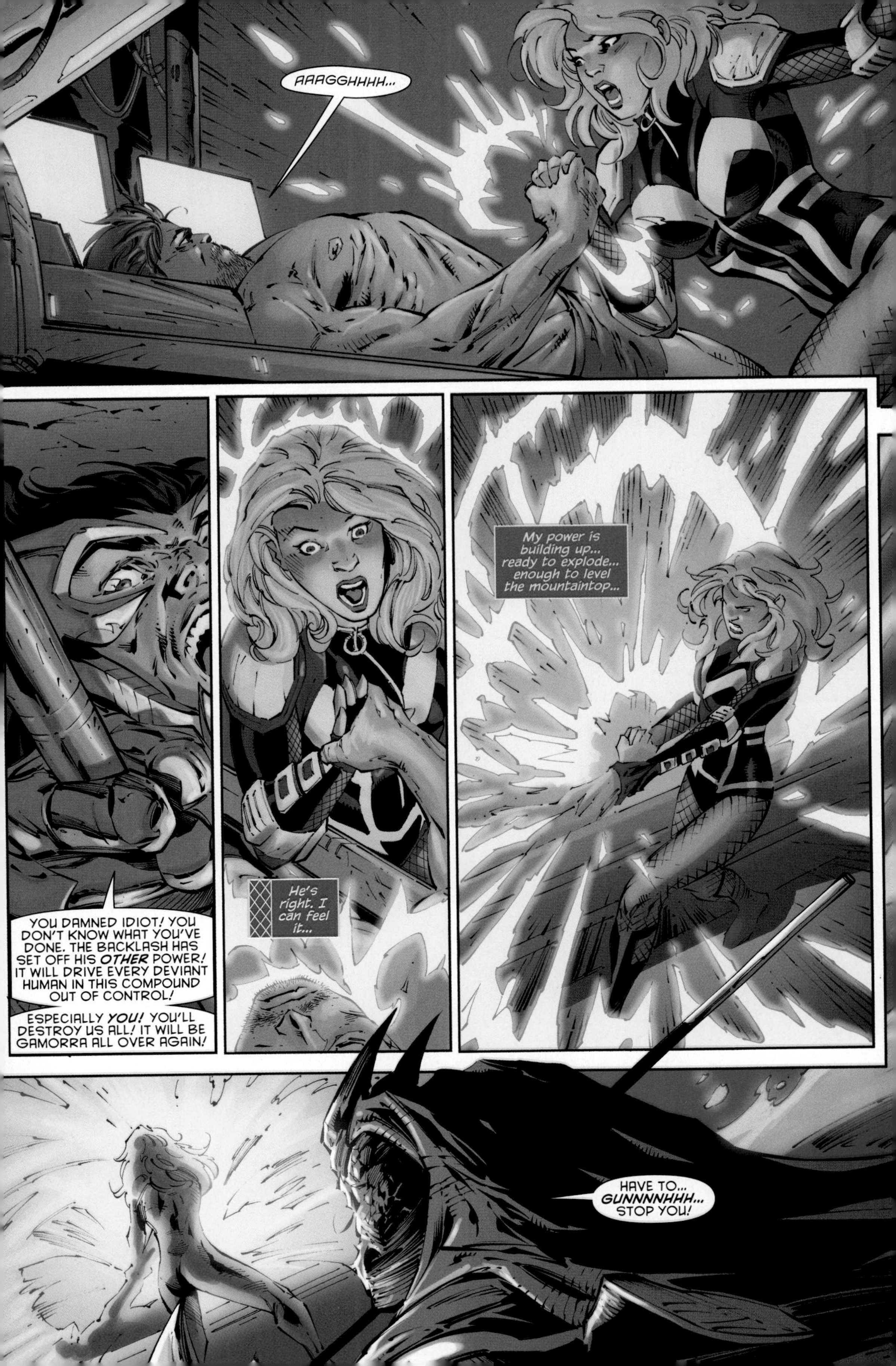
AAAGGHHHH...
YOU DAMNED IDIOT! YOU DON'T KNOW WHAT YOU'VE DONE. THE BACKLASH HAS SET OFF HIS *OTHER* POWER! IT WILL DRIVE EVERY DEVIANT HUMAN IN THIS COMPOUND OUT OF CONTROL!
ESPECIALLY *YOU!* YOU'LL DESTROY US ALL! IT WILL BE GAMORRA ALL OVER AGAIN!
He's right. I can feel it...
My power is building up... ready to explode... enough to level the mountaintop...
HAVE TO... *GUNNNNHHH...* STOP YOU!

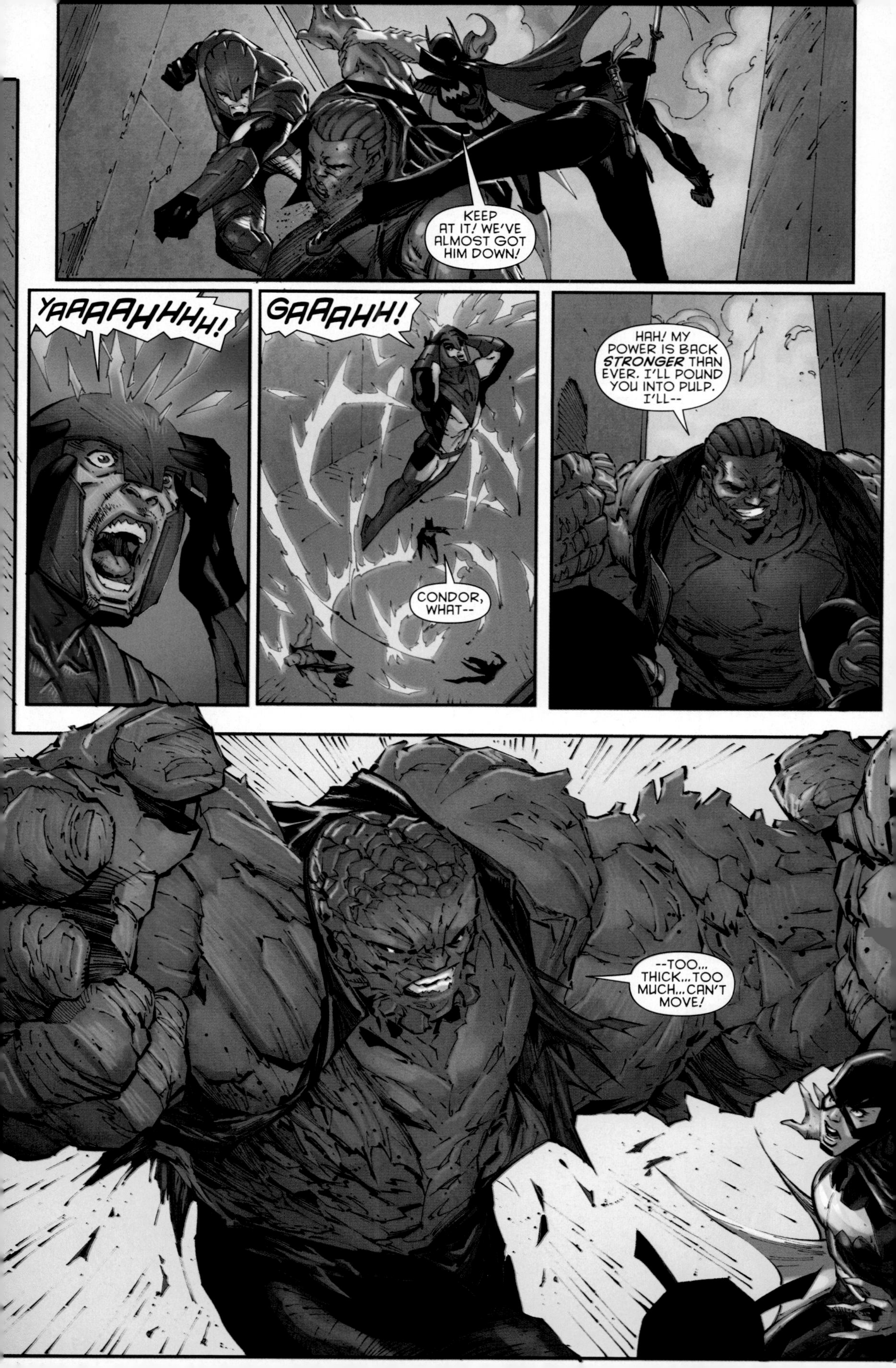
KEEP AT IT! WE'VE ALMOST GOT HIM DOWN!
YAAAAHHHH!
GAAAHH!
CONDOR, WHAT--
HAH! MY POWER IS BACK **STRONGER** THAN EVER. I'LL POUND YOU INTO PULP. I'LL--
--TOO... THICK...TOO MUCH...CAN'T MOVE!

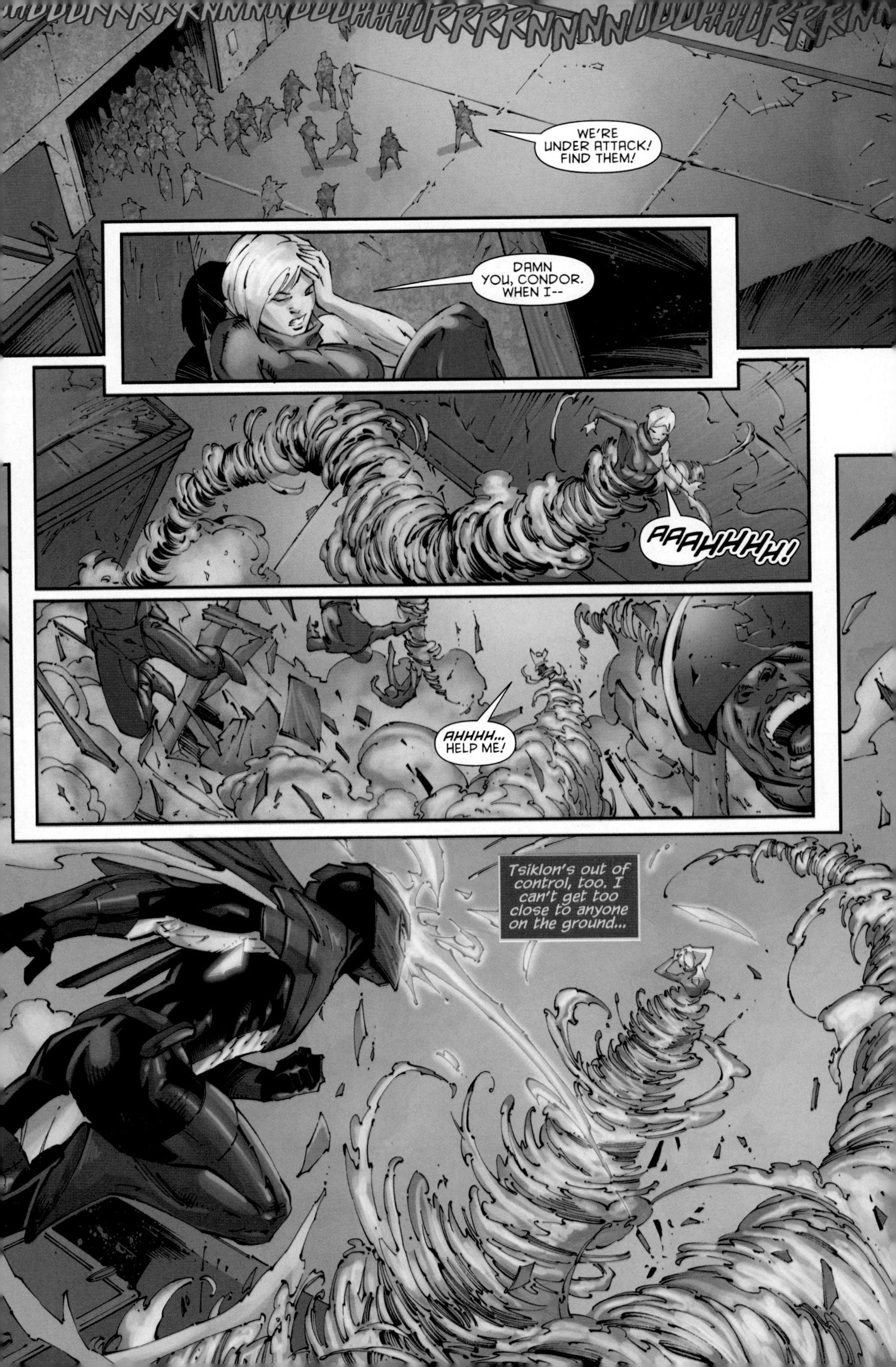
WE'RE UNDER ATTACK! FIND THEM!
DAMN YOU, CONDOR. WHEN I--
AAAHHHH!
AHHHH... HELP ME!
Tsiklon's out of control, too. I can't get too close to anyone on the ground...

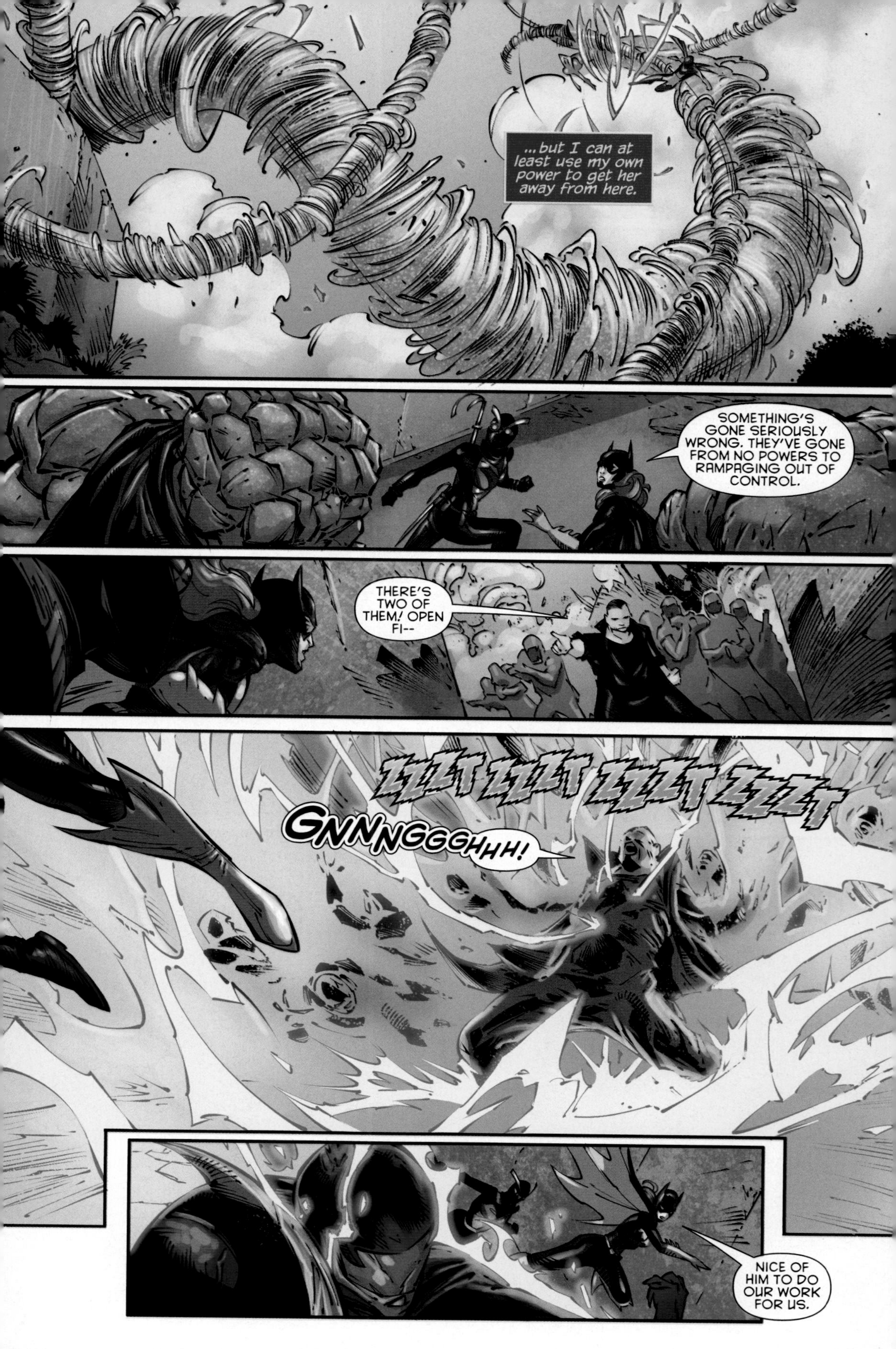
...but I can at least use my own power to get her away from here.
SOMETHING'S GONE SERIOUSLY WRONG. THEY'VE GONE FROM NO POWERS TO RAMPAGING OUT OF CONTROL.
THERE'S TWO OF THEM! OPEN FI--
ZZZZT ZZZZT ZZZZT ZZZZT
GNNNGGGHHH!
NICE OF HIM TO DO OUR WORK FOR US.

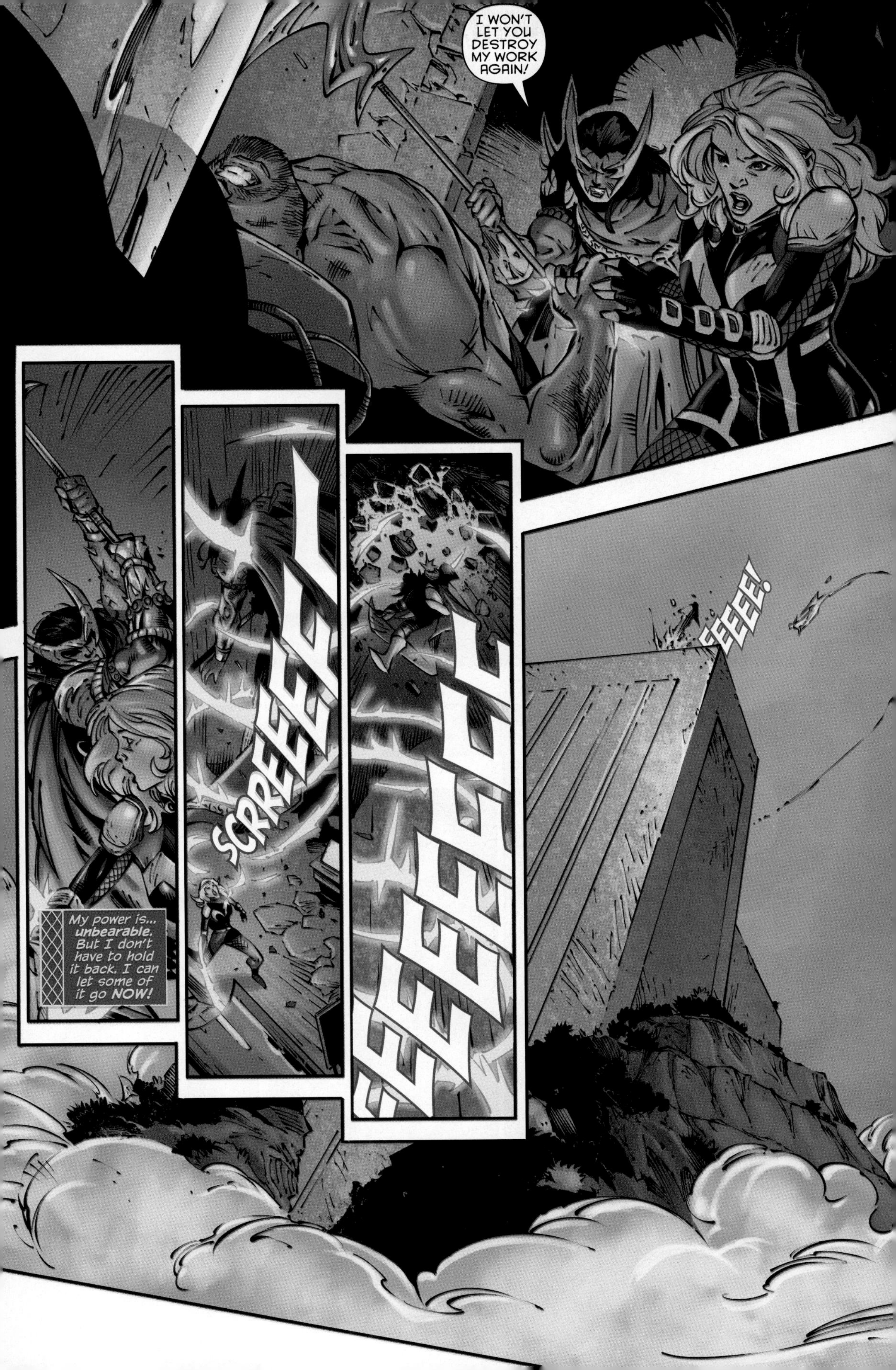

I WON'T LET YOU DESTROY MY WORK AGAIN!
My power is... unbearable. But I don't have to hold it back. I can let some of it go NOW!
SCREEEEE
EEEEEEEEE
EEEEE!

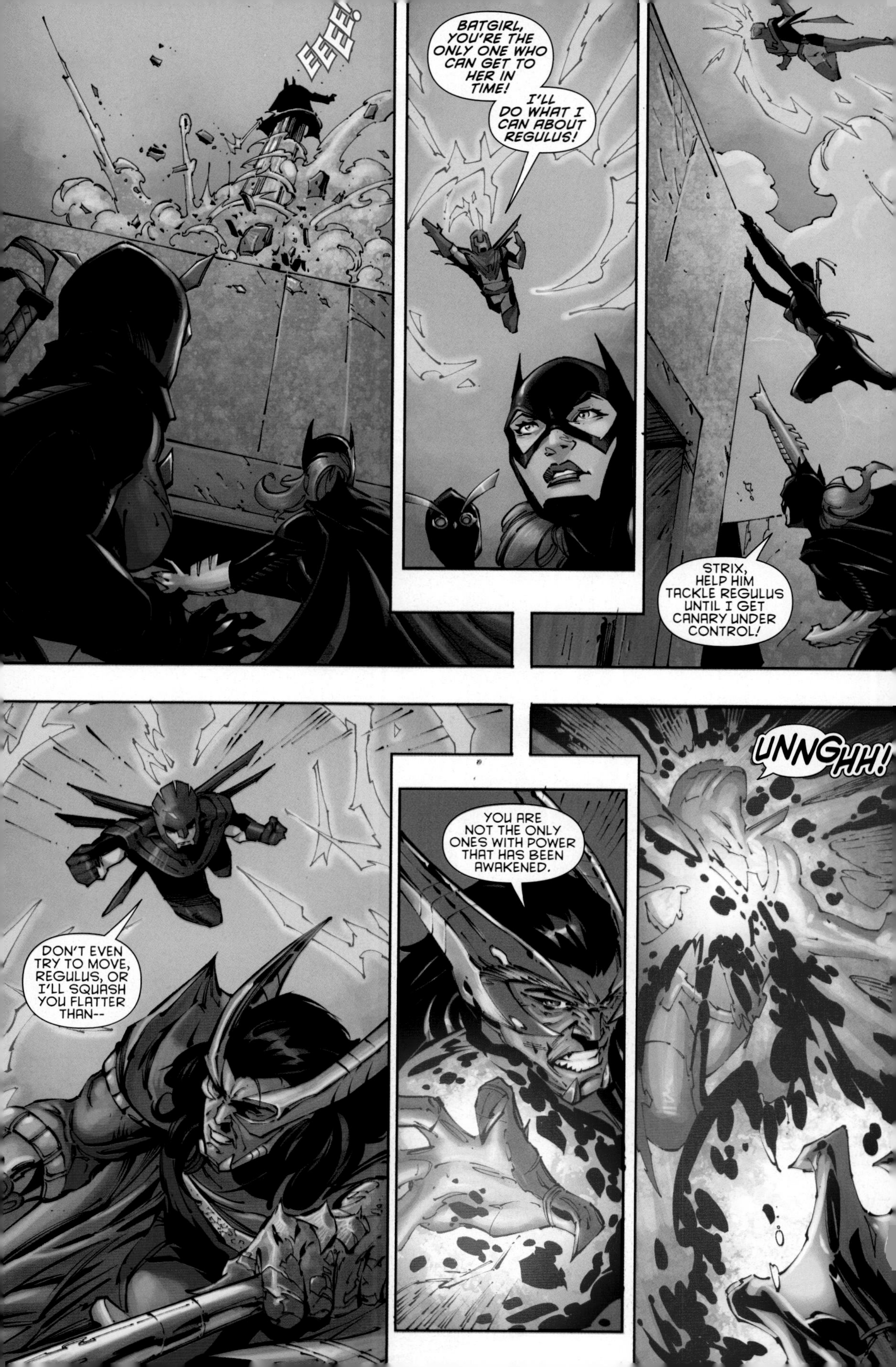
EEEE!
BATGIRL, YOU'RE THE ONLY ONE WHO CAN GET TO HER IN TIME!
I'LL DO WHAT I CAN ABOUT REGULUS!
STRIX, HELP HIM TACKLE REGULUS UNTIL I GET CANARY UNDER CONTROL!
DON'T EVEN TRY TO MOVE, REGULUS, OR I'LL SQUASH YOU FLATTER THAN--
YOU ARE NOT THE ONLY ONES WITH POWER THAT HAS BEEN AWAKENED.
UNNGHH!

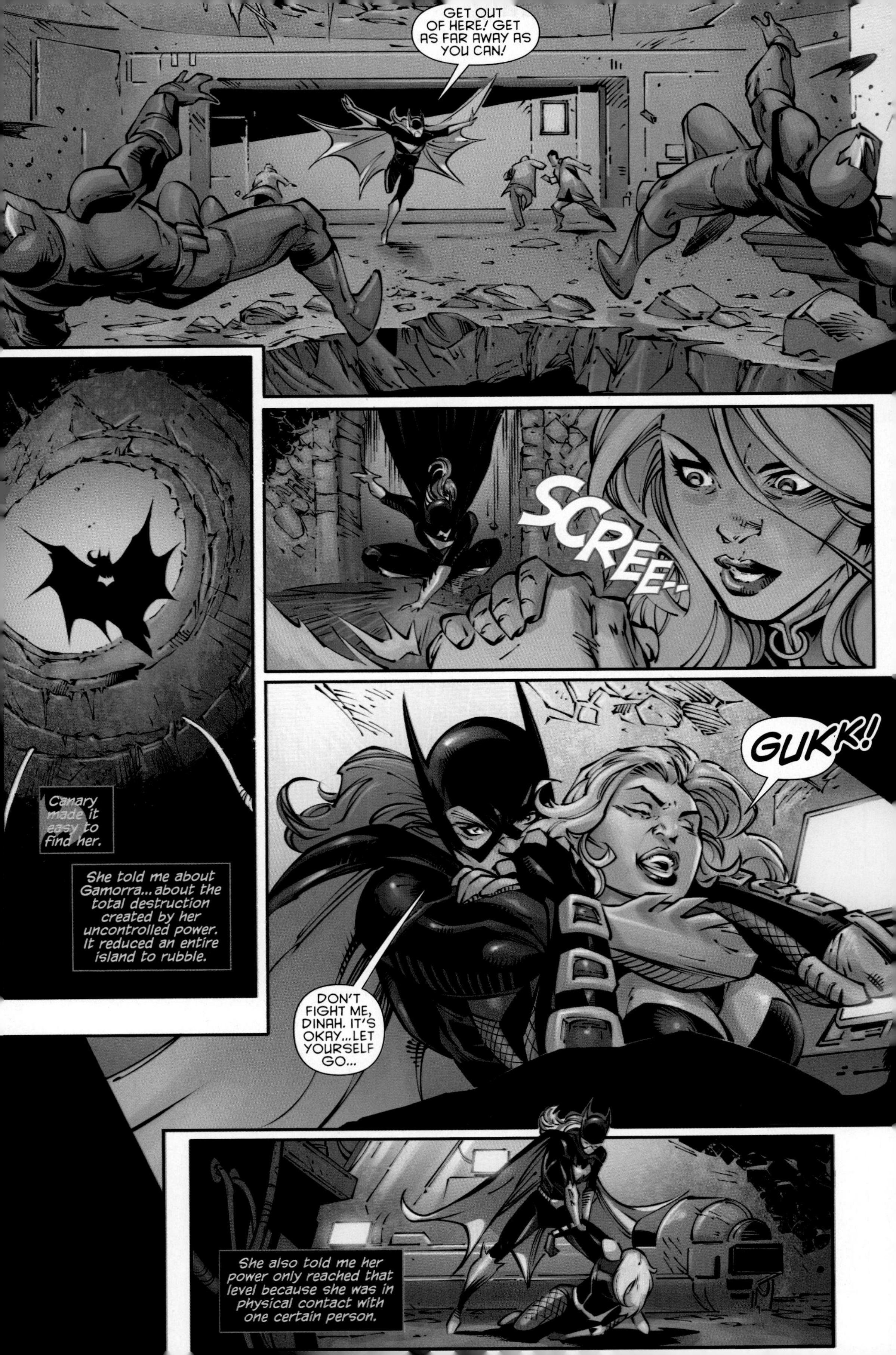
GET OUT OF HERE! GET AS FAR AWAY AS YOU CAN!
Canary made it easy to find her.
She told me about Gamorra...about the total destruction created by her uncontrolled power. It reduced an entire island to rubble.
SCREE...
GUKK!
DON'T FIGHT ME, DINAH. IT'S OKAY...LET YOURSELF GO...
She also told me her power only reached that level because she was in physical contact with one certain person.

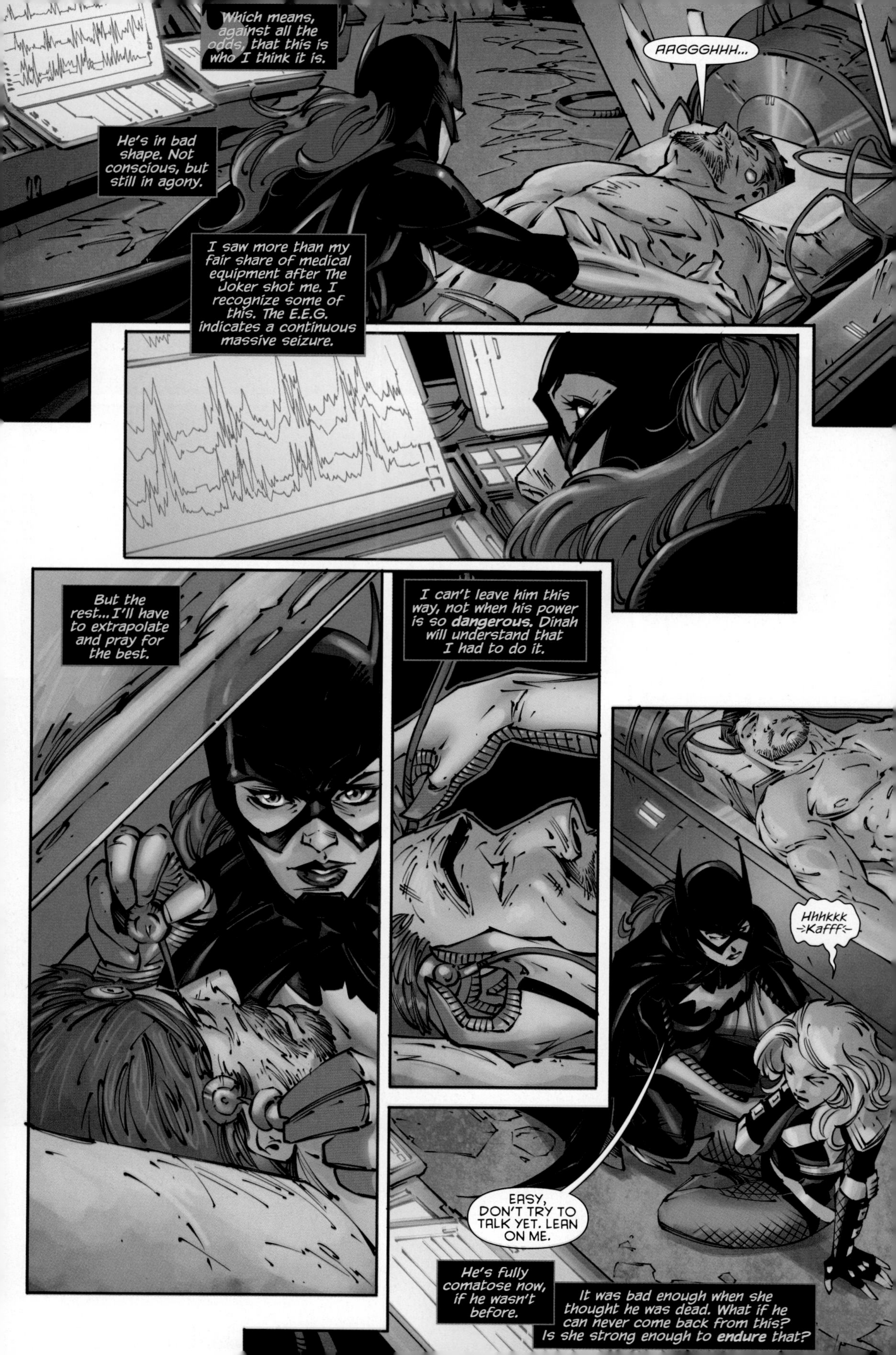

Which means, against all the odds, that this is who I think it is.
AAGGGHHH...
He's in bad shape. Not conscious, but still in agony.
I saw more than my fair share of medical equipment after The Joker shot me. I recognize some of this. The E.E.G. indicates a continuous massive seizure.
But the rest... I'll have to extrapolate and pray for the best.
I can't leave him this way, not when his power is so dangerous. Dinah will understand that I had to do it.
Hhhkkk Kafff
EASY, DON'T TRY TO TALK YET. LEAN ON ME.
He's fully comatose now, if he wasn't before.
It was bad enough when she thought he was dead. What if he can never come back from this? Is she strong enough to endure that?

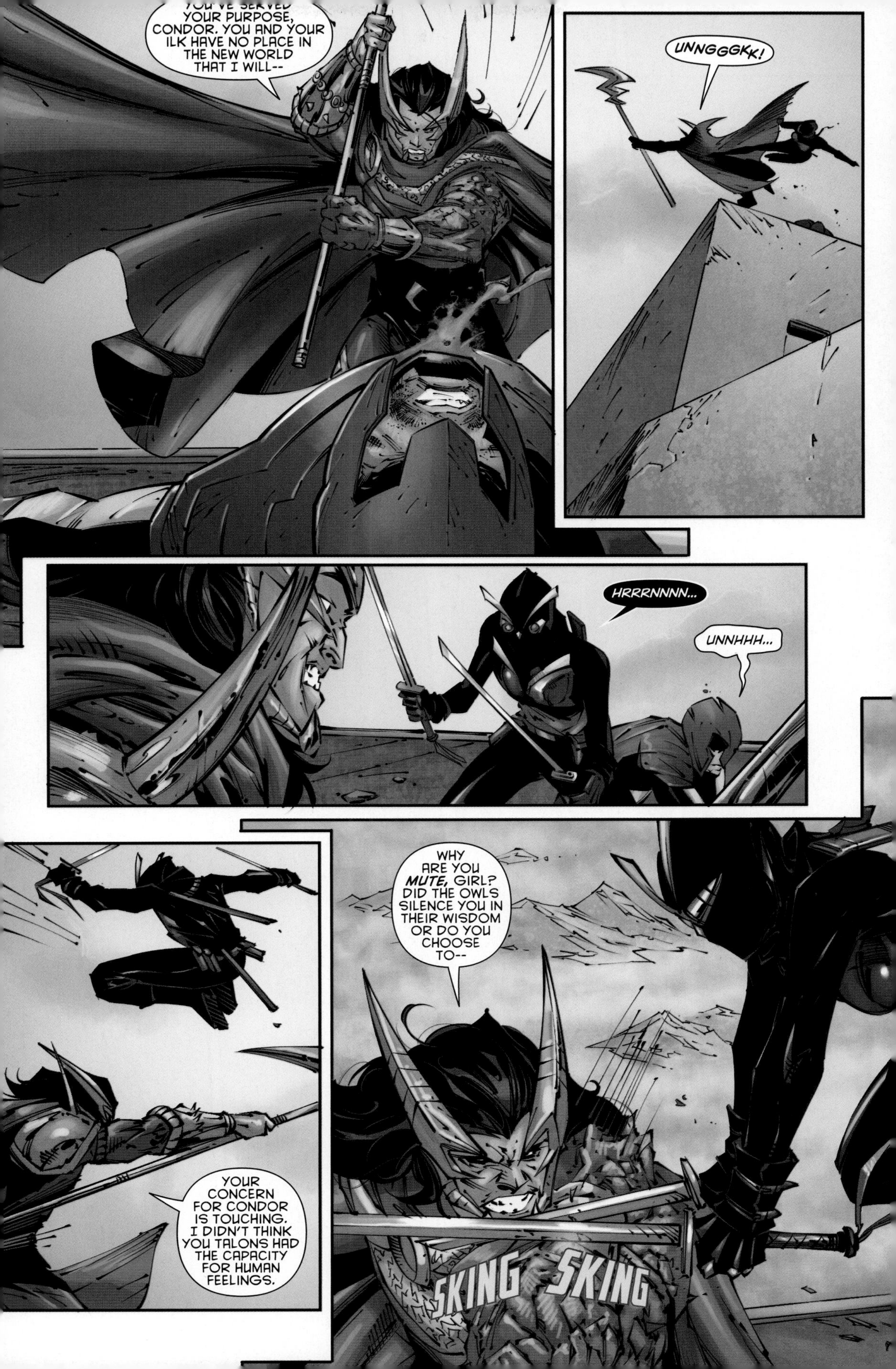
YOU'VE SERVED YOUR PURPOSE, CONDOR. YOU AND YOUR ILK HAVE NO PLACE IN THE NEW WORLD THAT I WILL--
UNNGGGKK!
HRRRNNNN...
UNNHHH...
WHY ARE YOU MUTE, GIRL? DID THE OWLS SILENCE YOU IN THEIR WISDOM OR DO YOU CHOOSE TO--
YOUR CONCERN FOR CONDOR IS TOUCHING. I DIDN'T THINK YOU TALONS HAD THE CAPACITY FOR HUMAN FEELINGS.
SKING SKING

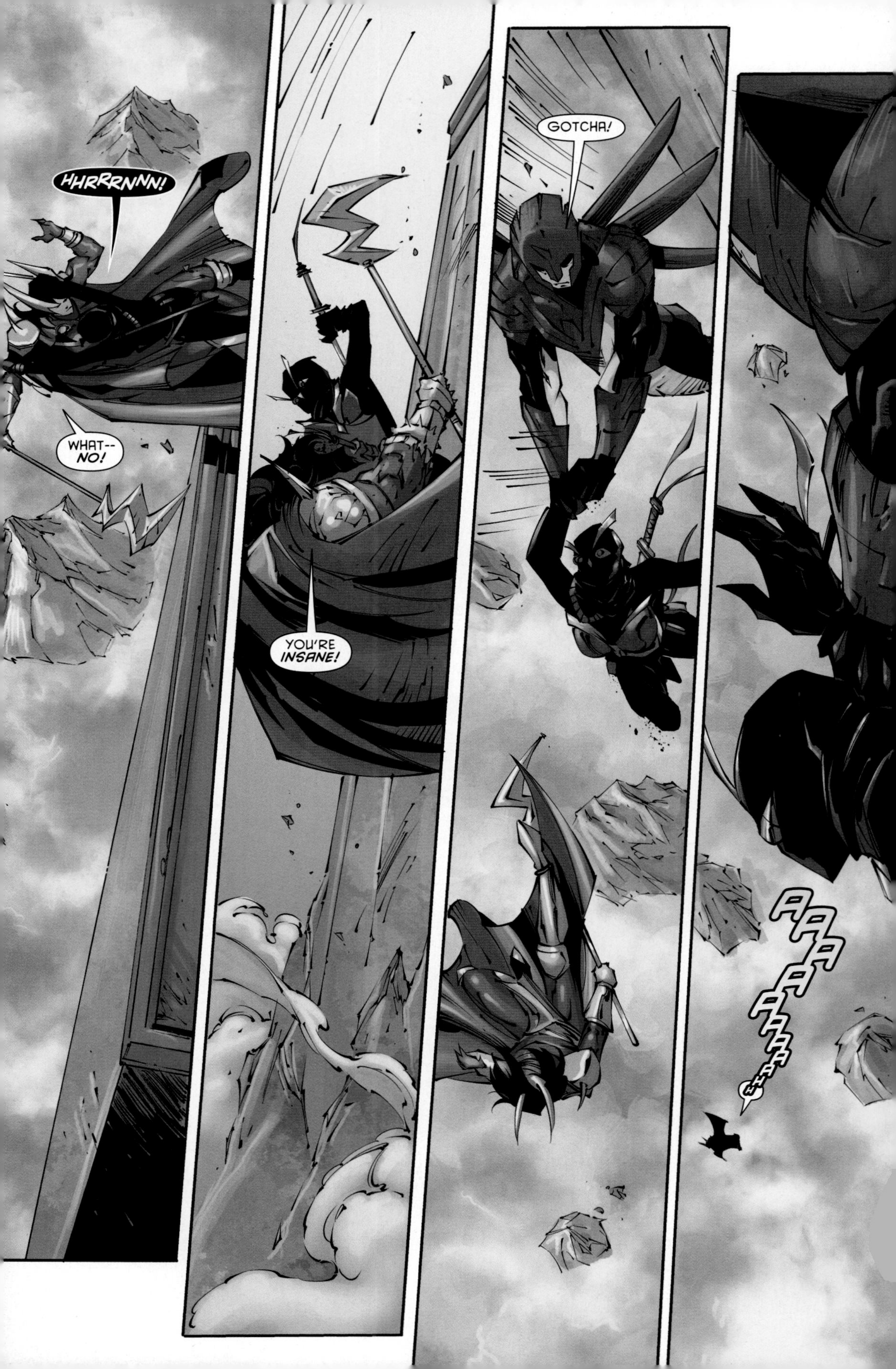
HHRRRNNN!
WHAT-- NO!
YOU'RE INSANE!
GOTCHA!
AAAAAAAAAAAAAH

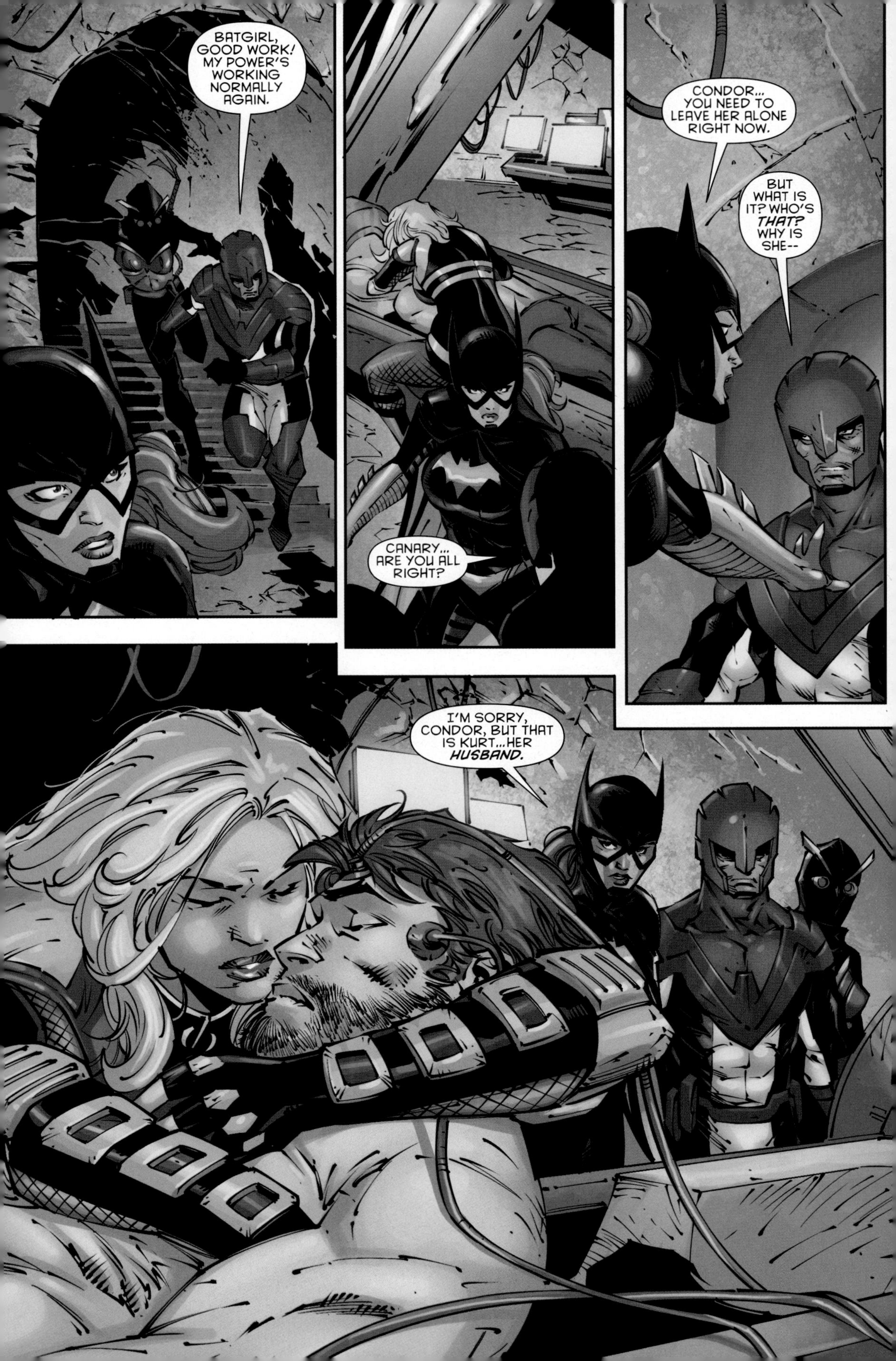
BATGIRL, GOOD WORK! MY POWER'S WORKING NORMALLY AGAIN.
CANARY... ARE YOU ALL RIGHT?
CONDOR... YOU NEED TO LEAVE HER ALONE RIGHT NOW.
BUT WHAT IS IT? WHO'S *THAT?* WHY IS SHE--
I'M SORRY, CONDOR, BUT THAT IS KURT...HER *HUSBAND.*

Full spread cover art for BIRDS OF PREY #19 by Ardian Syaf, Vicente Cifuentes & Chris Sotomayor

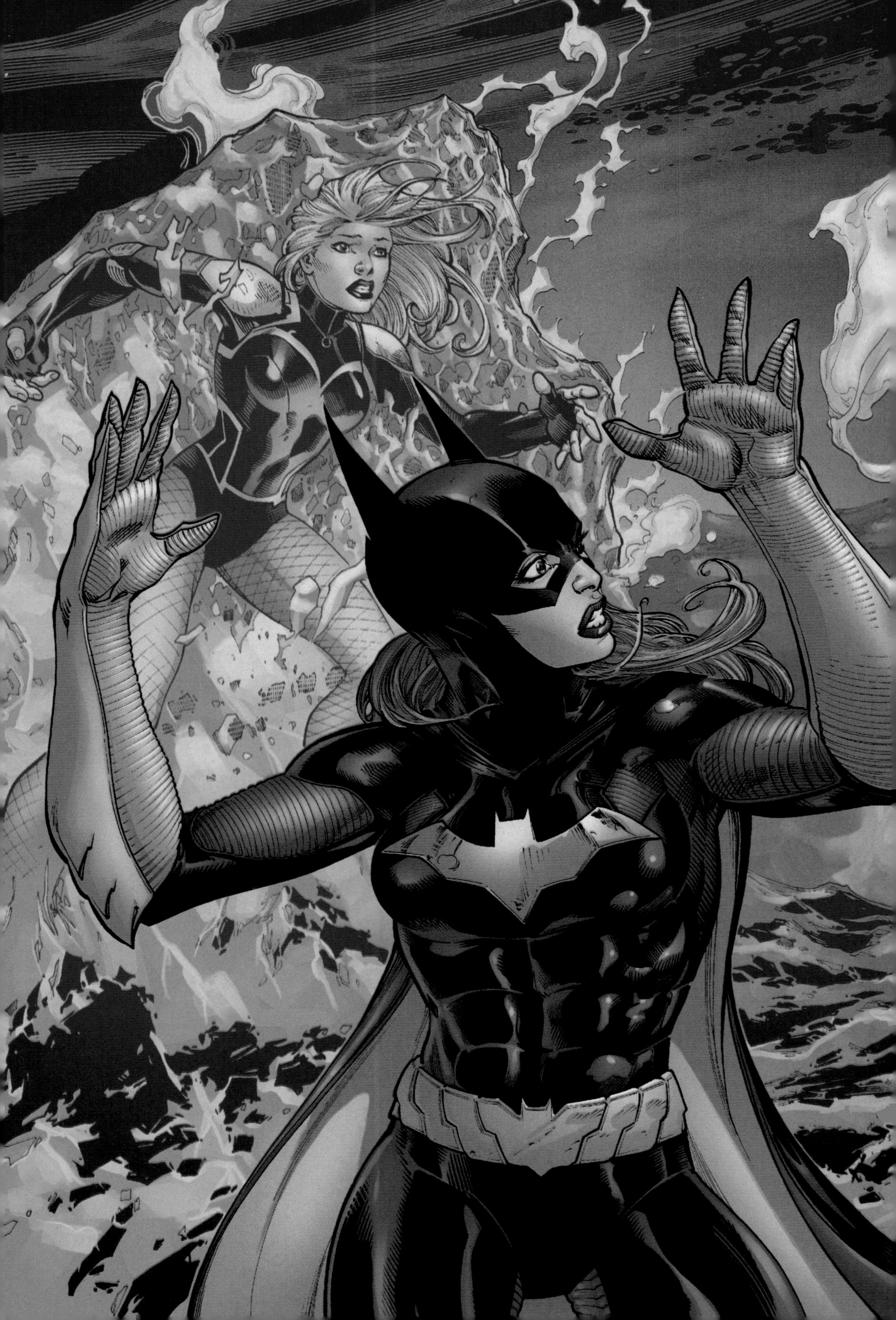

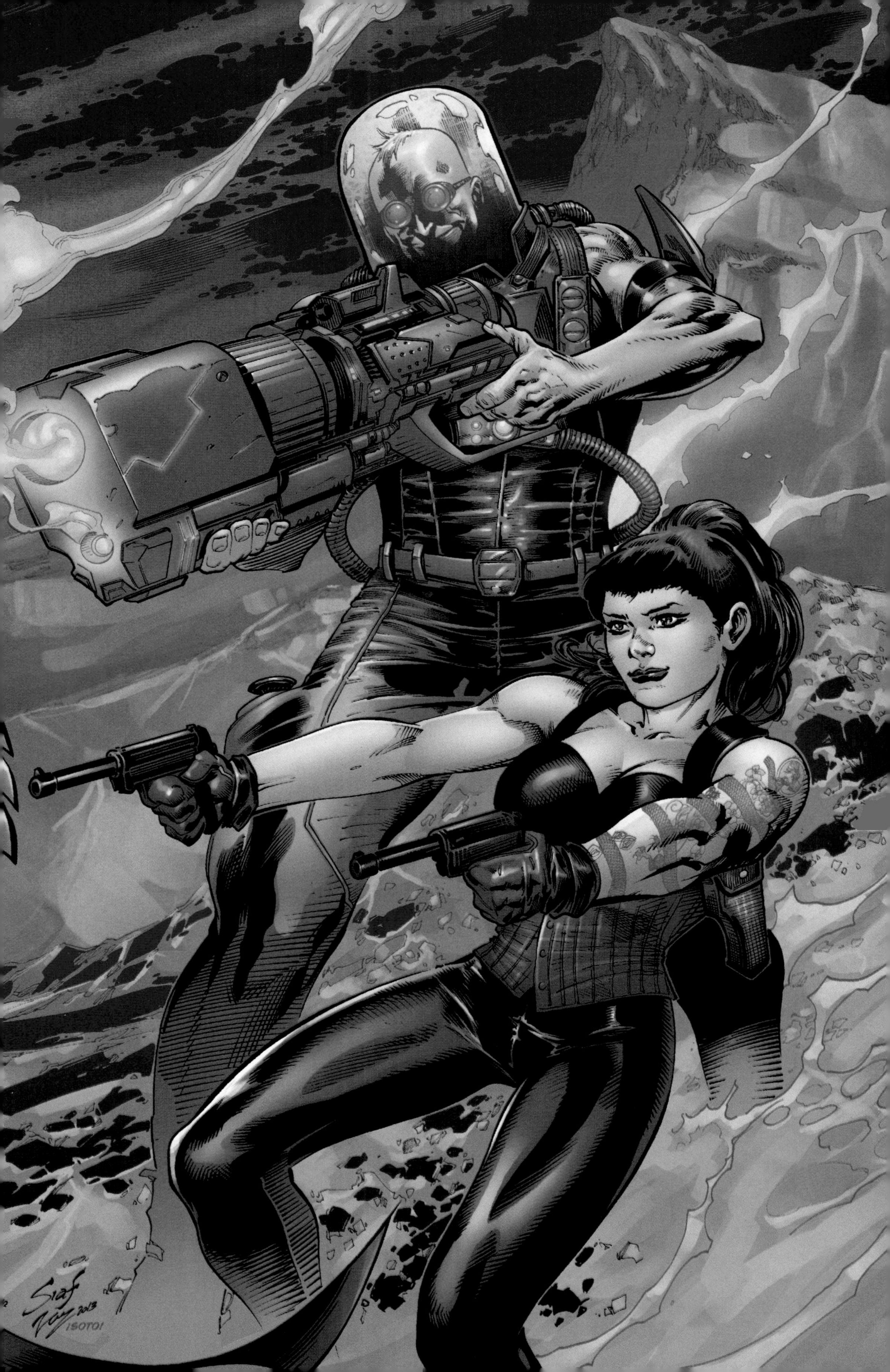

Sketches for issue #20 cover by Romano Molenaar

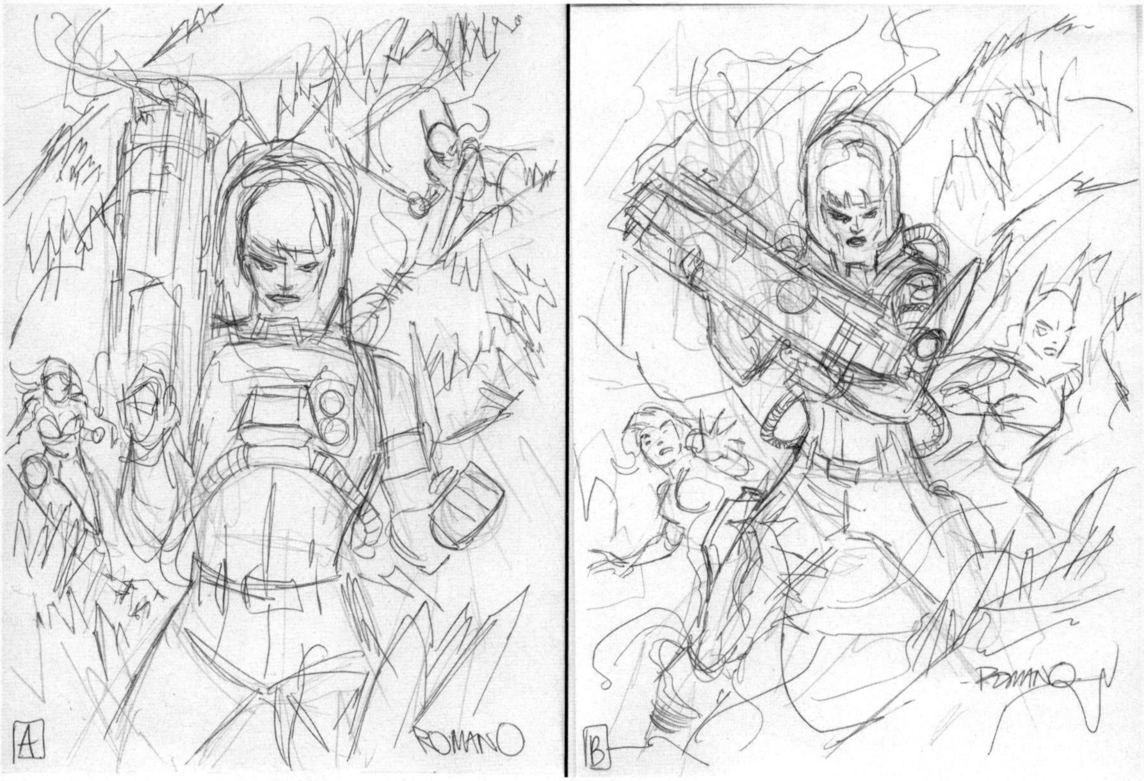
A
ROMANO
B
ROMANO

Sketches for issue #21 cover by Romano Molenaar

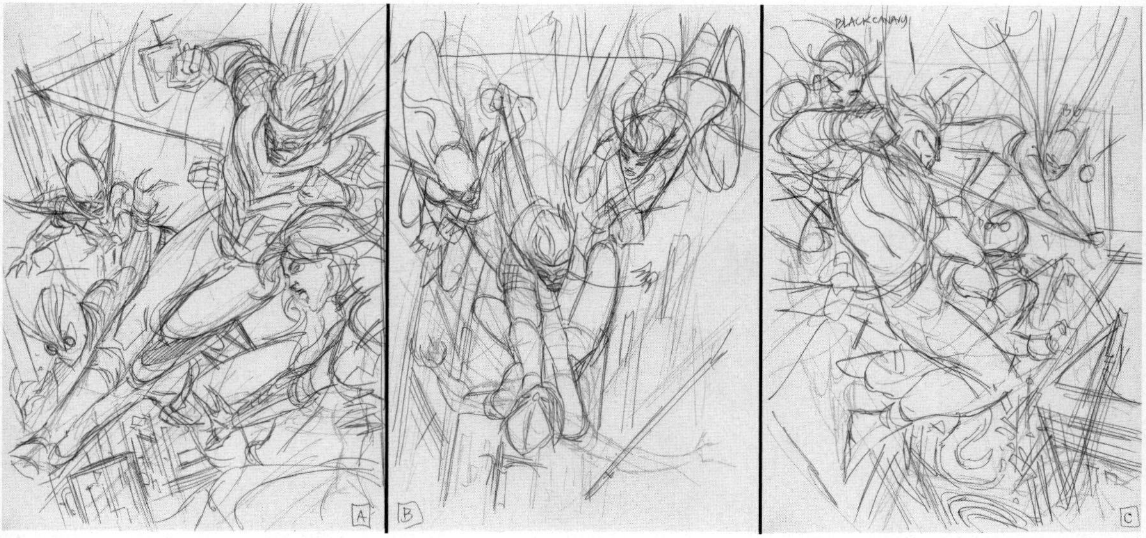
A
B
BLACKCANARY!
C

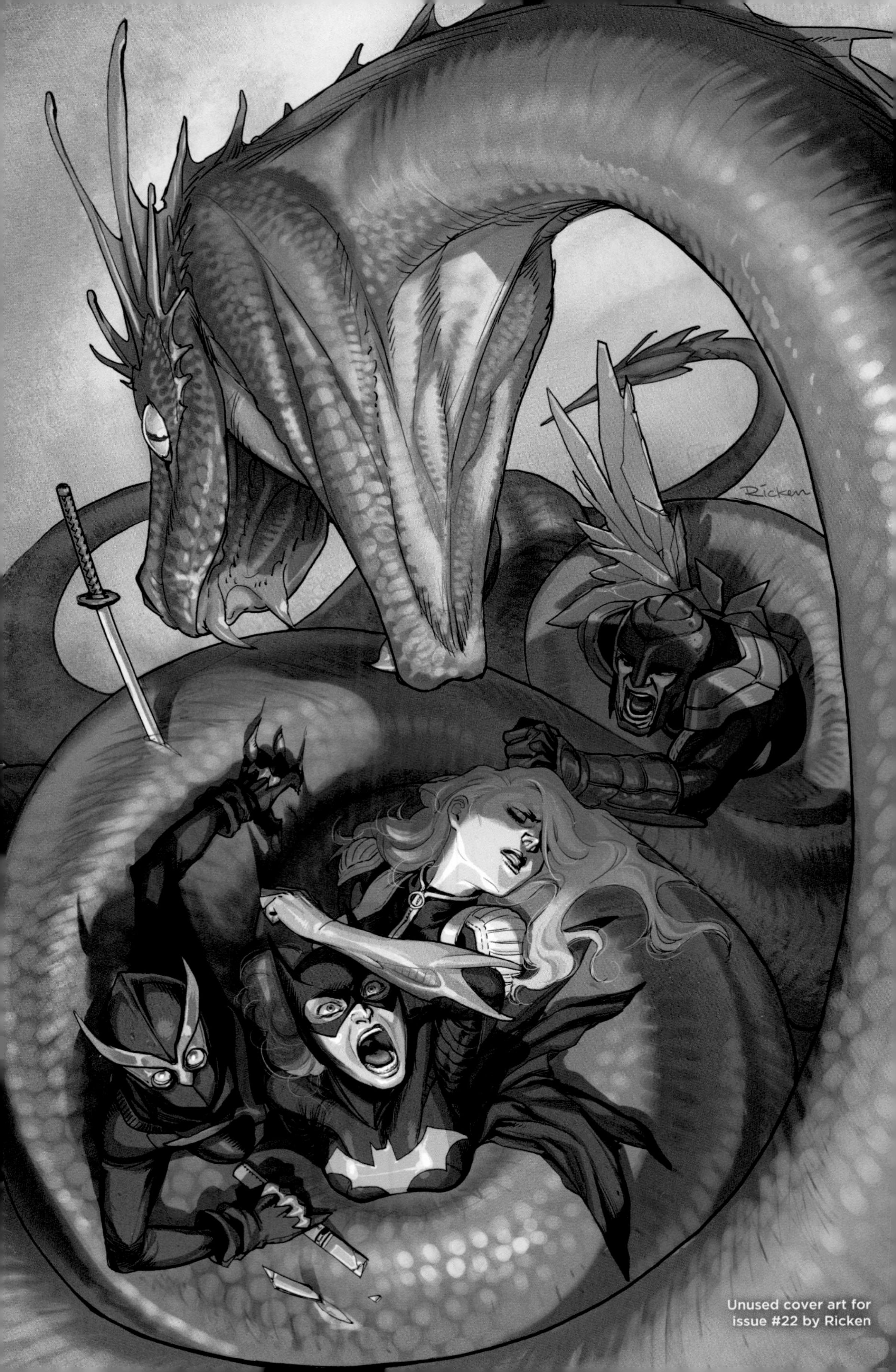
RICKEN
Unused cover art for
issue #22 by Ricken

Sketches for issue #24 cover by Jorge Molina

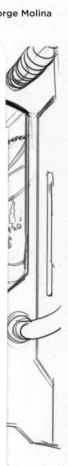